Welcome to the Fall 2017 issue of *Acoustic & Digital Piano Buyer*, a semiannual publication devoted to the purchase of new, used, and restored acoustic pianos and digital pianos. Published since 2009, *Piano Buyer* is the successor to the well-known reference *The Piano Book*, and its *Annual Supplement*, which from 1987 to 2009 were the principal consumer guides to buying a piano in the U.S. and Canada. Partially supported by advertising, *Piano Buyer* is available free online at www.pianobuyer.com. It can also be purchased in print from the website and in bookstores.

Piano Buyer is a hybrid book/magazine. The "book" part consists of a collection of how-to articles on the many aspects of buying a piano. These basic articles are repeated in every issue to serve the many new buyers continually entering the piano market. The "magazine" part consists of features that change with each issue to cover topics of more temporary or niche interest, and to provide variety. Each issue contains several of these excellent features, many of which remain relevant for years. If you missed any of them, you'll find them under the website's Reprints & Archive tab. The brand, model, and price reference material in the second half of the publication is updated, as needed, with each issue.

In this issue we offer several new articles for your reading pleasure. At only 40 years old, the Italian piano maker Fazioli is by far the youngest of the world's makers of high-end concert instruments. Yet, as pianist Alex McDonald remarks in his review of the company's larger grands, "Few piano makers generate more buzz among pianists and piano enthusiasts. . . . In a profession dominated by established composers, teachers, performers, styles, and instrument makers, many now consider Fazioli to be firmly established as a premium piano maker, in the same echelon as Steinway and Bösendorfer." Read McDonald's thoughts about the Faziolis, and how their tone and touch compare to those of Steinway instruments (p. 80).

Dealers in new pianos sometimes report customers requesting an instrument right out of the box or crate, rather than the demonstrator model on the sales floor that has been played by other prospective buyers. But in "Dealer Preparation of New Pianos: Should I Buy a Piano 'Out of the Crate'?," *Piano Buyer*'s Contributing Editor and Piano Industry Consultant Steve Cohen—a piano dealer himself—states that "the jostling and environmental changes that occur during the shipping of the instrument from the factory would ensure that it would arrive at the dealer in less than optimal condition. Bringing the instrument back to the level of musicality intended by the manufacturer is the responsibility of the dealer. . . . Why pay for a fine instrument and settle for anything less?" (p. 47).

Piano Buyer's Piano Review Editor, Owen Lovell, admits that he has never owned a software piano—piano sounds that reside on your computer and are played via your digital piano's keyboard—and, until recently, had always viewed them as a somewhat nutty fringe phenomenon. Noting, however, software pianos' growing prevalence and diversity in the global market, he reviews several of them in "Six Software Pianos Under $150: A Sampling." His conclusion? Lovell finds that, though a bit cumbersome to install, and sensitive to your computer's processing power, software pianos are a great way to "own" instruments one could never hope to afford. In addition, he writes, "Software pianos are a means of breathing new life into older gear for an affordable price, and they sound better and more realistic than almost every hardware-based digital piano I've played" (p. 122).

Piano Buyer's ratings of new pianos are probably the publication's most read, most misunderstood, and most controversial feature. As the quality of low-end pianos rises, and the differences between brands become increasingly subtle and subjective, our ratings have come to represent less our judgments of the instruments than our sense of how manufacturers and dealers position them in the marketplace—partly by price, but also by reputation and country of origin. But we've never been completely satisfied with this, in part because readers who lack the time, interest, and/or ability to make their own judgments frequently ask that we help them by recommending specific models. We've risen to the challenge with "Staff Picks," our unapologetically subjective assessments of the best in today's acoustic, digital, and hybrid pianos (p.41).

(continued on page 2)

Acoustic & Digital Piano Buyer is published semiannually, in March and September, by:

Brookside Press LLC
P.O. Box 601041
San Diego, CA 92160 USA

619.738.4155
619.810.0425 (fax)
info@pianobuyer.com
www.pianobuyer.com

Distributed to the book trade by Independent Publishers Group,
814 North Franklin St., Chicago, IL 60610
(800) 888-4741 or (312) 337-0747

FALL 2017
Supplement to
THE PIANO BOOK

Publisher and Editor
Advertising Director
Larry Fine
larry@pianobuyer.com

Piano Review Editor
Dr. Owen Lovell
owen@pianobuyer.com

Contributing Editor and
Piano Industry Consultant
Steve Cohen
steve@pianobuyer.com

Design and Production
Julie Gallagher, Harry St. Ours

Acoustic Piano
Technical Consultants
Sally Phillips
Del Fandrich

Digital Piano
Technical Consultants
Alden Skinner
Stephen Fortner

Copyeditor
Richard Lehnert

Contributors to this issue:
Ori Bukai, Brian Chung,
Steve Cohen, George Litterst,
Owen Lovell, Alex McDonald,
Sally Phillips, Alden Skinner,
Chris Solliday, Christopher
Storch

See www.PianoBuyer.com
for more information.

(continued from page 1)

Don't forget to explore the rest of our website. If you're shopping for a new piano, our two searchable online databases of 3,000 acoustic and more than 200 digital models will help you quickly home in on the instruments that match your requirements for size, furniture style, budget, and features. If you're shopping for a used instrument, try our Piano Buyer Classifieds; using its powerful search engine, browse among thousands of used pianos for sale. If you're in need of piano-related services—tuning, rebuilding, sales, teaching, or moving—use our Local Services Directory. And when you're ready to take a break, treat yourself to some comic relief with our blog, *Piano-Buying Stories.*

(continued on page 264)

FEATURE ARTICLES

by Steve Cohen and **Piano Buyer** staff

"Most pianos are not adjusted at the factory to 100% of their musical capability. Even if one were, the jostling and environmental changes that occur during the shipping of the instrument from the factory would ensure that it would arrive at the dealer in less than optimal condition. Bringing the instrument back to the level of musicality intended by the manufacturer is the responsibility of the dealer. . . . Why pay for a fine instrument and settle for anything less?"

by Alex McDonald, DMA

"Few piano makers generate more buzz among pianists and piano enthusiasts than the Italian company Fazioli. In a profession dominated by established composers, teachers, performers, styles, and instrument makers, many now consider Fazioli to be firmly established as a premium piano maker, in the same echelon as Steinway and Bösendorfer—a remarkable achievement, given that Fazioli was founded only as recently as 1978."

by Dr. Owen Lovell

"Software pianos are a means of breathing new life into older gear for an affordable price, and they sound better and more realistic than almost every hardware-based digital piano I've played. However, the installation process for each is tedious, with many steps, and once you've got your software piano running, you're going to spend time tweaking your computer's settings to find an acceptable balance of stability and performance."

Inside This Issue

PRACTICE MAKES PERFECT. You've probably heard that saying a hundred times, especially if you've ever studied the piano. Mom said it, so it must be true, right?

Well, hold on a minute—nothing against Mom, but let's get real: "Practice makes perfect" is a terrible motto for piano players. First of all, it's incorrect—how can anything become "perfect" if, every time, you practice it *wrong*? And second, it can't even come close to capturing the prodigious power of playing the piano. So, with all due respect to that venerable axiom, trash it—and make way for a motto that proclaims the *real* benefits of piano playing: *Practice makes prosperous.*

People usually associate the word *prosperous* with wealth. While that's certainly part of its meaning, many dictionaries suggest a broader definition: to be *prosperous* is to *flourish*, to *thrive* . . . to *be successful*. Therefore, the phrase *practice makes prosperous* declares boldly that *those who play the piano are far more likely to flourish, thrive, and experience success in life than those who do not.* Quite a stretch, you say? Read on.

Thriving Children

Consider what happens when eight-year-old Bobby decides to embrace serious piano practice. Not only does he embark upon a wondrous musical adventure (possibly the greatest benefit of all) but, perhaps unconsciously, he acquires a diversity of skills far beyond the musical notes:

- **He learns to *work hard*.** Anyone who excels at the piano has made a commitment to practice with vigor and determination.

- **He learns to *focus*.** In a world where iPods, MySpace, Facebook, Twitter and mobile texting have made multi-tasking the de facto way of life, young people are at risk of losing the art of concentration. Piano practice reminds Bobby how to focus on *one thing*—and do it well.

- **He learns to be *responsible*.** Serious pianists learn that faithful, consistent practice—even when they don't *feel* like doing it—will bring great satisfaction over time.

- **He learns to *pay attention to details*.** As his skills mature, Bobby learns to observe the fine points and use the most subtle nuances to create art.

- **He learns to be *self-reliant*.** While practicing, Bobby can't always rely on Mom and Dad for help. To succeed, he must learn to work well on his own.

- **He learns to be *creative*.** Creativity is a musician's lifeblood. Pianists use it not only to express musical ideas, but also to conquer the physical and mental obstacles that arise when learning new music.

- **He learns to *persevere*.** There is little satisfaction in learning only *half* of a piece of music. The determined pianist finds joy in following through to the very end.

These are only some of the skills Bobby will acquire as he devotes himself to diligent piano practice. So, how will such practice make him prosperous?

Ask employers what they look for when interviewing young job candidates for their top positions. Most are looking for a well-defined set of character traits. Specifically, they want people who know how to work hard, can focus well and avoid distractions, are responsible, will pay attention to details, are self-reliant and creative, and will persevere on a project from start to finish. Sound familiar?

You see my point. The skills Bobby learns by practicing the piano will be of immeasurable value to him not only in job interviews, but in every area of his life. People who have these skills are more likely to flourish in college, thrive in the work world, advance in their careers—and generally enjoy success in any field of endeavor.

Test scores support this contention. Studies show that students of music typically score higher on SATs than do non-music students—on average, 57 points higher on the verbal section and 41 points higher in math.[1] Further, a 1994 study showed that college undergraduate students who majored in music had the highest rate

> **Those who play the piano are far more likely to flourish, thrive, and experience success in life than those who do not.**

---

[1] *Profile of SAT and Achievement Test Takers.* The College Board, compiled by Music Educators National Conference, 2001.

KAWAI

Celebrating 90 Years of Tradition and Bold Innovation

of acceptance to medical school (66%).[2] *Practice makes prosperous.* Prepare your children for success in life: Introduce them to the piano.

Thriving Adults

But how about *you*? Are you among the 82% of adults who have always wanted to learn how to play an instrument?[3] Did you know that adults can gain as much as younger people from playing the piano?

Even if you've already achieved career success and significant wealth, there can be *so* much more to a prosperous life. Consider what happens when Nancy, a baby boomer and successful business owner, decides to join a recreational group piano class for adults:

---

[2] Peter H. Wood, "The Comparative Academic Abilities of Students in Education and in Other Areas of a Multi-focus University," ERIC Document ED327480 (1990).
[3] *U.S. Gallup Poll*. 2008 Music USA NAMM Global Report (August, 2008): 139.

- **She immediately feels *relief from stress*.** After hours of intense daily pressure at work, Nancy finds it easy to unwind at the piano. The class moves at a comfortable pace and no one is ever required to play solo—which means zero stress. In her personal practice and in class, Nancy can just relax and have fun.

- **She's *making new friends*.** Because recreational piano classes are taught in groups, Nancy enjoys getting to know others who share a common interest. Many of her classmates are professional people like her who, after raising a family, are finally getting to try the things they've always wanted to do. The warm camaraderie among class members is a wonderful surprise.

- **She enjoys *playing her favorite songs*.** Nancy always dreamed of learning her two favorite Beatles tunes. Now, she's thrilled to play these and many other classic hits for friends and family.

- **Her *mind and spirit are enlivened*.** The process of learning something completely new has been intellectually and emotionally stimulating for Nancy. She enjoys a sense of adventure when exploring new musical concepts and genres with her classmates. Playing the piano has made her feel more fully alive.

Studies have shown that recreational group music-making can significantly improve the quality of life and personal well-being among those who embrace it. So even when you're playing the piano just for fun, *practice makes prosperous* in meaningful ways that far exceed the balance in your 401(k).

To give the piano a whirl, contact a local music store or independent piano teacher to find out about recreational piano classes in your area. Whether you're young or old, striving for success or just playing for fun, the prodigious power of playing the piano can change your life.

How about you?
Are you among the 82% of adults who have always wanted to learn how to play an instrument?

Brian Chung is Senior Vice President of Kawai America Corporation and a leading proponent of the benefits of making music. He is also a pianist, and co-author (with Dennis Thurmond) of *Improvisation at the Piano: A Systematic Approach for the Classically Trained Pianist* (Alfred Publishing, 2007). Visit his website at www.brianchung.net.

ACOUSTIC OR DIGITAL:
What's Best for Me?

ALDEN SKINNER AND LARRY FINE

SHOULD YOU BUY an acoustic (traditional) piano or a digital (electronic) piano? For many, there will be no easy answer to this question. Many factors play into this seemingly simple decision, some practical, some not. Ideally, perhaps, the answer should be "Both"— take advantage of the "organic" qualities and connection with tradition of the acoustic piano, as well as the extreme flexibility of the digital. But assuming that, for a variety of reasons, "Both" isn't an option, careful consideration of the advantages and disadvantages of each will probably quickly reveal which will be best for you.

The advantages of the acoustic piano start with the fact that it's the "real thing," inherently capable of nuances that are difficult for the digital piano to emulate. The experience of playing an acoustic piano— the harmonics, the vibrations, the touch, the visual appeal, the interaction with the room, the connection with tradition—is so complex that digitals cannot reproduce it all. And, provided that it's a decent instrument and properly maintained, the acoustic will continue to serve you or a subsequent owner for several generations, after which it might be rebuilt and continue to make music.

If you're a beginner, the tone and touch of a good-quality digital piano should not interfere with the elementary learning process for a while, but is likely to become less satisfactory as you advance. If your aspiration is to play classical piano literature, the choice is clear: A digital may serve as a temporary or quiet-time practice instrument (some well-known classical pianists request that a digital piano be placed in their hotel rooms for practice and warmup), but the first time you play an acoustic piano that stirs your soul, there will be no turning back. Although digitals continue to draw closer to the ideal, there is, as yet, nothing like the total experience of playing a fine acoustic instrument.

The downside of an acoustic piano? Initial cost is generally higher, they're harder to move, the best ones take up a lot of space, and tuning and maintaining them adds several hundred dollars a year to their cost. And—most important—*all they will ever be or sound like is a piano.*

So why do sales of digital pianos outnumber sales of acoustics by more than two to one? Because, in addition to making a piano sound, digitals can also sound like any other instrument imaginable. State-of-the-art digital pianos can allow a player with even the most basic keyboard skills to sound like an entire orchestra. Many models have features that will produce an entire band or orchestra accompanying you as the soloist. Digital pianos can also be used as player pianos. They can enhance learning with educational software. They can be attached to a computer, and you can have an entire recording studio at your fingertips, with the computer printing the sheet music for anything you play. Many fine players whose main piano is a quality acoustic also have a digital, providing the technology for band and/or orchestral compositions, transcriptions, and fun!

Add to all that the advantages of lower cost, convenience, lack of maintenance expense, the ability to play silently with headphones, meeting the needs of multiple family members, the obvious advantages for piano classes, and computer connectivity, and you have a powerful argument for the digital.

While digital pianos have a lot of advantages, it's important to also consider the disadvantages. In addition to those related to learning and playing classical music, mentioned above, the life expectancy of a good digital piano is limited, primarily by obsolescence (digitals haven't been around long enough to know how long they will physically last), while the life expectancy of a good acoustic piano is upward of 50 years. Acoustic pianos hold their value rather well, while digitals, like other electronics, quickly drop in value. Obviously, then, if you're buying a starter instrument and plan to upgrade later, from a financial perspective you would do better to start with an acoustic piano.

Both variations have places in our musical lives. Now, which is right for you?

Both variations have places in our musical lives. Now, which is right for you?

(If you're still unsure, you might want to consider a hybrid piano—see our story on the subject in this issue.)

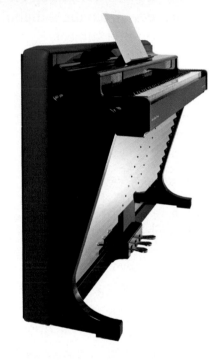

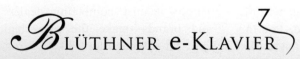

Introduction

The purpose of this article is to provide an overview of the process of buying an acoustic (traditional) piano, with an emphasis on the decisions you'll have to make along the way, and on the factors that will affect any purchase of an acoustic piano. References are given to other articles in this publication, or to *The Piano Book*, for further information on selected topics. For an overview of the process of buying a digital (electronic) piano, please read our **article** on that subject.

Why Is Buying a Piano So Hard?

An acoustic (traditional) piano can be one of the most expensive—and difficult—purchases most households will ever make. Why so difficult?

Lack of qualified advice. A person who sets out to buy a piano is unlikely to have a social support network of family and friends who are knowledgeable about pianos to serve as advisors, as they might if buying a car, house, or kitchen appliance. A "modern" piano is essentially a 19th-century creation about which few people know very much, and about which much of what they *think* they know may not be accurate or current. Even music teachers and experienced players often know little about piano construction or the rapidly changing state of piano manufacturing, often relying on their past experience with certain brands, most of which have changed significantly over the years.

Confusing array of choices. Acoustic pianos are marketed nationally in the United States under some 70 different brand names from a dozen countries (plus dozens of additional names marketed locally), with thousands of models available in dozens of furniture styles and finishes—and that's just new pianos! Add in more than a century's worth of used pianos under thousands of brand names in an almost infinite variety of conditions of disrepair and restoration. Just thinking about it can make one dizzy.

> An acoustic piano can be one of the most expensive—and difficult—purchases most households will ever make.

Value for the money unclear. New pianos vary in price from $2,000 to $200,000. But unlike many other consumer items, whose differences can be measured or are readily apparent, most pianos, regardless of price, look very similar and do pretty much the same thing: they're shiny and black (or a wood color), play 88 notes, and have three pedals. The features advertised are often abstract, misleading, or difficult to see or understand. For this reason, it's often not clear just what you're getting for your money. This can lead to decision-making paralysis.

Confusing sales practices. While many piano salespeople do an honest and admirable job of guiding their customers through this maze, a significant minority—using lies, tricky pricing games, and false accusations against competing dealers and brands—make the proverbial used-car salesman look like a saint. And once you get through haggling over price—the norm in the piano

For once, words can describe
how beautifully our pianos play.

"I like the Ritmüller pianos,

and think that the transformation of the Ritmüller line over the last few years has been one of the more **authentic and musically successful changes in the piano industry."**

~ Larry Fine

Publisher & Editor of **Piano Buyer**

When a prestigious publication like **Piano Buyer** calls our pianos "hands-down favorites in this category," it's a source of pride. From the quality of the components to the exacting craftsmanship, every Ritmüller piano reflects the vision our master piano designer and engineers, earning the praise of accomplished musicians worldwide. To learn more, visit RitmullerUSA.com.

Ritmüller
Since 1795

Guangzhou Pearl River Piano Group Co., Ltd. | Distributor in North America: GW Distribution, LLC. (845) 429.3712

business—you may be ready for a trip to a Middle East bazaar.

Vertical or Grand?

Probably the most basic decision to make when buying a piano—and one you may have made already—is whether to buy a vertical or a grand. The following describes some of the advantages and disadvantages of each.

Vertical Advantages

- Takes up less space, can fit into corners
- Lower cost
- Easier to move

Vertical Disadvantages

- Sound tends to bounce back into player's face, making subtle control of musical expression more difficult.
- Action is not as advanced as in grand; repetition of notes is slower and less reliable in most cases, and damping is sometimes less efficient.
- Keys are shorter than on grands, making subtle control of musical expression more difficult.
- Cabinetwork is usually less elegant and less impressive.

Vertical pianos are suitable for those with simpler musical needs, or where budget and space constraints preclude buying a grand. Despite the disadvantages noted above, some of the larger, more expensive verticals do musically rival smaller, less expensive grands. They may be a good choice when a more subtle control of musical expression is desired, but where space is at a premium.

Grand Advantages

- Sound develops in a more aesthetically pleasing manner by bouncing off nearby surfaces and blending before reaching player's ears, making it easier to control musical expression.

A LITTLE BIT OF THE TECHNICAL

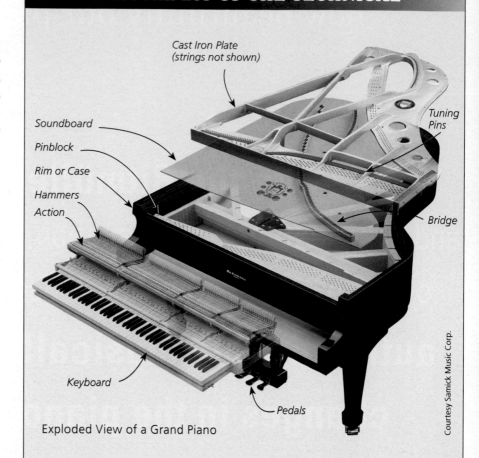

Cast Iron Plate (strings not shown)

Soundboard

Pinblock

Rim or Case

Hammers

Action

Tuning Pins

Bridge

Keyboard

Pedals

Courtesy Samick Music Corp.

Exploded View of a Grand Piano

A little bit (but not too much) of technical information about the piano is useful to have while shopping for one. Important words are in **boldface**.

A piano can be thought of as comprising four elements: mechanical, acoustical, structural, and cabinetry.

Mechanical: When you press a piano **key** (usually 88 in number), the motion of your finger is transmitted through a series of levers and springs to a felt-covered wooden **hammer** that strikes the strings to set them vibrating. This complex system of keys, hammers, levers, and springs is known as the **action**. Also, when you press a key, a felt **damper** resting against each string lifts off, allowing the string to vibrate. When you let the key up, the damper returns to its resting place, stopping the string's vibration. **Pedals**, usually three in number and connected to the action

and dampers, serve specialized functions such as sustaining and softening the sound. The right-foot pedal is called the **damper** or **sustain pedal**; it lifts all the dampers off all the strings, allowing the strings to ring sympathetically. The left-foot, **soft pedal** (on a grand piano, the **una corda pedal**) softens the sound. The function of the middle pedal varies depending on the type and price level of the piano. As a **sostenuto pedal**, it selectively sustains notes or groups of notes, a function required only rarely in a small percentage of classical compositions. Other possible functions for the middle pedal include a damper pedal for the bass notes only (**bass sustain**), and a mute or **practice pedal** that reduces the sound volume by about half.

Acoustical: Piano **strings** are made of steel wire for the higher-sounding notes (**treble**), and steel wire wrapped

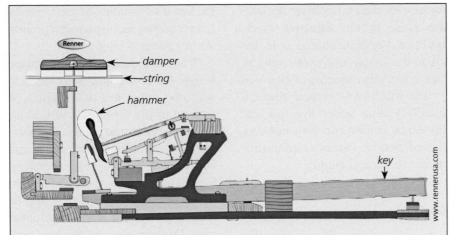

The key and action parts of a single note from a grand piano

[For online animation, click here.]

with copper for the lower-sounding notes (**bass**). They are graduated in thickness, length, and tension, and strung tightly across the structural framework of the piano. Each note has one, two, or three strings associated with it. Each such set of strings is known as a **unison** because all the strings in a set sound the same note. The strings lie across narrow hardwood **bridges** that transmit their vibrations to a wooden **soundboard**, usually made of spruce. The relatively large area of the soundboard amplifies what would otherwise be a rather weak sound and broadcasts the sound to the ears. The dimensions, arrangement, and positioning of all the acoustical elements in a piano is known as the piano's **scale design**. The scale design varies with the model and is a major determinant of the piano's tone.

Structural: The strings are strung across a gold- or bronze-colored **plate** (sometimes called a **frame** or **harp**) of cast iron, which is bolted to a substantial wooden framework. This heavy-duty structure is necessary to support the many tons of tension exerted by all the taut strings. A **vertical**, or upright, piano is one in which this structure stands vertically, and is most commonly placed against a wall. A **grand** piano is one in which this structure lies horizon-

tally. In a vertical piano, the wooden framework consists of vertical **back posts** and connecting cross beams; in a grand, wooden beams and the familiar curved **rim** comprise the framework. One end of each string is anchored to the plate toward the rear of a grand or the bottom of a vertical piano. The other end is coiled around a **tuning pin** embedded in a laminated hardwood **pinblock** hidden under the plate at the front (grand) or top (vertical). A piano is **tuned** by turning each tuning pin with a special tool to make very slight adjustments in the tension of its string, and thus to the string's frequency of vibration, or **pitch**.

Cabinetry: The piano's **cabinet** (vertical) or **case** (grand) provides aesthetic beauty and some additional structural support. A grand piano's rim is part of both the wooden structural framework and the case. Accessory parts, such as the music desk and lid, are both functional and aesthetic in purpose.

Although the acoustical and structural elements have been described separately, in fact the plate, wooden framework, soundboard, bridges, and strings form a single integrated unit called the **strung back**. A piano, then, consists of a strung back, an action (including keyboard), and a cabinet or case.

- More sophisticated action than in a vertical. Grand action has a repetition lever to aid in the speed and reliability of repetition of notes, and is gravity-assisted, rather than dependent on artificial contrivances (springs, straps) to return hammers to rest.
- Longer keys provide better leverage, allowing for significantly greater control of musical expression.
- Casework is usually more elegant and aesthetically pleasing.

Grand Disadvantages

- Takes up more space
- Higher cost
- Harder to move

What Size?

Both verticals and grands come in a wide variety of sizes. The important thing to know here is that size is directly related to musical quality. Although many other factors also contribute to tonal quality, *all else being equal*, the longer strings of larger pianos, especially in the bass and midrange sections, give off a deeper, truer, more consonant tonal quality than the strings of smaller pianos. The treble and bass blend better and the result is more pleasing to the ear. Also, longer grands usually have longer keys that generally allow superior control of musical expression than shorter grands. Therefore, it's best to buy the largest piano you can afford and have space for. Small differences in size between models are more significant in smaller pianos than in larger ones. However, a difference in size of only an inch or so is not generally significant, as it could be merely due to a larger cabinet or case.

Verticals

Vertical pianos are measured from the floor to the top of the piano.

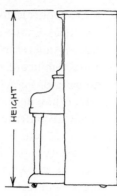

Verticals less than 40" tall are known as spinets. They were very popular in the post–World War II period, but in recent years have died out. Verticals from 40" to about 43" or 44" tall are called consoles. Spinet and console actions must be compromised somewhat in size or placement within the piano to fit them into pianos of this size. The tone is also compromised by the shorter strings and smaller soundboard. For this reason, manufacturers concentrate on the furniture component of small verticals and make them in a variety of decorator styles. They are suitable for buyers whose piano needs are casual, or for beginning students, and for those who simply want a nice-looking piece of furniture in the home. Once students progress to an intermediate or advanced stage, they are likely to need a larger instrument.

Studio pianos, from about 44" to 47" tall, are more serious instruments. They are called studios because they are commonly found in the practice rooms of music schools. Manufacturers make them in both attractive furniture styles for the home and in functional, durable, but aesthetically bland styles for school and other institutional use. If you don't require attractive furniture, you may save money by buying the school style. In fact, many buyers prefer the simple lines of these models.

Verticals about 48" and taller, called uprights, are the best musically. New ones top out at about 52", but in the early part of the 20th century they were made even taller. The tallest verticals take up no more floor space than the shortest ones, but some buyers may find the taller models too

massive for their taste. Most uprights are made in an attractive black, traditional or institutional style, but are also available with exotic veneers, inlays, and other touches of elegance.

The width of a vertical piano is usually a little under five feet and the depth around two feet; however, these dimensions are not significantly related to musical quality.

Grands

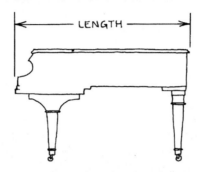

Grand pianos are measured (with the lid closed) in a straight line from the very front of the piano (keyboard end) to the very back (the tail). Lengths begin at 4' 6" and go to over 10' (or even longer in some experimental models). Widths are usually around 5' and heights around 3', but only the length has a significant bearing on musical quality.

Grands less than 5' long are usually somewhat musically compromised and are mainly sold as pieces of furniture. Grands between about 5' and 5½' are very popular. Although slightly compromised, they can reasonably serve both musical and furniture functions and are available in many furniture styles. (By the way, piano professionals prefer the term *small grand* to *baby grand*. Although there is no exact definition, a small grand is generally one less than about 5½' long.) Above 5½', pianos rapidly improve, potentially becoming professional quality at about 6'. Pianos intended for the home or serious professional top out at about 7' or 7½'. These sizes may also satisfy

the needs of smaller concert venues. Larger venues require concert grands, usually about 9' long.

When considering what size of piano is right for your home, don't forget to add two to three feet to the length of a grand or the depth of a vertical for the piano bench and pianist. Shoppers tend to underestimate what will fit and buy smaller pianos than necessary. Sometimes, the next-size-larger instrument can give you a great deal of tonal improvement at little additional cost. Dealers can usually lend you templates corresponding to different piano sizes to lay down on your floor so you can measure what will fit.

Budget

Your budget is probably the most important factor in your choice of piano, but it's hard to make a budget when you don't know how much pianos cost. Here is some rule-of-thumb information to get you started:

- Most new vertical pianos sell in the range of $4,000 to $10,000, though some higher-end ones cost two or three times that, and a few cost less.
- New small, inexpensive grand pianos generally go for $7,000 to $12,000; mid-size, mid-priced grands from $12,000 to $30,000; and high-end grands for $40,000 to $100,000 or more.
- Unrestored but playable used pianos cost from perhaps 10% to 80% of the cost of a comparable new instrument, depending on age and condition, with 15-year-old used pianos coming in at about 50%. The cost of restored instruments is discussed below.

More complete and accurate information can be found in the articles on new and used pianos, and in the "Model & Pricing Guide" reference section, elsewhere in this issue.

Rent or Buy

If the piano is being purchased for a beginner, there is a significant possibility that he or she will not stick with playing the piano. To handle this and other "high-risk" situations, most dealers offer a rental/purchase program. In the typical program, the dealer would rent you the piano you are considering purchasing for up to six months. You would pay round-trip moving expenses upfront, usually $400 to $600, plus a monthly rental fee, typically $70 to $120 for a vertical piano. (Rental/purchase programs do not usually apply to grand pianos.) Should you decide to buy the piano at any time before the end of the six-month term, all money paid up to that point would be applied to the purchase. Otherwise, you would return the piano and be under no further obligation.

Two pieces of advice here: First, make sure you rent the piano you ultimately wish to buy, or at least rent from the dealer who has that piano, and not simply the piano or dealer with the lowest rental rate—if you eventually decide to buy from a different dealer, you'll forfeit the rental payments already made to the first dealer. However, if you decide to buy a different piano from the same dealer from whom you rented, it's possible that dealer would agree to apply some or all of the rental payments to the new piano—but check on this in advance.

Second, clarify issues of price before you decide whether to rent or buy. Specifically, find out whether you'll be allowed to apply the rental payments toward, for example, today's sale price, rather than toward the regular price six months from now—or conversely, if you'll be held to today's price should there be a sale six months from now. Keep in mind, however, that a "sale" is generally a reduction in price designed to entice you to buy now.

Quality

Like just about everything else you can buy, pianos come in a range of quality levels. When we speak of *quality* in a piano, we are referring to how it sounds, plays, and looks, and how well it will hold up with time and use.

As you can imagine, any discussion of quality in pianos is likely to involve a lot of subjectivity and be somewhat controversial. However, a useful generalization for the purpose of discussing quality can be had by dividing pianos into two types: performance grade and consumer grade. *Performance-grade* pianos are made to a single, high quality standard, usually in relatively small quantities, by companies that strongly favor quality considerations over cost. *Consumer-grade* pianos, on the other hand, are built to be sold at a particular price, and the design, materials, level of workmanship, and manufacturing location are chosen to fit that price. Most consumer-grade pianos are mass-produced at a variety of price levels, with materials and designs chosen accordingly. Throughout much of the 20th century, the United States produced both types of piano in abundance. Presently, however, most performance-grade pianos are made in Europe and the United States, while virtually all consumer-grade pianos are made in Asia. Due to globalization and other factors, the distinction between the two types of piano is beginning to blur. This is discussed at greater length in the article "The New-Piano Market Today," elsewhere in this issue.

The above explanation of quality in pianos is very general, and some aspects of quality may be more applicable to your situation than others. Therefore, it pays to take some time to consider exactly what you expect from your piano, both practically and in terms of lifestyle. Practical needs include, among others, the level of expressiveness you require in the piano's tone and touch, how long you expect the instrument to satisfy your evolving needs, and what furniture it must match—as well as certain functional considerations, such as whether you use the middle pedal, desire a fallboard (key cover) that closes slowly, or need to be able to lock the piano. Lifestyle needs are those that involve the prestige or artistic value of the instrument, and how ownership of it makes you feel or makes you appear to others. Just as a casual driver may own a Mercedes, or one devoid of artistic abilities may own great works of art, many who don't play a note purchase expensive pianos for their artistic and prestige value.

A couple of the practical considerations require further discussion. Concerning expressiveness: What kind of music do you play or aspire to play? One can play any kind of music on any piano. However, some pianos seem better suited in tone and touch than other pianos to some kinds of music. Quality in piano tone is often defined in terms of the instrument's ability to excel at pleasing players of so-called "classical" music because this kind of music tends to make the greatest expressive demands on an instrument. So if you aspire to play classical music seriously, you may wish to one day own a fine instrument capable of the nuanced tone and touch the music demands. On the other hand, if classical music isn't your thing, you can probably get away with a less expensive instrument.

> A useful generalization for the purpose of discussing quality can be had by dividing pianos into performance grade and consumer grade.

Wm. Knabe & Co.

ESTABLISHED 1837

Exceptional. Elegant. Extraordinary.

"They reflect monumental credit on
American achievement; they are perfection."

- Richard Strauss,
Renowned German composer

HOW LONG DOES A PIANO LAST?

A note about how long a piano will last—a question I hear every day. The answer varies for pianos almost as much as it does for people. A piano played 16 hours a day in a school practice room might be "dead" in ten years or less, whereas one pampered in a living room in a mild climate might last nearly a century before requiring complete restoration to function again. A rule-of-thumb answer typically given is that an average piano under average conditions will last 40 to 50 years. If past experience is any guide, it would not be unreasonable to predict that the best-made pianos will last about twice as long as entry-level ones, given similar conditions of use and climate.

However—and this is the important point—most pianos are discarded not because they no longer function—in fact, they may go on to long lives as used pianos for other people—but because they no longer meet the needs or expectations of their owners or players. A player may have musically advanced beyond what the instrument will deliver, or the owner may now be wealthier and have higher expectations for everything he or she buys—or perhaps no one in the house is playing anymore and the piano is just taking up space. Thus, the important consideration for most buyers, especially buyers of new or relatively young pianos, is how long the piano in question will meet their needs and expectations, rather than how long that piano will last.

A key factor concerns how long you want to keep the instrument: Is it for a beginner, especially a youngster, and you're not sure piano lessons will "stick"? Is it a stepping stone to a better piano later on? Then an inexpensive piano may do. Do you want this to be the last piano you'll ever buy? Then, even if your playing doesn't yet justify it, buy a piano you can grow into but likely never grow out of.

You'll get a better sense of what quality means in a piano if you play a wide variety of them, including ones that cost less than what you plan to spend, as well as ones you can't afford. Warning: The latter can prove dangerous to your bank account. It's not unusual for a buyer to begin shopping with the intention of buying a $3,000 vertical, only to emerge some time later with a $30,000 grand!

New or Used?

The next choice you'll have to make is whether to buy new or used. The market for used pianos is several times the size of the market for new ones. Let's look at the merits of each choice:

New Piano Advantages

- Manufacturer's warranty
- Little chance of hidden defects
- Lower maintenance costs
- Easier to shop for
- Usually more local choices
- Longer piano life expectancy
- Greater peace of mind after purchasing

New Piano Disadvantages

- Higher upfront cost
- Significant depreciation loss if resold within first few years
- Limited choice of attractive older styles and finishes

Used Piano Advantages

- Lower upfront cost
- Greater choice of attractive older styles and finishes
- Can be more fun and interesting to shop for (if you like shopping for old things)
- Restorer may detail instrument to an extent that rivals new piano
- Piano likely to be already significantly depreciated, resulting in little or no loss if resold

Used Piano Disadvantages

- No manufacturer's warranty (though there may be a dealer's or restorer's warranty)
- Greater chance of hidden defects (unless completely restored)
- Higher maintenance costs (unless completely restored)
- Shorter piano life expectancy (unless completely restored)
- Can be maddeningly difficult and confusing to shop for
- Need to pay technician to examine and appraise it
- Possible need to size up restorer's ability to do a good job

Despite the longer list of disadvantages, most people buy used because of the lower upfront cost and because they feel they can manage the risks involved. The most important rule by far in managing risk is to have the piano professionally examined and appraised by a piano technician prior to purchase. This is especially important when buying from a private-party seller because there is no warranty, but it can also be done for peace of mind when buying from a professional seller, particularly if the piano is over ten years old. This will cost between $100 and $200 and is well worth the money. If you don't already have a piano technician you trust, hire a Registered Piano Technician (RPT) member of the Piano Technicians Guild (PTG). You can locate one near you on the PTG website, www.ptg.org. (To be designated an RPT, a technician must pass a series of tests. This provides the customer with some assurance of competence.)

It helps to remember that a new piano becomes "used" the moment it is first sold. Although junk certainly exists, used pianos actually come in a bewildering variety of conditions and situations, many of which can be quite attractive, musically and financially. However, pianos offered for a few hundred dollars or for free on websites such as Craigslist are usually a very poor option. They almost invariably need a great deal of work to bring them into playable condition, and are not worth the considerable cost of moving them. See also our article "Advice About Used Pianos For Parents of Young Beginning Piano Students" for a list of brands of used piano probably best avoided.

The subject of used pianos is vast. *The Piano Book* has a chapter devoted to it, including how to do your own preliminary technical examination of a piano. A summary of the most important information, including a description of the most common types of used pianos, where to find them, and how much to pay, can be found in the article "Buying a Used or Restored Piano" elsewhere in this issue. See also our archive of past feature articles for additional articles about buying a used or restored piano.

The Piano Dealer

The piano dealer is a very important part of the piano-buying experience, for several reasons:

- A knowledgeable and helpful salesperson can help you sort through the myriad possibilities and quickly home in on the piano that's right for you.
- A dealership with a good selection of instruments can provide you with enough options to choose from that you don't end up settling for less than what you really want (although you can make up for

BUYING A RESTORED PIANO

A subset of used pianos consists of instruments that have been professionally restored. The complete restoration of a piano is known as *rebuilding*. There is no universally agreed-on definition of what is included in a rebuilding job, so you have to ask specifically what has been done. A minimal partial restoration is called *reconditioning*—often just cleaning up the piano, replacing a few parts, tuning, and adjusting the action as needed. Vertical pianos are almost never completely rebuilt because the cost cannot be recouped in the sale price. However, verticals are frequently reconditioned. A complete rebuilding of a top-quality grand piano by a top-notch rebuilder generally costs from $20,000 to $40,000—and that's if you own the piano. If you're buying the piano too, figure a total cost of from 75% to more than 100% of the cost of a new piano of similar quality. A partial rebuilding of a lower-quality brand might cost half that, or even less.

Buying a used or restored piano is generally more difficult than buying a new one because, in addition to making judgments about the underlying quality of the instrument, you also must make judgments about its condition or about the skill and trustworthiness of the restorer—there's a greater concern about being burned if you make a mistake. Some find this too stressful or time-consuming. Others find the hunt fascinating, and end up discovering, in their community or online, an entire world of piano buffs, and piano technical and historical trivia.

this to some extent by shopping among a number of dealers).

- All pianos arrive from the factory needing some kind of pre-sale adjustment to compensate for changes that occur during shipment, or for musical finishing work left uncompleted at the factory. Dealers vary a great deal in their willingness to perform this work. There's nothing worse than trying to shop for a piano, and finding them out of tune or with obvious defects. It's understandable that the dealer will put the most work into the more expensive pianos, but a good dealer will make sure that even the lower-cost instruments are reasonably playable.
- A good dealer will provide prompt, courteous, skilled service to correct any small problems that occur after the sale, and act as your intermediary with the factory in the rare event that warranty service is needed.

Knowledge, experience, helpfulness, selection, and service—that's what you're looking for in a dealer.

Shopping Long-Distance via the Internet

The question often arises as to whether one should shop for a piano long-distance via the Internet. It turns out that this is really two different questions. The first is whether one should locate a dealer via the Internet, possibly far away, then visit that dealer to buy a piano. The second is whether one should buy a piano sight unseen over the Internet.

If you're shopping for a new piano, you'll probably have to visit a dealer. This is because dealers are generally prohibited by their agreements with manufacturers from quoting prices over the phone or via the Internet, or from soliciting business from customers outside their "market territory," the definition of which differs from brand to

brand. But once you set foot in the dealer's place of business, regardless of where you came from, you're considered a legitimate customer and all restrictions are off, even after you return home. There are no such restrictions for advertising or selling used pianos. (Exception: If a brand of new piano is one that the dealer owns or controls—known as a *house brand*—you may be able to purchase it without ever visiting the dealer.)

Customers, of course, don't care about "market territories." They just want to get the best deal. Given the ease of comparison shopping via the Internet, and the frequency with which people travel for business or pleasure, dealers are increasingly testing the limits of their territorial restrictions, and more and more sales are taking place at dealerships outside the customer's area. This is a delicate subject in the industry, and the practice is officially discouraged by dealers and manufacturers alike. In private, however, dealers are often happy when the extra business walks in the door (though they hate like heck to lose a sale to a dealer outside their area), and some manufacturers are choosing to look the other way.

There are obvious advantages to shopping locally, and it would be foolish not to at least begin there. Shopping, delivery, and after-sale service are all much easier, and there can be pleasure in forging a relationship with a local merchant. That said, every person's lifestyle and priorities are different. A New Yorker who frequently does business in San Francisco may find it more "local" to visit a piano dealer in downtown San Francisco, near his or her business meeting, than to drive all over the New York metropolitan area with spouse and children on a Saturday morning. In the marketplace, the customer is king. As people become more and more at ease with doing business of all kinds long-distance with the aid of the Internet, it's likely that piano shopping will migrate in that direction as well.

Buying a piano sight unseen (which, in view of the above discussion, is likely to involve used pianos, not new) is something entirely different. Obviously, if you're at all musically sensitive, buying a piano without trying it out first is just plain nuts. But, as much as I hate to admit it, it may make sense for some people, particularly beginners or non-players. In the piano business, we like to say—and I say it a lot—that a piano is not a commodity; that is, a product of which one example is more or less interchangeable with another. Each piano is unique, etc., etc., and must be individually chosen. But for someone who is buying a piano for a beginner, who has no preference in touch and tone, and who just wants a piano that's reasonably priced, reliable, and looks nice, a piano may, in fact, actually be a "commodity." I might wish it were otherwise, just as an audiophile might wish that I wouldn't buy a stereo system off the shelf of a discount department store, but we're all aficionados of some things and indifferent about others, and that's our choice. Furthermore, just as people who buy electronic keyboards frequently graduate to acoustic pianos, the person who today buys a piano over the Internet may tomorrow be shopping at a local dealer for a better piano with a particular touch and tone. Although it isn't something I'd advise as a general rule, the fact is that many people have bought pianos via the Internet without first trying them out and are pleased with their purchase (and some people, probably, are not so pleased).

If you're thinking of making a long-distance purchase, however, please take some precautions (not all of these precautions will apply to every purchase). First, consider whether it's really worth it once you've taken into account the cost of long-distance shipping. Find out as much as you can about the dealer. Get references. Get pictures of the piano. Hire a piano technician in the dealer's area to inspect the piano (to find a technician, use the Piano Technicians Guild website, www.ptg.org) and ask the technician about the dealer's reputation. Make sure the dealer is experienced with arranging long-distance piano moves, and uses a mover that specializes in pianos. Find out who is responsible for tuning and adjusting the piano in your home, and for repairing any defects or dings in the finish. Get the details of the warranty, especially who is responsible for paying the return freight if the piano is defective. Find out how payment is to be made in a way that protects both parties. And if, after all this, you still want to buy long-distance, my best wishes for a successful purchase.

It bears emphasizing that the above discussion was about buying a piano over the Internet from a *commercial dealer*, against whom you have at least some possibility of recourse if something goes wrong in the transaction. If buying long-distance from a *private individual*, in addition to the above advice, consider use of an escrow service, such as that provided by Piano Buyer Classifieds and Pianomart.com. The escrow service will hold your funds and not release them to the seller until you've had an opportunity to make sure that the piano you received is in the condition you expected.

Negotiating Price and Trade-Ins

The prices of new pianos are nearly always negotiable. Only a handful of dealers have non-negotiable prices. If in doubt, just ask—you'll be able to tell. Some dealers carry this bargaining to extremes, whereas others start pretty close to the final price. Many dealers don't like to display a piano's price because not doing so gives them more latitude in deciding on a starting price for negotiation. This makes shopping more difficult. Use the price information in the "Model & Pricing Guide" of the current issue

of *Acoustic & Digital Piano Buyer* to determine the likely range within which a given model will sell. Don't give in too quickly. It's quite common for the salesperson to call a day or two later and offer a lower price. If there's an alternative piano at another dealership that will suit your needs just as well, it will help your negotiating position to let the salesperson know that.

Due to the high cost of advertising and conducting piano megasales (such as college sales, truckload sales, etc.), prices at these events are often actually *higher* than the price you could negotiate any day of the week, and the pressure to buy can be substantial. Shop at these sales only after you've shopped elsewhere, and look for the real bargains that can occasionally be found there.

If you're buying a new piano to replace one that's no longer satisfactory, you'll probably want to trade in the old one. Dealers will usually take a trade-in, no matter how bad it is, just to be able to facilitate the sale. In fact, in many cases the dealer will offer you what seems like a king's ransom for the old one. The downside is that when a generous trade-in allowance is given on the old piano, the dealer is then likely to offer you a less-generous price on the new one. To see if you're being offered a good deal, you'll have to carefully analyze the fair-market value of the old piano and what would be a likely price for the new one without a trade-in. Sometimes it will be to your advantage to sell the old piano privately, though in that case you'll need to take into account the hassle factor as well.

For more information about new-piano prices and negotiating, see the introduction to the "Model & Pricing Guide," elsewhere in this issue, as well as in *The Piano Book*.

Used-piano prices may or may not be negotiable. If the used piano is being sold by a dealer who primarily sells new pianos at negotiable prices, then the used-piano prices are probably also negotiable. Prices of restored pianos sold by the restorer are less likely to be negotiable, as technical people are usually less comfortable with bargaining. Prices of pianos for sale by private-party sellers are usually negotiable, in part because the seller often has little idea of what the piano should sell for and has made up a price based only on wishful thinking. But even knowledgeable sellers will usually leave a little wiggle room in their price.

Electronic Player-Piano Systems

Prior to the Great Depression, most pianos were outfitted with player-piano mechanisms—the kind that ran on pneumatic pressure and paper rolls. Today's player pianos are all electronic; they run on smartphones, iPads and other tablets, notebooks and laptops, MP3s, CDs, or electronic downloads from the Internet, and are far more versatile and sophisticated than their pneumatic ancestors. Now you don't have to wait until Junior grows up to hear something interesting from the piano! A substantial percentage of new pianos, especially grands, are being outfitted with these systems. In fact, many pianos are being purchased as home-entertainment centers by buyers who have no intention of ever playing the piano themselves.

Several companies make these systems. Yamaha's Disklavier and Steinway's Spirio are built into select Yamaha, Steinway, and Bösendorfer models at these companies' factories. PianoDisc and QRS PNOmation, the two major aftermarket systems, can be installed in almost any piano, new or used, typically by the dealer or at an intermediate distribution point. Properly installed by a trained and authorized installer, none of these systems will harm the piano or void its warranty. However, such

The control box for some electronic player-piano systems is attached to the underside of the keybed.

installations are complicated and messy and must be done in a shop, not in your home.

The most basic system will play your piano and accompany it with synthesized orchestration or actual recorded accompaniment played through speakers hidden underneath the piano. The aftermarket systems generally add $5,500 to $7,000 to the price of the piano. Add another $1,500 to $2,000 to enable the piano to record your own playing for future playback. For a little bit more, you can mute the piano (stop the hammers from hitting the strings), turn on a digital piano sound, and listen through headphones—a great alternative for late-night practicing. The range of prices reflects the variety of configurations and options available, including what music source you use (smartphone, iPad, CD, MP3 player, etc.). Higher-level systems that reproduce music in audiophile quality cost $15,000 or

more. For more information, see the article "Buying an Electronic Player-Piano System," elsewhere in this issue.

Furniture Style and Finish

Although for most buyers the qualities of performance and construction are of greatest importance in selecting a piano, a piano is also a large piece of furniture that tends to become the focal point of whatever room it is placed in. This is especially true of grands. Add to that the fact that you'll be looking at it for many years to come, and it becomes obvious that appearance can be an important consideration. For some buyers, it may be the most important consideration.

Vertical pianos without front legs are known as *Continental* style (also called *contemporary, European contemporary,* or *Euro style*). They are usually the smallest (42" to 43" high) and least expensive pianos in a manufacturer's product line.

Pianos with legs supported by *toe blocks* (struts that connect the body of the piano to the front legs) are sometimes known as *institutional* or *professional* style, particularly when the cabinet also has little in the way of decoration or embellishment.

School pianos are a subset of the institutional-style category. Generally 45" to 47" in height, these are institutional-style pianos made specifically for use in school practice rooms and classrooms. They usually come equipped with long music racks for holding multiple sheets of music, locks for both the lid and the fallboard, and heavy-duty casters for easier moving. They are generally available in ebony or satin wood finishes. Sturdy and sometimes plain-looking, they are also often purchased for home use for less furniture-conscious locations. (If you're buying a piano for an institution, please read "Buying Pianos for an Institution," elsewhere in this issue.)

Continental Style

Wyman/Orla

Institutional or
Professional Style

Samick Music Corp.

Decorator Style:
French Provincial Cherry

Pramberger Piano Co.

School Style

Pramberger Piano Co.

Hybrid Style

Wyman/Orla

Decorator Style:
Mediterranean Oak

Samick Music Corp.

Decorator Style:
Traditional Mahogany

Pramberger Piano Co.

Vertical pianos with free-standing legs not reinforced by toe blocks are generally known as *decorator* style. Common decorator styles are Queen Anne and French Provincial, generally in cherry (or Country French in oak), all with curved legs; Italian Provincial, typically in walnut with square legs; Mediterranean, usually in oak with hexagonal legs; and Traditional, most often in mahogany or walnut, with round or hexagonal legs. Matching music racks and cabinet decoration are common furniture embellishments. Furniture-style preference is an entirely personal matter. A practical consideration, however, is that front legs not supported by toe blocks have a tendency to break if the piano is moved frequently or carelessly.

Hybrid styles, containing features of both institutional and decorator styles, are common, especially in Asian pianos.

Grand pianos come in far fewer styles than verticals. As you shop, it's likely you'll see only a few different styles, in a number of woods and finishes.

The traditional grand piano case is likely familiar to everyone. It has rather straight or slightly tapered legs, often flaring slightly just above the floor (called a *spade* leg), and usually a rather plain, solid music rack.

Victorian style (sometimes called *classic* style) is an imitation of a style in fashion in the late 1800s, with large, round, fluted legs and a fancy, carved music desk. Variations of the Victorian style have "ice-cream cone" or other types of round-ish legs.

As with verticals, grands also come in Queen Anne and French Provincial styles, with curved legs, and in other period styles. In addition to the leg style, these usually differ in the treatment of the music rack and cabinet embellishment as well.

Pianos come in a variety of woods, most commonly ebony (sometimes called ebonized), which is not actual ebony wood, but an inexpensive, sturdy veneer that has been finished in black; as well as mahogany, cherry, walnut, and oak. Exotic woods include bubinga, rosewood, and many others, available on higher-priced uprights and grands. In pianos of lesser quality, sometimes a less expensive wood will be stained to look like a more expensive one. Pianos are also available in ivory or white, and it's often possible to special-order a piano in red, blue, or other colors.

In addition to the wood itself, the way the wood is finished also varies.

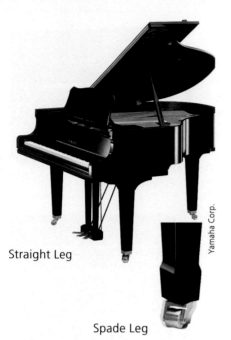

Straight Leg

Spade Leg

Yamaha Corp.

Queen Anne Style

Samick Music Corp.

Victorian Style
with Ice-Cream Cone legs

Petrof

Piano finishes come in either high polish (high gloss) or satin finishes. Satin reflects light but not images, whereas high polish is nearly mirror-like. Variations on satin include matte, which is completely flat (i.e., reflects no light), and open-pore finishes, common on European pianos, in which the grain is not filled in before finishing, leaving a slightly grainier texture. A few finishes are semigloss, which is partway between satin and high polish. As with furniture style, the finish is an entirely personal matter, though it should be noted that satin finishes tend to show fingerprints more than do high-polish finishes.

Most piano finishes are either lacquer or polyester. Lacquer was the finish on most pianos made in the first three-quarters of the 20th century, but it is gradually being supplanted by polyester. In my opinion, lacquer finishes—especially high-gloss lacquer—are more beautiful than polyester, but they scratch quite easily, whereas polyester is very durable. (Lacquer finishes can be repaired more easily.) Hand-rubbed satin lacquer is particularly elegant.

Touch and Tone

Touch, in its simplest form, refers to the effort required to press the piano keys. Unfortunately, the specifications provided by the manufacturers, expressed in grams, don't do justice to this complicated subject. The apparent touch can be very different when the piano is played quickly and loudly than when it is played softly and slowly, and this difference is not captured in the numbers—if you're a player, be sure to try it out both ways.

Advanced pianists tend to prefer a touch that is moderately firm because it provides better control than a very light touch, and strengthens the muscles. Too light a touch, even for a beginner, can cause laziness, but too firm a touch can be physically harmful over time. The touch of most new pianos today is within a reasonable range for their intended audience, but the touch of older pianos can vary a lot, depending on condition. A piano teacher may be able to assist in evaluating the touch of a piano for a beginner, particularly if considering an entry-level or used piano.

Piano *tone* is also very complex. The most basic aspect of tone, and the one most easily changed, is its brightness or mellowness. A *bright* tone, sometimes described by purchasers as *sharp* or *loud*, is one in which higher-pitched overtones predominate. A *mellow* tone, sometimes described as *warm*, *dull*, or *soft*, is one in which lower-pitched overtones are dominant. Most pianos are somewhere in between, and vary from one part of the keyboard to another, or depending on how hard one plays. The key to satisfaction is to make sure that the tone is right for the music you most often play or listen to. For example, jazz pianists will often prefer a brighter tone, whereas classical pianists will often prefer one that is mellower, or that can be varied easily from soft to loud; i.e., that has a broad dynamic range. However, there is no accounting for taste, and there are as many exceptions to these generalizations as there are followers. A piano technician can adjust the brightness or mellowness of the tone to a limited degree through a process known as *voicing*.

Another aspect of tone to pay

attention to is *sustain*, which is how long the sound of a note continues at an audible level while its key is depressed before disappearing. Practically speaking, this determines the ability of a melodic line to "sing" above an accompaniment, especially when played in the critical mid-treble section.

Most pianos will play loudly quite reliably, but providing good expression when played softly is considerably more challenging. When trying out a piano, be sure to play at a variety of dynamic levels. Test the action with your most technically demanding passages. Don't forget to test the pedals for a sensitivity commensurate with your musical needs.

The Piano Warranty

Most pianos never generate a warranty claim. That said, few people would sleep well if worrying about potential problems arising in such a major purchase. Key warranty issues are: what is covered, for how long, and who stands behind the warranty.

The overwhelming majority of new-piano warranties cover the cost of parts and labor necessary to correct any defect in materials or workmanship. The warrantor (usually the manufacturer or distributor) also generally reserves the right to replace the piano should it choose to in lieu of repair. The warrantee (the customer) generally makes warranty claims to the dealer who, upon approval of the warrantor, makes the necessary repairs or replaces the instrument, as applicable. If the dealer has gone out of business, or if the customer has moved, warranty claims are made to the new local dealer of that brand, if any, or directly to the warrantor.

Warranties are in effect from the date of purchase and generally run between five and fifteen years, depending on the manufacturer. Note that there is little correlation between

the length of the warranty and the quality of the piano, as decisions on warranty terms are often made based on marketing factors. For example, a new manufacturer might well offer a longer warranty to help bolster sales.

The Magnuson-Moss Warranty Act mandates that warranties be either *full* or *limited*. In the piano industry, the only significant difference is that full warranties remain in effect for the entire stated term, regardless of piano ownership, whereas limited warranties cover only the original purchaser. If you plan on possibly selling or trading up within a few years, a full warranty offers protection to the new owner, increasing the piano's value to them, and may justify a little higher selling price or trade-in value.

The final key issue about piano warranties concerns who stands behind the warranty. In most cases the

warranty is backed by the actual manufacturer. This is advantageous, as the manufacturer has a major capital investment in its factory and has probably been in business for many years. The likelihood is that it will be around for the entire five- to fifteen-year period of your warranty. In today's piano market, however, many brands are manufactured under contract for a distributor, and the warranty is backed only by that distributor. Often, the distributor's only investment is a small rented office/warehouse and a few dozen pianos. Pianos are also often made to order for a particular dealership under a private brand name and are sold—and warranted—only by that dealership and/or its affiliates. In those cases, the warranty is further limited by the financial strength of the distributor or dealership, which can be difficult

for the shopper to evaluate. In these situations, caution is called for.

When purchasing a used or restored piano, there is no warranty from a private, non-commercial seller, but a commercial seller will usually provide some kind of warranty, even if for only a few months. Pianos that have been completely restored typically come with a warranty with terms similar to that of a new piano, though of course it is backed by only the restorer.

Miscellaneous Practical Considerations

Bench

In all likelihood, your purchase of a new piano will include a matching bench. Benches for consumer-grade pianos are usually made by or for the piano manufacturer and come with the piano. Benches for performance-grade pianos are more often provided separately by the dealer.

Benches come in two basic types: fixed-height and adjustable, and in single and "duet" widths. Consumer-grade pianos usually come with fixed-height duet benches that have either a solid top that matches the piano's finish, or a padded top with sides and legs finished to match the piano. The legs of most benches will be miniatures of the piano's legs, particularly for decorative models. Most piano benches have music-storage compartments. School and institutional-type vertical pianos often come with so-called "stretcher" benches—the legs are connected with wooden reinforcing struts to better endure heavy use.

Adjustable benches are preferred by serious players, and by children and adults who are shorter or taller than average. The deeply tufted tops come in a heavy-duty vinyl and look like leather; tops of actual leather are available at additional cost. Adjustable benches vary considerably in quality. The best ones are expensive ($500 to $750) but are built to last a lifetime.

Finally, if the piano you want doesn't come with the bench you desire, talk to your dealer. It's common for dealers to swap benches or bench tops to accommodate your preference, or to offer an upgrade to a better bench in lieu of a discount on the piano.

For more information, see "Benches, Lamps, Accessories, and Problem Solvers," elsewhere in this issue.

Middle Pedal

As I mentioned near the beginning of this article, the function of the middle pedal varies. In some circumstances, you may need to consider whether the function of the middle pedal on a particular instrument will meet your musical needs.

On most new vertical pianos, the middle pedal operates a mute that reduces the sound volume by about 50%, a feature often appreciated by family members of beginning students. If your piano lacks this feature, after-market mute mechanisms are available for grands and verticals through

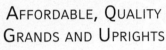

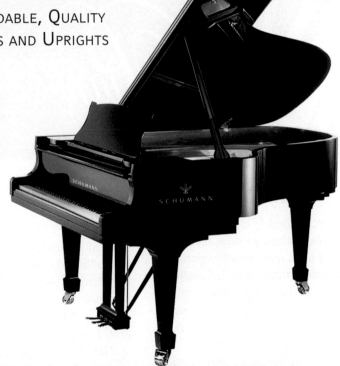

piano technicians or dealers. On older verticals and a few new ones, the middle pedal, if not a mute, usually operates a bass sustain, although occasionally it's a "dummy" pedal that does nothing at all. I've never known anyone to actually use a bass-sustain pedal, so it might as well be a dummy.

On most grands and a few expensive uprights, the middle pedal operates a sostenuto mechanism that selectively sustains only those notes whose keys are down at the moment the pedal is pressed. This mechanism is called into action for only a relatively few pieces of classical music, yet it is generally considered obligatory for any "serious" instrument. Only inexpensive new and used grands omit the sostenuto, usually in favor of a bass sustain. (The obligatory nature of the sostenuto pedal—or any middle pedal—on a grand piano is a largely American phenomenon. Until fairly recently, many "serious" European pianos made for the European market had only two pedals.)

Fallboard (Keyboard Cover)

Vertical pianos use one of three basic fallboard designs: the Boston fallboard, a sliding fallboard (both of which disappear when open), or a one-piece "drop" fallboard with integrated music shelf.

The Boston fallboard is found on most furniture-style pianos and characteristically is a two-piece, double-hinged assembly. It is easily removed for service, and the rigidity provided by the hinges keeps the fallboard and the piano's side arms from being scratched when the fallboard is opened or closed.

The sliding fallboard, a one-piece cover that slides out from under the music desk to cover the keys, is considerably less expensive. However, if it is pulled unevenly and/or upwardly, it can scratch the fallboard or the inside of the piano's side arms.

The one-piece "drop" fallboard is commonly found on larger uprights. It is simply hinged at the back and lifts up to just past vertical, where it lies against the upper front panel of the piano. Attached to its underside is a small music shelf that is exposed when the fallboard is opened, then manually unfolded.

Grand pianos have a smaller, one-piece "drop" fallboard that opens under the music desk. Fallboards on most newer grands (and some newer verticals) are hydraulically damped to close slowly over the keys, eliminating the possibility of harming the player's or a young child's fingers. Aftermarket kits are available for pianos that lack this feature.

Slow-Close Grand Piano Lid

A relatively new device adds hydraulic damping to a grand piano lid, substantially reducing the effort needed to raise and lower this extremely heavy part of the piano, and reducing the chance of injury when doing so. This is a standard feature of a few piano brands, but can also be retrofitted to most grand pianos. For more information, see our review. 🎹

THE NEW-PIANO MARKET TODAY

LARRY FINE

WHEN I BEGAN servicing pianos during the 1970s, most pianos sold in the U.S. (with the important exception of the growing number of pianos from Japan) were made in the U.S. by about a dozen different makers, which together turned out hundreds of thousands of pianos annually. By current standards, many were not particularly well made. Today, only three companies make pianos in the U.S. in any real quantities, which combined amount to no more than a few thousand instruments per year. However, over 30,000 new acoustic pianos are sold here annually under some 70 different brand names, made by more than 30 companies in a dozen countries. The quality is the best it's ever been. Here are the highlights of what's happened:

- The Japanese "invasion" of the 1960s onward was followed by a wave of pianos from Korea in the 1980s and '90s. Together, these imports put most low- and mid-priced American makers out of business.
- Rising wages in Korea in the 1990s caused much of that country's piano production to move to Indonesia and China.
- The economic emergence of China during the 2000s resulted in a new wave of low-priced, low-quality pianos appearing in the U.S. and globally.
- Foreign firms and investors have combined low-cost Chinese and Indonesian labor with high-quality design and manufacturing expertise, parts, and materials from Western countries to greatly increase the quality of low-priced Chinese and Indonesian pianos.
- Cheaper equipment for computer-aided design and manufacturing has allowed for their more widespread use by small and large firms alike, with a consequent increase in precision of manufacturing at all price levels.
- Since the 1990s, a dozen or more European makers of high-quality pianos have been aggressively marketing their pianos in the U.S., challenging entrenched interests and creating more choice and higher quality in the high end of the piano market.
- To better survive in a global economy, high-end companies have diversified their product lines to include low- and mid-priced pianos, setting up factories or forming alliances with companies in parts of the world where labor is cheaper. At the same time, makers of low- and mid-priced pianos are creating higher-priced models using parts and expertise usually associated with the high-end companies, thus blurring the line between the high and low ends of the piano market.

Over 30,000 new acoustic pianos are sold here annually under some 70 different brand names, made by more than 30 companies in a dozen countries.

China

The first piano factory in China is said to have been established in 1895, in Shanghai (perhaps by the British?). During the 1950s, the Communists consolidated the country's piano manufacturing into four government-owned factories: Shanghai, Beijing, and Dongbei (means "northeast") in the northern part of the country, and Guangzhou Pearl River in the south. Piano making, though industrial, remained primitive well into the 1990s. In that decade, the government of China began to open the country's economy to foreign investment, first only to partnerships with the government, and later to completely private concerns.

As China's economy has opened up, the nation's rising middle and upper classes have created a sharp increase in demand for pianos. Tempted by the enormous potential of the Chinese domestic market, as well as by the lure of cheap goods manufactured for the West, foreign interests have built new piano factories in China, bought existing factories, or contracted with existing factories for the manufacture of pianos. The government has also poured money into its own factories to make them more competitive and to accommodate the growing demand.

Except for the government involvement, the piano-making scene in China today is reminiscent of that in the U.S. a century ago: Hundreds of small firms assemble pianos from parts or subassemblies obtained from dozens of suppliers and sell them on a mostly regional basis. The government factories and a few large foreign ones sell nationally. Most of the pianos sold in the Chinese domestic market are still primitive by Western standards. Primarily, the quality has markedly improved where foreign technical assistance or investment has been involved; only those pianos are good enough to be sold in the West.

Although in China the government factories have long had a monopoly on sales through piano dealers, that hold is gradually being eroded, and the government entities are experiencing great competitive pressure from all the smaller players. Combined with the inefficiencies and debt inherent in government operations, the current competitive situation is probably making the government think twice about continuing to subsidize the piano industry. Already, one of its factories, Dongbei, has been privatized through its sale to Gibson Guitar Corporation, parent of Baldwin Piano Company; and another, Guangzhou Pearl River, has successfully completed an initial public offering to become a public company.

Besides Baldwin, Pearl River, and the government-owned factories, other large makers in China for the North American market are Parsons Music (Hong Kong), Yamaha (Japan), Young Chang (Korea), and, for the Canadian market, Kawai (Japan)—all of whom own factories in China. Other foreign-owned companies that own factories in China or contract with Chinese

manufacturers to make pianos for the U.S. market include AXL (Palatino brand), Bechstein (W. Hoffmann Vision brand), Blüthner (Irmler Studio brand), Brodmann, Cunningham, Heintzman, Perzina, Schulze Pollmann, and Wilh. Steinberg. Many American distributors and dealers contract with Beijing, Pearl River, and other makers, selling pianos in the U.S. under a multitude of names. Steinway & Sons markets the Essex brand, designed by Steinway and manufactured by Pearl River.

And one company, Hailun, is owned and operated by a Chinese entrepreneur, Chen Hailun.

From about 2000 to 2005, most sales of Chinese pianos in the U.S. were based on the idea of luring customers into the store to buy the least expensive piano possible. Dealers that staked their business on this approach often lost it. A growing trend now is to manufacture and sell somewhat higher-priced pianos that have added value in the form of better components, often imported to China from Europe and the U.S., but still taking advantage of the low cost of Chinese labor. The best ones are not just a collection of parts, however, but also have improved designs developed with foreign technical assistance, and sufficient oversight to make sure the designs are properly executed.

The oversight is especially important. Chinese piano manufacturers have been quite aggressive in acquiring piano-making knowledge, and are happy to use their alliances with Western distributors in furthering that end. There has been a tendency, however, for Chinese factory managers to ignore the advice and requests of Western distributors once their inspectors leave the factory, resulting in product that does not meet the standards or specifications contracted for. The distributors have gradually discovered that the only way to overcome this problem is

to own the factory themselves, to maintain a constant presence at the factory, or to constitute such a large percentage of the Chinese company's business that they, the Westerners, can control production. Alternatively, a Western company can examine all the pianos in its home country before sending them on to dealers, but this is less satisfactory than stopping problems at the source. Western distributors of Korean pianos used to complain of a similar problem with Korean factory managers during the height of that country's piano industry in the 1980s and '90s. As in Korea, the situation in China is rapidly improving as the Chinese become accustomed to Western ways of doing business and more focused on quality control.

Pianos made in China now dominate the North American market, constituting more than a third of all new pianos sold in the U.S. A decade ago, most were just barely acceptable technically, and musically undesirable. Over the years, however, both the technical and musical qualities have taken big leaps forward. While some remain at the entry level, others rival the performance of more expensive pianos from other parts of the world. Reports sometimes suggest less consistency than with pianos from other countries, and a continuing need for thorough pre-sale preparation by the dealer (who sometimes must weed out the bad ones and return them to the factory), but otherwise few major problems. The prices of the better models are rising, but for entry- and mid-level buyers, many Chinese brands are still good value.

Indonesia

Indonesia is China's closest competitor in terms of price and quality. But unlike China, in which many small and large companies, domestic and foreign, are involved

EVERY PIANO SHOWROOM READY OUT OF THE BOX!

KF228 NOW AVAILABLE

KINGSBURG PIANOS: QUALITY, RELIABILITY AND VALUE

KINGSBURG is proud to introduce the most wonderful experience for you — KU, KG, KF, from classic to luxury. Kingsburg pianos utilize some of the finest components in the world, are built to last and are showroom ready out of the box.

KINGSBURG
QUALITY | RELLABILITY | VALUE

in piano manufacturing, virtually all pianos made in Indonesia are the products of three large, foreign players: Yamaha, Kawai, and Samick. For the U.S. market, Yamaha makes an entry-level grand and most of their smaller verticals in Indonesia; Kawai makes all its small and medium-sized verticals there, and one entry-level grand; and Samick makes all its pianos for sale in North America there, both grand and vertical.

Overall, the manufacturing quality is similar to China's, but Indonesia got to this level of quality more rapidly and is perhaps more consistent. This may have been due to the smaller number and, on average, larger size of Indonesia's piano manufacturers, as well as to cultural and political differences between the countries. Development of manufacturing in Indonesia was aided by the fact that the country was already a democratic (more or less), capitalist nation with strong ties to the West, and accustomed to Western ways of working and doing business, with English widely spoken. The government does not own or manage the factories.

One of the big challenges in Indonesia, as in the rest of tropical Asia (which includes southern China), is climate control inside the factories, and the proper handling of wood to avoid problems later on when the instruments are shipped to drier countries and the wood dries out. All three companies, as well as Pearl River in southern China, have done a good job of meeting this challenge, but caution and proper climate control by the consumer are especially advised when these pianos are to be used in very difficult, dry indoor climates.

Korea

The Korean piano industry has had a tumultuous history, from its beginnings in the war-torn 1950s through its meteoric global rise in the 1980s; through labor unrest, the Asian economic crisis, and the abrupt collapse of the country's piano industry in the 1990s; and most recently through bankruptcies, reorganizations, aborted takeovers, and more bankruptcies. Today, both Samick and Young Chang seem to be on relatively stable financial footing, the latter having just emerged from bankruptcy after being purchased by Hyundai Development Company. As mentioned earlier, due to high labor costs in Korea, both companies have moved most of their manufacturing elsewhere, limiting production at home to the more expensive models.

Quality control in the Korean models is now nearly as good as in pianos from Japan, but getting there has taken 30 years of two steps forward, one step back. The reasons for the slow development are probably numerous, but undoubtedly some are cultural in nature: Western piano-company personnel have often reported that their Korean counterparts can be proud people, reluctant to take advice from Americans (not that they necessarily should—unless they're trying to sell products to Americans).

Musically, the two companies' pianos have never really gained clear, aesthetic identities of their own, other than as very acceptable musical products. Periodic redesigns by German engineers, or American engineers with Germanic names (always sought by piano makers), have brought some progress, but never as much as was hoped for. Part of the reason for the lack of identity may be that there have been such a multitude of product lines made in different factories to constantly changing specifications that nothing has settled down long enough to stick. Internal politics and dealing with quality-control problems have also taken up much energy over the years.

Things are settling down now for both companies. Samick, in its upper- and mid-level lines, is producing some of its nicest pianos ever. Young Chang is playing catch-up, but also has some good designs, with new ones in the pipeline. Both companies' top-level products have much to offer at good prices.

Japan

Japan's two major piano manufacturers, Yamaha and Kawai, began making pianos around 1900 and 1927, respectively, with export to the United States beginning in earnest in the early 1960s. The first few years of export were spent learning to season the wood to the demands of the North American climate, but since then the quality control has been impressive, to say the least, and the standard to which other piano manufacturers aspire. Both companies also have outstanding warranty service, so customers are never left hanging with unsatisfactory instruments. As in Korea, labor costs in Japan have risen to the point where both companies have been forced to move much of their manufacturing elsewhere, making only their more expensive models in Japan. With some exceptions, their grands and tallest uprights are made in Japan, small and mid-sized verticals in other Asian countries.

> **Quality control in the Korean models is now nearly as good as in pianos from Japan, but getting there has taken 30 years of two steps forward, one step back.**

The tone of Japanese pianos tends to be a little on the bright and percussive side (Yamaha more than Kawai), though less so than in previous years, and pleasing in their own way. In addition to their regular lines, both companies make high-end lines with more "classical" qualities, as well as entry-level lines that reflect a compromise between price and quality. The pianos are very popular with institutions and are real workhorses. Although more expensive than most other Asian pianos, a Japanese-made Yamaha or Kawai piano is hard to beat for reliability. Kawai also manufactures the Boston brand, designed by Steinway and sold through Steinway dealers.

United States

Only three companies manufacture pianos here in any numbers: Steinway & Sons, Mason & Hamlin, and Charles R. Walter. A few boutique makers, such as Ravenscroft, build high-end pianos to order. Baldwin, for a century one of the largest American producers, finally ceased most production at its American factory in 2009, having moved nearly all piano production to its two plants in China.

Steinway & Sons has been making high-quality pianos in New York City since its founding in 1853 by German immigrants. For most of the past century, the company has had little competition in the U.S.: when one desired to buy a piano of the highest quality, it was simply understood that one meant a Steinway. The last decade or two has seen a gradual erosion of that status by more than a dozen European firms and our own Mason & Hamlin. Although each by itself is too small to make a dent in Steinway's business, their combined effect has been to claim a substantial share of the market for high-end pianos in the home. (Steinway still dominates the concert-grand market and, to some extent, the institutional market.) This has been made easier by the fact that in certain respects these European-made pianos are visibly and audibly of higher quality than American-made Steinways (to be distinguished from Steinways made at the company's branch factory in Hamburg, Germany, which are of the highest quaity). Steinways have classic designs and use proven materials and methods of construction, but the musical and aesthetic finishing of the American-made pianos has too often been left uncompleted at the factory in the expectation, frequently unmet, that the dealers would finish it off. Fortunately, the past few years have seen a reversal of this trend in the form of many small improvements at the factory, as well as perhaps better performance by dealers. Though there is room for further improvement, the ratio of compliments to complaints, in my experience, has become more favorable. The recent replacement of American Steinway management by personnel from Steinway's European branches may also be having a salutary effect.

Mason & Hamlin, Steinway's principal competitor in the early part of the 20th century, went into a long period of decline after the Great Depression. After a series of bankruptcies and reorganizations in the 1980s and '90s, Mason & Hamlin was purchased in 1996 by the Burgett brothers, owners of PianoDisc, a leading manufacturer of player-piano systems. Since then, from an old brick factory building in Haverhill, Massachusetts, the Burgetts have completely restored the company to its former excellence, and then some. They and their staff have designed or redesigned a complete line of grand pianos and modernized century-old equipment. Rather than compete with Steinway on Steinway's terms, Mason & Hamlin has repositioned itself as an innovator, seeking out or developing high-quality but lower-cost parts and materials from around the world, and combining them with traditional craftsmanship to produce a great piano at a somewhat lower price.

Charles R. Walter, a piano design engineer by profession, has been making high-quality vertical pianos in Elkhart, Indiana, since the 1970s, and grands for over ten years. The factory is staffed in large part by members of his extended family. The instruments are built using the best traditional materials and construction practices. Right now, times are tough for small companies such as this, which produce an excellent product but are neither the high-priced celebrated names nor the low-cost mass producers. If you're looking to "buy American," you can't get any more American than Charles R. Walter.

Europe

European makers that regularly sell in the U.S. include: Bechstein, Blüthner, August Förster, Grotrian, Sauter, Schimmel, Seiler, Steingraeber, and Wilh. Steinberg (Germany); Bösendorfer (Austria); Fazioli and Schulze Pollmann (Italy); Estonia (Estonia); and Petrof (Czech Republic). Most

The rush to sell to Americans has caused some European companies to reconsider the tonal designs of their instruments.

are of extremely high quality; even the least of them is very good. Until two decades ago, most of these brands were virtually unknown or unavailable in the U.S., but as the European demand for pianos contracted, many of the companies found that Americans, with their large homes and incomes, would buy all the grand pianos they could produce. The liberation of Eastern Europe resulted in an increase in the quality of such venerable brands as Estonia and Petrof, which had suffered under Communist rule, and these brands, too, became available and accepted here.

The rush to sell to Americans has caused some European companies to reconsider the tonal designs of their instruments and to redesign them for better sound projection, tonal color, and sustain—that is, to sound more like American Steinways. Considering that some of these companies are five or six generations old and have redesigned their pianos about that many times in 150 years, this degree of activity is unusual. Some of the redesigns have been great musical successes; nevertheless, the loss of diversity in piano sound is to be mourned.

Several German companies have started or acquired second-tier lines to diversify their product lines, and have gradually shifted much of their production to former Soviet-bloc countries with lower labor costs, producing brands such as W. Hoffmann (by Bechstein) in the Czech Republic, and Wilhelm Schimmel, formerly Vogel (by Schimmel), in Poland. Today, there is enough commonality in business practices, laws, and attitudes toward quality among the countries of Europe that the distinction between Eastern and Western Europe carries little meaning—except for labor costs, where the savings can be great.

Globalization, Quality, and Value

The worldwide changes in the piano industry are making it more difficult to advise piano shoppers. For many years, the paradigm for piano quality has been an international pecking order: pianos from Russia, China, and Indonesia at the bottom; followed by Korea, Japan, and Eastern Europe; and, finally, Western Europe at the top, with pianos from the U.S. scattered here and there, depending on the brand. This pecking order has never been foolproof, but it has served a generation of piano buyers well enough as a rule of thumb.

Now this order is being disturbed by globalization. High-end and low-end makers are, to some extent, adopting each other's methods and narrowing the differences between them. On the one hand, some Western European and American makers of high-end pianos are partially computerizing the manufacture of their "hand-built" pianos, quietly sourcing parts and subassemblies from China, and developing less expensive product lines in Eastern Europe and Asia. On the other hand, some Korean and Chinese makers are importing parts and technology from Germany, Japan, and the U.S., producing pianos that sometimes rival the performance of more expensive pianos from the West. Global alliances are bringing new products to market that are more hybridized than anything we've seen before. Although the old pecking order still has some validity, the number of exceptions is increasing, causing temporary confusion in the marketplace until a new order emerges.

The worldwide changes in the piano industry are making it more difficult to advise piano shoppers.

At the same time that the range of quality differences is narrowing, the range of prices is widening, bringing into greater prominence issues of "value." Eastern European brands have emerged as "value" alternatives to Western European brands, the latter becoming frightfully expensive due to high labor costs and the rapid appreciation of the euro against the dollar. Some of the better pianos from China, Korea, and Indonesia have become value alternatives to Japanese pianos. Brands that don't scream "value" are being squeezed out of the market.

As mentioned above, one of the consequences of globalization is that parts and materials formerly available only to high-end makers are now for sale to any company, anywhere, that's willing to pay for them. Thus, you'll see a number of Asian firms marketing their pianos with a list of well-regarded brand-name components from Germany and North America, such as Renner, Röslau, Mapes, and Bolduc. The question then naturally arises: Given that high-end pianos are so expensive, and that today one can buy for so little a Chinese-made piano with German design, German parts, and perhaps even a German name, is it still worth buying a performance-grade piano made in the West? Are there any differences worth paying for?

There's no question that high-end components, such as Renner hammers and Bolduc soundboards, add to the quality and value of consumer-grade pianos in which they're used. But in terms of quality, components such as these are only the tip of the iceberg. Although the difference between performance- and consumer-grade

pianos has narrowed, in many ways the two types of manufacturers still live in different worlds. Differences are manifested in such things as the selection, drying, and use of wood; final regulation and voicing; and attention to technical and cosmetic details.

Makers of performance-grade pianos use higher grades of wood, selected for finer grain, more even color, or greater hardness, strength, and/or acoustical properties, as the use requires. Wood is seasoned more carefully and for longer periods of time, resulting in greater dimensional stability and a longer-lasting product. Veneers are more carefully matched, and finishes polished to a greater smoothness. Action assemblies purchased from suppliers may be taken apart and put back together to more exacting tolerances than originally supplied. The workspace is set up to allow workers more time to complete their tasks and a greater opportunity to catch and correct errors. Much more time is spent on final regulation and voicing, with an instrument not leaving the factory, in some cases, until a musician has had an opportunity to play it and be satisfied. Of course, the degree to which these manifestations of quality, and many others not mentioned, are present will vary by brand and circumstance, but underlying them all is this philosophical difference: with performance-grade pianos, the driving force behind decision-making tends to be the quality of the product; with consumer-grade pianos, cost is a greater factor.

A MAP OF THE MARKET FOR NEW PIANOS

The chart and commentary that follow are intended to provide the newcomer to the piano market with a simple summary of how this market is organized. This summary is not, strictly speaking, a ranking of

PERFORMANCE-GRADE PIANOS	
Iconic *Verticals:* $30,000–$70,000 *Grands* *5' to 7':* $75,000–$150,000	C. Bechstein Blüthner Bösendorfer Fazioli Steingraeber & Söhne Steinway & Sons (Hamburg)
Venerable *Verticals:* $20,000–$40,000 *Grands* *5' to 7':* $60,000–$105,000	August Förster Grotrian Sauter Steinway & Sons (New York)
Distinguished *Verticals:* $17,000–$35,000 *Grands* *5' to 7':* $50,000–$90,000	Bechstein (B) Estonia Haessler Shigeru Kawai Mason & Hamlin Petrof Schimmel (Konzert/Classic) Seiler (Germany) Yamaha (CF)
Notable *Verticals:* $16,000–$24,000 *Grands* *5' to 7':* $45,000–$80,000	W. Hoffmann (Tradition/Professional) Rönisch Schulze Pollmann (Masterpiece) Wilh. Steinberg (Signature) Charles R. Walter Yamaha (SX)

Notes: Unless otherwise stated, brand names refer to both grand and vertical models. Prices are Suggested Maximum Prices (SMP) of vertical models, and of grand models from 5' to 7' in length, regular style, lowest-price finish (usually polished ebony). Substantial discounts from these prices are common—see p.188 for further explanation. The prices shown for a category reflect, in round numbers, the approximate range into which most of the brands and models in that category fall, but a few models may fall outside the range. Also, keep in mind that an individual brand's price range may be narrower than that of the category it is listed under.

quality; rather, it is intended as a description of how manufacturers and dealers position their products in the marketplace. That is, if a dealer carried every brand, how would he or she position those brands, in terms of relative quality, when presenting them to prospective purchasers?

For pianos intended for consumer use, this positioning is usually done along lines of price; for high-end and luxury instruments—where price is

	Samick/ Young Chang	Yamaha/Kawai	Other Companies
Professional *Verticals:* $10,000–$20,000 *Grands 5' to 7':* $28,000–$55,000		Boston (Japan) Kawai (GX) grands Kawai verticals (Japan) Yamaha (CX) grands Yamaha verticals (Japan)	Brodmann (AS) J.F. Hessen W. Hoffmann (Vision) Hupfeld (Europe) grands Irmler (Professional) grands Kayserburg (Artist) Wilhelm Schimmel
Premium *Verticals:* $6,000–$13,000 *Grands 5' to 7':* $14,000–$40,000	Wm. Knabe (Concert Arist) J.P. Pramberger (Platinum) Samick (International) Seiler (ED) Albert Weber	Boston verticals (118S) Kawai (GL) grands Kawai verticals (UST-9) Yamaha (GC) grands Yamaha verticals (P22)	Baldwin Brodmann (PE) Cunningham Fandrich & Sons Feurich Hailun Heintzman verticals Hupfeld verticals Hupfeld (Studio) grands Irmler verticals Irmler (Studio) grands Perzina Ritmüller (Premium) Schulze Pollmann (Studio) G. Steinberg Wilh. Steinberg (P) Wertheim (Euro/Platinum)
Mid-Range *Verticals:* $4,500–$8,000 *Grands 5' to 7':* $11,000–$21,000	Wm. Knabe (Academy) Pramberger (Signature) Johannes Seiler Weber Young Chang	Kawai verticals (Indonesia) Yamaha verticals (Indonesia) Yamaha (GB) grands	Brodmann (CE) Cline Essex Heintzman grands Gerhard Heintzman verticals Kingsburg Palatino Ritmüller (Performance) verticals Story & Clark (Signature) Wertheim (Gold)
Economy *Verticals:* $3,500–$6,500 *Grands 5' to 7':* $9,000–$15,000	Wm. Knabe (Baltimore) Pramberger (Legacy)	*Note: This chart is **not**, strictly speaking, a rating of pianos by quality. Consumer-grade pianos are listed here by price range, performance-grade pianos are listed by general reputation. For explanation, see the accompanying article. See also **Staff Picks**, p.41, for recommendations of specific models.*	Cristofori/Paul A. Schmitt A. Geyer Hallet, Davis & Co. Hardman, Peck Gerhard Heintzman grands Pearl River Ritmüller (Classic) Ritmüller (Performance) grands Story & Clark (Heritage)

Notes: Unless otherwise stated, brand names refer to both grand and vertical models. Prices are Suggested Maximum Prices (SMP) of vertical models, and of grand models from 5' to 7' in length, regular style, lowest-price finish (usually polished ebony). Substantial discounts from these prices are common—see p.188 for further explanation. The prices shown for a category reflect, in round numbers, the approximate range into which most of the brands and models in that category fall, but a few models may fall outside the range. Also, keep in mind that an individual brand's price range may be narrower than that of the category it is listed under.

WHY WE DON'T PRECISELY RATE PIANO QUALITY

Why don't we strictly judge piano quality in *Piano Buyer*? During the last half of the 20th century, a great many pianos, especially low-end instruments manufactured in the U.S. and in developing countries, had significant defects that made separating good instruments from bad relatively easy. That is no longer the case. Due to globalization and the computerization of manufacturing, virtually all pianos now sold in the West are competently made and without major defects, and the differences between them are increasingly subtle and subjective. While it's still clear that high-end pianos are better than entry-level ones, comparisons of instruments that are closer in price are less conclusive, and much more subject to the whims of personal preference, how well the pianos have been prepared for sale, room acoustics, and so forth.

In addition, the definition of *quality* itself is extremely vague. Depending on the buyer's priorities, *quality* could refer, among other things, to a piano's musical performance, to the aesthetics of its furniture, to its ability to hold up under the demands of heavy use in a school, or to its ability to survive in difficult climates. If *quality* refers to its musical performance, is that in a concert venue, a teaching studio, or a living room? If in a concert venue, solo or with an orchestra? For playing Mozart, Debussy, Rachmaninoff, or Gershwin? And whose preferences in tone and touch should we enshrine as the standard by which all pianos should be measured? Each answer to those questions will produce a different ordering of pianos by quality. Furthermore, even those responsible for the technical design of pianos often can't agree on which features and specifications produce the best instruments.

In such a context of extreme subjectivity, varying priorities, and contradictory expert opinions, making too fine a distinction among brands based on their quality tends to give a false impression of scientific objectivity, and inhibits shoppers from making their own judgments and possibly discovering something wonderful for themselves. For these reasons, we have chosen to take a less active but, we think, more honest approach to giving piano-buying advice, by providing newcomers to the market with a simple frame of reference and a few personal recommendations (see our "Staff Picks" section), and otherwise letting them explore and discover for themselves what appeals to them.

of the distinctions listed in the chart. Note that there may be quality differences within a single product line that, for the sake of simplicity, we do not indicate here; and a few brands have been omitted due solely to lack of sufficient information about them. **Within each group, the brands are listed in alphabetical order. No judgment of these brands' relative quality should be inferred from this order.**

Prices shown for each group represent, in round numbers, a typical range of Suggested Maximum Prices (SMP) of new pianos in the least expensive styles and finishes—smaller models toward the low end of each range, larger models toward the high end. (Significant discounts from these prices are likely—see the Model & Pricing Guide.)

Performance-Grade Pianos

Performance-grade pianos generally have several of the following attributes:

- They are built to a single high standard, almost without regard to cost, and the price charged reflects whatever it takes to build such a piano and bring it to market.
- A greater proportion of the labor required to build them is in the handwork involved in making custom refinements to individual instruments, often with fanatical attention to detail.
- Most are made in relatively small quantities by firms that have been in business for generations, often under the ownership of the same family. As a result, many have achieved almost legendary status, and are often purchased as much for their prestige value as for their performance.
- These are the instruments most likely to be called into service when the highest performance level is required, particularly for classical music.

less likely to be a buyer's primary concern—there is a rough pecking order based on reputation. As will be discussed later, while price and reputation are often associated with quality, that association is far from perfectly consistent. Nevertheless, in the larger picture and speaking very generally, price and reputation are associated with quality closely enough that this chart can be used as a *rough* guide to the quality of today's new pianos, though not as a precise or authoritative one.

The key to proper use of this chart, then, is not to follow it religiously, but to understand that, given its nature, it should be used only as a learning tool. In addition, use common sense when comparing one brand with another. Compare verticals with other verticals of similar size, and grands with similarly sized grands, or models whose selling prices fall within the same range. Don't get hung up on small differences between one group and the next—the distinctions can be quite subtle. Furthermore, the preparation of the piano by the dealer can be at least as important to the quality of the product you receive as some

- Most performance-grade pianos are made in Europe or the United States; a few are now made in Japan.

Performance-grade pianos are divided here into four groups, based on our perception of their reputation in both the musical and technical spheres of the piano business. (Of course, our perceptions are ultimately subjective, and reasonable people, especially outside the U.S., may disagree with our rankings to varying degrees.) The first two groups are reserved for those brands whose prestige figures prominently in their value. Brands labeled *Iconic* are those that seem, by general agreement, to be the ones that would be the flagship line of any dealer that carried them—they are, so to speak, the Maseratis and Lamborghinis of the piano industry. Those labeled *Venerable* are not quite Iconic, but have a virtually uninterrupted period of 150 years or more of very high quality, and some have been owned by the same family for generations. (The word *venerable* carries a connotation of respect due in part to age.) Of course, the prestige of these two groups is based in large part on their extremely high quality, but marketing success and historical accident also play important roles in the reputations of these and other high-end brands.

The brands in the third group, *Distinguished*, are also of very high quality, but are either fairly recent arrivals to the Performance-Grade category, or have returned to very high quality in the last 20 years or so after a period of decline. Though not Iconic or Venerable, they are nonetheless excellent in every way. Preferences among performance-grade pianos in general are greatly dependent on musical taste in tone and touch. For these reasons, a number of brands in the third group have devoted followings and, practically speaking, may be just as good despite not having as much prestige associated with their names.

The last group in this category, *Notable*, consists of a few brands that are less often thought of as Performance Grade, but by price and reputation should probably be separated from the Consumer-Grade category. Most of these are also considerably less expensive than those in the other groups, and may be a better value when the highest levels of quality or prestige are not needed.

Consumer-Grade Pianos

Consumer-grade pianos are built to be sold at a particular price, and adjustments to (i.e., compromises in) materials, workmanship, and method and location of manufacture are made to meet that price. Most are mass-produced in Asia, with less in the way of custom refinement of individual instruments.

Consumer-grade pianos are grouped here mostly by price range. As mentioned earlier, in the larger picture, price is a reasonably good guide to quality. But as one focuses more closely on smaller areas of the market, the association of price with quality breaks down somewhat. For example, some brands may offer a better value than others because they are reduced in price to gain a larger market share, or because they are made in a country with lower labor costs. Some brands or models, especially those that are new to the market, may be mispriced because their manufacturers haven't yet learned from experience what the public is actually willing to pay for them. Two brands that are roughly equal in price and overall quality may have different blends of strengths and weaknesses. In fact, some lower-priced models may appeal to you more than some higher-priced ones because of their particular characteristics or features.

As can be expected, upper-level consumer-grade pianos generally have premium components and better performance than lower-level instruments. The best of them are made in Japan or Europe, or are partly made in China or Indonesia and then shipped to Europe for completion. Some have become so advanced in their designs, materials, and manufacturing technologies that they now rival some performance-grade pianos in musicality, and are sometimes recommended as substitutes for them, often at considerably lower prices. The economy models, on the other hand, are basic, no-frills pianos suitable for beginners and casual users, but which a conscientious student may outgrow in a few years.

STAFF PICKS
by Piano Buyer staff

Due to the highly subjective nature of piano ratings, in "A Map of the Market for New Pianos" (page 40), we purposely avoided making too many judgments about the quality of the various brands. Instead, we provided, as a frame of reference, a summary of the way pianos are presented in the marketplace by manufacturers and dealers. However, we feel we owe some *specific* recommendations to the many readers who have requested them, in part to simplify the buying process for shoppers who lack the time, ability, or interest to make their own discoveries. To emphasize the subjective nature of these recommendations, we provide them in this list rather than through the Map. This way, too, we don't have to pass judgment on each and every brand and model.

It's important to understand that in any artistic field, "expert" recommendations are only partially recognitions

Brand/Model	Classics/ Perennial Favorites	Musical Standouts	Good Values	Price ($)	Comments
ACOUSTIC PIANOS **Verticals 43"–45"**					
Hardman, Peck & Co. R45F (45")			✔	4,790	Beautiful cabinet, well constructed.
Perzina GP-112 Kompact (45")			✔	8,000	Impressive low-bass performance from a small, inexpensive vertical.
Walter, Charles R. 1520/1500 (43"/45")	✔	✔		18,000	Proof that a 43" piano can be musical, and it's made in the U.S.A.
Yamaha Silent Piano b2SG2 (45")			✔	9,498	An affordable acoustic with the flexibility of a digital.
Verticals 46"–52"					
Bechstein, C. Concert 8 (51.5")	✔	✔		70,070	One of the all-time great upright pianos.
Hailun HU5-P (50")		✔	✔	9,316	A "total package"—balanced tone, responsive action.
Hessen, J.F. 123 (48")		✔		12,800	
Kawai K300 (48")	✔		✔	9,990	
Kawai K500 (51")		✔		12,790	
Kayserburg KA-132 (52")		✔		16,190	Lovely, singing tone.
Knabe, Wm., WKV132MD (52")		✔	✔	9,198	
Pearl River EU122 (48")			✔	5,590	
Perzina GP-122 (48")		✔	✔	9.090	
Perzina GP-130 (51")		✔		11,460	A vertical piano that can hold its own against some far more expensive peers.
Petrof P125F1 (49.25")		✔		19,900	
Ritmüller UH-121RA (48")		✔	✔	7,790	One of our favorite vertical pianos at this price.
Schimmel K132 (52")		✔		35,794	
Schulze Pollmann SU122A (48")		✔		10,390	A warm, round tone quality and beautiful case finishes.
Yamaha U1 (48")	✔	✔		11,199	The standard against which every 48" vertical is inevitably compared.
Grands 4' 10"–5' 4"					
Cunningham Studio Grand (5' 4")		✔	✔	20,890	
Geyer, A. GG-150 (4' 11")			✔	9,590	
Ritmüller GH-148R (4' 10")		✔	✔	11,590	Amazingly good performance for such a small piano.
Seiler, Johannes, GS-160 (5' 3")		✔	✔	18,798	Pleasantly mellow with an elegant look.
Story & Clark H60A (5' 3")			✔	17,495	When you take into account all the technology it comes with (player piano and MIDI record), this piano is a great value.
Weber W150 (4' 11")		✔	✔	11,580	Surprisingly musical and satisfying tone for such a short grand.
Grands 5' 5"–5' 11"					
Baldwin BP178 (5' 10")			✔	23,390	
Estonia L168 (5' 6")		✔	✔	39,608	Estonia grands are an excellent value among high-end pianos.
Hailun HG178 (5' 10")		✔	✔	22,312	
Kawai GX-2BLK (5' 11")	✔			34,990	A must-try for those shopping for a grand under 6' long.

(continued)

Brand/Model	Classics/ Perennial Favorites	Musical Standouts	Good Values	Price ($)	Comments
ACOUSTIC PIANOS (continued) **Grands 5' 5"–5' 11"** (continued)					
Mason & Hamlin A (5' 8")	✔			61,255	
Perzina GBT-175 (5' 10")			✔	19,640	Nicely balanced scale. Some of the nicest wood-veneer case finishes we've seen at this price.
Pramberger PS-175 (5' 9")			✔	15,598	
Steinway & Sons M (5' 7")	✔			69,700	
Steinway & Sons O (5' 10.5")	✔			78,400	
Grands 6'–6' 10"					
Baldwin BP190 (6' 3")			✔	27,790	
Bösendorfer 200 (6' 7")	✔			132,598	A lovely and distinct chamber instrument.
Brodmann PE187 (6' 2")		✔	✔	20,380	Design said to be based on that of a Steinway model A.
Estonia L190 (6' 3")		✔	✔	48,139	The tone has lyrical beauty and is without harshness.
Estonia L210 (6' 10")		✔	✔	57,949	
Förster, August, 190 (6' 4")		✔		63,578	
Grotrian Cabinet Grand (6' 3")		✔		86,117	Uniquely diverse timbre. Subject of book Grand Obsession, by Perry Knize.
Haessler 186 (6' 1")		✔		74,233	
Mason & Hamlin AA (6' 4")		✔		69,779	
Seiler ED-186 (6' 2")		✔	✔	33,198	Clear treble tone and good sustain.
Steinway & Sons A (6' 2")	✔			89,700	
Weber W185 (6' 1")		✔	✔	16,980	Satisfyingly beautiful tone at a good price.
Yamaha C3X (6' 1")	✔			51,470	A workhorse in countless teaching studios and institutional practice rooms.
Yamaha C5X (6' 7")		✔		57,198	
Grands over 6' 10"					
Blüthner 2 (7' 8")	✔	✔		124,350	
Bosendorfer 214VC (7')		✔		147,998	Updated design combines improved projection with classic Bosendorfer sound.
Boston GP215PE (7' 1")		✔		51,400	
Kawai, Shigeru, SK-6 (7')		✔		78,600	
Mason & Hamlin BB (7')	✔	✔		79,047	Prodigious bass register sounds like that of a concert grand.
Sauter 220 "Omega" (7' 3")		✔		135,000	An incredibly capable tool for any serious pianist—and for fun, take a look under the lid.
Schimmel C213 (7')		✔		62,264	
Schimmel K219 (7' 2")		✔		80,800	A fantastic instrument from Schimmel's new Konzert series.
Wilh. Steinberg Signature 212 (6' 11")		✔		55,932	
Steingraeber & Söhne C212N (7')		✔		133,041	Remarkable tonal subtlety.
Steinway & Sons B (6' 10.5")	✔	✔		101,800	Very popular model in college and conservatory teaching studios, and the standard against which other high-end grands are measured.
Yamaha C7X (7' 6")	✔			73,598	Very popular in recording studios; musically versatile in the hands of the right technician.
Yamaha CF6 (7')		✔		119,598	A 7' grand that can compete with the best in the world.

(continued)

Brand/Model	Classics/ Perennial Favorites	Musical Standouts	Good Values	Price ($)	Comments
DIGITALS & HYBRIDS					
Blüthner e-Klavier PRO-88 EX		✔		3,326	An interestingly-styled slab with a unique piano sample.
Casio CGP-700			✔	799	Huge feature set and powerful speaker system.
Casio Privia PX-5S			✔	999	A professional instrument at a consumer price.
Casio Privia PX-160	✔		✔	499	One of the first models mentioned when considering better entry-level digital pianos.
Casio Privia PX-860			✔	999	Impressive sound from a shallow cabinet.
Kawai CN37			✔	2,599	New display and samples are a noteworthy improvement over the previous model CN35.
Kawai CA97		✔		4,655	Solid action performance, Soundboard Speaker System, and nice variety of piano samples.
Kawai VPC1		✔		1,849	Not a digital per se, but rather a dedicated controller keyboard for software (virtual) pianos, with Kawai's great RM3II action.
Kurzweil CUP-2		✔		2,999	An extremely compact contemporary design conceals a wealth of voices and features.
Roland FP-30			✔	699	A fine example of high-end piano sound generation trickling down to an economy model.
Roland HP504			✔	2,199	A way-above-average starter instrument with Ivory Feel keyboard.
Roland V-Piano Grand (GP-7)		✔		19,950	Enclosed in an elegant grand-piano cabinet, the V-Piano gives you the technology to design your own piano.
Yamaha Clavinova CVP-705		✔	✔	6,455	A price/performance sweet spot in ensemble digital pianos.
Yamaha Arius YDP-181	✔		✔	1,700	A direct descendant of the venerable YDP-223 from 2002. A perennial best-seller.
Yamaha AvantGrand N2/N3X		✔		12,635/ 18,816	A game changer that redefined our expectations for the sound and feel of a non-acoustic piano.

of inherent quality; in other ways, they are simply personal preferences. Thus, while you can probably count on pianos recommended by us to be "good" instruments, it doesn't follow from that that you will necessarily like them as much as we do. Our recommendations also say virtually nothing about brands and models that are *not* on the list. Either we haven't had the opportunity to try them out (or, at least, not under favorable conditions), or they just didn't stand out to us as being really special—but that doesn't mean there's anything wrong with them, or that you wouldn't want to take one home with you.

This list focuses on home- and studio-size instruments and does not include concert grands. A work in progress, it is by no means comprehensive, and will likely grow and evolve with future issues of *Piano Buyer*.

Classics/Perennial Favorites are models with a long-standing reputation for performance and durability. They are generally top sellers from well-known manufacturers.

Musical Standouts represent pianos that play and sound great to us. Although the list understandably tends to favor larger instruments, we've also included several smaller models that are noteworthy for having great sound for their size.

Good Values are pianos whose performance per dollar, in our opinion, is particularly attractive.

Vertical piano sizes are shown in inches, grand piano sizes in feet and inches. Prices shown for acoustic pianos are the Suggested Maximum Prices (SMP) of the least expensive style and finish (significant discounts from these prices are likely—see page 188 for explanation). Prices shown for digitals and hybrids are the Estimated Prices of the least expensive finish (see page 247 for explanation). 🎹

PRAMBERGER

SIGNATURE SERIES

Building on *Seven Generations* of *Piano Artistry*

www.prambergerpianoco.com

*A*fter a piano is assembled, and while it's still at the factory, it will be tuned and musically adjusted—that is, converted from an assemblage of parts into a functioning musical instrument. Generally speaking, as the quality and price of a piano rise, so do the amounts of tuning and adjusting that take place during manufacture. However, most pianos are not adjusted at the factory to 100% of their musical capability. Even if one were, the jostling and environmental changes that occur during the shipping of the instrument from the factory would ensure that it would arrive at the dealer in less than optimal condition. Bringing the instrument back to the level of musicality intended by the manufacturer is the responsibility of the dealer—or, once the piano has settled into its new home, of the buyer's technician. Any such work performed by the dealer before the piano is delivered to the customer is known as dealer preparation, or *dealer prep*.

Tuning

When a piano is in tune, its strings pull on the instrument's supporting wood and metal structure with a combined tension of 16 to 22 tons. Some of that tension is also converted to downbearing pressure on the wooden bridges and soundboard. A new piano typically takes a year or two to stabilize—for the strings to stop stretching, and for the bridges, soundboard, and structure to stop settling. During that time, of course, the piano will also be responding to seasonal—and sometimes daily—changes in humidity, as all acoustic pianos do. For these reasons, keeping the piano in tune on the dealer's showroom floor can be a challenge. Part of dealer prep consists of tuning the piano a few times while it's on display, sometimes even tuning it a little sharp, so that it falls toward the correct pitch as it settles. New pianos should also be tuned immediately before delivery to the customer, and again within a month or two after delivery, after the piano has had some time to acclimate to its new environment. The more the piano has been tuned by the dealer, the less frequently it will need to be tuned by the customer in the first year or two after purchase.

Action Regulation

A piano is said to have as many as 12,000 parts (it depends on how you count them), and most of them are the moving parts of the piano's key-and-action assembly. The accuracy of this assembly, and its fine adjustment—known as *action regulation*—significantly affect the quality of the piano's performance. A fine regulation allows the player to play both loudly and very softly, to repeat notes as rapidly as needed, and to take full advantage of the tonal properties built into the piano's musical design.

Most of the major piano manufacturers take steps to stabilize the action regulation before the piano leaves the factory, usually with "pounding" machines that play each note hundreds of times. This compresses the many cloth and felt action parts, and also helps stabilize the tuning. After this breaking-in process, the action requires regulating to restore its original design dimensions. This stabilization process continues on the dealer's

showroom floor as potential buyers play the instrument and the dealer touches up the regulation as needed, due to additional settling and environmental changes. The amount of regulating by the dealer that a piano will need will depend on the quality of its cloth and felt, the amount of playing-in it gets at the factory and dealer, and how long it sits on the dealer's showroom floor before being sold. Interestingly, the higher-quality cloth found in the better pianos, though providing quieter performance in the long run, is softer and so may take longer to settle. The pianos that spend the most time on the dealer's floor before being sold are likely to have the most stable regulation when delivered to the customer. Pianos that receive less playing-in or regulating before sale may need regulating by the customer sooner to perform their best.

Voicing

The tonal quality of the piano can be optimized by adjusting the hardness and density of the hammer felt, improving the accuracy of the strings' termination points, and adjusting the strike points of the hammers on the strings—all parts of a process called *voicing*. These adjustments allow the pianist to musically express him- or herself to the maximum extent permitted by the piano's design. While even the most skilled piano technician can't make an entry-level piano sound like a performance instrument, tone and touch in even the least expensive pianos can usually be significantly improved through regulation and voicing. This is true for both grands and uprights, although the potential for improved performance is usually greater for grands. However, rather than make wholesale changes in timbre between bright and mellow, which can take hours or even days, most voicing done as part of dealer prep is intended to merely even out the tone from note to note, which can be done in a matter of minutes.

Finish Polishing and Touchup

Almost all pianos arriving in a crate or box will need some polishing to remove slight blemishes caused by the packing materials. Larger dents or dings can also usually be fixed by skilled technicians to be virtually undetectable. Buyers should keep in mind, however, that if you look closely enough, it's possible to find slight blemishes on almost any piano—perfection is not an option.

A Multi-Level Approach to Dealer Prep

To describe the appropriate levels of dealer prep, it's helpful to divide the piano market into three segments: economy-priced instruments (e.g., Cristofori; Hardman, Peck; Pearl River); mid-priced instruments (e.g., most consumer-grade models from Baldwin, Kawai, and Yamaha), and high-end instruments (e.g., Bechstein, Bösendorfer, Steinway).

Economy-Priced Pianos

Economy pianos are designed to satisfy the needs of the beginning student (the first two to three years) or casual user, and to do so for a relatively low price. Until about 2010, most such entry-level pianos arrived at the dealer needing about eight hours of work to be brought up to a decent standard of performance. Some still do, but today, because of advances in the computerization of manufacturing, many come out of the crate or box needing tuning and only two to three hours of additional work to be playing at a level that would satisfy the beginning student.

At a minimum, an economy piano in the dealer's showroom should be in tune, holding a tuning reasonably well, and its tone should be clear and uniform across the keyboard. The action should be regulated such that the slightest downward motion of a key begins to move its corresponding hammer, and the touchweight across the keyboard should be smoothly graded from heavier in the bass to lighter in the treble. Keys, hammers, and other parts should be assembled with uniform spacing, and the keyboard should be level. While it's worth performing a basic level of regulation and voicing on an economy piano, it's generally not cost-effective to do a fussier job, not only because of the piano's low price, but also because the additional refinement usually won't result in musical improvement significant enough to be worthwhile.

Mid-Priced Pianos

A complete dealer prep of a mid-priced instrument includes the standards of the economy prep. In addition, the action should be regulated so that it is easily controlled even during the fast passages and varying volumes attempted by an advancing, intermediate-level student. It should repeat as rapidly as a reasonably accomplished amateur pianist can play.

These instruments should be voiced to optimize the manufacturer's scale design. That is, if the piano was designed to sound bright, crisp, and clear, it should be as bright as possible without being tinny or harsh. If, on the other hand, the piano is designed to have strong lower harmonics in addition to the fundamental, it should have a full-bodied, robust tonal quality. In simpler terms, the piano should be voiced to optimally sound the way it was designed to sound.

Many mid-priced instruments, especially those made in Japan, are prepped very well at the factory to the standards described above, and these popular instruments disappear quickly from the dealer's floor. Therefore, they're likely to need the least dealer prep of all three segments of the market.

High-End Pianos

Many brands of high-end piano receive extensive prep at the factory and arrive at the dealer in impeccable condition, hardly needing tuning. From this, one might conclude that these instruments need little or no dealer prep, but this turns out not to be necessarily true.

For one thing, though they may need little or no prep work when they arrive, over time, like all pianos, high-end instruments will go out of tune and regulation. And because these pianos, with their high prices, appeal to only a small segment of buyers, they may sit on dealers' showroom floors for months, even years—all that time having their tuning, regulation, and voicing touched up as needed. Second, the buyers of these instruments are often accomplished pianists who won't tolerate anything short of an exacting amount of optimization, and may additionally make special requests to suit their individual musical preferences. Last, the high-end design of these instruments will amply reward with superior musical results any additional musical finishing work done on them by a good technician.

The optimal dealer prep of a performance-grade piano should enable the piano to perform almost beyond human capabilities. That is, it should provide control greater than most accomplished, professional pianists can play, and it should leave all players wishing they could play better. In particular, it should enable the pianist to control dynamics (volume) such that very soft passages can be played with greatly controlled nuance, to repeat notes as rapidly as needed, and to take advantage of every musical advantage offered by the instrument's scale design.

Here are a few examples of pieces that require extreme repetition speed coupled with great control of dynamics. A high-end piano should be capable of executing these pieces (provided, of course, that the pianist is capable of playing them!):

▶ *Valentina Lisitsa playing the third movement, Presto agitato, of Beethoven's Piano Sonata 14 in C-sharp Minor, Op.27 No.2, "Moonlight"*

▶ *Yuja Wang playing Schubert-Liszt's "Erlkönig"*

When being prepped for the showroom prior to sale, the high-end instrument should, in addition to being finely regulated, be voiced to represent the characteristic tone of its brand as closely as possible. If the factory voicing was sufficient in this regard, it should be left alone or only slightly touched up. This is because buyers of these instruments are often familiar with—and expect—a certain sound from a particular brand, and may not be happy to find one brand voiced, usually unsuccessfully, in an attempt to make it sound like another. A Steinway should meet or exceed the expectations of a player familiar with and enthused by the Steinway tone and touch, for example, while a Bösendorfer should please players who are endeared to Bösendorfer's characteristic sound and feel. While this is somewhat subjective, the dealer's piano technician has likely tuned and voiced dozens of identical or similar models, and is in the best position to exercise that judgment. Once an instrument is sold, however, the buyer should be encouraged to provide input on voicing decisions; the pre- and post-delivery service of the high-end piano will be determined by a combination of the technician's judgment and the buyer's taste.

Post-delivery service of a high-end piano will usually include a couple of service calls within the first year, for tuning, touch-up regulation, and voicing.

■ ■ ■

To a certain extent, the levels of dealer prep described above represent ideals; the reality may be quite different. Some of the factors that may interfere with these ideals include:

- Pianos arrive on the dealer's showroom floor in widely varying conditions, depending in part on how long the instruments have been in inventory at the manufacturer, in a distributor's warehouse, or in the dealer's own storage area.
- Some dealers have technicians on staff; others contract out for technical services. The technicians, especially if under contract, may not always be available precisely when they're most needed. This means that some pianos may remain on the floor unprepped for a long time following delivery, or untuned after a seasonal change in humidity has put all the pianos out of tune. It also means that if you're fussy about your pianos, it helps to call the dealership in advance to let them know what you're looking for, so they can schedule a technician to touch up a few instruments in preparation for your visit.
- It's not cost-effective for a dealer to do a perfect job of prepping every instrument. In the case of low-priced pianos that arrive needing a lot of work, the dealer may do nothing more than make sure that there are no obvious mechanical problems, that the piano is

reasonably in tune, and perhaps even out the voicing a bit, if badly needed.

- Although, in theory, a dealer can significantly change the tone of a piano through voicing, practically speaking, the dealer can't be expected to completely revoice a piano to suit a customer until after the customer has bought the instrument. It's prohibitively expensive to completely revoice, and could result in a tone that other prospective buyers don't care for. Therefore, it's best for a buyer to find a piano whose tone is a pretty close match to his or her ideal. The dealer will then usually be happy to even out the tone a little from note to note, if needed.

Can I Safely Buy a Piano "Out of the Crate"?

Although the online sale of even such high-ticket items as acoustic pianos is not yet common, the world is trending in that direction. If a piano is sold this way by a dealer who's performed proper dealer prep, and who then hires a technician in the buyer's area to provide post-delivery service, this may work out just fine. But occasionally we hear of a manufacturer selling or shipping directly to consumers, delivering pianos to buyers in the manufacturer's packaging and bypassing the dealer—and the dealer prep—entirely. Unless the manufacturer increases the amount of factory prep to compensate, this can have costly consequences for the consumer, in terms of both cost and performance.

As we've seen, most pianos need several additional tunings before the tuning is stable; and regardless of the piano's quality, the regulation and voicing can almost always be improved. These improvements will provide better touch and tone for years to come. Although a local technician hired by the manufacturer can provide some of this prep work, the manufacturer is unlikely to pay for numerous service calls over an extended period of time—especially for the economy brands, which are most likely to be sold directly to the consumer. As a result, when the additional service is accounted for, the buyer may end up paying much more than he or she bargained for, or might forgo the service and be left with an instrument that never performs well.

In a similar vein, some shoppers at bricks-and-mortar piano stores request a new piano fresh out of the crate instead of a "floor sample," based on the misconception that a crated piano must be in perfect condition, whereas a piano that has been handled by the dealer and other shoppers is somehow compromised. In reality, the opposite is true: Most pianos fresh out of a crate or box need at least several hours of attention, technical and cosmetic, before they can meet the customer's expectations.

Pianos on display at a dealership get relatively little use, and are generally kept in tune, ready to be evaluated by prospective buyers. The extra tunings, the small amount of breaking-in of the action by prospective buyers, the optimizing of regulation and voicing by the dealer's technician, a little attention to cosmetics—all provide value to the wise shopper, who thus will always prefer a floor model to an unseen instrument still in its crate or box. Also, because acoustic pianos—even ones of identical make and model—tend to vary slightly from one another in their musical characteristics, choosing a floor model you've actually played will ensure that you receive an instrument with the sound and touch you expect.

It's possible that some mid-priced pianos, especially Japanese-made uprights, may lend themselves better than other types to being delivered to the customer "out of the crate," especially if the sale is followed by one or two service calls within six months for tuning and touch-up regulation and voicing. Instruments of this type generally need much less remedial prep than do low-priced pianos, let alone the level of specialized prep required by high-end pianos. In addition, these uprights tend to be musically very uniform from unit to unit of the same model.

However, even with these brands, this is not a good way to buy a piano. Service calls to a customer's home are much more expensive for the dealer than having the work done at the store, so even if the manufacturer or dealer provides post-delivery service for a piano uncrated in the home, that service is usually limited to the minimum needed to make the piano playable. In addition, many home-service technicians aren't capable of performing cosmetic repairs, and movers will be unwilling to take responsibility for cosmetic issues that aren't evident in exterior damage to the crate, so some of the risk of poor landed (delivered) quality is likely to be borne by the buyer. For all these reasons, the service departments of brands that are sometimes sold this way report that customers who buy a piano out of the crate are more likely than others to say they are unhappy with their purchase.

Good dealer prep results in an instrument that performs at or near its musical potential. Why pay for a fine instrument and settle for anything less?

Steve Cohen owns Jasons Music Center, a third-generation, family-owned piano dealer, and has been a consultant to the piano industry for over 40 years. His clients have included Bechstein, Samick, Yamaha, and Young Chang, among others. He is also *Piano Buyer*'s Contributing Editor and Piano Industry Consultant, and lead appraiser for its Seller Advisory Service.

BUYING A USED OR RESTORED PIANO

LARRY FINE

(This article is adapted from Chapter 5, "Buying a Used Piano," of The Piano Book, Fourth Edition, *by Larry Fine. Before reading this article, be sure to read "Piano Buying Basics"—especially the section "New or Used?"—elsewhere in this publication.)*

WHAT TO BUY: A Historical Overview

1700–1880

The piano was invented about 1700 by Bartolomeo Cristofori, a harpsichord maker in Padua, Italy. Cristofori replaced the plucking-quill action of the harpsichord, which can pluck only with unvarying force and hence unvarying volume of sound, with a newly designed striking-hammer action, whose force could be precisely controlled by the player. Thus was born the *gravicembalo col piano e forte* (keyboard instrument with soft and loud). This name was later shortened to *pianoforte*, then *fortepiano*, and finally just *piano*. In the 1700s the new instrument, made mostly by craftsmen in their shops, spread quietly through upper-class Europe. A number of different forms of piano action and structure were invented, such as the Viennese action, the English action, the square piano, and so on. Replicas of early

Cristofori Piano, circa 1720

fortepianos are popular among certain musicians who prefer to play the music of that period on the original instruments for which that music was written.

In the 1800s the piano spread more quickly through the middle classes, and across the ocean to North America. Riding along with the Industrial Revolution, piano-making evolved from a craft into an industry. Many important changes took place during the 19th century: The upright piano was invented; the modern grand piano action was invented, incorporating the best aspects of the previous rival actions; the cast-iron plate was invented, vastly strengthening the structure and allowing the strings to be stretched at a higher tension, thus increasing the power and volume of sound; the range of the instrument was extended from about five octaves to the present seven-plus octaves; and, toward the end of the century, the square piano died out, leaving just grands of various sizes and the full-size upright. By 1880, most of these changes were in place; the pianos made today are not very different from those of a hundred or more years ago.

In your search for a piano, you're unlikely to run across instruments made before 1880, with two exceptions. The square piano, or square grand, as it is sometimes called, looks like a rectangular box on legs (see illustration), and was very

popular as a home piano during the 19th century. Its ornate Victorian case makes very pretty furniture—but it also makes a terrible musical instrument for 21st-century playing and practicing. Tuning, servicing, and repair are difficult and expensive, very few piano technicians know how to do it, and parts are hard to come by. Even at their best, these instruments are unsuitable to practice on, even for beginners.

Another piano to avoid is a type of upright made primarily in Europe from the middle to the end of the 19th century. The dampers on these piano are positioned *above* the hammers and actuated by wires in *front* of the action—the reverse of a modern-day upright. This over-damper system has been nicknamed the "birdcage action" because the damper wires form an enclosure that resembles a bird cage. Besides being very difficult to tune and service through the "bird cage," these pianos are usually so worn out that they won't hold a tuning longer than about ten seconds, and their actions work erratically at best. Many of these pianos were cheaply made to begin with, but they often have ornate cabinets and fancy features,

Square Grand, 19th Century

such as candlestick holders, that make them attractive to antique collectors.

Although most pianos you'll come across made prior to 1880 will have little practical or financial value, the few that have historical value are best left to specialists and collectors who can properly conserve them.

1880–1900

The years from 1880 to about 1900 were a transition period, as some old styles were slow to fade. But some pianos from this period may be suitable for you. A piano with only 85 instead of 88 notes may be perfectly satisfactory if you don't anticipate ever needing the highest three notes. The resale value of such a piano may be slightly lower than its modern equivalent, but so should be the price you pay for it. A piano with an old-style cast-iron plate that, while extending the full length of the piano, leaves the pinblock exposed to view is, for all practical purposes, just as structurally sound as one in which the plate covers the pinblock.

Avoid, however, the so-called "three-quarter-plate" piano, in which the plate ends just short of the pinblock. These pianos have a high rate of structural failure. Pianos with actions that are only very slight variations on modern actions are fine as long as the parts are not obsolete and absolutely unobtainable.

Most pianos this old will need a considerable amount of repair and restoration to be fully usable, so the best candidates from this period will be those instruments that justify the expense involved, such as Steinway, Mason & Hamlin, Bechstein, and Blüthner grands, or, in rare instances, a more ordinary brand that has been exceptionally well preserved. With occasional exceptions, the vast majority of uprights and cheaper grands that survive from this period are not worth repairing, unless for historical or sentimental reasons.

1900–1930

The period from about 1900 to 1930 was the heyday of piano manufacturing in America. The piano held an important place in the national economy and as a symbol of culture and social status. Hundreds

An old-fashioned, pneumatically driven player piano with punched-paper music roll and pumping pedals

www.antiqueplayerpiano.com

of small firms turned out millions of pianos during this time; in fact, far more pianos were made annually then than are made today. If you're shopping for a used full-size upright or a grand, some of the pianos you'll see will probably be from this period. Smaller pianos weren't introduced until later. Although some well-preserved instruments from this period may be usable as is, most will need rebuilding, or at least reconditioning.

Those in the market for a used piano often ask for recommendations of specific brands from this period. This is a problem, because the present condition of the piano, the kind of use you'll be giving it, and the cost of the piano and repairs are far more important factors than the brand when considering the purchase of an old piano. Even a piano of the best brand, if poorly maintained or badly repaired, can be an unwise purchase. Time and wear are great levelers, and a piano of only average quality that has not been used much may be a much better buy. Nevertheless, since that answer never satisfies anyone, I offer a list (see box) of some of the brand names of the period that were most highly regarded. Please note that this list, which is by no means complete—or universally agreed on—applies only to pianos made before about 1930, since in many cases the same names were later applied to entirely different, usually lower, quality standards.

During this period, a large percentage of the pianos made were outfitted with pneumatically driven player-piano systems. When these mechanisms eventually fell into disrepair, they were often removed. Although there is still a small group of technicians and hobbyists dedicated to restoring these fascinating relics of the past, in most cases it is not economically practical to do so except for historical or sentimental reasons.

GRAY-MARKET PIANOS

If you're looking for a piano made within the last few decades, there is usually a plentiful supply of used Yamaha and Kawai pianos originally made for the Japanese market. However, there has been some controversy about them. Sometimes called "gray-market" pianos, these instruments were originally sold to families and schools in Japan, and some years later were discarded in favor of new pianos. There being little market for these used pianos in Japan—the Japanese are said to have a cultural bias against buying any used goods—enterprising businesspeople buy them up, restore them to varying degrees, and export them to the U.S. and other countries, where they are sold by dealers of used pianos at prices significantly lower than those of new Yamahas or Kawais. Used Korean pianos are available under similar circumstances. (Note: The term "gray market" is used somewhat erroneously to describe these pianos. They are used instruments, not new, and there is nothing illegal about buying and selling them.)

Yamaha has taken a public stand warning against the purchase of a used Yamaha piano made for the Japanese market. When Yamaha first began exporting pianos to the United States, the company found that some pianos sent to areas of the U.S. with very dry indoor climates, such as parts of the desert Southwest and places that were bitterly cold in the winter, would develop problems in a short period of time: tuning pins would become loose, soundboards and bridges would crack, and glue joints would come apart. To protect against this happening, Yamaha began to season the wood for destination: a low moisture content for pianos bound for the U.S., which has the greatest extremes of dryness; a higher moisture content for Europe; and the highest moisture content for Japan, which is relatively humid. The gray-market pianos, Yamaha says, having been seasoned for the relatively humid Japanese climate, will not stand up to our dryness. The company claims to have received many calls from dissatisfied owners of these pianos, but cannot help them because the warranty, in addition to having expired, is effective only in the country in which the piano was originally sold when new.

My own research has led me to believe that while there is some basis for Yamaha's concerns, their warnings are somewhat exaggerated. There probably is a greater chance, statistically, that these pianos will develop problems in conditions of extreme dryness than will Yamahas seasoned for and sold in the U.S. However, thousands of gray-market pianos have been sold by hundreds of dealers throughout the country, in all types of climates, for many years, and, while there have been problems, particularly in sections of the country with temperature and humidity extremes, I haven't found evidence of anything close to an epidemic. In mild and moderate climates, reported problems are rare. There are, however, some precautions that should be taken.

These pianos are available to dealers in a wide variety of ages and conditions. The better dealers will sell only those in good condition made since about the mid-1980s. In some cases, the dealers or their suppliers will recondition or partially rebuild the pianos before offering them for sale. Make sure to get a warranty that runs for at least five years, as any problems will usually show up within that period if they are going to show up at all. **Finally, be sure to use some kind of humidity-control system in situations of unusual dryness.** Remember that air-conditioning, as well as heating, can cause indoor dryness.

It's not always possible to determine visually whether a particular instrument was made for the U.S. or the Japanese market, as some original differences may have been altered by the supplier. The dealer may know, and Yamaha has a utility on its website (**www.yamaha.com/ussub/pianos/SerialNumberlookup.aspx**) that will look up the origin of a particular Yamaha piano by serial number.

1930–1960

The rise of radio and talking pictures in the 1920s competed with pianos for the public's attention and weakened the piano industry, and the Great Depression decimated it. During the Depression, many piano makers, both good and bad, went bankrupt, and their names were bought up by the surviving companies. Sometimes the defunct company's designs continued to be used, but often only the name lived on. Still, piano making in the 1930s, though reduced in quantity from earlier years, was in most cases of a similar quality.

To revive the depressed piano market in the mid-1930s, piano makers came up with a new idea: the small piano. Despite the fact that small pianos, both vertical and grand, are musically inferior to larger ones, the public decided that spinets, consoles, and small grands were preferable because they looked better in the smaller homes and apartments of the day. There has always been a furniture aspect to the piano, but the degree to which piano makers catered to that aspect from the mid-'30s onward marked a revolution in piano marketing.

During World War II, many piano factories were commandeered to make airplane wings and other wartime products, and what piano making there was fell somewhat in quality because of a lack of good raw materials and skilled labor. Things changed for the better in the postwar period, and you'll sometimes find used pianos from this period, still in reasonably good condition or needing some reconditioning, from such brands as Steinway, Baldwin, Mason & Hamlin, Sohmer, Everett, Knabe, and Wurlitzer.

1960–Present

In the 1960s, the Japanese began exporting pianos to the U.S. in large numbers. Although at first they had some difficulty building pianos to the demands of our climate, by the mid- to late-'60s their quality was so high and their prices so low that they threatened to put all U.S. makers out of business. In response, most of the mid-priced American makers cheapened their product to compete. As a result, the 20 years from about 1965 to 1985 are considered, from a quality standpoint, to be a low point in U.S. piano manufacturing. In any case, the Americans were unable to compete. The international takeover of the U.S. piano market accelerated in the 1980s as the Koreans began to export here, and by 1985 all but a few U.S. piano makers had gone out of business. As in an earlier period, some of their brand names were purchased and later used by others.

Please see the article "The New-Piano Market Today" for more information on the post-1960 period. See also the article "Advice About Used Pianos for Parents of Young Beginning Piano Students" for a list of specific brands of this period to avoid.

A used piano made within the past few decades can often be a very good deal, as these instruments may still show very few signs of age and wear, but with a price far below that of a new piano. The most recently made used pianos may even come with a warranty that is still in effect. Also, the influx of new, low-priced, Chinese- and Indonesian-made pianos has driven down the price of used pianos, in some cases rather substantially, as the imports offer the opportunity to buy a new piano for a price only a little higher than a decent used one previously commanded. If you're considering a piano from this period, you may wish to read applicable articles in this publication about new pianos, as well as current and past editions of *The Piano Book*. See also the accompanying article about so-called gray-market pianos.

CRACKED SOUNDBOARDS: MYTH and REALITY

Solid spruce soundboards swell and shrink with seasonal changes in humidity and, over time, can develop cracks. One of the problems that comes up most frequently in buying a used piano is judging the significance of a cracked soundboard.

Contrary to popular belief, cracks in the soundboard, while often unattractive, are not necessarily important, as long as the tone is acceptable. Very extensive cracking, however, can indicate that the piano has suffered great climatic extremes, and that its life expectancy may be short. In such a case, other symptoms of this will usually be evident elsewhere in the piano. If the cracks have been filled with wooden shims, this means that, at some point, the piano was rebuilt and the cracks repaired.

The ribs run perpendicular to the grain of the soundboard, and therefore perpendicular to any cracks. Any separation of a rib from the soundboard at a crack is a potential source of buzzing noises. A piano with a cracked soundboard should be carefully checked for rib separations before purchase. Repair of rib separations can usually be done at reasonable cost without rebuilding the piano.

When manufactured, the soundboard has built into it a curvature or *crown*. In a traditionally made, solid spruce soundboard, the crown is maintained by the compression of the wood fibers, whose elasticity causes the crowned soundboard to push back against the downbearing pressure of the strings on the bridges. Together, these two opposing forces enhance the tone of the piano. Over many years, because of the drying out of the wood and the loss of the wood's elasticity, the soundboard loses some or all of its crown, a condition that can be accompanied by the appearance of cracks.

A related condition is that of *compression ridges*. When a soundboard's compression exceeds the elastic limit of the wood fibers, those fibers may become crushed, producing slightly raised ridges in the soundboard's surface. This can happen, for example, in humid climates, or due to conditions related to the soundboard's manufacture. Compression ridges are quite common, and do not necessarily affect the piano's tone. However, when crushed, wood fibers lose their elastic properties, so the compression ridges are likely to turn into cracks as the soundboard's crown diminishes over time.

Although, in theory, cracks and a loss of crown should result in a deterioration of tonal quality, the actual results vary greatly from piano to piano; therefore, the tone quality of each such instrument must be evaluated on its own merits. In addition, your tolerance for such imperfections will depend on how expensive the piano is, and on your use of and expectations for it.

For more information on this subject, see *The Piano Book*.

Though in each decade both good and bad pianos have been produced, and each piano must be judged on its own merits, this brief historical overview may give you some idea of what to expect to see as you shop for a used piano. You can determine the age of a piano by finding its serial number (*The Piano Book* tells how) and looking it up in the *Pierce Piano Atlas* (www.piercepianoatlas.com), or perhaps by asking a piano dealer or technician to look it up for you.

How to Find a Used Piano

Finding a used piano essentially involves networking, a concept very much in vogue these days. Some networking can be done by computer, and some with old-fashioned phone calls and shoe leather. Here are some of your options—you may be able to think of others.

■ *Contact piano technicians, rebuilders, and used-piano dealers*

People who service pianos often have customers who want to sell their instruments. Some technicians also restore pianos for sale in their shops. Contacting these technicians or visiting their shops is a good way to acquaint yourself with local market conditions, to better understand what's involved in piano restoration, and to see an interesting slice of life in your community you might not otherwise encounter. If you decide to buy from a technician, you may pay more than you would a private party, but you'll have the peace of mind of knowing that the piano has been checked over, repaired, and comes with a warranty. Even though you trust the seller, it's a good idea to hire an independent technician to inspect the piano before purchase, just as you would if the piano were being sold by a private party, because even the best technicians can differ in their professional abilities and opinions.

■ Visit dealers of new pianos

New-piano dealers take used pianos in trade for new ones all the time, and need to dispose of them to recoup the trade-in allowance they gave on the new piano. Although many of the trade-ins will be older pianos, it's quite common for a customer to trade in a piano purchased only a few years earlier for a bigger or better model, leaving a nearly new piano for you to buy at a substantial discount on its price when new. Again, you may pay more than you would from a private party—usually 20 to 30 percent more—but it may be difficult to find something like this from a private party, and the dealer will likely also give some sort of warranty. Some of the best deals I've seen have been acquired this way. If you're also considering the option of buying a new piano, then you'll be able to explore both options with a single visit. On the other hand, sometimes dealers advertise used pianos just to get customers into the store, where they can be sold on a new

piano. The used piano advertised may be overpriced, or may no longer be available. When you have a used piano inspected, make sure the technician you hire owes no favors to the dealer who's selling it.

■ Shopping via the Internet

The best way to use the Internet to shop for a used piano is to look for sellers, both commercial and non-commercial, within driving distance of your home. That way, you can more easily try out the piano, develop a face-to-face relationship with the seller, and get a better sense of whether or not you want to do business with them. Craigslist (www.craigslist.org), though not a piano-specific site, seems to have become the preferred classified-ad site for this purpose, as it's both free and is organized by city. If you travel frequently, you should check out sellers in other cities, too—easy to do on Craigslist. Other popular piano classified-ad sites include www .pianoworld.com (which also has extensive forums for exchanging information and getting answers to your questions), www.pianomart .com (smartly organized for easy searching), and our own Piano Buyer Classifieds (www.pianobuyer.com), which uses the Pianomart database and search engine. These sites either charge a monthly fee to list or a small commission upon sale, but are free to buyers.

You'll also find pianos for sale on the Internet auction site eBay. Search on a variety of keywords, as each keyword will bring up a different group of pianos for sale. This can be frustrating, as either too broad or too specific a search term may yield unsatisfactory results. The bidding process generally provides a window of time during which you can contact the seller for more information, see the piano, and have it inspected before placing a bid. This is definitely not a good way to buy a piano unless

you have the opportunity to first try out the piano and have it inspected. On both eBay and the classified-ad sites mentioned above, many listings that appear to be non-commercial will actually turn out to have been placed by commercial sellers, who may have many more pianos for sale than the one in the ad you answered.

The website of the Piano Technicians Guild (www.ptg.org) has a listing of dealer websites and other resources that may be useful in locating used or restored pianos. If your situation is such that finding a local source of used pianos is unlikely, one reliable source that ships nationwide is Rick Jones Pianos in Beltsville, Maryland (www .rickjonespianos.com).

If you're thinking of making a long-distance purchase, the precautions mentioned in the section "Shopping Long-Distance via the Internet," in the article "Piano Buying Basics," bear repeating: First, take into account the cost of long-distance shipping and consider whether it's really worth it. If buying from a commercial source, find out as much as you can about the dealer. Get references. If you haven't actually seen the piano, get pictures of it. Hire a technician in the seller's area to inspect the piano and ask the technician about a commercial seller's reputation. Make sure the dealer has experience in arranging long-distance moves, and uses a mover that specializes in pianos. Find out who will be responsible for tuning and adjusting the piano in your home, and for repairing any defects or dings in the finish. Get the details of any warranty, especially who is responsible for paying the return freight if the piano is defective. Find out how payment is to be made in a way that protects both parties.

■ Non-Internet Techniques

In this age of the Internet, it's important not to forget older, more

Spirit of a great artist
Samick Pianos

conventional methods of networking that still work, such as placing and answering classified print ads in local newspapers and want-ad booklets; and posting and answering notices on bulletin boards anywhere people congregate, such as houses of worship, community centers, laundromats, etc. Other, more aggressive, techniques include contacting movers and storage warehouses to see if they have any pianos abandoned by their owners; attending auctions; contacting attorneys and others who handle the disposition of estates; and just plain old asking around among coworkers, friends, and acquaintances.

Restoring the piano case to like-new condition

■ *Obtaining a Piano from a Friend or Relative*

It's nice when pianos remain in the family. I got my piano that way. But pianos purchased from friends and relatives or received as gifts are as likely as any others to have expensive problems you should know about. It's very hard to refuse a gift, and perhaps embarrassing to hire a piano technician to inspect it before you accept it, but for your own protection you should insist on doing so. Otherwise you may spend a lot of money to move a "gift" you could have done without.

Which of these routes to finding a used piano you end up following will depend on your situation and what you're looking for. If you have a lot of time and transportation is no problem, you may get the best deal by shopping around among private owners or in out-of-the-way places. If you're busy or without a car but have money to spend, it may be more convenient to shop among piano technicians, rebuilders, or dealers, who may be able to show you several pianos at the same time and spare you from worrying about future repair costs and problems. If you travel a lot to other cities or have few piano resources in your local area, the Internet can be a big help in locating an appropriate commercial or non-commercial source far away. (See the ads in this publication for movers that specialize in long-distance piano moving.) The best route also depends on where you live, as some communities may have a brisk trade in used pianos among private owners but few rebuilding shops, or vice versa, or have an abundance of old uprights but few grands.

Buying a Restored Piano

Three terms are often used in discussions of piano restoration work: *repair*, *reconditioning*, and *rebuilding*. There are no precise definitions of these terms, and any particular job may contain elements of more than one of them. It's therefore very important, when having restoration

work done on your piano or when buying a piano on which such work has been done, to find out exactly what jobs have been, or will be, carried out. "This piano has been reconditioned" or "I'll rebuild this piano" are not sufficient answers. One technician's rebuilding may be another's reconditioning.

Repair jobs generally involve fixing isolated broken parts, such as a broken hammer, a missing string, or an improperly working pedal. That is, a repair does not necessarily involve upgrading the condition of the instrument as a whole, but addresses only specific broken or improperly adjusted parts.

Reconditioning always involves a general upgrading of the entire piano, but with as little actual replacement of parts as possible. For instance, reconditioning an old upright might include resurfacing the hammer felt (instead of replacing the hammers) and twisting (instead of replacing) the bass strings to improve their tone. However, definitions of *reconditioning* can vary widely: Many technicians would consider the replacement of hammers, tuning pins, and strings to be part of a reconditioning job in which more extensive work is either not needed or not cost-effective; others would call such work a partial rebuild.

Rebuilding is the most complete of the three levels of restoration. Ideally, *rebuilding* means putting the piano into "like new" condition.

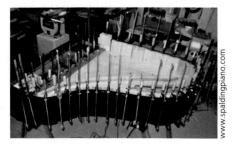

Gluing a new soundboard into the rim of a grand piano

GRAND PIANO REBUILDING CHECKLIST

The following is a list of the tasks that might comprise a fairly complete rebuilding of a grand piano. Any particular job may be either more or less extensive than shown here, depending on the needs and value of the instrument and other factors, but this list can serve as a guide. See also *The Piano Book* for information about specific rebuilding issues pertaining to Steinway and Mason & Hamlin pianos.

Notice that the restoration can be divided into three main parts: the soundbox or resonating unit, the action, and the cabinet. The *soundbox* (also known as the *strung back* or *belly*) includes the soundboard, ribs, bridges, strings, pinblock, tuning pins, plate, and the structural parts of the case; the *action* includes the keyframe and action frame, keys and keytops, hammers, dampers, trapwork, and all other moving action parts; the *cabinet* includes cosmetic repair and refinishing of the case and of the nonstructural cabinet parts and hardware. Note that the damper parts that contact the strings are restored with the soundbox, whereas the damper underlever action is treated with the rest of the action.

There is very little overlap among the three types of work; each of the three parts could be performed alone or at different times, as technical conditions permit and/or financial considerations require. In a typical complete rebuilding job, restoration of the soundbox might comprise 45 percent of the cost, the action 30 percent, and the cabinet 25 percent, though these percentages will vary according to the particulars of the job.

Soundbox or resonating unit

- Replace or repair soundboard, refinish, install new soundboard decal (if not replacing soundboard: shim soundboard cracks, reglue ribs as necessary, refinish, install new soundboard decal)
- Replace pinblock
- Replace bridges or bridge caps
- Replace or ream agraffes, restore capo-bar bearing surface
- Refinish plate, paint lettering, replace understring felts
- Replace strings and tuning pins, tune to pitch
- Replace damper felts, refinish damper heads, regulate dampers

Action

- Replace hammers, shanks, and flanges
- Replace or overhaul wippen/repetition assemblies
- Replace backchecks
- Replace front-rail key bushings
- Replace balance-rail key bushings or key buttons
- Replace or clean keytops
- Replace key-end felts
- Clean keys
- Clean and refelt keyframe
- Replace let-off felts or buttons
- Clean and, if necessary, repair action frame
- Regulate action, voice
- Overhaul or replace damper underlever action and damper guide rail
- Overhaul pedal lyre and trapwork, regulate

Cabinet

- Repair music desk, legs, other cabinet parts, as needed
- Repair loose or missing veneer
- Strip and refinish exterior; refinish bench to match piano
- Buff and lacquer solid-brass hardware, replate plated hardware

In practice, however, it may involve much less, depending on the needs and value of the particular instrument, the amount of money available, and the scrupulousness of the rebuilder. Restringing the piano and replacing the pinblock in a grand, as well as repairing or replacing the soundboard, would typically be parts of a rebuilding job. In the action, rebuilding would include replacing the hammer heads, damper felts,

and key bushings, and replacing or completely overhauling other sets of parts as well. Refinishing the piano case is also generally part of the rebuilding process. Because of the confusion over the definitions of these terms, sometimes the term *remanufacturing* is used to distinguish the most complete rebuilding job possible—including replacement of the soundboard—from a lesser "rebuilding." However, there is no substitute for requesting from the technician an itemization of the work performed.

When considering buying a rebuilt piano, or having a piano rebuilt, particularly an expensive one, the rebuilder's experience level should count heavily in your decision. The complete rebuilding of a piano requires many dissimilar skills. The skills required for installing a soundboard, for example, are very different from those required for installing a new set of hammers or for regulating the action. Mastering all of these skills can take a very long time. In a sense, you should be shopping for the rebuilder as much as for the piano.

Many rebuilders contract out portions of the job, particularly the refinishing of the piano's case, to others who have special expertise. Although this has always been so, more recently groups of technicians, each with his or her own business and shop, have been openly advertising their close, long-term collaboration with one another on rebuilding jobs. In a typical collaboration of this type, one person might rebuild the strung back or soundbox (soundboard, bridges, pinblock, strings, tuning pins, cast-iron plate); another would rebuild the action and do the final musical finishing, such as regulating and voicing; and the third would refinish the case.

Collaboration of this kind is a positive development, as it means that each technician does only what he or she does best, resulting in a better job for the customer. But make sure you know with whom you are contracting or from whom you are buying, and which technician is responsible for making things right if problems arise.

It may occur to you that you could save a lot of money by buying an unrestored piano and having a technician completely restore it, rather than buying the completely restored piano from the technician. This is often true. But the results of a rebuilding job tend to be musically uncertain. That is, if you are particular in your taste for tone and touch, you may or may not care for how the instrument ultimately turns out. For that reason, especially if a lot of money is involved, you might be better off letting the technician make the extra profit in return for taking the risk.

"Vintage" . . . or New?

"Vintage" pianos are those made during the golden years of piano-making in the United States—roughly, from 1880 to World War II. More specifically, the term usually refers to the Steinway and Mason & Hamlin pianos made during that period, though it's occasionally applied to other great American makes as well. In the last few decades the demand for these pianos, and consequently their prices, has mushroomed due to a (until recently) strong economy, increased entrepreneurial activity on the part of rebuilders and piano brokers, allegations by rebuilders and others that today's new pianos are not as well made as the older ones were, and the purchase of many older Steinways by Steinway & Sons itself for rebuilding in its factory.

What makes these vintage pianos so alluring? Many musicians and technicians believe that these instruments, when rebuilt, sound and play better than new pianos. However, no one knows for sure why this should be so, since most of the components in the piano are replaced during rebuilding. Some point to the fact that Steinway operated its own plate foundry until about World War II, afterward using a commercial plate foundry (which it now owns). Because this radical change in the manufacture of such an important component roughly corresponds with the end of the vintage era, and because the plate is one of the few original parts to survive the rebuilding process, some speculate that it holds the key to the difference. Others say it has to do with changes in the quality of the wood available to Steinway and other companies. Still others say it wasn't any single thing, but rather a combination of many fortuitous factors, including extremely skilled and talented craftsmen, that enabled these companies to make such special pianos during that period, but allegedly not afterward (though that doesn't explain why the rebuilt ones from that period should be better).

Steinway & Sons, for its part, disputes the entire idea that older Steinways are better, dismissing it as a romantic notion spread by purveyors of those pianos in their own financial interest. The company says it has done extensive testing of both plates and woods, and the idea that the older plates and woods were better has no scientific basis. It says it has also carefully inspected hundreds of older Steinways at its factory rebuilding facility, which is the largest Steinway rebuilding facility in the world, and finds no evidence that the older pianos were built better than today's—in fact, it believes that just the opposite is true. Steinway acknowledges that some pianists may prefer the sound of specific older pianos for subjective artistic reasons, but says that those considering the purchase of a restored, older instrument should do so to save money, not to seek better quality.

For more discussion of this topic, and of specific technical issues applicable to the rebuilding of a Steinway or Mason & Hamlin, please see *The Piano Book*.

How Much Is It Worth?

The valuation of used pianos is difficult. Prices of used pianos vary

PRICES OF USED PIANOS (US$)					
	Private Seller			Dealer	
	Worse	*Average*	*Better*	*Reconditioned*	*Rebuilt*
Vertical, pre-1950, average brand	0–300	0–600	300–1,000	1,000–1,500	N/A
Vertical, pre-1950, better brand	0–500	300–1,200	700–1,200	1,200–2,000	N/A
Vertical, pre-1950, best brand	500–2,000	1,000–3,500	2,000–5,000	3,000–6,000	N/A
Vertical, 1950–1985, average brand	0–600	400–1,000	1,000–2,000	1,200–2,500	N/A
Vertical, 1950–1985, better brand	0–800	700–1,500	1,000–2,500	2,000–4,500	N/A
Vertical, 1950–1985, best brand	700–2,000	1,500–4,000	2,000–5,000	4,000–7,000	N/A
Vertical, 1985–	Use Depreciation Schedule				
Grand, pre-1950, average brand, 5'	0–500	700–1,500	1,000–2,500	1,500–3,500	N/A
Grand, pre-1950, average brand, 6'	500–1,200	1,500–2,000	2,000–3,000	3,000–4,500	N/A
Grand, pre-1950, average brand, 7'	800–1,500	1,500–3,500	3,000–5,000	4,000–7,000	N/A
Grand, pre-1950, better brand, 5'	500–1,000	2,000–3,000	2,500–4,000	5,000–8,000	N/A
Grand, pre-1950, better brand, 6'	1,000–2,500	2,000–4,000	3,000–6,000	7,000–10,000	15,000–25,000
Grand, pre-1950, better brand, 7'	1,800–3,500	3,500–7,000	5,000–10,000	8,000–15,000	18,000–30,000
Grand, pre-1950, best brand, 5'	3,000–6,000	6,000–9,000	8,000–18,000	15,000–23,000	18,000–35,000
Grand, pre-1950, best brand, 6'	6,000–8,000	7,000–15,000	12,000–20,000	15,000–28,000	28,000–50,000
Grand, pre-1950, best brand, 7'	7,000–10,000	12,000–18,000	22,000–35,000	20,000–40,000	35,000–65,000
Grand, 1950–1985, average brand, 5'	500–1,200	1,000–2,500	1,500–3,000	3,000–5,000	N/A
Grand, 1950–1985, average brand, 6'	500–2,000	2,000–3,000	3,000–5,000	3,500–6,000	N/A
Grand, 1950–1985, average brand, 7'	1,500–3,000	2,500–4,000	4,000–6,000	4,000–8,000	N/A
Grand, 1950–1985, better brand, 5'	800–2,000	2,000–4,000	2,000–6,000	5,000–9,000	N/A
Grand, 1950–1985, better brand, 6'	1,500–3,000	2,500–5,000	4,000–8,000	8,000–12,000	12,000–22,000
Grand, 1950–1985, better brand, 7'	2,500–5,000	5,000–9,000	8,000–13,000	10,000–20,000	15,000–30,000
Grand, 1950–1985, best brand, 5'	4,000–9,000	7,000–14,000	9,000–18,000	15,000–21,000	20,000–35,000
Grand, 1950–1985, best brand, 6'	6,000–10,000	8,000–15,000	12,000–20,000	20,000–28,000	28,000–50,000
Grand, 1950–1985, best brand, 7'	8,000–12,000	14,000–22,000	18,000–28,000	20,000–40,000	35,000–65,000
Grand, 1985–	Use Depreciation Schedule				

APPRECIATE OR DEPRECIATE?

Some piano manufacturers market their instruments as "investments" and tout their potential for appreciation in value. If that's the case, then why a *depreciation* schedule? Do pianos appreciate or depreciate?

It depends on how you look at it. Imagine parking a sum of money in a savings account earning 2 percent interest at a time when inflation is at 3 percent. Each year, the balance in the account grows . . . and *loses* purchasing power. This is something like the situation with pianos. After a large initial drop in value during the first five to ten years (because, unless given an incentive to buy used, most people would prefer a new piano), used pianos lose value in comparison with similar new ones at about 1.5 to 2 percent per year. However, because the price of *everything* (including pianos) is rising in price at 3 or 3.5 percent per year (the rate of inflation), the value of your used piano will appear to *rise* by 1 to 2 percent per year (the difference between the depreciation and the inflation).

Why do we figure depreciation from a comparable new piano instead of figuring appreciation from the original price of the used one? Theoretically, it could be done either way. But the price of a comparable new piano is easier to look up—one might have to do a lot of research to find out what grandma paid for her piano. And the price of the new piano embodies all the inflation that has occurred between the original purchase of the used piano and the present, avoiding the trouble of having to look up the change in the cost of living during that time. The case is even stronger for using this method with foreign-made pianos: Tying the value of a used piano to the cost of a comparable new one makes it unnecessary to calculate the changes in the currency exchange rate—and sometimes changes in the currency itself!—that have occurred since the used piano was new.

Figuring depreciation from a comparable new piano is not without its own problems, however. With so many piano brands of the past now defunct or made to entirely different standards (usually in China), the task of figuring out what constitutes a "comparable" new piano can sometimes be formidable, if not impossible.

the appraisal process and determine the value of a piano within a reasonable range.

Fair market value is the price at which an item would change hands between a willing buyer and a willing seller, neither of whom is compelled to buy or sell, and each of whom has reasonable knowledge of the relevant facts.

Appraisers of used pianos and other consumer goods typically use three different methods to determine fair market value: *comparable sales*, *depreciation*, and *idealized value minus the cost of restoration*.

Comparable Sales

The *comparable sales* method compares the piano being appraised with recent actual selling prices of other pianos of like brand, model, age, condition, and location. Generally speaking, this is the most accurate method of determining value when one has access to a body of information on recent sale prices of comparable items. The problem here is that, with few exceptions, it's rare to find several recently sold pianos that are perfect matches for all these criteria. There is no central repository for sales information on used pianos, and each appraiser or technician, over a lifetime, sees pianos that are so diverse and scattered as to these criteria that they are likely to be of only limited value as appraisal guides. (Exceptions might be technicians or dealers who specialize in used Yamaha, Kawai, or Steinway pianos, brands that have attained near-commodity status in the piano business.)

To handle this problem, I and my staff have attempted to approximate the fair market value of pianos of various types, ages, and conditions by querying a number of piano technicians about their memories of comparable sales. The result is the accompanying chart, "Prices of Used Pianos," though I stress that we do not have enough data to do

wildly, depending on local economies, supply and demand, and the cosmetics and playing condition of the instrument at hand, including the amount and quality of any restoration work done. As if this weren't enough, it's almost a certainty that no two piano technicians or piano salespeople would return exactly the same verdict on any given piano's value. Art being what it is, beauty is in the eye and ear of the potential purchaser, and values are very much subjective.

In addition, when considering a used piano being sold by a private, non-commercial seller, keep in mind that many such sellers really have no

firm idea of how much their piano is worth, and have made up something based on little more than a wish. Therefore, don't let a high asking price keep you from making a more reasonable offer. Ask the seller how they arrived at their asking price. If you can back up your offer with your own technician's appraisal (including a list of the things that need to be fixed), credible listings of similar pianos, or other evidence of the piano's true value, you stand a good chance of getting the piano at or close to your price.

In this article, I've tried to assemble some information and tools to help buyers and sellers understand

more than make rough estimates. This chart is most useful for determining the approximate value of many brands of older piano for which it would otherwise be difficult to find enough comparable sales to determine a value. Understandably, however, the price ranges shown in the chart are quite broad. The chart is organized by categories of vertical and grand piano broken down by age (pre-1950 and 1950–1985), quality (Average, Better, Best), and condition (Worse, Average, Better, Reconditioned, and Rebuilt). For prices of pianos made since 1985, I suggest using the depreciation method, described later in this article.

The price ranges given reflect the wide possibilities a buyer faces in the used-piano market. At the low end of each range is a price one might find in a poor economy or a "buyer's market," where supply exceeds demand. At the high end, the prices are consistent with both a better economy and a higher demand for the type of instrument indicated. In some categories, the prices we received from our sources varied all over the map, and we had to use a considerable amount of editorial discretion to produce price ranges that were not so broad as to be useless as guidelines, and to retain at least a modicum of internal consistency in the chart. For that reason, you should expect to find some markets or situations in which prices higher or lower than those given here are normal or appropriate.

The prices given here for pianos that are not reconditioned or rebuilt (those labeled Worse, Average, Better) are the price ranges you might expect to find when buying pianos *from private owners*. The Reconditioned and Rebuilt categories represent prices you might encounter when shopping for such pianos *at piano stores or from piano technicians*, with a warranty given. In some cases

we have omitted the Rebuilt price because we would not expect rebuilding to be cost-effective for pianos of that general age and type. In every case, prices assume the least expensive style and finish; prices for pianos with fancier cabinets, exotic veneers, inlays, and so forth, could be much higher.

Quality

"Best brands" include Steinway, Mason & Hamlin, and the very best European makes, such as Bechstein, Blüthner, and Bösendorfer. "Better brands" include the well-regarded older names mentioned in the accompanying article for the pre-1930 period, such as Knabe and Chickering; and names such as Baldwin, Everett, Kawai, Sohmer, Yamaha, and others of similar quality for the 1950–1985 period. "Average brands" are pretty much everything else.

Condition

Worse, Average, and Better refer to the condition of the piano in comparison to the amount of wear and tear one would expect from the piano's age. However, even Worse pianos should be playable and serviceable. Note that because many buyers are quite conscious of a piano's appearance, pianos that are in good shape musically but in poor shape cosmetically will often sell at a price more consistent with the Worse range than with a higher one. This offers an opportunity for the less furniture-conscious buyer to obtain a bargain.

For a discussion of the definitions of *reconditioned* and *rebuilt*, please see the section "Buying a Restored Piano" in this article. **For the purposes of this chart, however, we have adopted the requirement that a piano has not been *rebuilt* unless its pinblock has been replaced, and that a piano that has been restrung, but without a new pinblock, is considered to have been *reconditioned*.**

Note that these definitions are not precise, and that both the quality and the quantity of the work can vary greatly, depending on the needs of the instrument and the capabilities of the restorer. These variations should be taken into account when determining the piano's value.

Depreciation

The *depreciation* method of determining fair market value is based on the fact that many types of consumer goods lose value over time at a more or less predictable rate. A *depreciation schedule*, such as the one here, shows how much an unrestored used piano is worth as a percentage of the actual selling price of a new piano of comparable

DEPRECIATION SCHEDULE			
Age in Years	Percent of New Value		
	Worse	*Average*	*Better*
5 or less	70	75	80
10	60	65	70
15	45	50	55
20	35	40	45
25	25	30	35
30	20	25	30
Verticals only			
50	5	10	15
70	0	5	10
Grands only			
50	10	15	20
70	5	10	15
Steinways			
5 or less	70	75	80
10	60	65	70
15	50	55	60
20	40	45	50
25	30	35	40
30	25	30	35
Verticals only			
50	5	10	15
70	5	10	15
Grands only			
50	15	20	25
70	10	15	20

quality. The problem here is that so many older brands are now made by companies different from the original, in different factories and parts of the world, and to different standards, that it can be difficult or impossible to determine what constitutes a "comparable" new piano. Thus, this method of figuring value is best used for pianos of relatively recent make when the model is still in production, or for older pianos whose makers have remained under relatively constant ownership, location, and standards, and for which, therefore, a comparable model can reasonably be determined.

Note that depreciation is from the *current* price of the model, not the original price, because the current price takes into account inflation and, if applicable, changes in the value of foreign currencies. The values are meant to reflect what the piano would sell for between *private, non-commercial parties.* I suggest adding 20 to 30 percent to the computed value when the piano is being sold *by a dealer,* unrestored, but with a warranty. These figures are intended only as guidelines, reflecting

our general observation of the market. "Worse," "Average," and "Better" refer to the condition of the used piano for its age. A separate chart is given for Steinway pianos. Other fine pianos, such as Mason & Hamlin, or some of the best European brands, may command prices between the regular and Steinway figures.

Idealized Value Minus the Cost of Restoration

This is the difference between the cost of a rebuilt piano and the cost to restore the unrebuilt one to like-new condition. For example, if a piano, rebuilt, would be worth $50,000, and it would cost $30,000 to restore the unrebuilt one to like-new condition, then according to this method the unrebuilt piano would be worth $20,000. This method can be used when a piano needs extensive, quantifiable repair work. It's not appropriate to use this method for an instrument that is relatively new or in good condition.

Other Types of Valuation

Several other types of valuation are sometimes called for:

Replacement value is what it would cost to replace the used piano with a brand-new one. This value is often sought when someone has purchased an insurance policy with a rider that guarantees replacement of a lost or damaged piano with a new one instead of paying the fair market value of the used one. The problem here, again, is what brand and model of new piano to consider "comparable" if the original brand and model are no longer being made, or are not being made to the same standards.

Here it may be helpful to consult the **rating chart** in the ***Piano Buyer*** article "The New-Piano Market Today." Choose a brand whose relationship to today's piano market is similar to that the original brand bore to the piano market of its day. Whatever brand and model you choose, depending on how high a replacement value you seek, you can use either the manufacturer's suggested retail price (highest), the approximate street price (lowest), or something in between. These prices, or information on how to estimate them, can be found in the "Model & Pricing Guide."

Trade-in value is what a commercial seller would pay for the used piano, usually in trade (or partial trade) for a new one. This is discounted from the fair market value, typically by at least 20 to 30 percent, to allow the commercial seller to make a profit when reselling the instrument. (In practice, the commercial seller will often pay the fair market value for the used piano, but to compensate, will increase the price of the new piano to the consumer.)

Salvage value is what a dealer, technician, or rebuilder would pay for a piano that is essentially unplayable or unserviceable and in need of restoration. It can be determined using the idealized-value-minus-cost-of-restoration method, but discounted, like trade-in value, to allow the commercial seller to make a profit.

Inspect, Inspect, Inspect

In closing, I'd like to remind you that your best protection against buyer's remorse is having the piano inspected by a piano technician prior to purchasing it, particularly if the piano is more than ten years old. Sometimes it will be sufficient to speak to the seller's technician about the piano, if he or she has serviced it regularly and has reason to believe that he or she will continue servicing it under your ownership. However, in most situations, you'll be better off hiring your own technician. You can find a list of Registered Piano Technicians in your area on the website of the Piano Technicians Guild, www.ptg.org.

More Information

If you're serious about buying a used piano, additional information in *The Piano Book* may be useful to you, including:

- How to remove the outer cabinet parts to look inside the piano
- How to do a preliminary inspection of a piano to rule out those that are not worth hiring a technician to inspect, including an extensive checklist of potential problem areas
- A discussion of issues that frequently come up in regard to the rebuilding of Steinway pianos
- A complete list of older Steinway models, from 1853 to the present
- How to locate the serial number of a piano
- A list of manufacturing dates and serial numbers for Steinway pianos.

History of Bush&Gerts Piano Company

1884, Establishment Of Bush&Gerts Piano Company

The Bush&Gerts Piano Company was a major player in the American piano industry. Established in 1884 by Wm.H.Bush, John Gerts and Wm.L.Bush. Bush&Gerts built excellent pianos in Chicago. In 1890, William·H·Bush, John Gerts and William·Lincoln·Bush changed the total investment to a corporation under the name of Bush and Gerts Piano Company, with $400,000 capital.

1892, Establishment of Bush&Gerts factory

The factory of Bush&Gerts, piano makers, occupies a block of ground at Dayton and Weed streets, Chicago. President Bush is one of the leading piano men of the United, States and has occupied high official positions in the National Piano Manufacturers' Association.

1893, World's Columbian Exposition

Bush&Gerts pianos have received numerous awards, One of the first is a quality gold medal in 1893 at the Chicago World's Fair at the Jackson Park and Midway Plaisance , with 27,300,000 Visitors.

1903, Bush&Gerts had branches all over the country with the expansion of Company scale

Bush was treasurer of the Conservatory and also president of the Bush&Gerts Piano Company of Texas and the Bush Temple of Music in Dallas. Bush&Gerts had branches in Boston, Dallas, Austin, and Memphis.

1912, Law against stencil pianos

For over forty years,strenuous efforts have been made by manufacturers of good pianos to put an end to the nefarious traffic in stencil pianos, and no one in the piano trade has been more earnest and active in this respect than William L. Bush.on January

1912, with the efforts of William.L.Bush, Mr. Campbell introduced his bill, according to the provisions of which"It shall be unlawful for any person, firm, company or corporation to place be unlawful for any person, firm, company or corporation to place upon the market for interstate or foreign commerce any product of manufacture, without printing, embossing, or stenciling the name and address of the manufacturer upon such article or commodity."

1924, Bush families turned to focus on the cause of music,Bush&Gerts pianos were actually built by the Haddorff Piano Company of Rockford, IL. Bush & Gerts enjoy the reputation of being very well made, and their earlier models are often very elaborate. The Haddorff Piano Company was established in 1901 by Charles A. Haddorff in Rockford, Illinois. Their factories were located at 55 Ethel Street. Haddorff was a large-scale manufacturer, and they built pianos for several other prominent piano manufacturers including Bush & Gerts and Clarendon.

From 1925 to 1940, Bush&Gerts Piano Company turned from global sales to only accepting high-end private hand-built pianos. In 1925, especially after the Great Depression, coupled with the company's strategic changes and the overall decline in the piano production industry in the United States, Bush&Gerts Piano company turned from global sales to only accepting high-end private hand-made pianos. The promotion of the balanced skills of the keyboards ensured the piano quality to have reached a peak during this period.

1928, Encounter with Vladimir Horowitz.

Horowitz was born in 1903, after finished the Europe road show and gained great welcome, he reached America in 1928. Cooperating with New York Philharmonic conducted by sir Thomas Beecham, Horowitz played the Tchaikovsky Piano Concerto at a Bush&Gerts piano, which made a splash to the world. The master really appreciated the improved Bush&Gerts, since then Bush&Gerts has been known as one of eight exclusive pianos at the world-class concert.

1940, the Conn Company bought out the Haddorff Piano Company including Bush&Gerts piano of Rockford in Illinois. Bush&Gerts Piano company accepted the operation of the new company and began to sell worldwide from 1941 to 1942. 900 pianos were produced annually during World War II, with an annual increase of 540%.

From 1942 to 1945, the Pearl Harbor incident led to the outbreak of the Pacific War, and the United States formally got involved in the Second World War. In the later years of the war, the handicraft factory of Bush&Gerts Piano Company was ordered to give up all the prepared and dried wood their lumber yard held for war production. From 1945 to 2015, Bush&Gerts Piano Company resumed its production of pianos. 1970, Charles R. Walter, former employee of Conn Company, purchased the Conn piano line and established the Walter Piano Co. in Elkhart, Indiana.Meanwhile, the Bush&Gerts Piano company became independent to be re-managed by the fourth generation descendant William J. Bush of the Bush family. Then only private customized manufacturing was accepted for professionals to ensure the quality of the piano, with an average of an annual production of more than 40 high-end private pianos by hand-made piano factory. (series number from 75000-78000)

In 2000, after seeing the broad prospects for developing in the Chinese market, Bush family's fifth generation descendant John Bush prepared a series of work in the establishment of some factories and marketing centers, and determined to enter the Chinese market as the first step before exploring the global market.

In August 2015, Christopher Hunter, manager of the Bush&Gerts Piano Company and the company president"Clive in China, officially

Bush&Gerts
http://en.bushgerts.com

Bush & Gerts
Chicago.

announced the entry into the Chinese market after 15 years of preparatory work. At the same time, the Bush family moved to New York with his hand-made piano factory, and start a strategic cooperation with Shanghai Bu Ge musical instrument company. The Chinese factory of the company started to produce the first batch of Bush&Gerts pianos in the Asian market, with the White House series and the Chicago series. Some models are sold back to America. The piano is numerated from 78001. The legitimate trademark of Bush&Gerts (It's writed 布什&戈尔茨 in Chinese characters) in China, is owned by the America Bush And Gerts Co.,Ltd only, and we suggest consumers identify the Bush&Gerts logo protected by law and be ware of imitations!

In 2016, the Bush&Gerts marketing center was established, which conducted a certain promotion in the world, announcing the acceptance of private customized business worldwide. At the same time, China's Bush&Gerts Piano factory launched Horowitz commemorative collection. At the end of the year, several new collections of pianos began to be manufactured by the Bush&Gerts handmade factory in Selangor, Malaysia. Bush&Gerts piano won the industry's praise as a national treasure piano brand with a hundred-year American original technology and piano craft after the musical instruments exhibitions in Shanghai, Guangzhou and other cities in China. At the end of 2016, the 200-acre new plant Bush&Gerts piano (China) company began to be constructed in phases, with its production capacity expected to reach 40,000 high-end pianos.

E-Mail:bushgerts@outlook.com

Web:http://en.bushgerts.com

Office Add:1 Radisson Plz #800,NewRochelle,New York

Bush & Gerts Company Launched Several New Series Of Pianos To The Market Worldwide

Model	Size	MSRRP(USS)*
CH-1	47"2	11,200
CH-2	47"6	12,400
CH-3	48	11,900
CH-5	49"2	13,900
WH-2	50"	22,800

Nowadays, Bush&Gerts Piano Co., Ltd. achieves the strategic cooperation with Shanghai Bu Ge Musical Instrument Company, the factory's address is selected in China , and the piano's configuration is purchased from world's top suppliers, which is also equipped with the unique patent piano action technology of Bush&Gerts. Bush&Gerts achieves the united cooperation with Germany ABEL\FFW (Hammer), ROSLAU (Strings), STRUNZ (Soundboard) and other suppliers, which jointly provides technical support for the perfect sound quality, rich expressiveness, etc. of Bush&Gerts Piano, inheriting the tradition for more than one hundred years of hand-made; the long-term accumulation and cultivation of production process make Bush & Gerts Piano perfect.

CH-1

CH-5

WH-2

There are many common misconceptions about buying pianos for young students, and one of them is that a suitable piano can be had for only a few hundred dollars. The truth is that, to progress, young students need *better* pianos, not worse.

Parents may not want to invest a lot of money in a piano—after all, the child may lose interest—so an older, cheaper piano may seem the logical place to start. However, a bad purchasing decision at this point in a student's learning tends to be a self-fulfilling prophecy. In many cases a piano that is too old, too small, or simply not good enough will soon become useless to the student. Students don't have enough experience to distinguish between a bad piano and their own lack of ability. When a piano's action can't be regulated to the correct touch, or its strings tuned to a harmonious sound, the student, unable to duplicate what was taught in a lesson, will become frustrated and discouraged, and will lose interest. *No amount of practice on such an instrument can overcome its shortcomings.* And when you include other factors—the costs of moving, tuning, and repairs; an older piano's shorter remaining life; lack of warranty protection; the need to hire experts to make repeated trips to evaluate the conditions of various older pianos—a new or more recently made instrument may start to look like a bargain in the long run.

For these reasons, I would encourage the financially able family to look at good-quality new pianos, or better used pianos no more than 15 years old. And with a young talented student, moving up to a quality grand is never a mistake. If an older piano is chosen, it should be one that was of good quality to begin with, and has been restored to like-new condition. If you're concerned

about a child's continuing interest, I suggest renting a new instrument now, with an option to purchase it later. Most reputable piano dealers offer month-to-month rental programs.

Although good *and* bad pianos have been made in every decade, and every used piano must be evaluated on its own merits, certain decades or categories of piano frequently found in today's used-piano market should raise red flags:

Old uprights—These are usually 48" to 60" high and somewhere around 100 years old. Many buyers will purchase an old upright with the idea that it might have antique value, then quickly find out that it doesn't. In some instances, buyers fascinated by old uprights see them as an opportunity to tinker with and learn something about pianos. There's nothing wrong with this—as long as a young student is not saddled with it.

Most pianos that are a century old and have not been discarded will need extensive restoration before they can be useful to the student, but few are worth enough to have such work performed on them. Many have difficulty holding a tuning, and/or desperately need new strings, hammers, dampers, or pedal repairs—or all of the above. Parents who purchase these deteriorating instruments as practice pianos for beginners will probably face a constant stream of complaints and subsequent repairs. In most cases, this category of used piano should be avoided for use in serious practice.

PIANO BRANDS TO AVOID

Here are some brand names from the 1960s, '70s, and '80s—and others from a little earlier and later—that are probably best avoided by students, though some may be acceptable for casual use if carefully serviced or reconditioned.

Aeolian

The following were some of the many brand names owned and made by the Aeolian Corporation, which went out of business in 1985. Many of these, and other names not listed, were "stencil pianos"—essentially identical instruments with different names applied to them, to meet dealers' needs. Note that this list applies to the use of these names only during the mid to late 1900s. Some of these names were used in earlier periods on fine pianos, and several are still being used today, but on pianos that have no connection to the ones warned about here.

Bradbury	J. & C. Fischer
Cable	Kranich & Bach
Duo Art	Melodigrand
George Steck	Pianola
Hallet, Davis & Co.	Poole
Hardman, Peck & Co.	Vose & Sons
Henry F. Miller	Winter & Co.
Ivers & Pond	

Other U.S.-made brands of the period

Betsy Ross (by Lester)	Kincaid (by Grand)
Brambach (by Kohler & Campbell)	La Petite (by Kimball)
Currier	Lester
Estey	Marantz (by Grand/ Marantz)
Grand	Rudolf Wurlitzer (by Wurlitzer)
Gulbransen	
Hobart M. Cable (by Story & Clark)	Westbrook (by Currier)
Jesse French (by Grand)	Whitney (by Kimball)

Foreign-made brands of the period

Belarus (Belarus)	Sojin (Korea)
Daewoo (Korea)	Suzuki (China)
Horugel (Korea)	Tokai (Japan)
J. Strauss (various countries)	

Small, cheap, American-made pianos from the 1960s, '70s, and '80s—During this period, American companies started feeling the competition from Japanese (and, later, Korean) makers who could undercut their prices. The result was that the few remaining American makers of inexpensive pianos began to cut as much cost as they could from their production. In addition, small pianos, especially spinets, were heavily promoted for their cabinet styling at the expense of their musical qualities.

Spinets, which are 36" to 40" high, have a recessed, or "drop," action that is connected to the keys with long "stickers" of wood or metal. These actions are difficult—and thus expensive—to repair. Also, during the 1950s and early '60s, many spinet actions were manufactured with connecting parts, called "elbows," made of plastic—a technology then in its infancy—which eventually deteriorated and broke off. Installing a set of replacement elbows can cost hundreds of dollars.

Spinets were usually the least expensive entry-level pianos a company would manufacture, and most are not worth repairing. Many of these small, cheap pianos were so poorly designed and constructed that, even when new,

and regulated and tuned as well as possible, they played poorly and sounded terrible.

The first wave of pianos from this era began to enter the used-piano market in the 1980s, as the people who originally purchased them began to retire. But many others were passed on to this generation's children, and now, as those children retire, a second wave of these instruments is entering the market. Even pianos from this period that were well made—and there were some—are now 30 to 50 years old, and so are likely to need some restoration before they will be suitable for the student. Caution should be used to separate those that have potential as good student instruments from those that don't. (See sidebar for some of the names from this period to be avoided.)

Early offerings from Korean and Chinese makers—Korean pianos made before the early 1990s, and Chinese pianos from before the early 2000s, often exhibit unpredictable, idiosyncratic problems. Quality control was erratic, and wood was often not properly seasoned, resulting in sticking keys and binding cabinet parts. Replacement parts can be difficult to obtain. Especially problematic were the small console pianos without legs (continental furniture style). These pianos tend to be plagued with sticking keys that repeat too slowly due to poor action design, a problem that can't be inexpensively corrected.

Of course, the used-piano market also offers many well-made pianos from the past, including some with famous names, that are of potential value to a student, but these can also present pitfalls for the unwary. Don't buy, without professional guidance, a piano that is not thoroughly playable and tunable, with the idea that you can simply have a few inexpensive repairs done once you get the piano home. Get repair estimates *before* you commit to purchasing any used piano. Every piano technician with any experience has stories of arriving at a tuning appointment to work on a newly acquired piano, only to find an unserviceable instrument. The fact that the instrument may have been rebuilt sometime in the past is not necessarily an advantage. A piano that was rebuilt 40 years ago is no better than a 40-year-old piano that has never been rebuilt, and if the rebuilding job was not competently done, it could be worse—it's more difficult to properly restore an instrument when certain critical design specifications have been modified due to a past restorer's mistakes.

Finally, don't rely on a private seller for important information about the piano you're thinking of buying. Even the best-intentioned sellers—including ones who play well—tend not to be knowledgeable about piano construction and mechanics, and may have absorbed erroneous information about the instrument, or forgotten important things about its history. Hire a piano technician to inspect any piano you're seriously considering buying. Sometimes, just a phone call to a technician will be enough to verify whether or not a particular instrument should be considered a serious candidate; if it is, the next step is an inspection by that technician.

Over the past 35 years, piano technician **Sally Phillips** has worked in virtually every aspect of the piano industry: service, retail, wholesale, and manufacturing. In her role as a concert-piano technician, she has tuned and prepared pianos for concert and recording work in such venues as Town Hall, Alice Tully Hall, and the Kennedy Center, and for the Cincinnati Symphony Orchestra, the BBC Concert Orchestra, and the Vienna Philharmonic. At present, Phillips lives in Georgia and works throughout the southeastern U.S. She can be contacted at sphillipspiano@hotmail.com.

PIANO ART

Steinway's
IMAGINE
John Lennon

To commemorate the 70th birthday of a true creative genius—legendary musician and songwriter John Lennon—Steinway & Sons proudly introduced the Imagine Series Limited Edition piano.

Like the songs of John Lennon, the Imagine Series is the perfect harmonization of music with creativity to achieve an end result that is much greater than the sum of its parts. The Imagine Series Limited Edition is modeled after the white Steinway grand piano that John presented to Yoko Ono on her birthday in 1971.

Inspiration Has a New Sound

At Yamaha, inspiration is born from the blending of traditional craftsmanship, exceptional artistry and modern innovation. The new Yamaha SX Series is crafted to produce an expanded natural tonal palette that generates warm, deep, expressive tones. Whether on stage, in a conservatory or at home, the Yamaha SX Series offers a rich sound that will inspire the player and enchant the audience.

SX SERIES

THE UNCOMPROMISING WORLD OF HIGH-END PIANOS

SALLY PHILLIPS

Those who've found themselves in a showroom full of beautifully crafted, prestige and high-performance pianos know that the experience can be both impressive and unnerving—impressive for obvious reasons, unnerving because of the extraordinary prices these instruments command—from $50,000 to $150,000 or more. Sometimes, novice buyers question whether the prices are justified—or are just the result of the clever marketing of well-known brand names. In this article, I explain what sets high-end pianos apart from less costly ones that might, at least superficially, look the same, and why the higher price can be justified. This discussion should be considered general in nature, however; actual differences will depend on the specific brands and models compared, and the differences in their prices.

The Definition of Quality

In the manufacture of medium-grade pianos, the term *quality* typically refers, in large part, to *quality control*; that is, that each example of a particular model is exactly like every other example. So, in theory, a model could have a satisfactory but unexceptional tonal design, and use satisfactory materials that meet structural specifications, and if all the pianos of that model are made to the same standards, the model could be considered to be of good quality.

In the manufacture of high-end pianos, however, *quality* means something more: Each instrument is judged not on its similarities to other examples of the same model, but on its excellence as a unique musical instrument. In fact, because the natural materials that pianos are made from are never completely uniform, and because the craftspeople who make these instruments are trained to maximize the musical potential of each instrument, any particular model of high-end piano is likely to exhibit small variations in performance characteristics from instrument to instrument.

• • •

So what do serious pianists, piano owners, piano technicians, and administrators of institutional music programs look for and expect in a high-end piano?

Tonal Quality

A piano with a singing tone, long sustain, and a wide dynamic range gives the pianist more latitude in creating musically expressive performances. The length of an

instrument's sustain is essential to the pianist's ability to make it "sing" in passages that require one note to connect with the next. In addition, the ability of a concert instrument to project to the back of today's large halls is critical to its success. Although a piano's tonal color (harmonic content) will vary depending on the tonal philosophy of the manufacturer, it should be consistent from note to note within each register, and transition smoothly from register to register across the instrument's entire range. Playing with different levels of force should produce predictable variations of tonal color and volume (see "Action Control," below). Professional pianos excel in these regards, and the technician's ability to artistically voice an instrument to bring out these elements of tone depends on the excellence of the soundboard wood, the rim stock, and the hammers.

At first, customers may feel they can't hear the difference between fine instruments and less-expensive models, but this is easily remedied with more exposure to the better instruments. Listen carefully to recordings, live concerts, and fine instruments at educational institutions, and your ear will begin to hear the difference.

Action Control

There are many opinions about the extent to which a pianist can affect the tone of a piano while playing, but it is a fact that, with the more sensitive actions of high-quality instruments, the skilled pianist is able to more reliably control the speed of the hammers' attack on the strings, and thus create a wider tonal palette, giving the audience a better and more nuanced musical experience. This is readily apparent at international piano competitions, at which many pianists, playing the same works on the same piano, can nonetheless bring forth very different tonal qualities from it. The ultimate experience of action control for the artist, possible with only the finest instruments, occurs when the piano becomes a seamless extension of the pianist's thoughts and feelings—the action seems to disappear, the music seeming to rise effortlessly from the instrument without the presence of an intervening mechanism.

Amateurs also benefit by discovering that many concepts discussed by more advanced pianists, such as phrasing, legato playing, and fast and reliable repetition, are now achievable when playing actions of more sophisticated design, longer keys, and parts that can be regulated more accurately.

Service and Maintenance

Because high-end pianos are more musically sensitive than less costly ones, they may require more frequent servicing if they are to be kept at peak performance levels. But this doesn't necessarily mean that they're delicate and finicky. Most of these expensive instruments are built to be taken down, moved, and set up constantly; played with vigor for many hours a day; and tuned and serviced regularly. In my experience, after an initial settling-in period, and a good regulation and tuning, high-end pianos are actually easier to maintain than less costly ones, requiring only slight touch-up adjustments on a regular basis. This comes as a surprise to many shoppers who are concerned that the maintenance of these instruments will be costly.

The reason is that high-end pianos usually have designs and materials that make their tuning and servicing easier, more accurate, and more stable. The woods used are more carefully chosen and processed with consideration for their ability to resist environmental changes, and more robust and careful construction of the piano's structural elements result in greater tuning stability and longevity. The action regulation and voicing are more likely to be stable because of better musical preparation at the factory, and higher qualities of cloth and felt in the action and hammers. More careful design and detailing of the piano at the factory mean fewer annoying problems to deal with later on.

• • •

High-performance pianos are much more expensive than consumer-oriented models because they are so much more costly to build. Moreover, when these higher costs, along with overhead and profit, are spread over the smaller demand for this type of piano, the cost difference per instrument is greatly magnified. In the manufacture of the best pianos, few economies of scale are available.

Materials

Many of the woods used in making high-end pianos—e.g., spruce, sugar pine, hard rock maple, beech, hornbeam, ebony, poplar, and rosewood—are chosen for specific properties: ability to transmit sound, strength-to-weight ratio, density, straightness of grain, etc. Woods used for components that will be visible to the buyer, such as soundboards and case veneers, must be visually flawless as well. High-end piano hammers will have tighter specifications for the wool used in their felt, as well as for their construction, to more predictably produce the tonal goals of that manufacturer. In less-expensive instruments, substitutions of less costly materials can often be made that will still result in instruments that are satisfactory for their less-demanding, intended use. But in a premium instrument, any such substitution that would compromise the piano's tone, stability, longevity,

High-End Pianos For 190 Years

We are proud to combine German classical hand craftsmanship with our industry leading innovations. Steingraeber & Söhne - seven generations since 1820!

Come and see us in our workshops in Bayreuth!

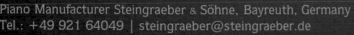

or appearance cannot be tolerated. Because makers of high-end pianos demand only the very best from their suppliers of parts and materials, but do not buy in large volume, they have little leverage over prices, which continue to rise as the choicest natural materials become more scarce.

The refinements of seasoning and quartersawing wood add more cost, but are necessary for maximum stability and longevity. Logs must be air dried for years, then kiln dried to a specific moisture content, so that the wood won't warp, twist, and crack later on, after installation in a piano. Quartersawing is a method of cutting boards from logs such that the grain is oriented in a direction that results in greater dimensional stability. However, it is a very inefficient use of the log, much of which cannot be used and thus is wasted. While all piano makers season and quartersaw wood to some extent, high-end makers are more fastidious in their selection and use of lumber. This contributes to pianos whose tunings and action regulations are more stable, even when in constant use in practice rooms, teaching studios, and recital halls, and under varying climatic conditions. Less-expensive pianos made primarily for home use won't survive such conditions nearly as well.

High-end companies use the same materials in all sizes of piano they make, with no compromises on the smaller pianos. This results in very expensive smaller grands and verticals.

Some less-costly brands claim that they use the same parts or materials that high-end brands do. Even when this is technically true, there can be a world of difference in how those materials are processed and/or the parts installed. For example, some less-costly brands advertise that they use the same Renner parts in their actions as are found in some high-end brands. But the high-end companies usually disassemble the parts and reassemble them to their own, stricter specifications, then custom-install them in the pianos, taking into account slight variations in the instruments that require slight repositioning of the parts. This process is too time-consuming and expensive for lesser brands, and may call for expertise that their workers simply don't have; they're more likely to use the parts just as they come from Renner, and install them according to a general formula. While this results in instruments that are good enough for most purposes, and perhaps better than those that use lesser-quality parts, it may not allow the actions to be regulated accurately enough for the most musically demanding uses. This example also highlights the error consumers make when comparing brands solely on the basis of features, specifications, and/or lists of parts and materials.

Design and Construction

In the interest of achieving better performance, appearance, or longevity, high-end piano makers are more likely to incorporate in their instruments unique or unusual construction methods or components, even though these may be more labor intensive and thus more expensive. Pianos that are more mass-produced, on the other hand, tend to include design compromises that enable faster or more efficient manufacturing. For example, the soundboards of most mass-produced pianos are shaped according to a design that is applied uniformly to every instrument of that model, whereas some high-end brands thin their soundboards by hand for best tonal quality, to compensate for slight variations in the wood.

Other examples of more expensive designs include unusual methods of bending or building up the rim, the use of multiple species of wood in rims or bridge caps, unique patented components for enhancing the tone, and more keys and/or strings than are found in a standard piano. Some of these design elements are present in part for reasons related to a brand's history, others purely for reasons of quality, but each is there because it serves the performance objectives of the manufacturer and is part of what makes each brand unique. All such idiosyncratic variations add considerably to the time and cost of manufacture.

Settling-in Time

A very necessary but expensive part of building a piano is the time it takes the components to settle between stages of construction, and these periods will generally be longer in a factory making high-performance instruments. On any visit to a piano factory, one may be puzzled by the sight of many pianos and components sitting around in various states of completion, not being worked on. This seems counterintuitive to anyone from an industry in which the main measure of efficiency is getting as many products out the door in as short a time as possible.

But in piano manufacturing, patience is crucial to getting good results. Grand-piano rims may have to sit for months after being bent, in order to stabilize before they can be worked on further. In between action regulations, pounding machines are used to compress the action cloth. The pianos must be tuned numerous times to stretch the strings, with settling time between tunings. Hammers must be voiced to perfection by hand. In the long run, the time it takes to let the 12,000 or so parts of a piano get used to each other pays off handsomely in the form of greater longevity and stability of action, tuning, and tone.

SEILER

— Family of Pianos —

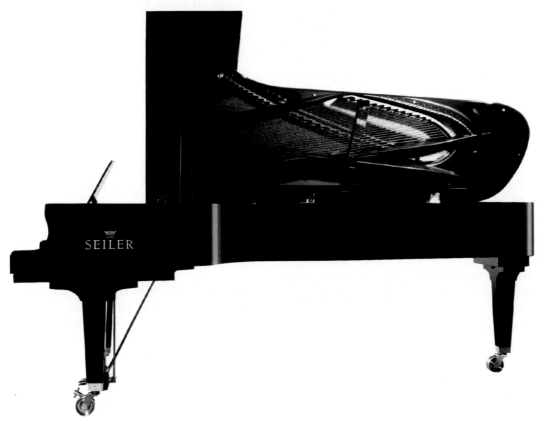

MASTERING THE ART OF PIANO BUILDING SINCE 1849

"The Seiler Concert is a new piano to the Nashville Opera. We love its elegant tone, crisp action and impressive durability through the rigors of long hours of Verdian opera."

- Amy Tate Williams, Nashville Opera Chorus Master & Accompanist

Enrico Caruso, Arthur Nikisch, Ruggiero Leoncavallo

www.seilerpianousa.com

Seiler Piano USA / 1329 Gateway Drive Gallatin, TN 37066 / Tel : 615-206-0077

Custom Musical Preparation

To maximize each instrument's potential once basic construction has been completed, high-end pianos are given much greater musical preparation—tuning, action regulating, and voicing—in the factory. This highly skilled, exacting work requires years of training. Performing extensive musical prep at the factory ensures that by the time the piano reaches the customer, its tuning will be stable, and the cloth and felt used throughout the action will have settled; as a result, the piano will need less initial servicing by the customer. Because the skill and experience of the craftspeople in a high-end factory are almost certainly greater than what is available to dealers or customers, this also ensures that every step in the piano's musical preparation has been performed, at least this first time, to a high standard, and that the instrument leaves the factory having fulfilled the manufacturer's performance objectives. In my experience, a piano that has been stabilized in this manner will wear more evenly, have fewer and less idiosyncratic problems, and will be easier and thus less expensive to service throughout its working life.

Worker Training, Experience, and Autonomy

The craftspeople in companies that produce high-end pianos are highly trained, and because of the enormous investment made in that training, companies are willing to pay a lot to employ these people over many years. It can take years of experience, for instance, to become a skilled voicer. The better companies have extensive programs that gradually move employees into areas of greater responsibility, so that skilled replacements are readily available when needed. This greatly increases the cost of labor over companies that make less-costly instruments, where workers need not be so highly skilled.

In the making of high-performance instruments, more autonomy is given to individual craftspeople to make changes or corrections as needed. For example, in a high-end factory, a voicer unhappy with the tone from a particular set of hammers has permission to replace them. This is in contrast with high-production factories, in which workers may pay less attention to mistakes or unsatisfactory results, and flawed instruments may go far down the assembly line before being caught (if they're caught at all), by which time making the correction may be too time consuming, and thus too expensive, to bother with.

Cabinet Detailing and Appearance

Between high-end and mass-produced pianos, there can be great differences in the quality of hardware (casters, hinges, pedals, screws), the thickness and surface preparation of the cabinet and plate finishes, the felt and cloth used in the case parts, and in the thickness and fit of the legs, lyre, and lid. Consumers may rarely notice these details, but they're important to the instrument's longevity, and affect the appearance and noiseless operation of all case parts.

• • •

Whether for a concert or for home, a professional pianist's choice of high-end piano is primarily based on the instrument's tone and touch: Does it sustain, to enable a singing line? Does it project the tone? Does it offer a wide range of dynamics and tonal color? Does the action repeat quickly and reliably, transfer power efficiently, and remain well within the player's control? For the amateur pianist, high-end pianos open up a wider world of sound and performance than is otherwise achievable—and having that range of expression literally at one's fingertips can lead to a tremendous joy in making music that is rarely experienced with lesser instruments. ▐▐▐▐

Over the past 35 years, piano technician **Sally Phillips** has worked in virtually every aspect of the piano industry: service, retail, wholesale, and manufacturing. In her role as a concert-piano technician, she has tuned and prepared pianos for concert and recording work in such venues as Town Hall, Alice Tully Hall, and the Kennedy Center, and for the Cincinnati Symphony Orchestra, the BBC Concert Orchestra, and the Vienna Philharmonic. At present, Phillips lives in Georgia and works throughout the southeastern U.S. She can be contacted at sphillipspiano@hotmail.com.

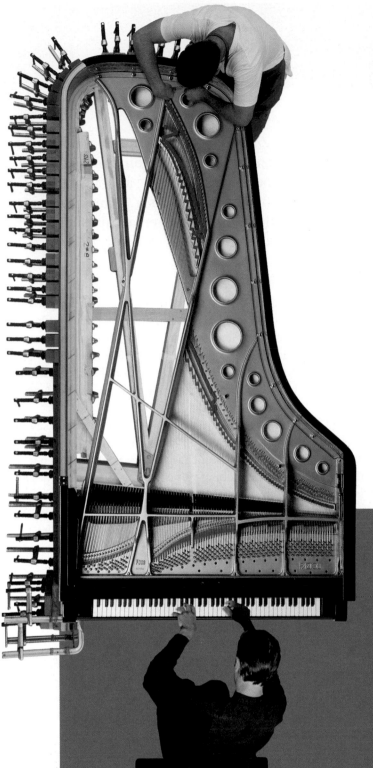

l'arte
per l'arte

We build our pianos with great passion out of a sheer love of music, not as commodities, but as instruments in the service of art: Pianos for those who love, play and dream of music.

Building pianos is our way to show our love of music.

FAZIOLI
www.fazioli.com

Few piano makers generate more buzz among pianists and piano enthusiasts than the Italian company Fazioli. In a profession dominated by established composers, teachers, performers, styles, and instrument makers, many now consider Fazioli to be firmly established as a premium piano maker, in the same echelon as Steinway and Bösendorfer—a remarkable achievement, given that Fazioli was founded only as recently as 1978.

Founder Paolo Fazioli, who had studied music and engineering as a youth, aspired to be a concert pianist. Instead, he found himself rising in the managerial ranks of the family business: a top Italian supplier of high-end office furniture. But the combination of his creative ambitions and his search for the perfect piano led Fazioli, with the help of experts, to design and build his own piano. In a very short time, his instruments were internationally recognized as being among the best in the world.

The Juilliard School, my alma mater, is famously known as an all-Steinway institution. Imagine the discussion, excitement, and even the hint of scandal when the faculty guided the school to purchase a Fazioli for Paul Hall, the main venue for student performances. Piano students rallied behind the two rival brands, with one of my teachers seemingly leading the charge for the Fazioli. I, too, had to choose. For my Doctor of Musical Arts (DMA) recital, a program of sonatas and fantasies by Mozart, Schumann, and Vine, would I play a New York Steinway or a Fazioli?

Think of it—a pianist actually having a say in choosing his instrument! Pianists are almost unique among instrumentalists in that we give nearly every performance on a piano not of our choosing. Sometimes we're blessed with a beautiful instrument that has been carefully nurtured by a knowledgeable technician. Other times, the instrument seems to work against us. Whatever the case

Fazioli models F212 and F228

may be, there is nothing the pianist can do about it; one must do the best one can with what has been given.

For this review, I spent roughly three hours at Collora Piano (collorapiano.com), a piano store near downtown Dallas that specializes in various European pianos, among others. Their Fazioli model F212 (7') had arrived only two weeks earlier, while the F228 (7' 6") had been performed on in their small concert hall for about a year and a half. I and several of my students had performed and recorded on it on multiple occasions before this session.

Fazioli's philosophy as an instrument maker could hardly be more different from Steinway's, and, given the widespread presence of Steinway pianos on the concert scene, in academia, and elsewhere, comparisons between the two are inevitable. However, I approached the instruments exclusively as a performer, with only the most limited knowledge of how they're built. (Someone seeking more technical information should ask an experienced technician or a Fazioli dealer, or see the company's profile in *Piano Buyer*.) The purpose of this review is to compare the Fazioli F212 and F228 to each other, and provide some comparisons with the New York Steinway model B (6' 10½").

The two Fazioli models had a lot in common—not surprising, as they're of the same brand, similar in size, and were both relatively new. Both had a beautiful consistency in touch and tone from top to bottom. The action was perfectly regulated at every point, as in a slightly heavy Yamaha (a compliment—everyone loves a Yamaha action); perhaps this was my favorite quality. Both the attack of the sound and its cutoff via the release of the damper were perfectly consistent from key to key. Executing ornaments in Bach's Prelude and Fugue in C-sharp Major (from Book I of the *Well-Tempered Clavier*) was pure joy. Similarly, the repetitions in Ravel's *Alborada del gracioso* were very clear and consistent—not a minor point, given that these repetitions are some of the most technically demanding in the classical repertoire. I often find that a consistent action is my number-one criterion in a piano, because the action is the foundation for how I manipulate tone: by understanding the key depth and key weight, the escapement point, and the release of key and damper. I find that a Steinway action can be equally responsive, but sometimes an attentive technician is required to bring out its best.

Also incredibly consistent, both between the Fazioli models and within each one, was the tone throughout the low, middle, and high registers. One of my few frustrations with Steinway is the occasional dead zone in the middle-high register, which is exactly where the melody tends to be. That said, because I play more Steinways

Fazioli Models Reviewed
Prices for models in polished ebony (US$)

Model	Size	MSRP*	SMP**
F212	7'	137,300	130,458
F228	7' 6"	153,600	146,415

*Manufacturers Suggested Retail Price

** Suggested Maximum Price. Most sales take place at a modest discount to this price. See Introduction to Model & Pricing Guide for more information. Models and prices subject to change; see Piano Buyer for updated information.

than Faziolis, I needed an adjustment period in my time with the Faziolis. For example, I immediately had to reduce my arm weight in the melody register. Whereas a Steinway may sometimes need a degree of arm weight for the melody to sing and project, the Fazioli seemed to project itself. When I leaned into either Fazioli model's upper register as I would on my 2005 Steinway O at home, I received a rather unpleasant noise that was far too loud for the space or the music. But after giving myself 30 minutes to recalibrate my technique, I found that both Faziolis responded beautifully. The registers mixed with each other admirably, but I had to play with a lighter touch and more internal release in order to allow everything to be heard.

I ran through passages from Mozart's Piano Concerto No.23 in A Major, K.488, and found the Faziolis to be ideal companions for Mozart's singing lyricism; the instruments were similarly well suited for executing Mozart's glistening passagework. Again, it took me some time to adjust my approach before finding a true *pianissimo* for Liszt's *Les Jeux d'Eau à la Villa d'Este*, but once pianist adjusted to instrument, the latter provided all the delicacy and translucence one could ask for. In sum, if I played the Fazioli like a Steinway, the sound was not ideal—and the reverse is almost certainly also true. A friend of mine compared playing a Fazioli to driving a Ferrari: the potency is tremendous, but it takes skill to achieve control. Given the Fazioli's incredible singing power and natural ability to project, I sometimes wonder if more skill might be required for a physically strong pianist to achieve a sweet ringing sound than for a smaller pianist.

Indeed, the Faziolis' consistency of clarity, sustain, and brilliance was addicting. But for me, there was a downside: I felt that the bass had an almost bright tinge, similar in sound to the middle or treble registers, such that it lacked a degree of depth, orchestral power, and even warmth found in many New York Steinways. Perhaps this was a tradeoff necessary to achieving its incredible upper registers, but in any case, it was particularly true of the F212. As I ran through passages of Liszt's Sonata in B Minor, the octaves of his *Funérailles*, and Stravinsky's *Pétrouchka*, I sometimes wished for a warmer or more resonant bass from the F212. Comparing the F212 and F228, there could be no denying that the F228 had more range and resonance in its bass; after all, in the world of pianos, bigger often means better bass. But while the sound of the Faziolis was always beautiful, it was not always warm. Sometimes the tone felt *too* perfect—but then, I was born and raised on a different sound. Metaphorically speaking, I prefer the somewhat more complex and romantic interpretations of Cliburn to the insightful clarity of Pollini; I always have and I always will.

In closing, I don't think there is an ideal piano any more than there is an ideal pianist. What is clear is that Fazioli pianos are impeccably made, with tremendous precision, consistency, and beauty. Given these qualities, it's not surprising that so many performers and teachers have found their voices through these remarkable instruments. 🎹

Alex McDonald holds a doctorate from the Juilliard School, and is festival director for Basically Beethoven, a thriving summer series of concerts in downtown Dallas that is now in its 37th season. He was Silver Medalist at the 2007 New Orleans International Piano Competition, and also competed in the 2013 Van Cliburn Competition. Dr. McDonald has soloed with the Mexican State Symphony Orchestra, the Louisiana Philharmonic, the Fort Worth Symphony, and the Utah Symphony; has been featured on PBS, NPR, WRR (Dallas), and WQXR (New York); and has performed throughout North America, as well as in South Korea, Japan, and Israel. He can be reached at mcdonaldpiano@gmail.com or through alexmcdonaldpiano.com.

SINCE THE PIANO'S INVENTION *by Bartolomeo Cristofori in 1700, its evolution has been driven by the desire to meet the changing musical needs of the times, by advances in technology, and by the business and marketing requirements of the piano manufacturers. High-end pianos exemplify this evolutionary process.*

Early pianos were limited by the technology of the day to a lightweight structure, and a design that produced a tone—bright and intimate, but with short sustain and low volume—that evolved from the sound of the harpsichord. This complemented both the musical styles favored by the Classical period, especially chamber music, and the smaller, more intimate venues in which music was then customarily performed. As technology advanced, it became possible—using cast-iron plates, stronger strings, and higher-tension scale designs—to produce more robust instruments capable of filling a large hall with sound. This suited the composer-virtuosos of the Romantic period, such as Liszt and Brahms, whose works for the piano demanded from the instrument greater power, and the ability to be heard above the larger orchestras of the day. However, this louder, more overtone-filled sound could also conflict with and overpower other chamber instruments and their performance settings.*

The great American pianos, having come of age during the Romantic era, tend toward the Romantic tonal tradition. The great European piano makers, however, embedded in a culture steeped in centuries of musical tradition, have long had to satisfy the conflicting tonal styles of different ages, and this has resulted in a wide variety of instruments with different musical qualities. As the American market for European pianos grows, the European companies are further having to reconcile remaining true to their own traditions with evolving to please the American ear. While all brands make full use of technological advances and are capable of satisfying diverse musical needs, some tend toward a more pristine tone, with plush but low-volume harmonics, perfect for chamber music or solo performances in small rooms; others are bright and powerful enough to hold their own above the largest symphony orchestras; and many are in between.*

The good news is that the best way to find the right piano for you is to play as many as you can—a simply wonderful experience!

What follows is a story with a valuable perspective from a well-respected dealer of performance-quality instruments.
—Editor

"I'm tone deaf," declared the husband. "I can't tell the difference between one piano and another."

His wife nodded in agreement. "He *is* tone deaf. And while I can hear some differences, it's all so confusing. All we want is a piano that our kids can learn to play on. We don't need a *great* piano."

A short conversation ensued in which I learned, among other things, that this couple had three children, ranging in age from seven years to six months.

"Our daughter just turned seven," the wife said. "She's interested in piano lessons, but we're not sure how committed she'll be."

"You know kids," the husband shrugged. "She may want piano lessons now, but in a few months' time . . . ?"

"You're right," I said. "Kids change their minds all the time. I started piano lessons at the age of six, and stopped only a few months later. But the piano stayed in our home, and at the age of 12 I was drawn back to it. I played a few tunes by ear, and after a while I started lessons again. But . . . would you like your youngest child to play the piano as well?"

They looked at each other. It seemed that the possibility of their six-month-old baby taking lessons sometime in the future was something they hadn't considered.

"This means that whatever instrument we choose, it will probably stay in our home for a very long time," the woman said to her husband. "Perhaps we should look at a greater range of instruments than just the few we had in mind . . . ?"

"But still," he said, turning to me, "is there enough difference in the tone of the pianos to justify a greater investment, and a possible increase in our budget?"

Such conversations are not rare. Some people feel they won't be able to hear the differences between pianos, or

that a high-end piano will be wasted on them. Others try to accommodate only what they perceive their needs to be at the time of purchase, rather than over the many years they may end up owning a piano.

Often, piano buyers form an idea of what they want and how much to spend, and consider only a few brands, without ever sufficiently researching the differences in manufacturers' philosophies and how these might affect the tone, touch, musicality, and price of the instrument. However, such information can help the consumer clarify his or her true needs and preferences. Many shopping for a piano all but ignore higher-end models, considering them beyond their needs or means. But for more than a few of these buyers, a better-quality piano may prove the better fit and value.

There are significant differences in manufacturing methods between performance-oriented instruments, which are often referred to as "handmade," and mass-produced instruments, in which some musical qualities are sacrificed to meet a lower retail price.

Performance-oriented manufacturers, especially at the highest level, are looking to capture a wide range of tonal characteristics. Some of these qualities, such as sustain, tonal variation, and dynamic range, are universally accepted as helping the playing of pianists of all levels sound more musical. All makers of high-end pianos strive to make pianos that excel in these areas. Other tonal characteristics, however, such as tonal color—the specific harmonic structure of the tone—can reflect a particular manufacturer's philosophy

of what the best piano should sound like, and are the elements that separate one high-end make from another. A piano maker's decision to emphasize certain musical qualities over others is manifested through differences in the instrument's design, in the instrument's resulting tone and touch, and in its appeal to a particular player or listener.

"Would you like to hear some higher-end instruments as well, just to compare?" I asked the couple.

"Yes, please," replied the woman.

And so we went on a tour of Piano Land, playing, listening to, and assessing the tone of a variety of instruments. "Ooohhh," said the wife in response to one particular make. "Aaahhh," sighed her husband, as the realization struck him: He actually *could* hear the differences between these pianos; not only that, he

Bösendorfer

Viennese Art of Piano Making Since 1828

had some rather clear preferences.

"But which is the *best* piano?" he asked. There are quite a few instruments here, all so beautiful, but so different from each other. Which *is* the best?

This is a question customers ask me again and again when visiting our showroom—we represent most of the high-end makers, and side-by-side comparisons are always possible. And while, time after time, our customers do find the absolute "best," for each of those customers the "best" is represented by a different make, according to his or her preferences. The combination of musical qualities emphasized by one piano maker may speak to one customer while leaving another indifferent—who, in turn responds enthusiastically to an instrument made by another manufacturer that has left the first customer cold. Some people

prefer a bold, outgoing, and powerful sound; others want a more delicate, clear, and melodic tone. Some like focused, defined, and pure tonal characteristics, while others look for instruments whose sound is more robust, deep, and dark.

At the top end of piano manufacturing, each instrument should have a high level of design, parts, materials, execution, workmanship, and attention to detail. However, it is personal preference—the buyer's response to the various manufacturers' interpretations of the "perfect sound"—that determines the answer to the question of "But which is the *best* piano?" The answer is different for every customer.

But which piano is the "best" is also a matter of other factors. Some high-end instruments might be considered the "best" in one setting, but not quite the best in another. A

piano that sounds its best in a large concert hall with hundreds of people may not necessarily be the right fit for the typical living room.

"The best instrument," I replied to the couple, "is the one that you'll most enjoy listening to as your children—and perhaps, before you know it, your grandchildren—play and develop their musical skills. The 'best' piano is the one you'll be happy with over the many years it will live in your home, and that one day, when you have the time, perhaps may tempt you to take lessons yourself. The best piano is the one that will deliver to you and your family the joy of music, now and over the long run."

Ori Bukai owns and operates Allegro Pianos in Stamford, Connecticut, which specializes in the sale of new and restored high-end pianos. Visit his website at www.allegropianos.com.

长江
Yangtze River

Voice of Glory
at the Top of the World
CGF-X1

Yangtze River Piano
Makes The Dreams Come True

A dream fulfilled, a passion pursued, challenge after challenge met – in elegance, honor and excellence, the Concert Grand Piano CGF-X1 stands in the spotlight as the world's most outstanding concert instrument.

The ideal combination of top-quality spruce, pioneering technology and extraordinary scientific design, the nine-feet concert grand piano has won great honors, praise and respect. In particular, Yangtze River Piano is the appointed piano of China Shenzhen International Piano Concerto Competition Week in 2014 and 2017. With a voice particularly rich in tone and timbre, Yangtze River Piano is the sound of perfection and makes musicians' dreams come true.

BUYING PIANOS FOR AN INSTITUTION

GEORGE F. LITTERST

[This article assumes you are already familiar with the basics of piano-shopping (see "Piano Buying Basics" and other appropriate articles in this publication), and treats only those aspects of the subject that are specific to the institutional setting.—Ed.]

Institutional Basics

Institutions vary so widely in size, makeup, and needs that it is impossible to cover in a single article all the variables that might apply. For example, the studio of a graduate-school piano professor might be 12 feet square, carpeted, and cluttered with bookshelves, desk, and chairs, but still needs a performance-grade instrument. A church sanctuary—often a carpeted, irregularly shaped room with a raised dais and filled with pews, glass windows, and lots of sound-absorbing people—needs a piano that can accompany the choir, be heard throughout a huge room, and also be used as a solo instrument for visiting artists. A school may need dozens of pianos for everything from tiny practice cubicles to a concert hall.

However, regardless of whether you're purchasing a piano for a church, school, performance space, or another institutional location, you need to start with some basic questions that will help identify the piano (or pianos) that are appropriate for your situation.

For example:

- Who will use the piano— beginners, advanced players, or concert artists?
- How often will the piano be played—in the occasional concert, or for 18 hours per day of intense student practice?

- How will the piano be used— lessons for graduate students? church services? recordings?
- Will the piano's location be fixed, or will it be moved often?
- In what size room will it primarily be used?

After answering these questions, this article will help you establish some basic parameters, including:

- Grand vs. Vertical
- Size
- New vs. Used
- Digital vs. Acoustic
- Traditional Acoustic vs. Acoustic with Record/Playback/Computer Features

Budget

Once you've narrowed down the parameters of your ideal instrument or group of instruments, you need to consider your budget. In doing so, it's best to remember that quality instruments properly maintained will last a long time. Accordingly, it's best to view the cost of each instrument not as a one-time expense, but as a total expense amortized over the life of the instrument.

When figuring out the true annual cost of an instrument:

- Spread out the instrument's purchase price over the span of its working life
- Factor in the cost of money, that is, the interest you would pay if you were to finance the purchase

(even if you don't actually plan to finance it)

Include costs of tuning (typically three to four times a year, but far more often for performance instruments), regulation, and repairs

When you figure the cost of an instrument this way, you may even discover that certain more expensive instruments are more affordable than you thought.

Once you've determined your budget, and the size and other features of the instruments you desire, you can use the **online searchable database** accessible through the electronic version of this publication to assist you in finding the specific brands and models that will fulfill your needs.

Grand vs. Vertical

Many situations are adequately served by vertical pianos, including:

- Practice rooms where the piano is used primarily by, or to accompany, non-pianist musicians
- Places where there is no room for a grand
- Instruments that are not used for intense playing or difficult literature

A number of features of vertical pianos are commonly sought by institutional buyers:

- Locks on fallboard and tops
- A music desk long enough to hold multiple sheets of music or a score
- Toe-block leg construction with double-wheel casters—particularly important if the piano will be moved often

- Heavy-duty back-post and plate assembly for better tuning stability
- Climate-control systems
- Protective covers

Grand pianos, however, have keys, actions, and tonal qualities that are more appropriate for practicing and performing advanced literature, and are therefore preferred in situations where they are largely used by piano majors or performing pianists. Grands are preferred by piano majors even for small practice rooms, because the students use these instruments primarily to develop advanced technical facility, something that's almost impossible to do on vertical pianos. Commonly sought features of grands are:

- Mounting on a piano *truck* (a specialized platform on wheels) for moving the piano easily and safely
- Protective covers to avoid damage to the finish
- Climate-control systems
- Lid and fallboard locks

Size

Carefully consider the size of your space. You can easily spend too much on a piano if it's larger than the space requires, and you can easily waste your money if you purchase an undersized instrument. For more information about how room acoustics might affect the size of instrument you should purchase, see "**Ten Ways to Voice a Room**," elsewhere in this issue.

Of course, the tonal quality and touch of the instrument are related, in large part, to its size. If you're purchasing pianos for teaching studios in which artist faculty are instructing graduate piano majors, or for practice rooms used primarily by piano majors, there may be musical reasons for choosing larger grands despite the fact that the spaces are small. You'll be able to capture most of the advantages of a larger grand's longer keys with an instrument six to six-and-a-half feet long. Any longer will be overkill for a small teaching studio or practice room. A larger teaching studio may be able to accommodate and make good use of a seven-foot grand. The size of the piano is much less important in the training of beginning pianists or

non-pianist musicians. There, other factors, such as the size of the room, will be the dominant considerations.

Vertical pianos made for institutions are almost always at least 45 inches tall. Smaller verticals may have inferior actions and tone, and cabinetry that is more prone to breakage. Verticals taller than about 48 inches are probably unnecessary for most small studio and practice rooms, but may be appropriate in larger spaces where a larger sound is needed but a grand is out of the question.

A special problem often occurs when a house of worship or small recital venue with limited funds tries to make do with a grand piano that's too small for the space. The pianist will tend to play much harder than normal, and overuse the sustain pedal, in an effort to make the piano heard at the back of the sanctuary or hall, causing strings and hammers to break and pedal systems to wear out prematurely. Generally, a small- to medium-size sanctuary will require a grand six to seven feet long to adequately fill the hall with sound, but this can vary greatly depending on the size of the hall, its acoustics, how large an audience is typically present, whether the piano is being used as a solo instrument or

The Yamaha model P22 has typical school-piano features, such as locks, a long music desk, toe-block leg construction, and double-wheel casters.

INSTITUTIONS
TRUST IN SCHIMMEL

There are many good reasons why Schimmel inst-ruments have been the best-selling German pianos for decades: For example, there are numerous inno-vations which provide pianists playing the smaller Schimmel grand pianos with the touch and sound characteristics of a full-size concert grand piano. Other reasons for their popularity are Schimmel's status as the German piano maker with the most awards from the musical press as well as the timeless design of their award-winning cabinetry. Above all, however, is the passion to create flexible, musically inspiring instruments which are built to last. Schim-mel pianos are created to support and respond to the pianist's demands to make uniquely beautiful and inspirational music. www.schimmel-piano.de

to accompany others, and whether the sound is amplified. A piano dealer can help sort out these issues and recommend an appropriate instrument.

New vs. Used

Excellent acoustic pianos that are well maintained should last for decades. Given this fact, should your institution consider purchasing used instruments and thus save some money? If this is something you're considering, read "Buying a Used or Restored Piano" in this issue before continuing. When comparing a used piano to a new one, consult a trusted piano technician to get a sense of the used instrument's condition and remaining useful life. Then amortize the cost of the pianos, including expected repair costs, over their expected lifetimes to determine which is the better value.

If considering a used acoustic piano with embedded electronics, such as an electronic player piano, be careful to avoid purchasing an instrument whose technology is so obsolete that you can't use it productively. On the other hand, if your intention is to use a player piano's MIDI features mostly in conjunction with a computer, you do have one protection against obsolescence on your side: Although MIDI has been around since 1982, it's still an industry standard that works well and shows no sign of disappearing in the near future. Accordingly, you can continue to upgrade the features of an older MIDI piano merely by upgrading the software you use on your computer.

Acoustic vs. Digital

Digital pianos continue to improve every year, and the benefits realized for every dollar spent on a digital piano continue to grow with advances in technology.

Yamaha

Here are some examples of institutional situations in which a digital piano is generally the preferred instrument:

- Class piano, where students and teachers wear headsets and the teacher controls the flow of sound in the room with a lab controller
- Multipurpose computer/keyboard labs where students need to work independently on theory, composition, and performance projects without disturbing others in the room
- A church that features a so-called "contemporary service" in which the keyboard player needs an instrument with lots of on-board sounds, registrations, and automatic accompaniments

In other situations, the preferred choice may not be so obvious. For example, if a school has a practice room largely used by singers and instrumentalists (not pianists), should you supply a digital piano or a vertical?

When weighing these and similar questions, keep in mind:

- In an institutional setting, a typical, well-maintained acoustic piano has a life expectancy of 20 to 40 years; a higher-quality instrument might last 30 to 50 years. Because the digital piano is a relatively recent invention, we can't be as certain how long they will last in an institutional setting. A reasonable estimate for a

good-quality digital instrument might be 10 to 20 years. However, digital instruments are subject to a rapid rate of technological advance that may eventually limit the instrument's usefulness, even though it still functions. On the other hand, the digital piano won't need tuning, and may go for years before it needs any other maintenance.

- Some digital pianos are simply a substitute for the acoustic equivalent. Others have additional features that may be highly desirable, such as connectivity to a computer, orchestral voices, and record and playback features.
- Some acoustic pianos are also available with digital-piano–like features, such as record and playback, and Internet and computer connectivity. If your choice comes down to an acoustic piano (for its traditional piano features of touch and tone) and a digital piano (for its embedded technologies), you may need to consider a hybrid digital/acoustic instrument. (See the article on hybrid pianos in this issue of *Piano Buyer*.)

Assessing Pianos Before Purchase

Assessing digital pianos is a relatively straightforward matter. You simply play and compare the features of various makes and models and make your selection. If you choose Model X, it doesn't matter if you take possession of the actual floor model that you tried: All Model X digital pianos will be the same.

Acoustic pianos are a different animal. There is more variation among pianos of the same model from a given manufacturer. However, it is important to note that some manufacturers have a reputation for producing uniformly similar instruments, while others have a reputation for producing more individually distinctive instruments.

If you're purchasing a single acoustic piano or a small number of acoustic pianos, you can and should take the opportunity to audition each one of them and make your selection carefully. If you're purchasing a concert or other very large grand, you may need to travel to the manufacturer's national showroom in order to make your selection. If so, factor the cost of the trip into your budget. In some situations it may be possible to audition a large grand in the space in which you intend to use it. This will give you an opportunity to know for sure that you're making the right decision. On the other hand, if you're purchasing a dozen practice room upright pianos, or are completely replacing your inventory of instruments,

it's more practical to audition just a sample of each model and make your purchase decision on that basis.

Keep in mind that any fine acoustic piano can be adjusted within certain parameters by a concert-quality technician. If a piano sounds too bright when it is uncrated, skilled needling of the hammers can result in a noticeable mellowing of the sound. Similarly, a new action may require some additional adjustment (called *regulation*) to provide you with a keyboard that is optimally responsive.

Preparation, Tuning, and Maintenance

All pianos require maintenance, and acoustic pianos more than digitals. New acoustic pianos need to be properly prepared before they're deployed. All acoustic pianos should be tuned regularly, and regulated as needed.

Acoustic pianos with record and playback systems also may need periodic calibration of their embedded systems. See the **accompanying article** for more information on the maintenance of acoustic pianos in institutions.

Who Should Make the Purchase Decision?

As the foregoing discussion suggests, there are many intersecting practical, artistic, and financial factors to be considered when making an institutional purchase of a piano or group of pianos. This raises the question: Who should make the purchase decision?

No single answer fits all situations. By tradition, a church's decision-making process may be handled by the music director, the pastor or priest, or perhaps by a lay committee. In a school

---

LOAN PROGRAMS:
AN ALTERNATIVE TO PURCHASING

Often, institutions find themselves needing to acquire a number of pianos at one time. Perhaps the institution needs to replace a large number of aging instruments or to furnish a newly expanded facility or program—or a school may want to acquire a number of new instruments each year to demonstrate to prospective students that it has a music program of high quality. Such situations can pose a budgetary dilemma—the simultaneous purchase of even a few pianos can cause fiscal stress. Fortunately, relief is sometimes available in the form of a school loan program.

On the surface, a school loan program may seem too good to be true: free pianos, loaned for an academic year. At the end of the year, the pianos are sold. More free pianos the next year.

In truth, a school loan program can work only when it makes sense for both the school and the local dealer. (Although the manufacturer may be a

participant in the program, the contract is normally with the local dealer.) Both sides of the agreement have obligations to the other.

For example, a school *may* receive any of the following, depending on the structure of the program:

- Free or very-low-cost use of a significant number of pianos
- Free delivery
- Free tuning and maintenance
- Name association with a prestigious manufacturer

A school may also have any of these obligations:

- Liability for damage
- Delivery charges
- Tuning and maintenance costs
- Requirement to purchase a certain percentage of the instruments
- Requirement to supply an alumni mailing list to the dealer for advertising purposes

- Requirement to provide space for an end-of-year piano sale

When evaluating a loan program, it's generally a good idea to consider:

- The quality of the dealership that stands behind the program
- The appropriateness of the mix of pianos offered
- The school's vulnerability if the program were to be discontinued by the dealership after the current year

That last point is a key issue. What happens if you replace your inventory of old pianos with loaned instruments and the loan program becomes unavailable the next year? Suddenly and unexpectedly, you are faced with having to buy replacement instruments.

Generally speaking, it is a good idea to include with your loan program a purchase component so that you are building your inventory of quality instruments over the course of the loan.

---

of music, decisions may be delegated to the chair of the piano department, the chair of the music department, the dean of fine arts, or some other individual or faculty committee.

In many instances, well-intentioned individuals with no knowledge of pianos find themselves having to make a final decision. It is important that those involved in the process commit themselves to understanding the intersecting issues, and bring into the decision-making process appropriate people from the artistic, technical, and/or financial sides. At a minimum, that means the piano technician, and the most advanced, or most frequent, professional users. If a digital-technology–based instrument is being considered, someone should be involved who can speak to those technical issues as well. A department chair who has not actually used the technology in question may or may not be in a position to evaluate it.

Negotiating a Purchase

Before negotiating a price or sending a proposal out to bid, it's usually a good idea to do some price research. This can be tricky, however.

For example, if you or someone you know simply calls up a dealer and asks for a price, you're unlikely to be told the lower "institutional price" that you might ultimately get. Some dealers are reluctant to quote prices over the phone, or are prohibited by their suppliers from doing so. Others will refuse to quote a price if they know that the purchase will ultimately go out to bid.

Your institutional purchase may benefit the dealer or manufacturer in ways other than the profit from the sale. Therefore, when discussing your possible purchase, don't hesitate to mention:

- How prominently positioned the instruments will be in your institution or in the community
- How many students or audience members will come in contact with the instruments on a regular basis
- How often you or your institution is asked for purchase recommendations
- How musically influential your institution is in the surrounding community

The bottom line is this: You won't know what the final price will be until an official representative of your institution actually sits down with the dealer principal or until bids are awarded. Before you reach that point, however, and for planning purposes, you can make discreet inquiries and put together some estimates. As a rule of thumb, and only for the purposes of budgeting, if you subtract 10% to 15% from the dealer's "sale" price, you will likely come close to the institutional price.

If you represent a school that's required to send purchase requests out to bid, you may not have much of a role to play in negotiating a price. However, the way in which you word your bid will have a lot to do with the bids that you receive and the instruments that the bidding rules will compel you to purchase.

For example, if you really want Brand X with features A, B, and C, be sure to write your bid description so that it describes—within acceptable guidelines—the instrument that you wish to purchase, and rules out instruments that don't fit your needs. If your bid description is loosely written, you may receive low bids for instruments that don't meet your requirements.

Because pianos can last a very long time, any piano-buying decisions you make today for your institution can have consequences for a generation or more. Therefore, it pays to take the time to think carefully about your institution's present and future needs, to budget sufficient funds for purchase and maintenance, and to consult with individuals both within and outside your institution who may have special expertise or be affected by your decision. If you take the time to do this properly, then your constituents—be they students, faculty, worshippers, or concert-goers—will enjoy the fruits of your work for years to come.

MUSEUM OF MAKING MUSIC

a Division of the NAMM Foundation

5790 Armada Drive
Carlsbad, CA 92008

http://www.museumofmakingmusic.org/

George Litterst (www.georgelitterst.com) is a nationally known music educator, clinician, author, performer, and developer of music software. In the last role, Mr. Litterst is co-author of the intelligent accompaniment program *Home Concert Xtreme*, the electronic music-blackboard program *Classroom Maestro*, and the long-distance teaching program *Internet MIDI*, all from TimeWarp Technologies (www.timewarptech.com).

PIANO MAINTENANCE IN INSTITUTIONS

CHRIS SOLLIDAY, RPT

THE ADEQUATE AND EFFECTIVE MAINTENANCE of pianos in institutional settings differs from the typical service needs of the home environment in two major ways. Pianos in schools, churches, and colleges are, first of all, usually subjected to heavy use, and second, are very often situated in difficult climatic environments. These pianos will require more frequent service by technicians with special skills, and greater attention to climate control.

In college and university settings, pianos are frequently used eight to twelve hours a day by many different players. Some students have practice habits that involve a great deal of repetition, which causes greater wear to the actions and keys of the instrument in a way that reflects the patterns of their practice. This can easily be ten times more patterned repetition than a piano normally receives in your home. The parts of piano keys and actions that will show the greatest wear are made of felt, leather, and wood, and there are thousands of them in each piano. These materials are chosen, designed, and treated by manufacturers to maximize their working life, and considering the repetitive nature of their use, it's a wonder they last as long as they do.

No matter how well made, however, the nature of these materials dictates that when the piano is used for many hours, day after day, week after week, the wear and deterioration can be extensive. To maximize their longevity, it is very important to keep these pianos in good regulation so that the wear proceeds more evenly. Along with tuning, regular regulation of

the action, pedals, and tone should be basic parts of any effective plan of piano maintenance. Without this, neglected instruments in such environments will quickly become impossible to regulate without extensive overhaul or replacement of parts.

At some point, of course, parts *will* have to be replaced, worthy instruments rebuilt, and unworthy ones replaced. But there is no need to hasten the inevitable by subjecting

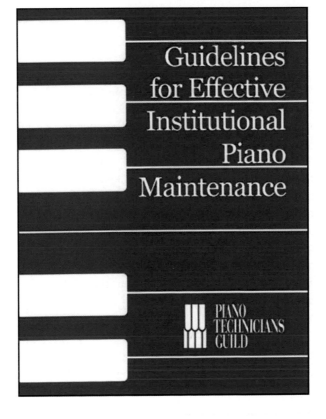

Guidelines for Effective Institutional Piano Maintenance

PIANO TECHNICIANS GUILD

pianos to the worst form of abuse: neglect. Frequent and regular servicing of pianos is a requirement for any institution that hopes to maintain an adequate performance or learning situation that will not only meet the needs of its members, but serve as a vehicle for the recruitment of new students.

Depending on the security and rules established for using the pianos, abuse can also come in the form of vandalism or simple carelessness. Rules should be established that keep food and liquids away from pianos. Procedures for the safe moving of pianos should be established and strictly enforced to protect the instruments as well as those who do the moving. Untrained personnel should never move a piano anywhere.

The single largest factor affecting the need for piano maintenance, however, is a fluctuating climate. While an environment that is always too hot or too cold, or too wet or too dry, can cause deterioration, pianos can usually (within reason) be regulated to reliably perform in such an environment. However, many institutions provide interior climates of constant change. It's not unusual to find a school or church whose HVAC system produces 80°F and 8% relative humidity during the winter heating season, but 76°F and 80% relative humidity in the summer. These systems' air-exchange devices can also create drafts that blow directly on the piano,

further varying the temperature and relative humidity by a great deal. Often, the temperature settings on these systems are changed during vacation periods. A good target for any piano's environment is 68° F and 42% relative humidity. Installation of inconspicuously-located climate-control systems for the pianos is almost always necessary in institutional environments. A plan for the daily monitoring of these systems should also be considered. [*See the article, "Caring For Your Piano," for more information on climate-control systems for pianos.—Ed.*]

The most important factor in maintaining the utility and longevity of any institution's pianos is the choice of piano technician. An institutional technician should possess the advanced skills and experience required to prepare pianos for public concerts, organize and manage a large inventory of instruments, deal daily with high-level pianists and educators, and be familiar with the techniques necessary for the time-efficient maintenance of practice-room pianos. An underqualified technician can contribute to an accelerated rate of deterioration and shorten the lives of the instruments under his or her care. Some fully qualified technicians, mostly manufacturer-trained, have no formal credentials. However, hiring a Registered Piano Technician (RPT) member of the Piano Technicians Guild (PTG) ensures that at least a minimum standard of expertise has been tested for and achieved. A good way to begin planning any institution's piano-maintenance program is to read PTG's *Guidelines for Effective Institutional Piano Maintenance*, available in printed form or as a free download from www.ptg.org.

Chris Solliday, RPT, services the pianos at several institutions, including Lafayette College, Lehigh University, and East Stroudsburg University. He lives in Easton, Pennsylvania, and can be reached through his website at www.csollidaypiano.com.

CARING FOR YOUR PIANO

LARRY FINE

A PIANO MAY LOOK large and imposing, but there is a great deal inside it that is delicate, and sensitive to both use and environmental changes. You have made a considerable investment in the instrument and now should protect that investment, as well as maximize your enjoyment of it, by properly caring for it. For most pianos in good condition receiving moderate use in the home, a budget of $300 to $500 per year should suffice for normal service.

If you bought the piano from a commercial seller, your first service will probably be a few weeks after delivery, by a technician associated with the seller. If you bought a used piano from a private seller and do not have a trustworthy recommendation to a technician, you can find the names of Registered Piano Technicians (RPT) in your area from the website of the Piano Technicians Guild (PTG), www.ptg.org. To become an RPT, one must pass a series of exams, assuring at least a minimum level of competence in piano servicing.

The following are the major types of service a piano needs on a regular or semi-regular basis. More information can be found in *The Piano Book*.

Tuning

Pianos go out of tune mostly because of seasonal changes in humidity that cause the soundboard and other parts to alternately swell and shrink. This happens regardless of whether or not the piano is played. Pianos vary in their responsiveness to fluctuations in humidity, but the variance is not always related to the quality of the instrument. People also differ in their sensitivity to tuning changes. New or newly restored pianos should be tuned three or four times the first year, until the strings are fully stretched out. After that, most pianos should be tuned between one and three times per year, depending on seasonal humidity changes, the player's sensitivity, and the amount of use. Pianos that receive professional levels of use (teaching, performance) are typically tuned more often, and major concert instruments are tuned before each performance. A regular home piano tuning typically costs between $100 and $200. However, if the piano has not been tuned regularly, or if it has undergone a large change in pitch, additional tuning work may be required at additional cost.

A piano has over 200 strings, each of which must be individually tuned.

Regulation

Pianos also need other kinds of service. Due to settling and compacting of numerous cloth and felt parts, as well as seasonal changes in humidity, the piano's action (key and hammer mechanism) requires periodic adjustments to bring it back to the manufacturer's specifications. This process is called *regulation*. This should especially be done during the first six months to two years of a piano's life, depending on use. If it is not done, the piano may wear poorly for the rest of its life. After that, small amounts of regulating every few years will probably suffice for most pianos in home situations. Professional instruments need more complete service at more frequent intervals.

The thousands of parts in a piano action need periodic adjustment, or **regulation**, to compensate for wear and environmental changes.

Randy Potter School of Piano Technology

Offering a complete course for beginning and intermediate students in piano tuning, repairing, regulating, voicing, apprentice training and business practices

Randy Potter School of Piano Technology, Inc.
61592 SE Orion Drive
Bend, OR 97702 USA
P 541.382.5411
F 541.382.5400

www.randypotterschool.com

Voicing

Within limited parameters, the tone of a piano can be adjusted by hardening or softening the hammers, a process called *voicing*. Voicing is performed to compensate for the compacting and wear of hammer felt (which causes the tone to become too bright and harsh), or to accommodate the musical tastes of the player. Voicing should be done whenever the piano's tone is no longer to your liking. However, most piano owners will find that simply tuning the piano will greatly improve the tone, and that voicing may not be needed very often.

Cleaning and Polishing

The best way to clean dust and finger marks off the piano is with a soft, clean, lintless cloth, such as cheesecloth, slightly dampened with water and wrung out. Fold the cloth into a pad and rub lightly in the direction of the grain, or in the direction in which the wood was originally polished (obvious in the case of hand-rubbed finishes). Where this direction is not obvious, as might be the case with high-polish polyester finishes, rub in any one direction only, using long, straight strokes. Do not rub in a circular motion, as

this will eventually make the finish lose its luster. Most piano manufacturers recommend against the use of commercially available furniture polish or wax. Polish specially made for pianos is available from

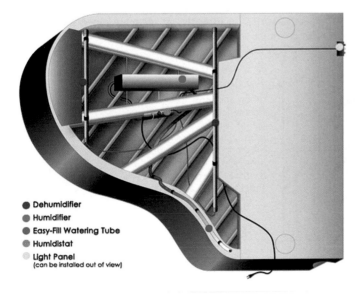

- ● Dehumidifier
- ● Humidifier
- ● Easy-Fill Watering Tube
- ● Humidistat
- ○ Light Panel
  (can be installed out of view)

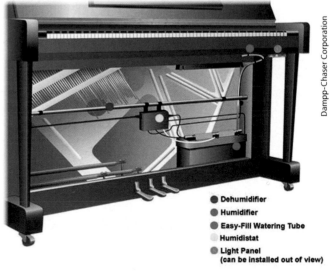

Dampp-Chaser Corporation

- ● Dehumidifier
- ● Humidifier
- ● Easy-Fill Watering Tube
- ○ Humidistat
- ● Light Panel
  (can be installed out of view)

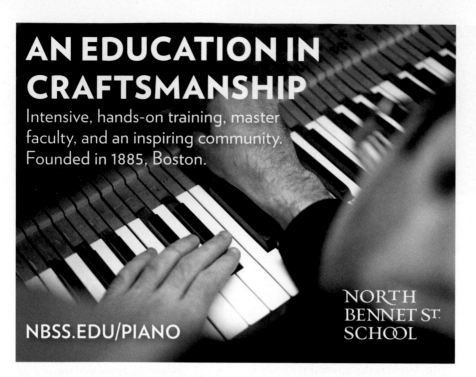
some manufacturers, dealers, and technicians.

To clean the keys, use the same kind of soft, clean cloth as for the finish. Dampen the cloth slightly with water or a mild white soap solution, but don't let water run down the sides of the keys. If the keytops are made of ivory, be sure to dry them off right after cleaning—because ivory absorbs water, the keytops will curl up and fall off if water is allowed to stand on them. If the black keys are made of wood, use a separate cloth to clean them, in case any black stain comes off (not necessary for plastic keys).

Dust inevitably collects inside a piano no matter how good a housekeeper one is. A piano technician can

WHEN SHOULD I HAVE MY PIANO TUNED?

When to tune your piano depends on your local climate. You should avoid times of rapid humidity change and seek times when the humidity will be stable for a reasonable length of time. Turning the heat on in the house in the fall, and then off again in the spring, causes major indoor humidity changes, and in each case it may take several months before the piano's soundboard fully restabilizes at the new humidity level.

In Boston, for example, the tuning cycle goes something like that shown in the graph. A piano tuned in April or May, when the heat is turned off, will probably be out of tune by late June. If it is tuned in late June or July, it may well hold its tune until October or later, depending on when the heat is turned on for the winter. If the piano is tuned *right* after the heat is turned on, however, say in October or November, it will almost certainly be out of tune by Christmas. But if you wait until after the holidays (and, of course, everyone wants it tuned *for* the holidays), it will probably hold pretty well until April or even May. In my experience, most problems with pianos in good condi-

tion that "don't hold their tune" are caused by poor timing of the tuning with the seasonal changes.

Note that those who live in a climate like Boston's and have their piano tuned twice a year will probably also notice two times during the year when the piano sounds out of tune but when, for the above reason, it should probably *not* be tuned. The only remedies for this dilemma are to have the piano tuned more frequently, or to more closely control the humidity.

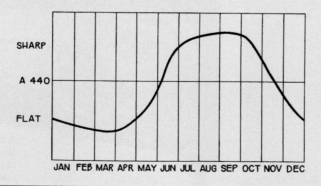

The pitch of the piano in the tenor and low treble ranges closely follows the annual cycle of indoor humidity. The graph shows how a typical piano in Boston might behave. Most areas of the country that have cold winters will show a similar pattern.

safely vacuum up the dust or otherwise clean the interior of the piano when he or she comes to tune it.

Humidity Control

Because pianos are made primarily of wood, proper control of humidity will greatly increase both the life span of the piano and your enjoyment of it. A relative humidity of 42% is sometimes cited as ideal for a piano, but any humidity level that is relatively constant and moderate will suffice. Here are some common steps to take to protect your piano from fluctuations and extremes of humidity:

- Don't place the piano too near radiators, heating and cooling ducts, fireplaces, direct sunlight, and open windows.

- Avoid overheating the house during cold weather.

- Use air-conditioning during hot, humid weather.

- Add humidity to the air during dry weather with either a whole-house humidifier attached to a central air system or with a room humidifier. Room humidifiers, however, have to be cleaned and refilled frequently, and some make a lot of noise. If you use a room humidifier, don't place it too near the piano.

Instead of the above, or in addition to it, have a climate-control system installed in the piano. They make no noise, require very little maintenance, and cost $350 to $500 for a vertical piano or $400 to $600 for a grand, ordered and installed through your piano technician or piano dealer. The illustrations on the previous page of the Dampp-Chaser climate-control system show how the system's components are discreetly hidden inside the piano. For more information about these systems, see **www.pianolifesaver.com**.

Another solution to the humidity-control problem is **Music Sorb**, a non-toxic silica gel that naturally attracts moisture from the air when humidity rises above 50%, and releases that same moisture when the humidity drops below 50%. It comes in cassettes or pouches sold through piano technicians or from the website **www.musicsorbonline.com**. A supply sufficient for a single piano costs about $125 and may need replacing once a year, depending on local humidity variations. 🎹

Benches

In all likelihood, your purchase of a new piano will include a matching bench. Benches for consumer-grade pianos are usually made by the piano manufacturer and come with the piano. Benches for performance-grade pianos are often provided separately by the dealer.

Benches come in two basic types: *fixed-height* or *adjustable*. Consumer-grade pianos usually come with fixed-height benches that have either a solid top that matches the piano's finish, or a padded top with sides and legs finished to match the piano. The legs on most benches will be miniatures of the piano's legs, particularly for decorative models. Most piano benches have music storage compartments. School and institutional-type vertical pianos often come with so-called "stretcher" benches—the legs are connected with wooden reinforcing struts to better endure heavy use.

Both solid-top and padded benches work well. The padded benches tend to be a little more comfortable, especially for those who have little natural padding of their own. They tend to wear more quickly, however, and are subject to tearing. Solid-top benches wear longer but are more easily scratched.

Adjustable benches are preferred by serious players who spend hours at the piano, and by children and adults who are shorter or taller than average. The standard height of a piano bench is 19" or 20". Adjustable benches typically can be set at anywhere from about 18" to 21". By adjusting the bench height and moving it slightly forward or backward, one can maintain the proper posture and wrist angle to the keyboard.

High-quality adjustable benches have a very heavy steel mechanism—so strong you could almost use it as a car jack! The duet-size bench (seats two) weighs well over 60 pounds. These benches are made of hard rock maple and come in most leg styles and finishes. The deeply tufted tops come in a heavy-duty vinyl and look like leather; tops of actual leather are available at additional cost. Both look great and wear well. The best ones, such as those made by Jansen, are expensive ($500 to $750) but are built to last a lifetime. Over the past few years, lesser-quality adjustable benches have come on the market. While these benches are adjustable within a similar range, the mechanisms aren't as hardy. They may be fine for light use, but most will not last nearly as long as the piano. A new style of adjustable bench, with steel legs, may be useful in high-use institutional settings.

A new type of adjustable bench on the market contains a hydraulic or pneumatic mechanism for raising or lowering the seat. There are different versions, but a typical one uses two nitrogen-gas cylinders, one on each side, and is good for 30,000 up-and-down cycles. The bench can be adjusted quickly and effortlessly by means of a handle on the side of the

www.pljansen.com

Padded Bench

Wood Top Bench

Steel Legs

Adjustable Bench with Steel Legs

www.benchworld.com

Adjustable Artist Bench

Stretcher Bench

Hydraulic Bench

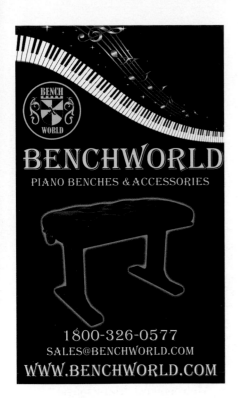

Balance Arm Lamp

Clip-On Lamp

bench. This can be an advantage to players whose wrists are easily fatigued by turning the knob of the traditional or standard type of adjustable bench, or for musicians who need to make height adjustments quickly and silently during a performance. These benches can also usually be set higher than the traditional kind. Most hydraulic or pneumatic benches are very stable, with metal legs (see photo), avoiding the wobbliness that can sometimes afflict four-legged wooden benches. Standard models range in price from $500 to $900; fancier versions, on which the metal is covered by wood, cost from $1,300 to $2,200.

Legs for both fixed-height and traditional adjustable benches are attached by a single bolt at the top of each leg. These bolts should be tightened anytime there is wobble in the bench. Don't over-tighten, however, as that might pull the bolt out of the leg.

Finally, if the piano you want doesn't come with the bench you desire, talk to your dealer. It's common for dealers to swap benches or bench tops to accommodate your preference, or to offer an upgrade to a better bench in lieu of a discount on the piano.

Lamps

Having adequate lighting for the piano music is critical. It's hard enough to learn how to read music without having to deal with a lack of illumination, or with shadows on the sheet music. The ideal solution is track lighting in the ceiling just above the player. In many homes and institutions, however, this is not feasible. In those instances, a piano lamp may well be the answer.

Piano lamps fall into two major groups: floor lamps and desk lamps. Floor lamps arch over the piano and hover over the music rack, while desk lamps sit directly on the piano or are attached to the music rack itself. Desk lamps are subdivided into three groups: a standard desk lamp that sits atop a vertical piano directly over the music rack; a "balance-arm" lamp that sits off to the side on a grand piano's music desk and has a long arm that hovers over the music rack; and a clip-on lamp that attaches directly to the music rack itself (see illustrations).

Piano lamps come in a variety of qualities, sizes, styles, finishes, and bulb types. The better ones are usually made of high-quality brass, while the least expensive are often made of very thin brass or are simply brass-plated. The light from incandescent-bulb lamps tends to be a tad harsh, but the bulbs are less expensive than those for fluorescent lamps, which, though pricier, emit a softer light.

Piano lamps are available through most piano dealerships as well as at lighting stores. A limited selection can

also be found at The Home Depot and Lowe's.

Accessories and Problem Solvers

Only a few accessories are used with pianos, and most are available at your local piano dealership. You might consider:

- **Caster Cups**. Caster cups are small cups that go under the wheels of vertical and grand pianos to protect the floor or carpet. They come in plastic or a variety of woods, and in clear acrylic that allows the carpet or hardwood floor to show through. If the caster cups have felt on the bottom, however, be careful, as the dye from the felt can bleed into carpeting, especially if it gets damp.

- **Piano Covers**. Used mostly in churches and schools (and homes with cats), piano covers are designed to protect the piano's finish from accidental damage, and are available to fit any size of piano. They come in vinyl or mackintosh (a very tight-weave fabric that is very water-resistant), brown or black on the outside, and a fleece-like material on the side that touches the piano. A thicker, quilted, cotton cover is available for use in locations where the piano is moved frequently or may get bumped.

Piano Covers

Bench Cushions

- **Bench Cushions**. Bench cushions are made in a variety of sizes, thicknesses (1" to 3"), fabrics, and colors. They are also available in tapestry designs, most with a musical motif, tufted or box-edged, and all have straps to secure them to the bench.

- **Pedal Extenders**. These extension devices are available for those whose feet do not comfortably reach the pedals. Some are nothing more than a brass pedal that bolts on to the existing pedal, while others are a box, finished to match the piano, that sits over the existing pedals and has pedals with rods to operate the piano's pedals.

- **Metronomes**. Many music teachers recommend using a metronome to improve students' timing. Any piano or musical-instrument dealership will generally have a wide selection, from the solid walnut, wind-up, oscillating metronome like the one your grandmother had on her piano, to a new, beeping digital model.

- **Grand Piano String Covers**. Wool string covers are available in a variety of colors that complement the piano's finish. When in place, they provide a reduction in sound volume, and protection against dust (and cats). Thicker

Lucite

Wood

Caster Cups

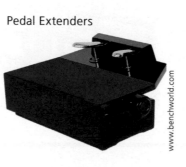

Pedal Extenders

Metronomes

sound-reduction covers and baffles are also available.

- **Lid and Fallboard Slow-Close Systems.** Raising and lowering the lid of a grand piano is frequently difficult, and can be downright dangerous. This is due to the combination of its weight, which can exceed 50 pounds, and its position, which makes it hard to reach. Enter a new product that solves at least the weight problem: Safety-Ease Lid Assist. Safety-Ease (now known as Magic Lid) consists of pneumatic cylinders that effectively counter-balance the weight of the lid and damp its movement so that it can be easily raised or lowered, even by a child. It mounts under the lid, between the lid hinges on the piano's rim, is finished in polished ebony to match most pianos, and requires no drilling or permanent installation. This unique system is sold and installed only by piano dealers or technicians. The installed price for small and mid-size grands is $500 to $600. More information is available at www.magic-lid.com.

The fallboard (keyboard cover) can also be a danger, not so much for its weight or position, but for the swiftness of its fall and because, when it falls, little fingers are likely to be in its path. Many new pianos today come with a pneumatically or hydraulically damped, slow-close fallboard. For those that don't, aftermarket devices are available from piano dealers or technicians.

- **Touch-Weight Adjustment Systems.** *Touch* or *touch weight* refers to the pressure required to press a piano key. Too little touch weight, or touch weight that is uneven from note to note, makes a piano action difficult to control; too much touch weight makes a

piano tiring to play, and can cause physical problems for the player over time. Touch-weight problems can be caused by poor action design, worn parts in older pianos, or incorrectly dimensioned replacement parts in restored pianos.

Historically, discussions, measurements, and adjustments in this area of piano technology have been about *static* touch weight—the force needed to make a piano key just begin to move slowly downward. Less well understood, and usually ignored, has been *dynamic* touch weight—the force required to press a key in actual normal, rapid playing. Here, the rapid movement of the key creates *inertia* (i.e., the tendency of a moving mass to keep moving in the same direction and at the same speed, and the tendency of a stationary mass to remain stationary.) Unlike static touch weight, which depends on the *relative* amount and positioning of mass on either side of the key's balance point, as well as on friction, dynamic touch weight depends on the *total* amount of mass in the system. Attempts to fix problems in static touch weight by adding mass to the front or rear of the key can cause problems with dynamic touch weight by creating excessive inertia.

Until fairly recently, technicians resorted to a patchwork quilt of homemade, trial-by-error remdies for problems with static touch weight; dynamic touch weight wasn't even on their radar. More recently, a greater understanding of touch weight has emerged, and more sophisticated techniques for solving touch-weight problems are being developed. The gold standard among these techniques is that of David Stanwood, who developed the first system for mathematically describing, measuring, and solving problems

related to dynamic touch weight. His system is applied by a network of specially trained technicians who, because of the comprehensive nature of the system and the remedies it suggests, tend to use it on higher-end instruments and those undergoing complete restoration. More information can be found at www.stanwoodpiano.com.

A simpler remedy, but only for heavy or uneven static touch weight on a grand piano, is a product called TouchRail, available through piano technicians. TouchRail is a rail with 88 individually adjustable springs that replaces a grand piano's key-stop rail. The springs press gently on the keys to the front of the balance point, enabling the technician to effectively "dial in" a desired touch weight and make it perfectly even from note to note. Because it's spring-based rather than mass-based, TouchRail won't add inertia to the action system, though of course it won't cure any pre-existing problems with excessive inertia, either. Installation requires no drilling, cutting, or other permanent modification of the piano, and the rail can be removed and replaced in seconds during routine piano service, just like a traditional key-stop rail. The installed price is around $795. See www.pitchlock.com for more information. ▐▐▌

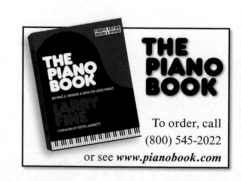

TEN WAYS TO VOICE A ROOM

CHRISTOPHER STORCH

*H*ave you noticed that your newly purchased piano doesn't sound quite the same as when you tried it in the showroom? The difference you notice between showroom and home may stem from the acoustics of the room in which the piano is placed. Not all problems with piano tone are best solved by voicing the instrument—it may be your *room* that needs voicing. Some of the factors that can significantly affect the sound of your piano room are: the size of the room, including ceiling height; the sound-absorbing and -reflecting materials in the room, which give it its reverberant character; and the number and orientation of objects in the room, which affect how sound is scattered or diffused.

Making the Distinction Between the Piano and the Room

It's important to distinguish between acoustical problems caused by the piano and those caused by the room. For instance, a problem of too much loudness is often caused by a piano that is too large for the room. This can be best addressed at or close to the piano, rather than by increasing the amount of sound-absorbing materials elsewhere in the room. On the other hand, such problems as harshness of tone, excess lingering sound, and hot and dead spots, can often be attributed to the room. Many of the following suggestions for loudness control or other acoustical adjustments are easily reversible; experiment with some of these before making more permanent changes to your piano or room.

Reverberation

Reverberation refers to the persistence of sound within a space after the source of the sound has stopped. Such prolongation of sound can help give music the qualities of blending, lushness, fullness, and breadth. Too much reverberation can make the music muddy and indistinct, and the buildup of reverberant sound can make the piano sound too loud. When there is too little reverberation, the room is said to sound "dry" or even "dead"; to compensate for this, the pianist might feel the need to overplay to achieve a lush, musical sound. In general, the larger the cubic volume of the space, the longer the reverberation time; the smaller the cubic volume, the shorter the reverberation time. The more sound-absorbing materials in the space, the shorter the reverberation time; the

fewer such materials, the longer the reverberation time. The length of reverberation is a matter of personal preference. Some pianists like having the room reverberation be part of the sound of their piano playing; others prefer keeping the sound of the room to a minimum, enjoying primarily the clear sound of the piano as modulated by their technique.

Hot or Dead Spots

Hot spots and dead spots are places in the room where certain frequencies or notes, though played with the same force, stand out more than other frequencies or notes. Problems of this type are best solved by installing sound-scattering objects: bookcases, furniture, wall hangings, and so forth. Reorienting the piano or moving it slightly can also help.

Below are ten ways to mitigate problems in piano sound other than by voicing the instrument, beginning with some relatively simple things to do nearby the piano itself:

 Buy a piano that's the right size for the room.

The first and best way to avoid problems with room acoustics is to buy a piano that's the right size for the room. Too large a piano can overload a room with sound, while one that's too small may not be heard equally well in all parts of the space. A rule of thumb: Assuming a ceiling height of eight feet, the combined lengths of the four walls should be at least ten times the length of a grand piano or the height of a vertical. However, it's not always possible to follow this advice—in many cases, the purchase decision will be dictated more by musical needs or budget than by room size. A small piano, for example, may have performance problems inherent to the instrument's size, such as poor bass tone or an unresponsive action, even when it's the right size for the room. Or, if you're longing for a large grand's growling bass, be aware that, even though such a piano is perfectly capable of producing that sound, your room may not be able to support it.

When the piano's size is not a good match for the room, try voicing the piano, or experimenting with one of the following tips:

 Move or reorient the piano within the room.

Most rooms have three pairs of parallel surfaces: two sets of opposing walls, and the ceiling and floor. Parallel surfaces tend to produce standing waves—certain frequencies that sound much louder than others at some points in the room, but that are virtually inaudible at other points. Moving the piano away from room corners

and partway along the length of a wall, and/or turning it at an angle this way or that, can sometimes mitigate this problem. You'll have to experiment, listening at different places within the room. Remember that the piano's sound when you sit at the keyboard will be different from its sound elsewhere in the room.

 Use a piano cover to directly reduce loudness.

Typical cloth string covers designed for grand pianos—that is, covers that lie directly on the strings—will only marginally reduce sound volume, especially if they have only a single layer of cloth. Most reports say that thin string covers are effective only for the highest notes, to take the edge off the sound. Thicker, sound-attenuating string covers, custom-made for a particular model of grand piano, work better. An even more effective mute for a grand would be a full-size, quilted cover that reaches the floor. However, this will require closing the lid completely and placing the music rack atop the cover—though unattractive, in some situations this is the only practical way to reduce excess loudness. For a vertical piano, a blanket or section of carpet can be attached to the piano's back.

 Place sound-absorbing material inside the piano, between the soundboard and the wooden structural support beams.

You may be able to drastically reduce a piano's loudness by inserting blankets or foam rubber blocks between a grand's soundboard and its wooden case beams, or between a vertical's soundboard and wooden posts. One possibility is to purchase the foam in sheets and cut shapes to fit. Your piano technician may have experience in doing this, and may also be able to help you avoid damaging the soundboard or creating the buzzes that can accompany this technique—ask for pointers. This method of loudness control won't be possible if you have a grand outfitted with a humidity-control system or an electronic player-piano system.

 Place a rug under a grand piano to absorb sound.

The sound of a grand piano is sent out into the room via the lid, which is propped up at an angle on the stick—and by a considerable reflection by the floor of sound emanating from the underside of the soundboard. If your floor covering is a sound-reflecting material such as wood, stone, or tile, the loudness can be greatly reduced by placing a rug under the piano. To absorb even more sound, place a thick pad under the rug.

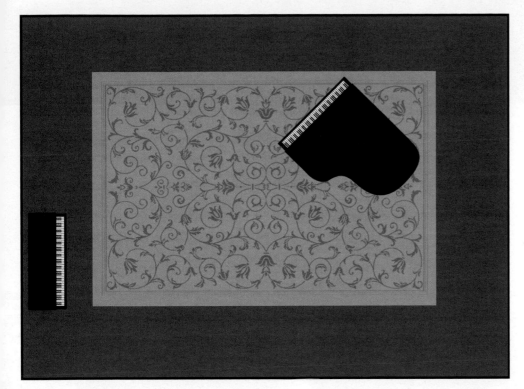

Moving the piano away from room corners and partway along the length of a wall, and/or turning it at an angle this way or that, can sometimes mitigate acoustic problems. Experiment and listen at different places within the room. If your floor is a sound-reflecting material, the loudness can be greatly reduced by placing a rug under the piano.

Experiment with the size of the rug or carpet and its orientation under the piano. Other, more temporary solutions: place a dog bed or a collection of throw pillows under the piano.

 6 *Place objects under a grand piano to scatter sound.*

Perhaps you don't want to absorb the sound coming out of the bottom of your grand piano, but just want to disperse it more evenly throughout the room. The space under a grand can be used for storage chests, plants, knickknacks, and the like.

Let's say you've tried some or all of these steps; you've noticed some improvement, but not enough. Here are some more advanced treatments for the room itself.

 7 *Cover or expose hard wall and/or window surfaces.*

Glass tends to reflect high-frequency sound, while allowing lower frequencies to pass right through, never to return. A room with a lot of exposed glass will often sound harsh and bright, as it accentuates the treble notes. Covering these windows can help to absorb higher-frequency sound energy and thus restore the balance of bass and treble. Heavy fabric such as velour, sewn into gathers, works best to absorb sound. Sheer, semitransparent fabrics are much less effective, but can have subtle acoustical effects, if that's all that's required, and can be used to "fine-tune" the room.

Large areas of exposed bare walls and ceiling can produce a similar effect as glass, but are more effective at preserving bass energy. In a room that sounds too muddy—i.e., it makes music sound indistinct—sound-absorbing wall coverings such as tapestries, or hanging rugs, might be worth a try. Also available are fabric-wrapped, sound-absorbing panels that will work well in homes, though their "professional" look lacks the personal touch of one's own home furnishings.

In a space with high ceilings, hanging banners, flags, or other materials from the ceiling can cut down on reverberation.

Be aware that most household sound-absorbing materials do not work very well below about 200 Hz (about middle C). If your acoustical problem occurs below this frequency, look to other techniques or materials to solve it, including professional acoustical materials designed specifically to address low-frequency sound.

 8 *Add or remove upholstered furniture and other sound-absorbing objects.*

Adding sofas, pillows, upholstered chairs, carpets, and other sound-absorbing décor can reduce excess reverberation and loudness, and removing such objects will

increase them. Even placing cloths over coffee and side tables will cut down the reflection of sound just a little bit. Plush, overstuffed furniture produces the greatest sound-absorbing effect. Upholstered furniture of leather, wood, or metal has less effect.

9 *Add or remove sound-scattering wall hangings, objects, and furniture.*

Be careful not to add *too* many sound-absorbing objects to the room—it's possible to go too far, making the room sound too dead, dry, or soft. Sometimes you don't want to absorb sound—you merely want to scatter or diffuse it more evenly about the room. The sound will then be more natural and less "hollow" without necessarily losing reverberation and loudness. In scattering sound, your goal is to use objects both large and small with complex shapes to break up large expanses of flat surfaces. Again, some experimentation is in order. Examples of sound-scattering objects are bookshelves (not too full), tables, chandeliers, room-dividing screens, and sculpture. Designing a space with ceiling beams can also scatter sound.

You've tried everything! Below is one last word of advice.

10 *Hire a professional.*

Some of the acoustical phenomena described here can be confusing to the untrained. Even worse, some problematic combinations of piano and room may have more than one of these problems. If you've tried everything and still don't hear an improvement, consider seeking expert help from a piano technician or a room-acoustics consultant (acoustician). Such professionals may be able to help you design or furnish the space for the best sound, suggest appropriate acoustical materials, and direct you to local suppliers for those materials.

Chris Storch, RPT, is an acoustician with 20 years' experience in the areas of architectural acoustics, noise and vibration control, and environmental noise abatement. Some of the more prominent projects on which he has consulted include Verizon Hall, in Philadelphia; Sibelius Hall, in Lahti, Finland; LG Arts Center, in Seoul, South Korea; and Fox Cities Performing Arts Center, in Appleton, Wisconsin. Storch is a 2009 graduate of the Piano Technology program at the North Bennet Street School, in Boston. He tunes and services pianos in the Boston area, and conducts research in piano acoustics in his spare time. He can be reached at chrisstor@aol.com.

BUYING A DIGITAL PIANO
An Introduction

ALDEN SKINNER and PIANO BUYER STAFF

IF, AFTER HAVING READ "Acoustic or Digital: What's Best for Me?," you've decided on a digital piano, the next step is to shop for and select the right model for your needs. There are currently some 200 models of digital piano on the market. Narrowing the field requires exploring some basic issues.

Style and Price

Digital pianos come in three basic physical styles: **slab**, **console** (also sometimes called vertical or upright), and **grand** (see illustrations). Which instrument style you choose will depend on use, space limitations, furniture requirements, and price.

Slab: A *slab* is simply a keyboard and, usually, pedal(s), without a stand. If you need to take the piano to a gig, or if home is a dorm room or a small studio apartment and you need to make the most efficient use of every square inch, you may opt for a slab that can be placed on a stand or table for practice, and stuck in a closet when not in use. Keep in mind, however, that slabs currently on the market weigh from 20 to 85 pounds, so be sure to choose one with a weight that you can handle.

Slabs generally come with a single pedal, but for many models, optional stands and three-pedal units are available. You may need to buy the slab, stand, and pedal unit separately and put them together, or a retailer you buy from may sell you all the parts as a package deal. Slab digital pianos start as low as $200, with most priced between $500 and $2,000, and a few as high as $7,000. An optional matching stand with integrated pedal assembly usually costs $200 to $300 more, but a simple, generic stand can be had for as little as $40. Note that some slabs don't come with a stand to hold your music; you might need to provide one.

Console: A *console* is a keyboard with a stand or cabinet that contains a built-in pedal assembly. A console may look like an upright acoustic piano or organ, or simply like a digital piano. Consoles generally have a stand and pedal assembly built in at the factory. However, as mentioned above, many slabs can effectively be turned into a console by separately buying a stand with an integrated pedal assembly.

Digital consoles

Roland

Slab pianos

Yamaha

Digital grand

kawai

The cabinetry of console models ranges from two flat side supports with a cross member for stability, to elegant designs that would look at home in the most posh surroundings. It's common for models in this category to be available in multiple finish options, including synthetic wood grain, real-wood veneers, and, on some of the better models, the lustrous polished ebony often found on acoustic pianos. Most of these models have the usual three pedals. Console digitals start at about $500, with most priced between $1,000 and $5,000, and a few as high as $10,000.

Grand: If the piano will be in elegant surroundings, you may choose a *grand*-style digital. Digital grands come in lengths of about three feet—just long enough to suggest the shape of a baby grand—to about five feet. Like some of the console models, these are often available in a variety of wood-grain finishes and the polished ebony finish common in today's acoustic grands. You will usually pay a premium for the elegant furniture. Grands start at $1,500, with most priced between $3,000 and $10,000, and a few as high as $20,000.

Note that there is little or no relationship between an instrument's physical style and its musical features—slabs are often used on stage by professional musicians, and grand-shaped digitals may have features no better than the non-grand versions they're based on. However, the larger spaces enclosed by a grand-piano cabinet and some console cabinets can accommodate more, larger, and more advantageously positioned speakers, particularly bass speakers (woofers). This, and the sympathetic vibration of a wood cabinet, may result in better sound quality from the onboard speakers of some cabinet models than that found in digitals without cabinets, especially slabs.

Speakers, Headphones, and Stage Pianos

Most people who buy a digital piano do so, in part, so that they can play with headphones and not disturb anyone. For that reason, *all* digital pianos come with headphone jacks. When used with headphones, most instruments' onboard (internal) speakers are silenced. Also, nearly all digital pianos can have the sound of their onboard speakers rerouted to an external amplifier and speakers if, for example, the onboard speakers are inadequate for the venue, or if you'd prefer to use the speakers of your home audio system.

Grado

Some slab digitals come *without* onboard speakers. These are called *stage pianos*, and are generally used by professional musicians in performance venues where an external amplifier and speakers are expected to be present. Not having onboard speakers saves a little bit in cost, weight, and space. However, if you're planning to use the instrument at home most of the time, the convenience of having at least some onboard speakers is generally worth the trade-off.

(Note: The *stage piano* category also includes a few models of electronic keyboard with fewer than 88 notes and/or with keys that are not weighted to feel like an acoustic piano. For our purposes, those models are not considered digital pianos and are not included in our database.)

Taking Stock of Your Musical Needs

Unless you expect to buy another piano in a year or so, you need to consider your long-term requirements. Who will be the piano's primary player today, and what are his or her musical interests and ambitions? If it's for the family, how long will it be until the youngest child has the opportunity to learn? Does Mom or Dad harbor any musical interests? If so, it's likely that one family member or another will use the instrument for many years to come. This argues for getting a higher-quality instrument, whose advantages of better tone, touch, and features will be appreciated over time.

If multiple players will use the instrument, it needs to meet the expectations of the most advanced player. At the same time, a beginner in the family will benefit from features that are of no interest to the advanced player, and still another family member may just want to fool around with the instrument once in a while. Easy-play features and educational software will keep these players happy—and you might be surprised how many people are enticed into learning to play as a result of these easy first steps. So, obviously, an individual player may search among a very narrow range of instruments, while a family may have to balance the different needs of several people. Fortunately, the wealth of available choices can easily accommodate any combination of individual and/or family needs.

Instrumental Voices (Sounds) and Ensemble Capabilities

Sounds in digital pianos are also known as *voices* or *tones*. Voices can include such sounds as:

- Individual musical instruments, such as piano, electric piano, guitar, flute, etc.
- Combinations of instruments, such as a string or brass ensemble
- Percussion sounds, such as snare drum or cymbals
- The human voice
- Unusual sound effects, such as gunshot or helicopter

Some digital pianos may contain more than one example of a

Great Digital Pianos Begin Here.

Relying on ninety years of experience in building fine acoustic pianos, Kawai creates digital pianos with the finest tone and touch… period.

We offer a variety of award-winning digitals perfect for stage, studio and home. Discover the difference these exceptional instruments will make in your music.

CA Series
The Finest Tone and Touch

CP Series
Elegant and Powerful

CN Series
Award-Winning Digital Pianos

ES8 · The Ultimate Portable Digital Piano

90th Anniversary
KAWAI

particular type of voice, especially piano, such as bright- and mellow-sounding pianos, or pianos that mimic the tonal characteristics of several different well-known makes of concert grand.

Standard or *traditional* digital pianos are designed mainly to emulate the acoustic piano, with the optional accompaniment of one or more other voices. Most will allow you to split the keyboard so that the right hand plays a melody in one instrumental voice while the left hand plays an accompaniment in another (such as piano and string bass); or to layer the sounds so that two or more instrumental voices sound together (such as piano and strings) when each key is played. These days, even the least-expensive standard digitals usually have at least a few different piano voices, as well as a dozen or two other instrumental voices, such as harpsichord, church and jazz organ, vibes, and strings. Many models contain hundreds of voices, built-in rhythms, sound effects like *reverb* and *chorus*, and a metronome for keeping time, among other features.

Other, slightly more expensive models, called *ensemble* or *arranger* digital pianos, generally have all the features of standard digitals, but also come with two other major features: Easy-Play and Auto-Accompaniment. With *Easy-Play*, playing as little as a single key will trigger the sound of an entire chord. With *Auto-Accompaniment*, an entire musical combo or orchestra (strings, horns, percussion, etc.) will back you up as you play, and automatically change its accompaniment to match your melody or changing chords. These backing tracks, known as *styles*, come in all kinds of musical forms, such as Swing, Latin, Rock, World, and so forth—with many different rhythms and special effects. The best of these styles are of a caliber that will please the most discerning ear.

You might not think you need the additional capabilities of an ensemble digital, but having them can enable the beginner, as well as family members who don't take lessons, to have a lot more fun and sound like pros with minimal practice. The instant gratification provided by auto-accompaniment might keep a player with low attention span more fully engaged. For an advancing player, the opportunities for musical creativity are significantly enhanced. On the other hand, if you're the only player and expect to play mostly classical piano music, you may not want to spend money on the ensemble feature.

When looking over the specs of digital pianos, it's easy to be impressed by the large number of voices that some models contain, and there was a time in the recent past when the number of voices was closely related to an instrument's quality and price. That's no longer necessarily true. First, the price of memory has plummeted to the extent that even the least expensive models can be outfitted with hundreds of voices. Second, the quality of the voices, which is related to the amount of memory they take up, varies considerably; more voices doesn't necessarily mean a better instrument. It's expensive for a manufacturer to create or purchase custom, high-quality sounds, and these sounds take up a lot of memory. When an instrument contains more than a few dozen voices, often most of the rest are from a standardized set of voices, sometimes usable only for playback of files created elsewhere, but not selectable from the instrument panel by the user; or from a company's library of legacy (older) voices; both usually using less memory, and therefore of lower quality than the company's latest offerings. That said, these additional voices can still come in handy for the power user who needs a certain unusual sound or combination of sounds, or for the playback of some music files that call for them. And ensemble digitals, with the diverse instrumentation contained in their many styles, can make good use of the extra voices. But most home users of standard digital pianos will find a dozen or two high-quality voices to be more than sufficient.

Keep in mind also that we've been speaking here only of an instrument's internal voices. These days, it's also possible to install additional high-quality piano and instrumental voices on your computer, and play them using your digital piano as a keyboard controller; or to download voices to the digital piano directly from the Internet via Bluetooth (both discussed later).

Piano Sound and Acoustic Piano Realism

Manufacturers create digital piano sounds either by recording actual pianos (known as *sampling*) or by using mathematical algorithms to mimic the acoustic properties of piano sounds (known as *physical modeling*). Some instruments employ a combination of the two methods. Whereas even the most expensive acoustic piano has only a single set of sound characteristics, many modestly priced digital pianos can reproduce the sounds of multiple sampled concert grands, pianos with different tonal characteristics, and imitations of vintage electronic keyboards, among others. Digital pianos that use physical modeling, and some that use sampling, may even allow the user to make extensive custom refinements to the built-in piano sounds.

Some kinds of music, especially classical, require a level of musical expression that traditional acoustic pianos have evolved to satisfy. For those who play, or plan to play, this music, the ability of a digital piano to imitate the sound, touch, and pedaling of an acoustic piano is important. For players of other kinds of music, however, the ability of a digital piano to sound or play like an acoustic one may be less important. Although virtually all digital pianos are designed to imitate acoustic pianos to *some* extent—that's why they're called *digital pianos*, not *electronic keyboards*—they vary

considerably in how accurately and thoroughly they do so.

The better digital pianos more accurately imitate an acoustic piano by, among other things:

- Re-creating the piano's acoustical resonance, and the sympathetic vibrations of the strings of an acoustic piano's *un*played notes—that is, the keys the player *hasn't* struck—especially when the

sustain pedal is depressed, as well as the sound of a vibrating string being silenced by a damper when a key is released: sounds that are subconsciously part of the acoustic-piano experience.

- Having a larger number of speakers, or speakers that are better positioned; or special features like a soundboard speaker system, in which an

acoustic-piano–style soundboard is used as a "speaker."

- Containing higher-quality key sensors to more accurately translate the speed with which a key is depressed into sound volume; re-creating the acoustic-piano action's feel of "escapement" as a key is depressed, and having wooden keys with keytops that imitate the feel of ivory, which absorbs sweat and so is less slippery to the touch than plastic.

- Including three pedals that perform the same functions as on an acoustic grand (soft, sostenuto, sustain), and a sustain pedal capable of half pedaling, a pedaling technique used by advanced players.

Note that all of the models that we consider to be digital pianos have 88 notes, the keys are weighted, and, in virtually all of them, the touchweights are graded (i.e., the resistance to your touch gradually decreases from bass to treble) across the range of the keyboard—all just as in an acoustic piano. Instruments with fewer than 88 notes, or with semi-weighted keyboards that depend on springs for their weight, should be avoided by those looking for a realistic acoustic-piano experience.

Connecting to a Computer

Virtually all digital pianos can be connected to a personal computer, allowing you to:

- Use computer software and a printer to record, notate (write), edit, and print the music you play
- Use software that will, for example, help you learn to play piano, train your musical ear, or teach you music history
- Use your digital piano as a keyboard controller for playing virtual instruments (i.e., instrumental sounds that reside on your computer)
- Play duets or practice with someone in a different location

Digital pianos communicate with a computer and each other via a music-technology language called Musical Instrument Digital Interface (MIDI). MIDI is not music—it's a stream of data commands that basically specify which notes are played, when, and how loudly, among other parameters. This common language allows music composed on one digital piano to sound more or less the same when played on another ("more or less" because, even when both instruments are playing their respective "piano" voice, for example, the tonal characteristics of the two "pianos" might be quite different from one another). MIDI also allows your digital piano to interact with music software on your computer.

Most digital pianos connect to a computer via a cable that plugs into USB ports on both ends. (The USB port on the digital piano is technically known as *USB to Host*.) A few of the less-expensive models rely on an older method: a cable from the MIDI ports of the piano to a USB port on the computer. The newest method of connecting to a computer is wirelessly via Bluetooth.

Bluetooth and Internet Connectivity

An increasing number of digital pianos are now equipped with Bluetooth, to link to the Internet using your smartphone or tablet as a hotspot. This feature is still in its infancy, so many of its potential uses are not yet known; here are some of the ways it's currently being used:

- Stream virtually unlimited music, sounds, rhythms, and styles from the Internet, and play along with them and/or record them for later playback
- Access an app on your smartphone to change your digital piano's touch, tone, and tuning
- Access an app on your smartphone for sophisticated recording in MIDI or digital audio
- Access sheet music from the Internet and use an app on your smartphone to turn pages
- Access apps and online video tutorials to learn to play piano, or to teach yourself a particular song
- Access the piano manufacturer's user guide, instructional videos, and apps to learn to use and customize your instrument

Recording and Playback

Most digital pianos allow you to record your playing for future playback. Here are some of the reasons you might want to do this:

- To critically review your own piano playing, possibly with a teacher
- To play a duet with a recording you previously made of yourself, or one made by someone else
- To create a "one-person band" by recording different instrumental parts from the same piece of music on separate tracks and combining them into a single performance
- To create a soundtrack for a home video

As mentioned earlier, digital pianos create and record music as a sequence of MIDI commands—thus the name *MIDI sequencer* for the most common form of internal recorder in a digital piano. This type of recording system is popular because it requires relatively little memory, and because of its simplicity and flexibility: If you later want to play the music back with different instrumental sounds, all you need do is specify the different voices, usually by pressing a button or two—you don't have to re-record the music.

Digital piano models vary in their internal recording (MIDI sequencing) capabilities from one track to about 16 tracks. However, the trend in the industry today is to output the music from the instrument to a computer, and to use computer software, not the piano's internal recorder, for sophisticated recording and music editing. This MIDI sequencing software is generally inexpensive, runs faster than the piano's internal recorder, and is constantly evolving in sophistication. Thus, most digital pianos today have no more than three to five internal recording tracks, and often as few as one or two. A minority of models still have as many as 16 tracks, and the larger number of tracks could be convenient if, say,

you wanted to sketch out an idea requiring many instrumental voices and a computer wasn't nearby. But a few tracks will be more than enough for most nonprofessional users.

If you want to create a very high-quality recording, however, it's generally necessary to record in a digital audio format, such as MP3 or .WAV, instead of MIDI; that is, to record the actual sound, rather than just the MIDI commands. This used to be the exclusive province of specialized, expensive workstations, but the ability to record in digital audio has now trickled down to many digital piano models. This type of recording is much more memory-consuming than MIDI sequencing, so it's usually stored on a USB memory device, such as a flash drive, plugged into the piano. The recording can then be transferred to a computer, where you could use it, for example, as the soundtrack of a home video, or upload it to social media, or e-mail it to family and friends.

SELECTED OTHER FEATURES

External Flash-Drive Storage

Some digital pianos allow you to store your recorded music and other files on USB flash drives or memory cards plugged into a port provided for this purpose. (This port is technically known as *USB to Device*.) These may be files you've recorded, files you've downloaded from the Internet, or files of additional rhythm patterns and styles, additional voices, and user data such as the instrument's internal settings.

Vocal Support

Some digital pianos feature a microphone connection, on the theory that many who love to play also love to

sing. At its most basic level, this feature simply uses the digital piano's audio system as a PA system for the singer. However, some models can also employ effects processing to enhance the performer's voice in some way, or can combine the vocal input with harmonizing to create four-part harmony. Some will also display karaoke lyrics, which, on some higher-end models, can also be output to a video display, such as a TV monitor. Without the vocal support feature, it would still be possible to run vocals through the instrument's speaker system via its line-in connection, but the microphone would require its own amplifier (or the use of an amplified mic), and the special effects mentioned above would not be available.

Educational Support

Some digital pianos include educational extras, such as digital piano lessons, a DVD, or a teaching app that can guide the beginner through a number of factory-installed or downloaded songs, even integrating with Internet connectivity to provide interactive coaching. While not a substitute for a private teacher or class lessons, these materials can be very useful to those who have only a casual interest in learning to play, or whose budget for lessons is limited.

In this tutorial, we've only barely scratched the surface of the amazing features of today's digital pianos. You can read about these and other features in greater depth in our online-only "Digital Piano Basics" articles. Read on for information and tips about the process of shopping for a digital piano.

Shopping Options

Your shopping options depend on the type of digital piano you've decided to buy and the region you live in. In North America, different categories of instruments are available through different types of outlets. Furniture-style models, particularly the higher-end models manufactured by the largest suppliers, are available mostly through traditional bricks-and-mortar piano dealers, though increasingly they're finding their way into other types of outlet. The lower-priced console, slab, or stage models, and some of the less widely distributed brands, are available from a cross section of traditional bricks-and-mortar music retailers, club and warehouse chains such as Costco, consumer-electronics chains such as Best Buy, big-box instrument stores such as Guitar Center, and online retailers such as Amazon, Kraft Music, Musicians Friend, and Sweetwater Music. If you enter into a search engine the specific brand and model of instrument you're looking for, and the name of the city you live in or near, the search results will usually show both online and local sources for that model.

At a bricks-and-mortar retailer, prices are usually somewhat flexible, and negotiating the price of a digital piano is no different from negotiating the price of an acoustic piano (as is discussed in "**Piano Buying Basics,**" elsewhere in this issue). But wherever you shop, you'll find that many of the simpler console digitals and nearly all slab and stage-piano models that are sold through a variety of local and online stores are virtually always sold at the same price. This is due to a pricing model called *minimum advertised price* (or MAP), that's used for many categories of products.

A manufacturer's or distributor's MAP is the lowest price at which a dealer is allowed to advertise an item. Since prices are easily compared and all retailers want an even chance at winning your business, everyone advertises at the MAP. And since the MAP is typically lower than the price at which the dealer might have preferred to sell the item, the selling price is rarely lower than the MAP. Therefore, MAP has become the standard pricing for all non-piano-dealer models of digital piano. (Note: In practice, retailers will often get around the MAP advertising restriction by offering discounts on accessories when you buy the instrument. Also, the restriction is only on the *advertised* price, not the selling price. With online retailers, it may be possible to get a lower price if you can speak with a salesperson over the phone.)

In deciding where to buy, consider what level of service and support you require. Do you:

- Want to try out an instrument before buying?
- Need the help of a salesperson in choosing an instrument or in learning how to use it?
- Need someone to come out to your home to install or set up the instrument?
- Want local warranty support in case you encounter a problem?

If the answer to any of these is "yes," then you should buy from a piano dealer, or other bricks-and-mortar music dealer, as these services will not be available from online retailers, and will be minimal at best from mass merchandisers like Costco. To some extent this will limit the models available to you, as bricks-and-mortar dealers are more likely to stock models whose higher prices and profit margin can support the services they provide. On the other hand, if you're experienced at buying music technology online, pretty much know what you want, or are a beginner with few requirements and just buying something inexpensive, you may find it quicker, easier, and cheaper to buy online.

Tips for the Serious Shopper

If you're going to be shopping for an instrument among local bricks-and-mortar music retailers, the following shopping tips may be useful:

- *Calibrate your ears.* Before you shop, "calibrate" your ears by listening to recordings of solo piano. Listen to whatever type of music you enjoy—and use the headphones you bought for your digital piano. This will embed in your mind, as a benchmark, the sound of high-quality acoustic pianos.
- *Evaluate the tone.* Evaluating an instrument's tone is very subjective, and judging the tone of instruments that have a lot of voices can be overwhelming. Your best bet is to select the five or six instrument voices you think you'll use most, and make them the standard for comparison as you shop. If you choose the digital piano on which those voices sound best to you, it's likely you'll find the other voices satisfying as well. Take detailed notes and use them to establish your favorite(s).
- *Turn off effects.* Be aware that the default voice settings of most digital pianos include some degree of reverberation. This isn't a bad thing, but it's worthwhile to listen to the piano voice, and any other voices that are important to

PX-870
PriviA

The PX-870 is the new flagship of the Privia family, designed to give you a true grand piano experience. With authentic piano sound and feel, a stylish and seamless new design, and the powerful new Sound Projection speaker system, the PX-870 is an outstanding instrument for inspiring brilliant performances.

you, with reverb and all other effects turned off. This will allow you to judge those voices without any coloration or masking from the effects.

- *Evaluate the touch.* Aside from sound, the most important element in the selection of an instrument is likely to be the feel of the action. You'll be selecting from a variety of actions that all try to emulate the feel of an acoustic piano—some lighter, some heavier. Just as there is no single correct piano sound, there is no single correct touch; rather, there is a range of acceptable touches. If you spend most of your playing time with a heavy action, then when you encounter an instrument with a lighter action, you'll play too heavily— and vice versa. The cure is to play

as many instruments as possible, as often as possible. Listen to how each piano responds and adjust your touch accordingly. With experience, you'll learn to adapt.

- *Use the salesperson.* Digital pianos are really computers disguised as pianos, and like some features of a PC, many of the capabilities of digitals are hidden from view, accessible by pressing a sequence of buttons or through multi-screen menus. While the owner's manual will explain how to access these features or sounds, it's impractical for you to study the manuals of every instrument under consideration. Enter the salesperson! This is one of those instances where a well-trained salesperson can be invaluable. But remember that the salesperson is not going home with you, so

don't be swayed by his or her talent. Listen to what they have to say, but focus your attention on the instrument itself.

- *Used digitals.* Because digital-piano technology advances at a blistering pace relative to acoustic-piano technology, there is much less interest in used digitals than in used acoustics. Many of today's digital pianos eclipse the capabilities of the models of even five years ago. Combine this technological advancement with the fact that support of older instruments may be limited—electronics manufacturers are required to maintain replacement parts for only seven years after production ceases—and investing in older models becomes worthy of serious second thoughts.

An Introduction to Software Pianos

MY OTHER PIANO IS A COMPUTER

ALDEN SKINNER

IF THE DIGITAL PIANO is thought of as a complete instrument that's ready to play right out of the box, piano software can be thought of as part of a "piano kit." The standard digital piano is completely self-contained in that it's made up of the memory and processing electronics required to produce the sound, the firmware (software residing on a chip) that is the source of the sound, a keyboard to control the sound, and, more often than not, the audio system needed to hear the sound. If viewed as separate components of a piano kit, however, a personal computer can take on the role of memory and processing, piano software becomes the sound source, a keyboard (very possibly your digital piano) provides control, and powered monitor speakers and/or headphones let you hear your new invention. If you have a digital piano (or an acoustic piano with hybrid features) and a personal computer (Mac or Windows), you already have most of the ingredients of a software-based piano.

The obvious question: If you already have a digital piano, why would you want to add a software piano? Most digital pianos are capable of producing more than one piano sound, but typically, all of these sounds are based on a single piano as a sample source. Think of it this way: If you could add a Bösendorfer, Blüthner, Fazioli, or Steinway to your palette of piano samples for only the cost of the software, would you do it? (I hear the sounds of pianos and computers being pushed together even now.) How about being able to virtually design your own instrument with piano software based on physical modeling? (See "Digital Piano Basics, Part 1" for more information on physical modeling.)

Adding a software piano to your existing piano, or building your own piano from a "piano kit," is a bit more involved than putting your computer and your piano in the same room—but not by much. Let's take a look at the requirements on both the computer and piano sides. Since the requirements for the piano are pretty simple, we'll start there.

Digital and Hybrid Piano Considerations

If your existing piano is going to serve as the basis for your extended piano family, the minimum requirement is that it have MIDI-out capability—USB MIDI makes it slightly easier, but regular MIDI connections will do as well. The good news here is that all currently available digital pianos and most acoustic hybrid pianos already have, or can add, this capability. The next step is to be able to get your existing "host" piano to stop producing its own sound. For digital pianos, this consists of a brief trip to the owner's manual to learn how to set it up as a

"controller" or "master" keyboard. Acoustic pianos must either be capable of "silent" mode or must be converted to enable it (see "Hybrid Pianos" in this issue).

Computer Considerations

Requirements for the computer vary considerably, depending on the piano software used and the choices you make in software settings. Just as with digital pianos, sample-based software is highly dependent on the size of the computer's memory, while physical modeling software—which creates the sound in real time rather than retrieving an existing sound sample—primarily depends on the speed of the computer's processor. At a minimum, hardware requirements will involve processor type and speed, and the amount of random-access memory (RAM) and hard-disk space. These requirements range from packages that can run on most recent-vintage mid-range computers, to those requiring higher-speed multi-core processors, 8 Gigabytes (GB) of RAM, over 250 GB of free hard-disk space (preferably on a fast SSD drive), and a dedicated sound card. Either way, you need to check the hardware requirements of the individual software package you'd like to run to make sure it will work properly on your computer—or use it as an excuse to get a new computer.

Aside from making sure that you have enough memory to store and run these packages, processor and sound-card choices will also keep latency in check. Latency is how long it takes the computer to produce a sound from the time you press a key. When latency becomes noticeable, your brain doesn't know whether to slow your playing so that the sound can catch up, or to speed up to make the sound happen faster. Neither of these works. (Anyone who plays the pipe organ knows what latency is, and will adapt to it without a second thought.)

Software

This is where the real fun starts. There are currently dozens of software-piano packages available, at prices ranging from under $50 to over $500. These include both sample-based packages and packages based on physical modeling. There are products on the market for Mac, PC, and even mobile-device platforms. Several host acoustic pianos (i.e., the sources of the samples) are available via software, including instruments made by Bechstein, Bösendorfer, Blüthner, Fazioli, Kawai, Steingraeber, Steinway, and Yamaha. If you'd like to add some period instruments to your palette, there are also packages with samples from historical fortepianos.

If you're not particularly into computers, software pianos may not be for you. But if you enjoy even a mild bit of tinkering, and have dreamed of owning a collection of the world's finest pianos or even of "designing" your own piano, you may find software pianos an irresistible temptation. If you're interested in following the world of piano software, it's discussed in Piano World's "Digital Pianos—Synths & Keyboards" forum. 🎹

A confession: Your humble Piano Review Editor has never owned a software piano. It gets worse: Outside of trade-show booths, I've never really tried them, even though I occasionally reread Alden Skinner's *Piano Buyer* article "**My Other Piano is a Computer.**" In the complex hierarchy of the piano universe, I'd always relegated users of software pianos to a tiny niche of self-described tweakheads, gearslutz, and a set of vocal outliers on Internet forums devoted to music and recording. The growing prevalence and diversity of software pianos in the global market, combined with the relative slowness with which hardware-based digital piano makers tend to improve their instruments' core sounds—a predictable cycle of offering the newest, most premium piano sounds in their flagship models, to be trickled down to midrange models a few years later, and to the entry-level stuff a year or two after that—requires *Piano Buyer* to take a more detailed, more frequent look at this growing sector of the piano industry.

Budget, Scope, and Equipment

As I began this journey, I wanted the result to be a little different from the typical articles primarily intended for power users of software pianos. I thought that there must be others out there like me: players bored or dissatisfied with the sounds of their no-longer-new digital pianos, but without the money to invest in a completely new hardware-based digital that would be appreciably better. I limited the budget to products with a list price of $150 or less. Furthermore, I wanted to focus on pianos that weren't resource hogs, but can run acceptably well on a consumer-spec, not-new computer. For this comparison, I used my MacBook Air laptop, mid-2012 revision with 4GB of RAM, a 1.7GHz Intel Core i5 processor, and a 128GB solid-state drive: nothing special nowadays. And, in addition to the all-important aspect of piano sound quality, other significant considerations in this comparison were ease of installation and use.

Besides a computer that meets the minimum specs for running a software piano, you need a digital piano or MIDI controller (I used my last-generation Blüthner PRO-88 digital piano), and a couple of connection cables between the digital piano, computer, and whatever speakers and amplifier you're going to use. From Monoprice (www.monoprice.com), a convenient source for low-cost cabling, I bought a USB Type A to B cable and a 1/8" stereo to dual ¼" mono cable for a total of less than $5 plus shipping. You can delete the speakers, amp, and

the last cable mentioned if you decide to use only headphones—and I ended up spending a good amount of late-night practice time with my trusty, warm-sounding, affordable Grado SR-60 open-back headphones, which are easily driven by a laptop without the need for an external headphone amp. If you want to use your digital piano's own speaker system and amplifier, you need to be sure that the piano has Line In jacks and the ability to set the keyboard in, as Skinner calls it, "controller mode" (something my Blüthner doesn't do); otherwise, you may also be shopping for powered monitor speakers, which tend to offer a significant increase in sound quality over the speakers built into entry-level and midrange digital pianos. Although you can buy "boxed" software pianos, in this age of high-speed Internet access most people select the download option for the software pianos tested.

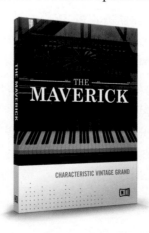

Galaxy Instruments: The Maverick and Vintage D

I began with Galaxy Instruments' fascinating list of virtual piano libraries (www.galaxy-instruments.com) and downloaded two of their nine current software pianos, The Maverick ($99) and the Vintage D ($139). This required also downloading Native Instruments' Native Access installer and Kontakt player interface (both are free), the latter of which operates Galaxy's products. Installation wasn't difficult, but it did require careful reading of the support documentation accompanying each product. Once the initial installation was complete, the Galaxy software pianos can run without an active Internet connection—convenient for users in remote areas. Not counting download time, I had The Maverick up and running in about an hour—the only immediate adjustments were selecting the correct MIDI input from an idiot-proof dropdown menu, and setting the latency (more about that later). The Maverick is a carefully sampled 1905 C. Bechstein grand.

If you've ever complained that digital pianos sound too sterile, unrealistically perfect, and lack personality, The Maverick will transform your experience. It's tempting to get lost in the specs: 2,500 individual samples, 18 velocity layers, etc. I'd rather describe these software pianos in less technical language. The Maverick has the character and quirks of a high-quality antique piano, along with a wide range of color and dynamics, and long sustain. As with a well-worn piano, each note is subtly different from its neighbors in terms of voicing and damping, and each register has its own tonal character, which some may find desirable and authentic. The high treble section has a velvety sound, not the typical "live" duplex-scaling sound of modern acoustic pianos. When pushed, The Maverick will snap back at you with a sharp initial attack, but the subtlety of sounds at mezzo-forte and below is what really got my attention—it was a significant improvement in realism and control over my Blüthner's hardware-based internal sounds. I was able to project and phrase the inner voices in the second of Ravel's charming *Valses Nobles et Sentimentales* as effectively as I could on a fine acoustic grand. There was a whisker too much pedal resonance (strings excited sympathetically) at the default setting, but that—and brightness of tone, dynamic behavior, lid position, and a huge amount of flexibility and options related to reverb—were all easily adjustable with the Kontakt control interface, and could be further adjusted in two submenu panes. Those familiar with high-end, hardware-based digital pianos will recognize these types of adjustments. But simpler entry-level models usually limit the player's ability to modify such parameters, often severely; using a software

The Maverick is based on a carefully sampled 1905 C. Bechstein grand.

piano opens up this world of customization at a fraction of the cost of a digital piano. One really helpful detail in the Kontakt interface is a display mode that describes everything you point to in a satisfying degree of detail, which saved me from hunting through the manual. Dozens of alternative presets are available for The Maverick; e.g., Levitating Maverick, Sparkling Maverick, Maverick on Tape. Any of these can be used as a starting point for endless tweaking of the sound.

With sound as realistic as The Maverick's, running most of the processing through your average laptop is not without drawbacks. At first, dropouts of the audio signal (heard as quiet clicks, or notes that suddenly stop sounding) were common through my older MacBook Air. Nor did this happen only when I was playing thick textures or fast passages. Following the instructions, I tried adjusting the Latency slider in the Options menu, to give the processor a bit more time to work before sending the sound to my headphones, but the problem persisted somewhat. A reboot, along with an increase in what Galaxy calls the instrument preload buffer size, almost completely cured the problem, but I suspect that harnessing the The Maverick's full capabilities takes a little more computing power than I had available. Even so, in terms of experiencing the often indescribable sensations of playing a real acoustic piano, The Maverick may have been my favorite of the six pianos I tested for this review.

I moved on to the Vintage D, a carefully sampled 1920 Hamburg Steinway concert grand. It certainly promised excitement—this piano, housed in a German recording

The Vintage D is based on a carefully sampled 1920 Hamburg Steinway concert grand.

studio, has been used in sessions by Chick Corea, Keith Jarrett, and other famous performers. According to Galaxy, it was sampled using a variety of modern and vacuum-tube microphones and special preamplifiers. Installing this piano involved a couple of extra steps, as the download was in three parts (.rar files), and required downloading free file-extraction software to stitch the three into a single uncompressed file on my computer's hard drive. After authentication—that is, after you've paid and are given a code as proof you're the rightful owner of the software license, which you then enter in the program—you import the library into the Kontakt control interface. Unfortunately, Kontakt wasn't able to locate the sound library on my computer. After an hour of fooling around late on a Friday afternoon, I sent an email to Galaxy's support site to see how quickly—or if—they would respond. I was pleasantly surprised to receive a reply on Sunday morning that explained what I needed to do to get things running.

Vintage D is an extremely tweakable platform. Although it's been around for some years now, and its interface might not look as beautiful as The Maverick's, just a little time spent with Vintage D shows why this software piano has a sizable following. The bass register is alive with believably rich overtones, while the treble tries to emulate the more immediate attack sound of the Hamburg Steinway. (Most pianists feel that the default voicings and tonal philosophies of the Hamburg- and New York–built pianos slightly differ from each other.) Tone controls, an easy-to-use compressor, reverbs, pads (i.e., non-piano sounds that can be combined with the piano sound), and setting presets are all present on the main screen or on a one-click submenu.

Then there's the Anatomy section, which includes adjustments of listening position, pedal behavior, and

tuning options that include historical temperaments (but only one choice for equal temperament, labeled Stretch). It also includes the most adjustable Velocity Curve I've seen, though it's not easy to make minor changes using a laptop's trackpad. (The Velocity Curve defines the correlation of the sound volume with how hard you hit the keys, which controls the perceived touchweight.) Finally, there are settings for various sounds that simulate the sometimes unwanted noises made by real acoustic pianos (and are parts of what our ears associate with realistic piano sound), such as pedal and damper noise and the impact noise of the hammers hitting the strings. Vintage D gives the user the ability to adjust these values infinitely—you're not limited to On and Off. The default Basic Grand sound is very dry, as in a recording studio, and so almost encourages you to immediately start adjusting things.

I'd be remiss if I didn't mention the Warp Machine submenu in the old version of the program's Pad setting (you get both an older and the newest version of Vintage D in the download for the OS X environment)—a psychedelic mixture of all sorts of effects and other goodies that I'm used to hearing from synths and stage pianos. I tried poking the Random Warp button repeatedly, to see what combination of sounds it would come up with, and when I looked up from my computer and piano, an hour had gone by.

VI Labs: American Grand, German Grand, and Italian Grand

VI Labs (www.vilabsaudio.com) offers four software pianos, mostly concert grands. Although VI Labs has recently been best known for their reproductions of the unique and expensive Ravenscroft 275 grand piano, the lower-priced products that met the criteria for this review were their American Grand, German Grand, and Italian Grand, each priced at $149 (or $349 for the bundle, called True Keys). Not counting download time, setup and installation took just under 90 minutes (I work slowly). To their credit, VI Labs offers a helpful installation video for first-time users; I opened that in a separate window, then paused and started the video as needed to complete each step of the installation. You need to establish an account with VI Labs (all the registrations and installers are free), then an account with the iLok license management service (http://ilok.com), then download a package of piano-related files from VI. Also, there's an installer for the VI Labs software, a piece of licensing software from iLok that you need, and finally the UVI Workstation control interface, which hosts and operates the pianos downloaded. Despite the many required downloads, steps, and registrations, as long as I followed

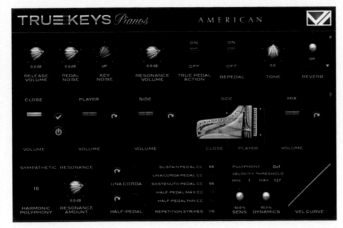

VI's American Grand is based on a New York Steinway model D concert grand.

VI's Italian Grand is based on a Fazioli F308 concert grand.

the installation video exactly, everything worked correctly the first time.

VI's American Grand is based on a New York Steinway model D concert grand, as you can tell pretty much immediately on trying it—the tonal complexity of each note and the big-piano bass are almost instantly recognizable. Though it had the hallmark sound of that brand, the default mode somehow didn't sound right as I played it . . . but that problem was immediately resolved when I hit the Settings button and noticed that all of these VI Labs pianos are able to faithfully reproduce the experience of hearing the instrument close-miked inside the piano (the default setting), or from the player's point of view, or from the audience's perspective, or any combination of those settings. Once I'd clicked the Player or Side (audience) points of view, or loaded my preferred vantage point from the list of presets, it all made a lot more sense to my ears.

As I worked on all eight Ravel waltzes for performance in the upcoming concert season, this piano worked beautifully for the grandiose seventh movement, with its somewhat virtuosic flourishes and occasional tendency to abject romanticism and a fullness of dynamics that remind me of Ravel's later orchestration of the set. (Fans of *La Valse* will hear similarities, too, but these waltzes are, thankfully, far easier to play). I looked away from the screen and was trying to get lost in the sound of the piano when another funny thing happened: I began to listen to The American Grand with my piano-technician ears. I began wondering if the octaves in the low bass were tuned too wide for my taste. I thought the midrange dynamics were a bit too bright too soon, and reflexively looked down at my tuning bag and voicing tool. I started comparing notes in chromatic scales, wondering why two or three were just too dull compared to their neighbors—and noting the rough transition at the bass/tenor break where the hammers could have been better fitted to the strings. These are really nit-picky criticisms of the preparation of the sampled piano—they're also a compliment to the degree of realism this lover of acoustic pianos heard in this software piano.

VI Labs' Italian Grand reminded me why many digital-piano enthusiasts and power users have embraced the growing trend in software pianos: you get to try pianos you couldn't possibly afford and may never get to play. At 10' 2", the Fazioli F308 is the largest current-production grand piano I know of. I've seen maybe three of them in the U.S., and played precisely zero. (The 9' 2" F278 concert grand is much easier to find.) I let it load up, and two seconds after playing, I was chuckling to myself—there was that cutting attack, that immediate, extroverted, in-your-face sound I know from having played Faziolis that had seen a good amount of use—though the bass register wasn't as voluminous as I'd guessed a 10'-long piano might be. The opening chords of the first Ravel waltz require an almost snare-drum–like percussiveness, and the Italian Grand was the perfect tool for the job.

Which brings us to adjustability. All three VI Labs pianos offer adjustments through a unified interface. I would suggest that you immediately change the default polyphony in the Settings pane from the minimum to the medium position, unless you're playing music with very thin textures and will seldom use the damper pedal—in romantic-style playing, you'll notice that limitation pretty quickly. In addition to the aforementioned mike placements and mixes, there are adjustments of reverb, dampers, pedal and key noise, resonance, tone brightness, detailed pedal calibrations (including half-pedal), equalization, and adjustments to the Velocity Curve. This allowed me to take a little edge off the Fazioli attack sound through moderate dynamic levels without significantly affecting the piano's ability to still make that edgy tone at the loudest dynamics.

The third of VI Labs' $149 software pianos is the German Grand, modeled on a modern Bechstein model A228 (7' 5") semiconcert grand. VI's presentation of this piano is a nice middle ground between the overtone-rich, voluminous American Grand and the cleaner, sharper Italian Grand, and the sample sounded as if the original instrument had been a bit newer or, from top to bottom, technically better prepared than the other two. I thought the German Grand's bass had the satisfying presence and richness of a big grand piano without overwhelming the treble, as in some actual concert grands, while the last few notes of the high treble weren't quite as focused as I'd prefer if I were playing the actual acoustic model. I ended up viewing the German Grand as the jack-of-all-trades of the three pianos in VI's True Keys collection—it was a bit milder-mannered than its rowdier American and Italian counterparts.

Because all three VI Labs pianos use the same UVI Workstation control interface and player, they all performed similarly with my older MacBook Air. The most obvious performance-related calibrations that I discovered in the program were hard-drive speed (four options) and cache size (a wide range of adjustment). As with the Galaxy Instruments pianos, I was getting occasional clicking noises and note dropouts. After fooling

VI's German Grand is modeled on a modern Bechstein model A228 semiconcert grand.

around with the hard-drive settings and increasing the default cache size by about 50%, I was able to achieve a result that was more stable but still not as error-free as a hardware-based digital piano—perhaps one little click for every two pages of music. With some additional time spent tweaking settings and/or a slightly more powerful computer, I feel pretty confident that I could get this setup to work well.

Garritan: Abbey Road Studios CFX Lite

Garritan's Abbey Road Studios CFX Lite ($79.95) is a less expensive version of their acclaimed CFX Concert Grand software piano ($199.95, full version), and one that is also less demanding of your computer's resources. The CFX in the product name refers to Yamaha's flagship 9' concert grand, which has become increasingly popular on concert stages and in international competitions. As you can also tell from the name, this particular CFX was recorded at Abbey Road, the same recording facility we associate with important tracks by the Beatles, Pink Floyd, and Howard Shore, to name a few. Installation of CFX Lite required registering a free account, downloading and unpacking the software (a .zip file for the Mac), running an installer program, activating the software with a virtual keycard, and downloading a control interface called the ARIA Player. Garritan has a well-developed support site for their virtual-instrument software, including user manuals, a list of tech-support topics and FAQs, a user forum, and e-mail support. Not counting download time, I was able to complete the installation process carefully in 45 minutes—less time than the others. The disk space used was roughly 25GB, which is a good bit more than the competition in the low-priced segment, but still reasonable in this era of ever-cheaper disk storage.

After I checked a box to indicate which MIDI input it should use, the program functioned correctly with my gear. Right from the start, CFX Lite ran with greater stability on my computer than the other softwares in this comparison, with fewer dropouts, but adjustments in RAM allocation and disk cache size had less effect on further reducing such problems than they did in the other programs. Even if they lacked the comparatively polished look and feel of the VI Labs and Galaxy Instruments user interfaces in the OS X environment, Garritan's user interfaces are pretty intuitive. CFX Lite can be used through either the standalone CFX Lite application or the ARIA Player application (after installation, you end up with both on your computer).

The first adjustment you'll want to make is to the stereo image, which defaults to Audience; the alternative

Garritan's Abbey Road Studios CFX Lite is a less expensive version of their acclaimed CFX Concert Grand software piano.

is Performer. In addition to simulating the sounds from those two positions, the aspect you'll hear most is too-hard separation of the bass and treble in the left and right channels. In Audience mode, low bass notes start moving to the right side of the stereo image—a little unsettling, until I figured out what was going on and switched to Performer mode! The Velocity Curve could be adjusted to a variety of presets, or customized with particular areas boosted or cut—I could get the CFX to behave just the way I wanted. Other adjustments included pedal behavior, resonance, a three-band equalizer, timbre, stereo image width, tuning (pitch and stretch), and ambience/reverb. The reverb control was very much like that on a mixing board, offering a good bit of customization but requiring a little extra time to learn how to use.

Compared to the other pianos in this review, the Abbey Road Studios CFX Lite had a more refined sound at most volume levels, pretty and unassuming. When I pushed the dynamics, the CFX Lite woke up and could make a more imposing and aggressive tone; still, I'd characterize this piano's sound as more of a blank canvas than one with a too-pronounced sonic signature that you'll either love or hate (such as VI's Italian Grand or Galaxy's The Maverick). The CFX Lite makes up for this with a handful of presets that, via effects, push the possibilities of this piano to a very different place and sound from the default settings. Presets like Dreamer, In My Life, Narrow Range, and the hilariously freaky Upside Down do a lot more than just adjust the settings available to the user— they're twisted, remixed, alternative pianos.

The Takeaway

Software pianos are a means of breathing new life into older gear for an affordable price, and they sound better and more realistic than almost every hardware-based digital piano I've played. Forget about comparing them to the sound qualities of entry-level or most midrange models—it's not even close. I spent many hours playing these under-$150 instruments, and had more enjoyment practicing on my used digital piano than I've ever experienced. Each of these software pianos comprises instantly recognizable samples from a very special instrument, with an array of tone qualities and possible adjustments—among them you'll probably find a piano you'll love. All of the manufacturer websites include libraries of recordings that you can listen to before you buy, to hear if the sound samples/models and effects are to your liking.

However, the installation process for each—starting with a lengthy, multi-gigabyte download—is tedious, with many steps. Once you've got your software piano running, you're going to spend time tweaking your computer's settings to find an acceptable balance of stability and performance—and even after hours of such tweaking, computers that meet the piano's minimum published specifications may *still* exhibit dropouts and other problems, possibly necessitating the purchase of a higher-performance computer or upgraded components. By comparison, new hardware-based digital pianos can often be up and running in seconds, without consulting the owner's manual. Lower-cost ones might have shorter sustain or noticeable looping, and more generic sound engines, but they always work as well as they can right out of the box.

This novice found the software-piano experience exciting and, at the same time, slightly frustrating. I liked them well enough that I'd definitely consider buying one—but if I do, that will also mean continuing to spend time configuring the software for better reliability, and/or upgrading my laptop—or waiting for the next versions to be released, hoping for quicker installations, and more trouble-free operation on my present computer.

Dr. Owen Lovell (owen@pianobuyer.com) is *Piano Buyer*'s Piano Review Editor, and Assistant Professor of Music at Georgia College.

HYBRID PIANOS

ALDEN SKINNER AND LARRY FINE

MENTION THE WORD *hybrid* today and most people think of cars that combine a traditional internal-combustion engine with an electric motor to improve gas mileage and reduce emissions. By definition, a hybrid—whether a rose, a breed of dog, or a car—results from the combination of two different backgrounds or technologies. Now the piano has joined the ranks of the hybrids.

A hybrid piano combines electronic, mechanical, and/or acoustical aspects of both acoustic and digital pianos, in order to improve or expand the capabilities of the instrument. While applying the term *hybrid* to piano designs is a recent development, the practice of combining elements from acoustic and digital pianos is more than 25 years old.

A hybrid piano can be created from either an acoustic or a digital piano, but we need to be clear about our definitions of *acoustic* and *digital*. The essential difference between acoustic and digital pianos is in how the sound is produced. In an acoustic piano, a sound is produced by the mechanical act of a hammer hitting strings, causing the strings to vibrate. In a digital piano, the sound is produced electronically, either from previously sampled acoustic pianos, or by physical modeling that employs a mathematical algorithm to produce sounds like those of an acoustic piano. (Here we're speaking only of that aspect of a digital piano that is designed to produce a piano-like sound. Digitals typically also can produce many other instrumental and non-instrumental sounds.)

Acoustic-based Hybrids: the MIDI Controller

On the acoustic side, the original hybrid instruments were not new pianos, but modifications of already existing pianos. In 1982, with the advent of Musical Instrument Digital Interface (MIDI), a computer language for musical instruments, instruments from different makers could "speak" to one another. Soon after, various kinds of mechanical contacts were invented for placement under the keys to sense keystroke information such as note, key velocity, and duration, and convert it into MIDI data. This MIDI information was then routed to synthesizers, which turned the information into whatever instrumental sounds the attached synthesizer was programmed to produce. When one instrument is used to control another in this manner through the transmission of MIDI information, the first instrument is called a MIDI controller. At the beginning, however, the sound of the acoustic piano could not be turned off, though it could be muffled in vertical pianos.

A hybrid results from the combination of two different technologies.

Early mechanical key contacts were subject to breakdown, or infiltration by dust, and their presence could sometimes be felt by sensitive players and interfere with their playing. The more advanced key contacts or sensors used today involve touch films or optical sensors that are more reliable and accurate, and add no significant weight to the touch. In time, also, mechanisms were invented for shutting off the acoustic piano sound entirely, either by blocking the hammers from hitting the strings, or by tripping (escaping) the action train of force earlier than normal, so that the hammers lacked the velocity needed to reach the strings. Headphones would block out any remaining mechanical noise, leaving only the sounds of the electronic instrument.

Not surprisingly, most makers of these MIDI controller/acoustic hybrid systems have been manufacturers of electronic player-piano systems. The same MIDI sensor strip used under the keys of these systems for their Record feature (which allows players to record their own playing for later playback) can also transmit the MIDI information to a digital sound source: either an internal source that comes with the piano (a *sound card*) or an external one, such as a synthesizer or a computer with appropriate software installed. All player-piano systems today allow, through MIDI control, for the accompaniment of the acoustic piano sound by digitally produced sound, be they other piano-like sounds, other instrumental sounds, or even entire orchestras.

In addition to the accompaniment function, it turns out that these hybrid systems in which the acoustic piano can be silenced potentially have another very practical function. If your playing is likely to meet with objections from neighbors or family, being able to silence the piano and then play as loudly as you want, while listening through headphones, can be very handy. Realizing this, the major player-piano manufacturers make the MIDI controller feature available—without the player piano—relatively inexpensively. These MIDI controllers include a MIDI sensor strip under the keys, or optical sensors for keys and hammers, but no hardware and electronics that would make the piano keys move on their own. Usually, these systems come with a "stop rail" or other mechanical device to prevent the hammers from hitting the strings, an internal digital sound source, and headphones. When you move a lever to stop the acoustic piano sound, you turn on the digital sound source, which is heard through the headphones. Yamaha calls this instrument Silent Piano; a version whose digital piano sound is broadcast by the acoustic piano's soundboard is called TransAcoustic. Kawai calls its hybrid-piano series (including one model with a soundboard speaker system) AnyTime. PianoDisc calls its two add-on systems QuietTime and ProRecord; QRS's version is called SilentPNO.

Yamaha's **Silent Pianos** have sensors associated with their keys, hammers, and pedals that record their movements in MIDI format and output the information through a digital-piano sound chip to headphones or speakers, or to a computer for editing. With the addition

Kawai's silent/hybrid pianos are known as **AnyTime** (ATX).

of Yamaha's Silent System, the acoustic piano can be silenced and the instrument used as a digital piano with a real piano action.

Two new Silent Systems are now available. The SG2 system is available in the b1, b2, and b3 vertical models and the GB1K grand. This system offers a CFIIIS concert grand piano voice, nine additional voices, can record and playback MIDI files, and has USB capability to preserve recorded performances. The SH system, used in all other piano models, offers a piano voice that uses binaural sampling of the CFX concert grand, 18 additional voices, can record and play back MIDI and audio files, and has USB capability to preserve recorded performances. SH grand models also incorporate a QuickEscape mechanism that automatically adjusts the action when the Silent System is engaged so that the touch feels the same whether the piano is being played acoustically or in silent mode.

Yamaha now also offers its **TransAcoustic** piano series, with several vertical and grand models. Like the Silent Piano, the TransAcoustic (TA) is an acoustic piano that can also send digitally sampled sounds, including Yamaha's CFX Concert Grand samples, directly to headphones, sound systems, mixers, etc. The TransAcoustic differs from the Silent Piano in having two transducers attached to the piano's soundboard. The transducers convert the digital signal into an electromechanical impulse that sets the soundboard vibrating—literally turning the soundboard into a loudspeaker. The soundboard, strings, and case provide a natural acoustic resonance for the digital samples, which can be played at even the softest volumes without the use of headphones and, when combined with the piano's normal acoustic sound, can produce a more richly textured sound.

Kawai's silent/hybrid pianos, known as **AnyTime** (ATX), are part of its K series of vertical pianos. The K15-ATX2 (44") is a basic model; the more advanced K200-ATX2 (45") and K300-ATX2 (48") use the digital sound engine from Kawai's top-of-the-line CA-95 digital piano, as well as optical key and hammer sensors for the most sensitive control. The K300-AT2X also has a soundboard speaker system, similar in concept to that of Yamaha's TransAcoustic piano.

QuietTime, from PianoDisc, can mute an acoustic piano and let the user hear his or her performance through headphones via sampled sound. The **QuietTime MagicStar V5 S Series**, introduced in 2013, has a slimline control unit that includes a touchscreen and iDevice compatibility. It also supports all three pedals, has a port for a USB stick, and comes with 80 demo songs. The control-unit sound module contains 128 sampled instruments, including a full General MIDI (GM) sound set, as well as 11 popular instrument presets, such as piano with strings. It also includes a built-in, adjustable metronome. A MIDI key-sensor strip is installed under the keys, and a padded mute rail prevents the hammers from hitting the strings while retaining the motion and feel of the piano action. The mute rail is activated by moving a small lever under the keyboard, which also turns on the sampled sound. MagicStar comes with a control unit, power supply, MIDI cable, MIDI strip, pedal switches, headphones, and mute rail. When the piano is to be used as a MIDI controller only (i.e., with no sound module or with a separate sound module), the MIDI key-sensor strip can be purchased from PianoDisc separately as ProScan, with or without the mute rail and headphones.

In late 2013, PianoDisc introduced another product in the QuietTime family: **ProRecord**. ProRecord uses fully optical, no-contact, high-speed key and pedal sensors to capture and record key and pedal movements. The system's sensitivity can be calibrated to a very fine level, allowing it to be customized to a particular piano action or player so that, for example, trills can be accurately reproduced when playing near the bottom or top of the key, even on a vertical piano. ProRecord comes with a tone generator with a GM2 128 + 100 instrument sound set and nine drum kits, including sympathetic string and damper resonance. The system is compatible with both Apple and Android smartphones, tablets, and apps, and with the PianoDisc iQ player-piano system. Like MagicStar, ProRecord comes with headphones, and a mute rail for muting the acoustic piano.

SilentPNO, from QRS, consists of the PNOscan record strip, a PNOmation II sound module, Wi-Fi adapter, and a stop rail for muting the acoustic piano. By muting the piano and turning on the soundcard, the pianist can play in privacy with headphones and enjoy the automatic recording features of PNOcloud and PNOmation, described in the article, "**Buying an Electronic Player-Piano System.**"

But the accompaniment and "silent" functions of a hybrid MIDI controller/acoustic piano are only the beginning of what it can do. Just as the MIDI signal can be sent to a synthesizer or sound card, it can also be sent to a personal computer or transmitted over the Internet. Regardless of whether a MIDI controller originates in an acoustic or a digital piano, it enables the instrument to interact with music software to record, produce notation, control instrumental voices on a personal computer, or interact with other pianos in the same room or on different continents. The potential for hybrids in creating and teaching music is limited only by the imagination of the user. Notation softwares—from MakeMusic's Finale, Avid's Sibelius, GenieSoft's Overture, and others—allow the hybrid piano's key input (playing) to be converted to music notation. This notation can be edited, transposed, split into parts for different instruments, played back, and printed out. The possibilities for teaching are perhaps even more powerful. Taking a lesson from a teacher in a different state or a master class from a performer in a different country becomes possible with hybrid technology, particularly when combined with the player-piano features. Exacting copies of performances can be sent to similarly equipped instruments for playback, and critiques—with musical examples—can be sent back to the student. Some systems enable this interaction in real time over broadband connections, complete with synchronized video.

As we've said, most of the activity in the field of acoustic hybrids has been among player-piano makers, whose offerings have been either specialized (Silent Piano) or add-ons (QuietTime, SilentPNO). However, MIDI capabilities are now standard in all acoustic pianos, vertical and grand, made by Story & Clark, a subsidiary of QRS, the only piano maker so far to have done this. If you add a stop rail to silence the piano (available from QRS) and a sound source, you could turn one of these instruments into a "silent" type of hybrid like those described above. But even without those additions, a Story & Clark piano can be used with a personal computer and music software for recording,

All Story & Clark pianos come with a factory-installed PNOscan MIDI strip beneath the keys.

notation, controlling computer-produced instrumental voices, or any of the myriad other uses possible with a MIDI controller.

Digital-based Hybrids: Replicating the Acoustic Experience

Now, you may wonder: If you're just going to use a piano to interact with a computer, play piano sounds silently, or make other instrumental sounds, why bother with an acoustic piano at all? Why not just use a digital piano or keyboard of some kind? The reason is: the *experience*. Digital pianos are long on functionality but short on, shall we say, atmosphere. For those used to the looks, touch, tone, or other, less tangible aspects of acoustic pianos, digital pianos, in their "pure" form, just don't cut it—so digital piano makers have spent a great deal of time, energy, and money trying to mimic one or more of these aspects of acoustic pianos. The closer they get to duplicating the experience of playing an acoustic piano, the more they earn the right to the *hybrid* designation—because, when you get down to it, the function of an acoustic piano *is* the experience.

The first aspect of an acoustic piano that digital piano makers mimicked was, of course, the looks, and a large segment of the digital piano market consists of acoustic piano look-alikes. But that alone isn't enough to earn the title *hybrid*. Next, the mechanism of the acoustic piano found its way into the digital piano. Much engineering has gone into the numerous action designs in digitals, always in the attempt to make their feel and response as close as possible to that of a "real" piano. For example, Yamaha's GranTouch line of digital pianos uses a slightly modified acoustic piano action to trigger the piano's sensors (the hammers are small and don't actually strike strings). With such an action, there's no need to simulate certain action processes, such as escapement, because it actually occurs mechanically. Many digital piano actions these days have weighted and/or wooden keys, and other enhancements that do a reasonable job of emulating an acoustic piano action; still, advanced pianists, especially classical ones, are unlikely to be satisfied by most of them.

Of course, digital piano makers have put more effort into copying the tone of the acoustic piano than any other aspect. How they've done this is beyond the scope of this article (see "Digital Piano Basics" for this information), but one interesting attempt is that of adding a soundboard to the digital. The Kawai CA-91, introduced in 2006, with its Soundboard Speaker System; and the Yamaha CGP-1000 Clavinova in 2007, with its Hybrid Active Soundboard System, both use an actual piano soundboard, set in motion by transducers, to augment the conventional speakers and impart a more natural tone to the instrument.

The latest entry in the hybrid arena is also the first instrument to be formally named a Hybrid Piano. Yamaha unveiled its Avant-Grand series in 2009. The Avant-Grand elevates the digital piano to a new level with a number of hybrid technologies, first of which is a real piano action. As mentioned above, this eliminates any discussion of whether or not it *feels* like an acoustic piano action—it *is* one. (However, whether or not the action feels *right* is still a legitimate topic of discussion.) This action controls the digital voices through the use of optical sensors, which measure the velocity of the keys and hammers without physically contacting any part of the action.

All three AvantGrand models have grand-piano actions, but whereas model N3 is also shaped like a grand, the cabinets of the lower-cost N1 and N2 are closer to that of a vertical piano (which brings up the interesting observation that the decision of whether to call a digital piano a "grand" or a "vertical" is not a simple one). In 2012, Yamaha introduced the model NU1 Hybrid Piano, the first digital piano with a real vertical-piano action.

One aspect of the traditional acoustic-vs.-digital argument that changes with the addition of a real action is the digital's advantage of rarely needing maintenance. While the AvantGrand and NU1 models will never need to be tuned, eventually their actions will require some degree of adjustment or regulation. (We'll bet the piano technician will be surprised when, on arriving to regulate an action, he or she finds the "piano" is a digital.)

But there's more to the feel of an acoustic piano than its action, and this brings us to the last attribute of acoustic pianos that designers of digitals have attempted to copy: the intangibles. With the AvantGrand, one "intangible"—the vibrations generated by the strings and transmitted throughout the instrument—has been made tangible. Yamaha has added this ingredient to the N2 and N3 by connecting transducers to the action to send the appropriate frequency

> **Many digital piano actions these days have weighted and/or wooden keys, and other enhancements that do a reasonable job of emulating an acoustic piano action.**

and degree of vibration to the player's fingers. This is where the experience of playing becomes a bit . . . spooky. Not unlike an amusement-park ride that convinces your brain that you're dodging asteroids while hurtling through space when you are, in fact, fairly stationary, the AvantGrand's Tactile Response System quickly convinces you that you're feeling the vibrations of nonexistent strings.

The illusions don't stop there. When you depress a digital piano's sustain pedal, you're pressing a spring with constant tension. This is not how the sustain pedal feels on most acoustic pianos, in which the initial movement meets little resistance as the pedal takes up a bit of slack in the mechanism that lifts the dampers. Once the mechanism begins to lift the dampers, the resistance increases. Here again, the AvantGrand does a convincing job of conveying the feel and, perhaps more important, the degree of control available with an acoustic's sustain pedal, including half-pedaling and incremental control. The N3's four-channel sample set and 12-speaker audio system are also convincing, easily tricking the ears into thinking that considerably more than four feet of piano are in front of you. The AvantGrand and NU1 models all use samples from Yamaha concert grands for their sounds.

One area in which digital pianos are not intended to emulate acoustics is that of price. The Hybrid Pianos, with the sound and, in some cases, perhaps the experience, of a Yamaha concert grand, are priced similarly to some of the company's least expensive acoustic grands and verticals. Actually, such comparisons are barely possible—the acoustics lack many of the digitals' features, such as onboard recording, USB memory, transposition, and alternate tunings.

Which Side Are You On?

As the market for hybrid pianos heats up, buyers will increasingly have to choose between acoustic pianos with digital enhancements and digital pianos that try to create the acoustic experience. Decisions will be made by weighing the relative quality, and importance to the buyer, of action, tone, looks, price, and features. More advanced classical pianists whose digital needs are modest, and buyers who, among other things, are looking to fill up a living room with a large, impressive piece of furniture, will probably tend to stick with the acoustic-based hybrid for now. Those whose musical needs are more general, or who have a strong interest in digital features, may find digital-based hybrids more cost-effective.

Another factor that may come into play is that of life expectancy. A good acoustic piano will typically function well for 40 or 50 years, if not longer. Few digital pianos made 15 to 20 years ago are still in use, due either to technological obsolescence or to wear. True, the relevant technologies have evolved, as has the design of digital pianos and the quality of their construction. Realistically, however, if past experience is any guide, pianos that are largely acoustic with digital enhancement may well last for many decades, while those that are digitals enhanced with acoustic-like features are unlikely to last as long.

The piano has evolved a great deal since Bartolomeo Cristofori invented it in 1700, and that evolution continues. Today it is possible to buy a piano with an ABS-Carbon action (Kawai), a carbon-fiber soundboard (Steingraeber Phoenix), or one that looks as if it was made for the Starship *Enterprise*! The hybrid piano's blending of acoustic and digital technologies is just another step—or branch—in that evolution.

Yamaha AvantGrand model N3

SOME OF YOU may have fond memories of gathering around Grandma's old upright player piano and pumping those huge pedals to make it play—until you could hardly walk! As with so many other devices, technology has revolutionized the player piano, replacing the pneumatic pressure and rolls of punched paper with electronics, smartphones, iPads, and MP3 files. Today, nearly one out of every four new grand pianos is sold with an electronic player-piano system installed.

The capabilities of these systems range from those that simply play the piano (often all that's desired for home use) all the way to those that allow composers to create, play, and print entire orchestral scores without ever leaving the piano bench. You can even watch a video of Billy Joel in concert on a screen built into your piano's music rack, or on your tablet or notebook, while, simultaneously, his performance, with orchestra, is faithfully reproduced on your own piano, "live" in your living room! The features and technological capabilities are already vast and are still evolving.

Before you begin to wade through the possibilities, you should carefully consider your long-term needs. Since many of the features of the more sophisticated systems are related to recording one's performance and composing, you should first decide whether or not you want the ability to record what you or others play on your piano, or to use the piano for music notation. In many typical family situations, the piano, just like Grandma's, is primarily used for children's lessons and for entertainment. If that's the case, one of the more basic systems, without recording capabilities, will likely be satisfactory. Most systems can be upgraded to add recording and other, more advanced features, should you later want to add those. However, as technologies advance, it may become increasingly difficult to upgrade your older system.

Some player systems can be added (retrofitted) to any new or used piano; others are available only on a specific make of piano. When installed in a new piano, some systems must be installed by the piano's manufacturer, while others can be installed by the dealer or at an intermediate distribution point. A factory-certified local installer of a retrofit can usually match the quality of a factory installation. Installation is somewhat messy and must be done in a shop, not in your home; but when done correctly, it won't harm the piano or void its warranty.

The player systems currently on the market can be described as falling into two categories: those that are used mostly in situations requiring only low- to medium-quality playback reproduction, and those whose playback and/or recording functions are of audiophile quality and are intended for the most discriminating or high-level professional users. The first category includes systems by PianoDisc, Pianoforce, QRS, and most Yamaha Disklaviers. When used as playback-only systems, these are suitable for home entertainment, and for commercial use in restaurants, hotels, assisted-living facilities, etc. When outfitted with recording capabilities and/or with a "silent" feature that mutes the acoustic piano's sound, they become more useful for students, and for lighter professional use for music notation or as a MIDI controller. The audiophile category includes the Bösendorfer CEUS, Steinway Spirio, and Disklavier Pro models. However, this classification scheme

The underside of a grand piano with solenoid rail (uncovered), power supply, and speaker installed.

QRS Music Technologies, Inc.

ELECTRONIC PLAYER SYSTEMS

HOW DO THESE THINGS MAKE THE PIANO PLAY?

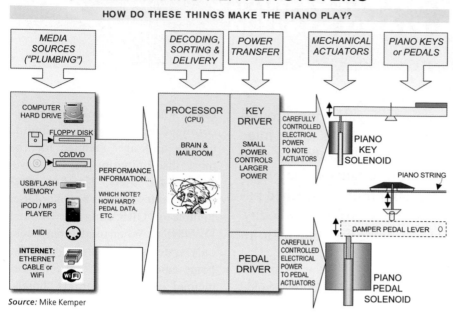

Source: Mike Kemper

doesn't entirely do justice to home entertainment systems, which can be more sophisticated in other respects, such as versatility and functionality, than some audiophile systems.

The quality of a piano performance, either by a sophisticated electromechanical reproducing system or by a human being, greatly depends on the overall quality and condition of the instrument being played. Thus, an out-of-tune and/or ill-voiced piano with a poorly regulated action would result in an unpleasant listening experience, whether played by human or machine. This, of course, emphasizes the importance of regular and proper maintenance of the instrument. When buying a piano, the performance quality of the player-piano system will be limited, to a large extent, by the performance quality of the piano itself. Don't scrimp on the piano, just to be able to afford a player system for it.

How a Typical Electronic Player-Piano System Works

Basic player systems consist of:

- a solenoid (electromechanical actuator) rail installed in a slot cut in the piano keybed (a shelf-like part of the piano that supports the keys and action)
- a processor unit and other electronics mounted out of sight under the piano
- Some models use a control box that plays MP3s, DVDs, and/or CDs (depending on the model), and is either mounted under the keybed at the front of the piano, or sits on or near the piano. In some models, the control box contains no disc drives and is hidden away under the piano, depending instead on your own CD player, MP3 player, or other device for the musical input. A remote-control device for operating the control box from a distance is also generally included with these units.
- In place of a control box, most newer models now use as the system's remote control an iPad or other tablet, or a smartphone, linked to a WiFi station such as Apple's Airport Express mounted

out of sight under a grand piano or inside an upright. A number of apps are available for operating and calibrating the system.

- One or more amplified speakers are installed out of sight under the grand piano or inside the upright models—unless you choose a system configuration that uses your own speaker system.

On the solenoid rail, there is one solenoid for each key. There is also a solenoid for the damper pedal and, sometimes, one for the una corda (soft) pedal. Each solenoid contains a mechanical plunger that, when activated by an electronic signal, pushes against a key or against the pedal trapwork, causing the appropriate keys and pedals to move up and down. When playing, one track contains the datastream that controls the piano solenoids; the other track provides an instrumental and/or vocal accompaniment that plays through a stereo system or through amplified speakers that come with the player system. The accompaniment may be in the form of synthesized or sampled sounds, or actual recordings of live musicians. A wide selection of piano solos is also available.

For recording, keystroke and pedaling information are recorded in MIDI format by a sensor strip installed beneath the keys and sensors attached to the pedals. Some systems also record hammer motions. This information can be stored for later playback on the same piano, stored on other media, sent to other MIDI-compatible devices, or imported into a computer.

The same sensors used for recording can turn the piano into a MIDI controller. Add headphones, a device for mechanically silencing the acoustic piano, and a sound card or other tone generator, and you essentially have a hybrid acoustic/digital piano you can play late

Treasure it. Play it.
Stand in awe of it.
ENTERTAIN WITH IT.

SPIRIO

Presenting the first high-resolution *player piano* worthy of the revered STEINWAY & SONS name. SPIRIO is a masterpiece of artistry, craftsmanship, and engineering that delivers all the nuance and passion of live performances by today's most renowned musicians from classical to jazz to rock.

WWW.STEINWAY.COM/SPIRIO

STEINWAY & SONS

ONE STEINWAY PLACE, ASTORIA, NY 11105 TEL. 718.721.2600 STEINWAY.COM

at night without disturbing anyone. Because this feature can be used independently of the player piano, most manufacturers of these systems make it available separately under such names as Silent Piano (Yamaha), QuietTime or ProRecord (PianoDisc), and SilentPNO (QRS). Of course, the MIDI controller can also be used with or without a tone generator to send a MIDI datastream to a computer for use with composing and editing software, among other applications. (For more information, see the article "**Hybrid Pianos**" elsewhere in this issue.)

Common Features

Basic player-piano systems share a number of features:

- live playback of piano music with a good reproduction of the artist's performance. The keys, and in some systems the pedals, actually move up and down.
- playback of piano music with a full band, orchestral, and/or vocal accompaniment (yes, it will sing!)
- a repertoire of thousands of songs and the ability to download music from the Internet
- connectivity to home audio or home-theater systems
- remote control

Other capabilities, in a variety of applications, are considered valuable tools for composers, educators, and students, as well as performers. They include:

- a system of sensing key and pedal motions that can capture and record the nuances of a live performance for later playback or editing
- playing every instrument of the orchestra (and then some!), using the piano keyboard coupled with an onboard and/or outboard sound module

- the ability to import and export performances through a variety of wired and wireless connections, including MP3s, iPads, the Internet, etc.
- synchronizing a solo-piano performance on your piano with a commercially available CD or DVD of a famous performing artist
- Internet radio that streams data specifically formatted for the player system, for a virtually unlimited supply of musical input
- connectivity to most computers, facilitating music editing, enhancing, and printing
- connecting to teachers and other players anywhere in the world via the Internet

In addition to bundling some amount of music software with the purchase of their systems, most manufacturers record and separately sell software for their systems as MP3 downloads from a website, or as CDs or DVDs. A significant caveat is that one manufacturer's software may, by design, not work unconditionally with another manufacturer's hardware.

Questions to Consider

To list and compare the wide variety of features and capabilities offered by each of the many player systems would be beyond the scope of this article. However, the most significant concerns, aside from price, are the following. Ask your dealer or installer about the ones that interest or concern you.

- *Installation:* Can the system be installed in (retrofitted to) any piano, or is it exclusive to a particular brand of piano? If exclusive, this will limit your options as to what brand of piano to buy.
- *Music Source:* Do you have a preference of source of music for

the system: smartphones, Internet downloads, iPads and other tablets, MP3s, CDs, etc.? This will influence your choice of system brand and configuration.

- *Recording:* Do you need recording capability, or the ability to use the system as a MIDI controller? The addition of an acoustic-piano silencing mechanism will allow you to play silently with headphones, or to connect to a computer to edit and transcribe music, among other benefits.
- *Playing Softly:* How well does the system play softly without skipping notes and without excessive mechanical noise? This is especially important if you plan to use the player piano for soft background music. If so, be sure to try out the system at a low volume level to be sure it meets your expectations.
- *Music Software:* How well does the available music software satisfy your needs?
- *Equipment:* Do you need a system with a CD player and/or iPad included, or will you be supplying your own? Do you need speakers or a video monitor, or will you be connecting the system to your own stereo system or home theater?
- *Software Compatibility:* Can it play the music libraries of other manufacturers' systems? It's important to note, however, that because competitors sometimes change their formats and encryption, the ability to play the data format of a particular competitor's software may not be guaranteed.
- *Dynamic Resolution:* How many gradations of volume can the system record and play back? Most systems record and play back in 127 increments, which is more than sufficient for most uses. Some pre-recorded CDs play back with as few as 16 levels

of expression—still probably enough for casual use, but you should test out the type of music you expect to listen to, to hear if it meets your musical expectations for dynamic resolution. A few systems can handle 1,000 or more increments. This may be desirable for high-level professional or recording applications, or for the most authentic playback of complex classical compositions. Likewise, some systems have higher processor speeds that scan the system a greater number of times per second for higher resolution. Some record by sensing only key movements, while others, for greater accuracy, also sense hammershank movements. It's important to note that some systems that are theoretically capable of playing back with high resolution nonetheless come with music that has been pre-recorded at lower resolution. Music can never be played back at a level of sound quality higher than that at which it was recorded.

- **Pedals:** Which pedals are played by hardware (solenoids) and which, if any, are mimicked by software? Hardware provides a more authentic piano performance, but duplication of pedal functions by software is simpler. Most important is hardware support for the sustain (damper) pedal, and all systems currently provide that. Only a few also provide hardware for the soft pedal (less important), and fewer still for the sostenuto (middle) pedal (unimportant).
- **Damper Pedal Performance:** Does the system record multiple damper-pedal positions, allowing for pedaling techniques such as "half-pedaling," or does it simply record an "on" or "off" position? As with dynamic resolution, the

recording and playback of multiple pedal positions is desirable for an authentic performance experience. The on/off mode is sufficient for casual or simple uses.

- **Pedal Functionality:** Some add-on (retrofit) systems, when installed, may alter the functionality or feel of the pedals, especially the middle pedal. If possible, try playing a piano on which a similar player system is installed to see if the pedal operation is okay for you. If only the middle pedal is affected, it might not matter to you, because this pedal is rarely used
- **Options:** What special features, advantages, and benefits are included or are optionally available? Examples include the ability to synchronize the piano with commercially available MP3s, CDs, and DVDs, features used for teaching purposes, a built-in video monitor, subscriptions to Internet music libraries or streaming radio that make available virtually unlimited input to your piano, bundled music software, and so forth.
- **Upgradability:** To what extent is the system upgradable? Most systems are highly upgradable, but the upgradability of some entry-level systems may be limited.

How Much Player-Piano Systems Cost

The costs of electronic player-piano systems vary enormously, not only from one system to the next, but even for the same system, depending on where it is installed and other factors.

A dealer has several ways of acquiring an add-on (retrofit) player system, which can affect the price at which the system is sold. Factory-installed systems—installed while the piano itself is being manufactured—are the least expensive for the dealer

to acquire. Several large piano manufacturers are authorized to do this. In addition, the companies that make the player systems may factory-install them in brands that they own; for example, QRS PNOmation in Story & Clark pianos, and Piano-Disc in Mason & Hamlin instruments. When installed this way, the difference in price between the piano alone and the piano plus player system may be moderate. The next more expensive options are when the player system is installed at an intermediate distribution point before reaching the dealer, or when a larger dealer, in his or her own shop, installs a system in a piano already on the showroom floor—with most brands of piano, either of these can be done. These installations require more labor that those done while the piano is being manufactured. More expensive yet is when the smaller dealer must hire a local independent installer to install a system in a piano that is on the dealer's showroom floor. The most expensive option is to have a system installed in a piano you already own. In that situation, you also incur the expense of having the piano moved to and from the installer's shop.

The cost can also vary because player systems are often used by dealers as an incentive to buy the piano. The dealer will charge well for an expensive piano, then "throw in" the player system at his or her cost. Or vice versa—the dealer lets the piano go cheaply, then makes it up by charging list price for the system. The more modular systems can also vary in price, according to which options and accessories the dealer includes.

For all these reasons, quoting prices for player systems without knowing the context in which they're installed and sold is difficult. Nevertheless, as a rule of thumb, one of the more popular, typically configured, factory-installed QRS or PianoDisc systems with playback and accompaniment might add $5,500 to $7,000 to the piano's street price, with recording capability adding another $1,500 or so. However, for the reasons given above, prices 20% lower or higher aren't unusual.

As for systems available only as factory installations, Yamaha Disklavier grands generally cost $10,000 to $15,000 (street price) more than the same Yamaha model without the player system. At the time of this writing, the Steinway Spirio is about $15,000 more expensive than the Steinway piano alone. At the high end, a Bösendorfer CEUS will set you back $65,000 to $75,000 (street price). The retail prices of these systems are included under their companies' listings in the "Model & Pricing Guide."

Mike Kemper, a Los Angeles-based piano technician and expert on electronic player-piano systems, contributed to the original version of this article. *Piano Buyer*'s Contributing Editor **Steve Cohen** contributed to this article's most recent revision.

THE SYSTEMS

BÖSENDORFER CEUS

See Bösendorfer in Acoustic Piano Brand & Company Profiles

PIANODISC

PianoDisc
4111 North Freeway Blvd.
Sacramento, California 95834
916-567-9999
www.pianodisc.com

PianoDisc makes retrofit player-piano and performance-capturing systems, including a newly released optical recording system, that can be added to virtually any acoustic piano—grand or vertical, new or used—and even some digital pianos. Pianos fitted with PianoDisc

systems maintain full functionality of all pedals, and playback (and optional record) of all 88 notes. Piano manufacturers offer factory-installed PianoDisc products, and piano dealers in over 60 countries have installations done at their locations by trained and certified Piano-Disc technicians.

PianoDisc's principal player-piano system is called **iQ**. The core technology of the iQ system, hidden within the piano body, can play back PianoDisc music using, as a source, almost any media player. The most popular configuration is the iQ iPad Air bundled with an Apple iPad and Airport Express for wireless control. With iQ, customers can operate all functions of the system from a single, familiar source that also allows them to take advantage of hundreds of apps (offered through Apple's App Store and Google Play) for additional enhancement and enjoyment. Unique within the industry, iQ features a patented method of detecting adjustments made in the volume of the music player to automatically match the piano's volume to it. Each PianoDisc system includes a free package of music and video software valued at $1,400, and a set of five CDs of the customer's choice from the PianoDisc catalog.

PianoDisc's high-resolution solenoid system, **SilentDrive HD**, is standard equipment on all current PianoDisc player systems. Each key's solenoid recognizes 1,024 levels of expression. SilentDrive HD offers quiet playback of original piano performances, and features a faster processor and streamlined architecture that improve timing, velocity, and dynamics. The ProPedal proportional pedal feature, introduced in 2013, is a low-profile, invisible pedal-drive system that uses the piano's original pedal trapwork without any modification of the piano's profile or operation.

Beginning in the second quarter of 2014, PianoDisc customers will be able to use the latest Android technologies, in addition to Apple and other smart devices, to stream audio music and videos directly from PianoDisc's vast library to their pianos, using a custom PianoDisc app or a media player such as Avia or DoubleTwist. In addition, customers will be able to purchase and play digitally delivered content directly from a smart device in a simple one-step process. With Android integration, customers can also project the synchronized videos using Google's Chromecast.

PianoDisc's live, free, streaming piano radio network, available 24/7 to all iQ-based systems, can play a customer's piano directly. Piano-Disc expects to soon add more stations with a greater variety of music programming. This service should be of special interest to hotels, restaurants, and other businesses that use PianoDisc to provide their customers with nonstop, royalty-free entertainment.

The **PianoDisc Remote** app is a utility for the iQ system with many custom features. Although piano and audio balance can be adjusted with the iQ Audio Balance Control, PianoDisc Remote lets users further customize the volume levels and balance of the piano and audio accompaniment, and to fine-tune their synchronization. Revamped with new features for 2014, this app is now available at a lower price ($24.99) through the Apple App Store.

iQ Flash, an entry-level system, is another addition to the Piano-Disc line. Basic operation is accomplished by playing PianoDisc MP3 or MIDI files from USB, SD, or MMC flash memory. All functions can be accessed either from the included remote control or via a few multifunction buttons on the face of the iQ Flash control box. Audio and piano balance controls are easily adjusted with the wheel next to the SD slot. An easy-to-read, high-contrast, backlit LCD display allows the user to view and make song selections, and to use the Repeat and Shuffle features. Incorporating the Studio Performance package into iQ Flash allows players to capture performances as MP3 files on their preferred media-storage devices. With an additional mixer and a powered microphone, vocals can be added to the recording.

For use with its systems, PianoDisc maintains a growing library of thousands of music titles available as digital downloads, CDs, DVDs, and high-definition Blu-ray discs. The library includes solo-piano performances by famous artists, piano with instrumental accompaniment (most of these are live recordings), and vocals in 28 different categories. PianoDisc has recently introduced over a dozen famous Chinese albums, including folk, popular, traditional, and classical Chinese music.

PIANOFORCE

Pianoforce Inc., U.S.A.
115 South Ohio
Sedalia, Missouri 65301
877-542-8807
sales@pianoforce.us
www.pianoforce.com

Pianoforce is a relatively new entrant in the player-piano market under its own name, but the company that makes it—formerly Ncode Ltd., now Pianoforce EU, of Bratislava, Slovakia—has been developing and manufacturing front-end controllers for the player-piano systems of other companies, such as Baldwin and QRS, since 1995. In 2005, Pianoforce was first offered as a complete system in the pianos of selected piano makers. In 2006, it was introduced as a kit retrofittable to any piano, new or old. Designed and built by Pianoforce in Europe,

iQ Flash, an entry-level system, is the latest addition to the PianoDisc line.

the kit is ordered through a piano dealer, and is typically installed in a new piano at a distribution point or at the dealer location.

Pianoforce says that its system differs from those of its competitors in that the main rail component also contains all the controlling electronics, eliminating the need for a lot of complicated wiring and making for a neater, simpler installation. Also, a technician using the remote handset can customize the system to the piano and to the customer's preferences through the adjustment of many playing parameters, such as solenoid force, note release, and pedal release. These custom settings can then be saved in the controller. With the help of a small sensor mounted on the soundboard, the system automatically calibrates itself to the piano's sound. The combination of automatic calibration and manual setup ensures the best playback performance for each individual piano.

In 2007 Pianoforce introduced its latest controller, the Performance. Expanding on the company's past experience in supplying control components for other manufacturers, the new controller contains some of the newest, most advanced features available in a player piano, such as the ability to read the softwares of other systems—including Yamaha Disklavier, QRS (except SyncAlong), and Web Only Piano—plus standard MIDI files; and onboard connections to the Internet via an Ethernet or wireless

hookup. There are three USB ports for greater versatility, such as plugging in flash drives or an external hard drive. There is an optical digital stereo output and a dedicated subwoofer output line. The system can now be controlled remotely, via WiFi, with the user's Android or Apple device, and Internet streaming radio is available 24/7 with piano accompanied by original audio tracks.

More recently, Pianoforce has introduced the Stealth Performer controller, which allows the controller to be hidden away, out of sight. With WiFi remote control, all of the functionality of the original Performance controller is available, but no hardware is visible on the front of the piano.

The system comes with 2GB of internal memory (expandable to 8GB), preloaded with approximately 20 hours of piano music.

KEESCAN, an optional recording feature, uses optical sensors to record key and sustain-pedal movements. Also available is the AMI box, which facilitates connection of a microphone, iPod, and other USB devices. In addition to the system's ability to play other makers' softwares, Pianoforce is building its own library of CDs.

SilentPlay, Pianoforce's newest feature, combines KEESCAN, the new SP1 sound module, and a special muting rail to permit silent play of the customer's vertical piano, while giving the performer unparalleled digital sound through headphones or speakers. Connection to a computer gives a composer complete control over his or her compositions, from editing individual notes to saving new music for later replay.

Pianoforce has offices in Europe (Pianoforce Europe) and the U.S. (Pianoforce Inc., U.S.A.); branches in Austria, Germany, Portugal, Spain, Switzerland, and the U.K.; and is represented in Australia, China, Hong Kong, and Macao.

QRS PNOmation

QRS Music Technologies, Inc.
269 Quaker Drive
Seneca, Pennsylvania 16346
800-247-6557
www.qrsmusic.com

PNOmation, and the new PNOmation Studio, are electronic player-piano reproducing systems that can be installed in virtually any piano, grand or vertical, new or used. Most manufacturers endorse the PNOmation system, and will install it, at a dealer's request, at one of their manufacturing or distribution points. Standard installation is also available at a dealer location by a QRS-trained and -certified technician. QRS also installs the system in many major brands of piano at its own U.S. factory. The factory installation conceals unnecessary wires, electronics, and the solenoid rail cover, for a more pleasing appearance, and the operation and feel of the piano's original pedal trapwork are retained.

Traditionally, electronic player pianos have been defined by the type of control box at the front of the piano, or by the controller's capabilities. PNOmation differs in integrating the core features of every controller, including the music, into the PNOmation engine, thereby eliminating confusing options as well as the need to have a box hanging under the piano or on the lyre. Instead of offering a modular approach to the equipment required for various features, PNOmation offers all features standard, and a modular approach to their use. For example, the user can log in to the PNOmation system through any web-enabled device, pull up the system's embedded web-app user interface, and begin to play the piano. For those more comfortable with inserting their music selections into the device, music can be delivered via a USB thumb drive; then you need only push Play on the system's remote control, or the Play button on the unit itself.

When PNOmation is integrated with the PNOscan optical sensor strip—a leading technology for recording performances on an acoustic piano—and a keystop rail to prevent the piano's hammers from striking the strings, the piano becomes a PNOmation Studio. The PNOscan strip doesn't touch the keys—it uses only reflected light to continuously measure key and pedal movements. By integrating PNOscan with PNOmation in a one-time setup operation, one need only play the piano and the piece is recorded—no login, no need to push Record or Stop. Just pull up a bench and play, and your performance is saved both locally (named according to your preset preferences) and uploaded to your personal QRS PNOcloud account. The file can also be sent to your favorite editing program or e-mailed to a friend—all without boxes or wires. Purchase of PNOscan also entitles the buyer to one year's worth of free piano lessons from the online piano-teaching software Piano Marvel.

Key to PNOmation's flexibility is the fact that it is simultaneously delivered in both a standalone-network mode, with its own network serving its own user interface, and in a network mode in which PNOmation is a client on your home network. One advantage of this arrangement is that if your home network is down, the PNOmation features can still be accessed. Other advantages include ease of setup, network updates, cloud account links, learning, archiving, and video streams.

As a client on a home network, a PNOmation-equipped piano can be controlled by accessing the web-app user interface via iPhone, iPad, iTouch, Android, Mac, Google Chrome browser, Kindle Fire, or any other similar piece of technology, as well as via the more unique Apple Watch and Amazon Echo. The web app gives the user full control of all parameters of the system and how music is played, so there is rarely a reason to call in a technician to make adjustments. Some customers are concerned only with whether a song is a solo performance or a performance with background music, which they can determine from the web-app screen. Other customers may want to manipulate a MIDI file to change the tempo or tuning, and some may want to upload a recorded performance to view or change. None of this is possible with an off-the-shelf MP3 playback engine, but all of it is easily done with QRS's PNOmation app. The QRS system also includes integrated Bluetooth MIDI and Bluetooth Audio. This gives you the ability to wirelessly use third-party apps in conjunction with your PNOscan, or third-party speaker systems for playback.

The web app also offers the customer several new ways to control the PNOmation engine, including better-controlled release of the sustain pedal, to give it a soft landing and eliminate the potential

The QRS PNOmation web app gives the user full control of all parameters of the system and how music is played.

QRS Music Technologies, Inc.

thump heard with the release of the damper tray. The same controlled-release technology has also been applied to the keys, improving the PNOmation's already quiet playback while adding much more lifelike fingering. Other features include trill timing compensation, delay compensation, pitch correction, and MIDI-output curve maps. While most customers will use the default settings, those who want to dial in the perfect performance will be able to do so.

QRS has been in the business of player-piano content since 1900, and offers one of the best player-piano libraries on the market, including SyncAlong, which allows the piano to play along with original artist content. All of the data that control the movements of the piano keys and pedals are in a non-compressed MIDI format (a high-definition MIDI format will soon be released). All music available for PNOmation—soon to number more than 10,000 tracks—can be purchased one song at a time or by the album, or users can purchase an All-Access Plan that provides access to the entire QRS music library and extends the warranty. QRS also offers an upgrade option for legacy QRS products and for competitors' systems that have a MIDI input, giving them many of the advantages of the latest PNOmation system.

STEINWAY SPIRIO

Steinway & Sons
1133 Avenue of the Americas
New York, New York 10036
646-356-3960
www.steinway.com

In 2016, Steinway officially launched the Spirio electronic player-piano system. Spirio is directly installed in a Steinway piano at the time of manufacture, ensuring no alteration in the exterior appearance of the instrument. Except for the power cord, Spirio requires no visible hardware on the piano. At the present time, Spirio is available on only three Steinway models, all in high-polish polyester finish: model B (available worldwide), model M (available in the U.S. and Canada), and model O (available in select European and Asian markets). The system adds about $15,000 to the list price of the instrument. At present, a recording option is not available.

This high-resolution system uses proprietary software to measure hammer velocity up to 800 times per second at up to 1,020 dynamic levels, as well as proportional pedaling for the damper and soft pedals at up to 100 times per second for as many as 256 pedal positions. As a result of this high-resolution sampling, delicate damper and key-shift pedaling, subtle phrasing, and soft trills are reproduced with great accuracy. Steinway says that the system's superior playback is a result of a combination of numerous patented developments, including closed-loop proportional pedaling, immunity to varying line voltages, sophisticated thermal compensation, and proprietary high-resolution drive techniques.

While many older player-piano systems use compressed, low-resolution MIDI data files, Steinway says that the Spirio catalogue is recorded at the highest resolution possible from any system available today. The library contains thousands of tracks—including classical, jazz, and contemporary—all recorded live by accomplished Steinway Artists in Steinway's master recording studio, and new music is continually being added. Playlists, themes, and genres are curated by Steinway & Sons, drawing on the company's extensive musical expertise. In a first for the player-piano industry, Steinway's entire catalog of performances is provided to Spirio owners at no additional charge. Spirio users access the library through the Steinway & Sons App on their iOS device—an iPad is included in the Spirio purchase price.

YAMAHA DISKLAVIER

Yamaha Corporation of America
P.O. Box 6600
Buena Park, California 90622
714-522-9011
800-854-1569
infostation@yamaha.com
www.yamaha.com

Disklaviers are Yamaha (and now Bösendorfer) pianos that have been outfitted with an electronic player-piano system. These mechanisms are installed only in new Yamahas and the Bösendorfer model 200, and only at the Yamaha and Bösendorfer factories. They cannot be retrofitted into older Yamahas or any other brand.

Disklavier differs from most aftermarket systems in that Disklavier is not modular. Whatever Disklavier features come with a particular model of piano are what you get (although software upgrades are possible). The sophistication of the key, hammer, and pedal sensing also varies, depending on which Disklavier version is associated with that particular piano model. For a number of years, the E3 has been the standard Disklavier version in the U.S. In 2016, it was replaced by the Enspire. However, many instruments with the E3 system are still on dealers' showroom floors.

The Enspire is available in the larger Yamaha upright models and in nearly all of the grand models, and is offered in three system variations: CL, ST, and PRO. The CL (Classic) is a playback-only system that omits the recording and Silent System functions found in the ST and PRO, and is offered only in the entry-level grand model GB1K, and only in select markets.

ST (Standard) systems are included in upright Disklaviers and in

The control panel of the Disklavier Enspire is nearly invisible from the front of the piano.

most grands under 6'. These systems have a noncontact optical sensing system featuring continuous grayscale shutters for each key, and window-style shutters on each hammer (grands only). Optical sensors are also used for the damper, soft, and sostenuto pedals. This sensor system allows users to capture their own performances in standard MIDI format. In addition, a built-in Silent System allows users to silence the acoustic-piano sound and, through headphones, access the instrument's digital sounds, which include binaurally captured samples of a CFX concert grand. A patented DSP servo-drive system monitors and controls key and pedal movements in real time to automatically compensate for environmental changes, or any other movement that doesn't correlate with performance data.

PRO systems, found in all grands over 6', are high-resolution systems that, in addition to the optical sensors mentioned in regard to the ST system, incorporate continuous grayscale shutters on each hammer to measure their speed and position. The additional sensors allow for even greater recording and performance accuracy: 1,024 levels of key and hammer velocity and 256 increments of pedal position. Enspire PRO systems also use an advanced DSP servo-drive system, called AccuPlay, to monitor and adjust performance reproduction.

Unlike the E3 system, the Enspire doesn't have a control-box style user interface, relying instead on a discreet control panel nearly invisible to the user. However, all functions and features can also be accessed and controlled by any compatible HTML5 browser; Yamaha recommends using an Apple iOS or Android device.

Enspire comes with 500 built-in songs, many of them in Yamaha's PianoSoft Audio format, which features stereo audio recordings that play in sync with piano performances. Users also have access to over 6,000 additional titles for purchase through the Yamaha MusicSoft online store,

directly accessible through the instrument's user interface.

Yamaha also offers Internet streaming services for the Disklavier Enspire, including Disklavier Radio, which provides over 30 channels of streaming piano music 24 hours a day; and DisklavierTV, a video streaming service that allows users to view live and on-demand musical performances that play in sync with their piano.

Additional Enspire features include:

- An included USB WiFi adapter that permits peer-to-peer connectivity with a mobile device or connectivity to a network via WPS
- Automatic system calibration and troubleshooting
- Digital tone generator with 16 playable voices and 480 ensemble voices (256-note polyphony)
- Direct-to-USB audio recording function
- V-sync technology, which allows users to create video recordings that sync to recorded piano performances
- USB storage connectivity
- MIDI connectivity via standard MIDI ports or USB
- Coaxial digital output

Online readers: For information about the E3 Disklavier, still on dealers' showroom floors, click **here**.

For simple playback, most player-piano systems now on the market are probably equally recommended. The Disklavier, however, has a slight edge in reliability, and its recording system is more sophisticated than most of the others', especially in the larger grands. For this reason, it is often the system of choice for professional applications such as performance and teaching, and much of Yamaha's marketing efforts are directed at that audience.

Two examples are especially noteworthy. Yamaha supports the Minnesota International e-Competition, in which contestants gather in several cities and play Disklavier concert grands. Their performances are recorded using Video Sync, then sent to judges in another location, who, rather than listen to recordings, watch and listen to the music reproduced perfectly on other Disklavier pianos.

A similar concept is a technology called Remote Lesson, which debuted in spring 2010 after years of development and testing. A student takes a lesson on one Disklavier while a teacher located far away teaches and critiques on a second Disklavier connected via the Internet, student and teacher communicating with each other in real time via videoconferencing. Initially, this feature will be made available only to selected universities and at additional cost. Details and timing regarding availability of this feature to individuals is still under discussion.

Yamaha's latest Disklavier offering is Disklavier TV, which uses RemoteLive technology. Disklavier TV makes it possible for Mark IV, E3, or Enspire Disklavier owners to receive video, audio, and piano data in perfect sync, so they can receive concerts in their home with their Disklavier playing the piano part in sync with the rest of the concert. During the 2013 NAMM trade show, Yamaha used this technology to hold a major concert in which Elton John was broadcast live, playing Disklavier pianos in many different countries simultaneously, in perfect sync with program audio and video.

Yamaha maintains a large and growing library of music for the Disklavier, including piano solo, piano with recorded "live" accompaniment, piano with digital instrumental accompaniment, and PianoSmart arrangements. The system will also play standard MIDI files types 0 and 1.

THIS SECTION contains brief descriptions of most brands of new piano distributed nationwide in the United States. Brands that are associated with only a single dealer, or otherwise have marginal distribution, are omitted unless I believe them to be significant in some respect. The contact information listed for each brand is that of the brand's U.S. distributor, or of the manufacturer itself if there is no separate U.S. distributor.

Note: Electronic player-piano systems are covered in "**Buying an Electronic Player-Piano System**," elsewhere in this issue.

BALDWIN

For current-model, new pianos:
North American Music, Inc.
11 Holt Drive
Stony Point, New York 10980
845-429-0106

For parts and warranty information on older pianos:
Baldwin Piano Company
309 Plus Park Boulevard
Nashville, Tennessee 37217
615-871-4500
870-483-6111 (parts)
800-444-2766 (Baldwin 24/7 consumer hotline)
www.baldwinpiano.com

Pianos made by: Baldwin (Zhongshan) Piano and Musical Instrument Co., Ltd., Zhongshan, Guangdong Province, China; Parsons Music Ltd., Yichang, Hubei Province, China

Baldwin Piano & Organ Co. was established in Cincinnati in 1862 as a retail enterprise and began manufacturing its own line of pianos in 1890. Throughout most of the 20th century, the company was considered one of the most successful and financially stable piano makers in the United States. Beginning in the 1980s, however, the quality declined, especially as a result of the relocation of action manufacturing to Mexico. In 2001, a combination of foreign competition and management problems resulted in bankruptcy, and purchase by Gibson Guitar Corporation.

Baldwin currently manufactures vertical pianos for the U.S. market in a factory it owns in Zhongshan, China, where it also maintains a major presence in the Chinese domestic, and other international, piano markets. It also contracts with Parsons Music, a large, well-respected manufacturer associated with a chain of music schools and stores in Hong Kong and China, to have grand pianos made under the Baldwin name.

In 2007, Baldwin purchased a formerly government-owned piano factory in Dongbei, China, and for a while made grand pianos there, but due to a dispute with the Chinese government, production at that factory has been temporarily halted.

The company ceased regular piano production at its only remaining U.S. factory, in Trumann, Arkansas, at the end of 2008, though the facility remains open as a U.S. distribution and service center. Pianos sold in the U.S. now bear only the Baldwin name; all other piano names Baldwin owns and has recently used, such as Hamilton, Wurlitzer, Chickering, Howard, and D.H. Baldwin, have been retired, although some pianos bearing those names may remain on showroom floors for quite some time until sold.

Baldwin has re-created versions of most of its former U.S. vertical models at its facility in Zhongshan. In most instances, the cabinet styling of the former models, but not the scale designs, have been copied. Models B342 and B442 are 43" consoles, in attractive furniture styles similar to those of the former Acrosonic models 2096 and 2090, respectively. Model B243 is similar to the famous Baldwin Hamilton studio, the most popular school piano ever built, with toe-block construction. Model B252 is a nearly exact replica of the former 52" model 6000 upright, with Accu-just hitch pins, though with a bass sustain instead of a sostenuto pedal. In addition to re-creating versions of former U.S. vertical models, Baldwin has also created a number of new models to fill various price points and meet consumer demand.

The Baldwin grands made by Parsons Music have some similarities to the former U.S.-made Artist grands in terms of cabinet styling and material specifications, but the scale designs have been changed. Premium features include a maple rim, sand-cast plate, solid Alaskan Sitka spruce soundboard, duplex scaling, real ebony-wood sharps, German Röslau music wire, German Abel hammers, and a slow-close fallboard. All grand models are now available in a hand-rubbed, satin ebony finish.

Baldwin has licensed the Magic-Lid (formerly known as Safety-Ease) slow-close grand lid system, which is now standard on the 5' 10" model BP178 and the 6' 3" model BP190.

Baldwin sells an electronic player-piano system called ConcertMaster, available only on Baldwin pianos.

Warranty: 10 years, parts and labor, to the original purchaser.

BECHSTEIN, C.

including W. Hoffmann

Bechstein USA
301 Upland Road
Williamsport, Pennsylvania 17701
570-337-8113
Glenn@BechsteinUSA.com
www.bechstein.de

Pianos made by: C. Bechstein Pianoforte Fabrik GmbH, Berlin and Seifhennersdorf, Germany; and C. Bechstein Europe Ltd. (former Bohemia Piano Ltd.), Hradec Králové, Czech Republic

---

Bechstein was founded in 1853 by Carl Bechstein, a young German piano maker who, in the exploding world of piano technology of his day, had visions of building an instrument that the tradition-bound piano-making shops of Berlin were not interested in. Through fine workmanship and the endorsement of famous pianists, Bechstein soon became one of the leading piano makers in Europe, producing over 5,000 pianos annually by 1900. The two World Wars and the Depression virtually destroyed the company, but it was successfully rebuilt. In 1963 it was acquired by Baldwin, and in 1986 Baldwin sold it to Karl Schulze, a leading West German piano retailer and master piano technician, who undertook a complete technical and financial reorganization of the company. In the early 1990s, Bechstein acquired the names and factories of Euterpe, W. Hoffmann, and Zimmermann. Pianos with these names are currently being sold in Europe, but only W. Hoffmann is sold in North America. In 2006 Bechstein purchased a controlling interest in the Czech piano maker Bohemia, and integrated it into a new entity called C. Bechstein Europe Ltd.

Bechstein says that all Bechstein-branded pianos are manufactured in Seifhennersdorf, Germany, and that W. Hoffmann pianos are made in the Czech Republic. Bechstein recently announced a technical-cooperation agreement with the Chinese piano maker Hailun, and it is widely believed in the industry that major components for some Bechstein and/or W. Hoffmann models are made outside Europe. With few exceptions, Bechstein prefers not to divulge where the components for its instruments are made, a policy that frustrates some industry observers who seek transparency. However, the company says that, whatever the origin, all parts are inspected and made to conform to its rigid standards; in my experience, all models, including the less expensive ones, continue to receive praise for their high quality.

Bechstein-branded pianos use Abel or Renner hammers, solid European spruce soundboards, beech or beech and mahogany for grand rims and some structural parts, and maple pinblocks. Three pedals are standard on all pianos, the grands with sostenuto and the verticals with practice pedal (sostenuto optional). Over the past decade, all Bechstein grands have been redesigned with a capo bar (eliminating the agraffes in the treble), higher tension scale, and front and rear duplex scales for better tonal projection and tonal color. Also, unlike older Bechsteins, which had an open pinblock design, in the redesigned grands the plate covers the pinblock area. For better tuning control, the higher-level pianos are without tuning-pin bushings.

Bechstein pianos are available in two levels of quality. The regular verticals and partially redesigned versions of the old grand models now comprise a lower-priced "B" series, and say only "Bechstein" on the fallboard. They were previously named the Academy series. The 51½" Concert 8 (one of my all-time favorite verticals), several smaller verticals, and the fully redesigned grands (models D, C, B, M/P, and L), are the higher-priced line and say "C. Bechstein" on the fallboard. The company says that both lines are made in Germany, though for cost-effectiveness some parts and components may originate in the Czech Republic.

The differences between the B series and C. Bechstein lines appear to be primarily in tonal philosophy and cabinetry. C. Bechstein grands were designed with a higher tension scale for better projection, and with various components that the company believed would result in the greatest usable palette of tonal color: tapered soundboard, vertically laminated bridges, hornbeam hammer shanks, solid keybed, thicker rim, and hammers with walnut moldings and AAA felt. The grand soundboard is installed after the inner and outer rims are joined. The ribs are tapered after being glued to the soundboard, and the heavy-duty rim posts are dovetailed and embedded in the rim.

The less-expensive, traditional, B-series grands have an untapered soundboard, solid beech bridge with beech cap, maple hammer shanks, expansion-type keybed, and hammers with mahogany moldings and AA felt. The same quality wood and strings are used in both. The rim parts are joined, and the soundboard and ribs installed, in a more efficient, less time-consuming manner than with the C. Bechstein models. C. Bechstein keys still use leather key bushings, whereas the B-series keys use the more conventional cloth bushings. Bone keytops are an option on the C. Bechstein pianos, and genuine ebony sharps are used on both series.

The company uses its own Silver Line action in the Bechstein series and, in the C. Bechstein series, its Gold Line action, which is made to slightly stricter tolerances. As part of its global strategy, the company uses multiple suppliers for nearly all parts; parts for the Gold Line action come from Renner in Germany, while Silver Line parts are sourced from several countries, including China. Both actions appear to be well made, and both are of the Renner design, with the smooth, responsive touch characteristic of that design. Of course, the parts from Renner are more time-tested than the others.

The C. Bechstein cabinetry is much sleeker and more sophisticated than the plain B series, though both cabinets are finished to the same standard. The C. Bechstein plates receive the royal hand-rubbed finish; the other plates are just spray-finished in the conventional manner.

When the two lines are compared side by side, there are differences in their finished quality and performance level. Although the B-series pianos are, generally speaking, very good instruments with a slightly warmer default tone quality, the C. Bechstein models clearly outperform this less expensive line, and are free of the small tonal inconsistencies and minor flaws we have observed in the B series. It's possible that the comparative shortcomings of the B-series instruments could be remedied by further technical work, but it's apparent that they are not prepped at the factory to the same standard as the C. Bechstein pianos.

C. Bechstein grands are impeccably made in Europe and are "orchestrally" voiced, a concept that the company says is related to the change of timbre at different velocities of touch. According to Bechstein, customers who do not explore this feature of tonal design often prematurely assume that the piano is voiced too bright for the American musical taste. (However, several of my colleagues had high praise for the wide dynamic range, tonal color, and responsive action of the redesigned 7' 8" model C grand.) The company maintains that since voicing is a matter of overall piano design, their pianos are voiced at the factory to their tonal standard and should not be significantly altered. Some customers may still prefer the slightly warmer sound of the B-series grands, which are also about half the price of the C. Bechstein models.

Bechstein engineers oversee production of the Bechstein-designed W. Hoffmann line of pianos in the company's Czech facility. This is a mid-priced line intended to compete with other mid-priced pianos from Eastern Europe and Japan. Currently it consists of grands and verticals in three series. The Tradition- and Professional-series instruments are entirely made in the Czech Republic. The Professional series has a higher level of design and components, and more customized musical preparation by the company's most experienced craftspeople. The Vision-series pianos are assembled in the Czech Republic, but their strung backs (the instruments' structural and acoustical parts) are imported from China.

Bechstein also sells the Zimmermann brand, designed by Bechstein and manufactured in China. It is not currently available in North America.

Bechstein has a silent-piano option, called Vario, that can be built into any of its instruments. This option allows you to mute the acoustic piano and turn on a digitized sound of a C. Bechstein concert grand, which can be listened to through headphones for silent play. Optical key and pedal sensors transmit MIDI information for the control of music software. The Vario system adds about $6,600 to the price of a vertical piano, and about $11,500 to the price of a grand.

Warranty: 5 years, parts and labor, to original purchaser.

BLÜTHNER

including Haessler. See also **Irmler** and **Rönisch**.

Blüthner USA LLC
5660 W. Grand River
Lansing, Michigan 48906
517-886-6000
800-954-3200
info@bluthnerpiano.com
www.bluthnerpiano.com
www.roenisch-pianos.de/en/
In Canada, contact Bluethner Piano Canada Inc.
604-264-1138
rrgarvin@telus.net
www.bluethner.ca

Pianos made by: Julius Blüthner Pianofortefabrik GmbH, Leipzig, Germany

Blüthner has been making pianos of the highest quality in Leipzig, in the eastern part of Germany, since 1853, and though nationalized in 1972, always remained under the management of the Blüthner family. Until 1900, Blüthner was Europe's largest piano factory. During World War II, the factory was bombed, but after the war the East German government allowed the Blüthner family and workers to rebuild it because the Blüthner piano was considered a national treasure (and because the Soviet Union needed quality pianos). With the liberation of Eastern Europe, Blüthner is again privately owned by the Blüthner family.

Blüthner pianos have beech rims (grands), solid spruce soundboards, Delignit pinblocks, Renner actions, Abel hammers, and polyester finishes. Pianos for export have three pedals, including sostenuto on the grands, and celeste (practice) on the verticals. Blüthner builds about 100 verticals a year in four sizes, and 500 grands a year in six sizes.

In addition to numerous specialized furniture styles and finishes, Blüthner has two recently issued special editions. In honor of the company's 150th anniversary, Blüthner introduced a Jubilee model with a commemorative cast-iron plate in the style of the special-edition pianos of a century ago. It is available in several sizes, in any style or finish. A Julius Blüthner edition honoring the founder of the company, now operated by the fifth generation of his family, is available in most grand sizes, and features, among other embellishments, brass inlays in the lid, round Victorian legs, and a very fancy, elaborately carved music desk in the styling designed by the founder.

Blüthner pianos incorporate several unique technical features. With aliquot stringing, the notes in the highest treble section (about the top two octaves) have four strings each instead of three. The extra string is raised slightly above the others and vibrates only sympathetically. The effect, heard mainly in medium to forte playing, is similar to that of a duplex scale, adding tonal color to the treble and aiding the singing tone. Another feature concerns the angled hammers, which may at first look odd, though the reason may not be readily apparent. It turns out that the angled hammers are actually cut at an angle to match the string line and mounted straight on the shanks instead of being cut straight and mounted at an angle like other brands. The company says that the effect is to more evenly distribute the force of the blow across both the strings and the hammers, and to make a firmer connection with the backchecks, which are also positioned in a straight line. Visually, the effect is an even, rather than a staggered, hammer line.

In what is perhaps a world's first, Blüthner has designed and built a piano for left-handed pianists. This is a completely backward piano, with the treble keys, hammers, and strings on the left and the bass on the right. When it was introduced, a pianist gave a concert on it after only a couple of hours of practice! It is currently available in the 6' 10" and 9' 2" sizes by special order (price not available).

With voicing, Blüthner pianos have a very full sound that is warm, romantic, and lyrical, generally deeper and darker than some of their German counterparts. Sustain is good, but at a low level of volume, giving the tone a refined, delicate character. The action is a little light, but responsive. The pianos are built of superb materials, and are favorably priced compared to some of their competitors.

In the 1990s a Haessler line of pianos was added to the Blüthner line. (Haessler is a Blüthner family name.) Created to better compete in the American market, Haessler pianos have more conventional technical and cosmetic features than Blüthner pianos and cost about 25 percent less. For example, the grands are loop-strung instead of single-strung, there is no aliquot stringing, and the hammers are cut and mounted in the conventional way. Case and plate cosmetics are simpler. The pianos are made in the Blüthner factory in Germany to similarly high quality standards.

In 2016, Blüthner added to its line a hybrid-piano option, known as "e-volution," (see **Hybrid Pianos**, elsewhere in this issue). This option, which comes with an optical MIDI strip, a digital sound source, and a piano-silencing system, can be added to any Blüthner upright or grand piano model. A piano outfitted with the e-volution system can be played as an acoustic piano, as a digital piano (with the sound of a Blüthner concert grand), or as both at the same time. It can also stream music via Bluetooth from another source through its built-in Bose sound system. The system adds about $8,000 to the price of a piano.

Blüthner also owns the Irmler brand (see under **Irmler**), and the Rönisch and Hupfeld brands (see under **Rönisch**).

Warranty: Blüthner and Haessler—10 years, parts and labor, to original purchaser.

BÖSENDORFER

Yamaha Corporation of America
P.O. Box 6600
Buena Park, California 90622
714-522-9415
info@boesendorferus.com
www.boesendorfer.com
Pianos made by: L. Bösendorfer Klavierfabrik GmbH, Vienna, Austria

Bösendorfer was founded in 1828 in Vienna, Austria, by Ignaz Bösendorfer. The young piano maker rose to fame when Franz Liszt endorsed his concert grand after being unable to destroy it in playing, as he had every other piano set before him. Ignaz died in 1858 and the company was taken over by his son, Ludwig. Under Ludwig's direction, the firm greatly prospered and the pianos became even more famous throughout Europe and the world. Ludwig, having no direct descendants, sold the firm to a friend, Carl Hutterstrasser, in 1909.

Carl's sons, Wolfgang and Alexander, became partners in 1931. Bösendorfer was sold to Kimball International, a U.S. manufacturer of low- and medium-priced pianos, in 1966. In 2002 Kimball, having left the piano business, sold Bösendorfer to BAWAG Bank, Austria's third largest financial institution. The bank encountered financial troubles unrelated to Bösendorfer and sold the piano company to Yamaha in 2008. Yamaha says it will not be making any changes to Bösendorfer's location or methods of production, and that its sales network will continue to be separate from Yamaha's. Bösendorfer manufactures fewer than 500 pianos a year, with close to half of them sold in the U.S.

Bösendorfer makes a 52" upright and eight models of grand piano, from 5' 1" to the 9' 6" Imperial Concert Grand, one of the world's largest pianos. The 5' 1" grand, new in 2012 and unusually small for a Bösendorfer, has the same keyboard as the 5' 8" grand, ensuring a good touch despite the instrument's small size. The company also makes slightly less expensive versions of four grand models known as the Conservatory Series (CS). Conservatory Series grands are like the regular grands except that the case receives a satin finish instead of a high polish, and some cabinet details are simpler. Previously, the CS models also had a satin-finished plate, and were loop-strung instead of single-strung, but in 2009, regarding these features, the specifications of the regular models were restored. All Bösendorfer grand pianos have three pedals, the middle pedal being a sostenuto.

One of the most distinctive features of the grands is that a couple of models have more than 88 keys. The 7' 4" model has 92 keys and the 9' 6" model has 97 keys. The lowest strings vibrate so slowly that it's actually possible to hear the individual beats of the vibration. Piano technicians say that it is next to impossible to tune these strings by ear, although electronic tuning aids can help accomplish this. Of course, these notes are rarely used, but their presence, and the presence of the extra-long bridge and larger soundboard to accommodate them, add extra power, resonance, and clarity to the lower regular notes of the piano. In order not to confuse pianists, who rely on the normal keyboard configuration for spatial orientation while playing, the keys for these extra notes are usually covered with a black ivorine material.

The rim of the Bösendorfer grand is built quite differently from those of all other grands. Instead of veneers bent around a form, the inner rim is made in solid sections of spruce and beech that are joined together. The outer rim has a solid core of quartersawn spruce that is grooved by Bösendorfer craftsmen so that it can be bent around the inner rim; after bending, the grooved sections are filled with spruce inserts. Because spruce is better at transmitting than reflecting sound, the extensive use of spruce in the rim has the effect of making the rim an acoustical extension of the soundboard, causing the entire body of the piano to resonate. This, along with the scale design, may be why Bösendorfers tend to have a more delicate treble, and a bass that features the fundamental tone more than the higher harmonics. Although the stereotype that "Bösendorfers are better for Mozart than Rachmaninoff" may be an exaggeration (as evidenced by the number of performing artists who successfully use the piano in concert for a wide variety of music), the piano's not-so-"in-your-face" sound is certainly ideally suited for the classical repertoire, in addition to whatever else it can do.

In recent years, Bösendorfer has made some refinements to its designs. The relatively newer 6' 1", 7', and 9' 2" models have been designed specifically to appeal to pianists looking for a more familiar sound. The last two models, now called the Vienna Concert (VC) series, have redesigned scaling and soundboard for greater sound projection, improved sustain, and a wider range of tonal color and dynamics. In all models, however, the distinctive Bösendorfer sound is still readily apparent.

In the past few years, Bösendorfer has introduced a number of interesting instruments in new cabinet styles. These include a Porsche-designed modern piano in aluminum and polished ebony (it can be special-ordered in any standard Porsche finish color); the Liszt, Vienna, and Chopin models of Victorian-styled pianos; and limited-edition models, such as the Liszt Anniversary, Beethoven, Mozart, Hummingbird, and Schönbrunn. Perhaps not to be outdone by Porsche, in 2009 Bösendorfer produced a model commissioned and designed by Audi on the occasion of that automaker's 100th anniversary.

Bösendorfer makes a unique electronic player-piano system called CEUS, no longer advertised in the U.S. but available by special order. The Bösendorfer model 200 is optionally available with a Yamaha Disklavier Enspire installed.

Perhaps the world's most expensive piano inch for inch, Bösendorfer grands make an eloquent case for their prices. They are distinctive in both appearance and sound, and are considered to be among the finest pianos in the world.

Warranty: 10 years, parts and labor, transferable to future owners within the warranty period.

BOSTON

Steinway & Sons
1133 Avenue of the Americas
New York, New York 10036
646-356-3960
boston@steinway.com
www.steinway.com/boston

Pianos made by: Kawai Musical Instrument Mfg. Co., Ltd.,
Hamamatsu, Japan and Karawan, Indonesia

In 1992 Steinway launched its Boston line of pianos, designed by Steinway & Sons and built by Kawai. Steinway's stated purpose in creating this line was to supply Steinway dealers with a quality, mid-priced piano containing some Steinway-like design features for those customers "who were not yet ready for a Steinway." In choosing to have a piano of its own design made in Japan, Steinway sought to take advantage of the efficient high-technology manufacturing methods of the Japanese while utilizing its own design skills to make a more musical piano than is usually available from that part of the world.

In 2009, Steinway launched the Performance Edition of the Boston piano with enhancements to the instruments' design and specifications, including a grand inner rim of maple for increased structural integrity and improved tone, the patented Octagrip® pinblock for smoother tuning and more consistent torque, and improvements to hardware and keytop material, among other things. Performance Edition models have model numbers ending in PE. In 2016, the company introduced Performance Edition II grands (PE-II), containing further improvements, including bubinga veneer on the inside rim of all ebony grands, improved finishes, a new plate color, and other cosmetic changes; and a lower-tension scale, resulting in a very clear bass, better treble sustain, and more transparency in the tenor range.

Sold only through select Steinway dealers, Boston pianos are currently available in three sizes of vertical and five sizes of grand. All are made in Japan, except the model UP-118S PE, which is made in Kawai's Indonesian factory.

Boston pianos are used by a number of prestigious music schools and festivals, including Aspen, Bowdoin, Brevard, Ravinia, and Tanglewood.

The most obvious visible feature of the Boston grand piano's design (and one of the biggest differences from Kawai pianos) is its wide tail. Steinway says this allows the bridges to be positioned closer to the more lively central part of the soundboard, smoothing out the break between bass and treble. This, plus a thinner, tapered, solid-spruce soundboard and other scaling differences, may give the Boston grands a longer sustain though less initial power. The wide-tail design may also endow some of the grands with the soundboard size normally associated with a slightly larger piano. The verticals are said to have a greater overstringing angle, for the same purpose. Over the last few years, the Boston verticals have been redesigned for greater tuning stability and musical refinement.

A number of features in the Boston piano are similar to those in the Steinway, including the above-mentioned maple inner rim, vertically laminated bridges for better tonal transmission, duplex scaling for additional tonal color, rosette-shaped hammer flanges to preserve hammer spacing, and radial rim bracing for greater structural stability. The Boston grand action is said to incorporate some of the latest refinements of the Steinway action. Cabinet detailing on the Boston grands is similar to that on the Steinway. Boston hammers are made differently from both Kawai and Steinway hammers, and voicers in the Kawai factory receive special instruction in voicing them. All Boston grand models come with a sostenuto pedal; all verticals have a practice (mute) pedal, except for the model UP-118S PE, which has a bass sustain.

Boston grands also have certain things in common with Kawai RX-series grands: tuning pins, grand leg and lyre assemblies, radial rim bracing, sostenuto pedal, and the level of quality control in their manufacture. The same workers build the two brands in the same factories. One important way they differ is that Kawai uses carbon-fiber–reinforced ABS Styran plastic for most of its action parts, whereas Boston uses only traditional wooden parts. Although similarly priced at the wholesale level, Kawai pianos tend to be a little less expensive to the retail customer than comparably sized Bostons due to the larger discounts typically given by Kawai dealers.

Steinway guarantees full trade-in value for a Boston piano at any time a purchaser wishes to upgrade to a Steinway grand.

Piano technicians are favorably inclined toward Boston pianos. Some find them to have a little better sustain and more tonal color than Kawais, while being otherwise similar in quality. When comparing the two brands, I would advise making a choice based primarily on one's own musical perceptions of tone and touch, as well as the trade-up guarantee, if applicable.

Warranty: 10 years, parts and labor, to original purchaser.

BRODMANN

Piano Marketing Group, Inc.
15203 Severyns Road
Tustin, California 92782
949-600-1476
657-266-0351 (fax)
peterh@BrodmannPianoUSA.com
www.BrodmannPianoUSA.com
Pianos made by: Parsons Music, Hong Kong/China

Joseph Brodmann was a well-known piano maker in Vienna in the late 18th and early 19th centuries. Ignaz Bösendorfer apprenticed in Brodmann's workshop and eventually took it over, producing the first Bösendorfer pianos there.

The modern-day Brodmann company was founded in 2004 by two former Bösendorfer executives. Brodmann, they say, was originally planned as a possible second line for Bösendorfer, but when that company abandoned the idea, the two executives pursued it on their own. In 2014, the Vienna-based Brodmann company filed for bankruptcy protection in Austria. However, manufacture and distribution of the Brodmann line continue unchanged. U.S. distribution rights to the Brodmann line are owned by Piano Marketing Group; for all other parts of the world, the factory sells directly through its own distributor network.

Brodmann says its mission is to produce a piano with high-end performance characteristics at an affordable price by using European components in key areas, strict quality control, and manufacturing in countries with favorable labor rates.

There are three lines of Brodmann piano, all manufactured, in whole or in part, in China by Parsons Music. The Professional Edition (PE) pianos, made entirely in China, are designed in Vienna and use European components such as Strunz soundboards, Abel hammers, Röslau strings, and Langer-designed (Chinese) actions (Renner in the model 228 grand). Several vertical models use carbon-fiber action parts, for greater uniformity and dimensional stability, and all grand models are now available with optional carbon-fiber actions. For quality control, Brodmann has its own employees from Europe working in the factory. The scale design of the 6' 2" model PE 187 is said to be similar to that of a Steinway model A and is often singled out for praise.

The Conservatory Edition (CE), for the more price-conscious buyer, is also made entirely in China, from parts sourced globally, and receives Brodmann quality control.

The Artist Series (AS) models, introduced in 2011 and available only in the larger grand sizes (including a concert grand) and the largest upright size, are based on German scale designs. They are partially made in China, then shipped to the Wilh. Steinberg factory (also owned by Parsons Music), in Eisenberg, Germany, where the Röslau strings and Renner actions are installed, and all musical finishing work is performed by German artisans. The rim is made of maple; the soundboard, ribs, and pinblock are from Bolduc, in Canada; and the piano uses a Renner action, Kluge keyboard, and Renner hammers.

Brodmann has discontinued its entry-level piano line, Taylor London.

Warranty: 10 years, parts and labor, to original purchaser.

CHERNOBIEFF

Chernobieff Pianos & Harpsichords
Lenoir City, Tennessee
865-986-7720
chrisppff@gmail.com
www.chernobieff.com

Reminiscent of some piano designs attempted 200 years ago, Chernobieff's Mammoth is one of the most unusual pianos being built today. Dubbed a Vertical Concert Grand, Mammoth's model VCG stands 7' 2" tall, weighs 1,200 pounds, and has the scale design and sound of a 9' concert grand.

The piano's immense structure includes six laminated wooden back posts and a welded steel frame, yet despite its bulk, the instrument appears quite attractive in its custom-made cabinet of Brazilian cherry. The soundboard and ribs are of Sitka spruce. The action, invented specifically for this piano, appears superficially to be like that of a vertical, but actually contains the double-escapement feature of a grand piano action.

Inventor-builder Chris Chernobieff got his start assembling dulcimer and harpsichord kits, and branched out into piano service and rebuilding about 15 years ago. Inspired by other technicians who built their own pianos, Chernobieff asked, "Why not me?" Having spent the last several years designing and building the Mammoth, he now has plans for a 6' vertical and some innovative grand models.

Mammoth model VCG retails for $98,000.

CLINE — See Hailun.

CONOVER CABLE — See Samick.

CRISTOFORI
including Paul A. Schmitt.

Jordan Kitt's Music
11726 Parklawn Drive
Rockville, Maryland 20852

301-770-9081
(Chris Syllaba)
info@cristoforipianos.com

Schmitt Music
2400 Freeway Blvd.
Brooklyn Center,
Minnesota 55430
763-566-4560 x5086
(Tom Wennblom)
www.cristoforipianos.com

Pianos made by: Guangzhou Pearl River Piano Group Ltd., Guangzhou, Guangdong Province, China

Originally issued under the name Opus II, the Cristofori and Paul A. Schmitt brands are a joint undertaking by Jordan Kitt's Music, which owns and operates four piano dealerships in the D.C. and Atlanta markets; and Schmitt Music, which has more than a dozen locations throughout the Midwest and in Denver. About 15 years ago, wanting to improve their entry-level product offerings, the two companies combined forces to negotiate upgrades of product features and quality control directly with the factory. Today, although the brands are identical, Cristofori is sold only in Jordan Kitt's stores, Paul A. Schmitt in Schmitt Music stores. Bartolomeo Cristofori (1655–1731) was, of course, the inventor of the piano.

The Cristofori and Paul A. Schmitt lines are manufactured by China's largest piano manufacturer, Guangzhou Pearl River Piano Group. The uprights come in numerous sizes, styles, and finishes, including a 43" decorator console in a French cherry cabinet, 45" and 46½" studios, and a 48" upright. The 48" professional upright, appropriate for home or institutional use, has front legs with toe blocks for strength, a large soundboard and long strings for bigger sound, and—new in 2012—a slow-close fallboard. Grands come in lengths of 4' 10", 5' 3", 5' 7", and 6' 2". The 5' 3" and 5' 7" sizes are wide-tail designs, which gives these mid-sized grands a larger soundboard area and, thus, a bigger sound.

The Cristofori and Paul A. Schmitt pianos are differentiated from Pearl River's own line of pianos by upgraded specifications such as the use of highest-quality German Röslau strings; all-spruce veneered soundboards of premium Siberian spruce; a different selection of cabinet styles; and a full, transferable warranty. U.S. technicians inspect every Cristofori and Paul A. Schmitt piano at the Pearl River factory prior to crating and shipping.

Warranty: 12 years, parts and labor, transferable to future owners within the warranty period.

CUNNINGHAM
Cunningham Piano Company
5427 Germantown Avenue
Philadelphia, Pennsylvania 19144
800-394-1117
215-438-3200
www.cunninghampiano.com

Pianos made by: Ningbo Hailun Musical Instruments Co. Ltd., Ningbo, Zhejiang Province, China; with Cunningham Piano Company, Philadelphia, Pennsylvania

Cunningham Piano Company began manufacturing pianos in 1891 and, in its time, was the largest piano maker in Philadelphia. The original Cunningham factory ceased production in December 1943. The company was reopened in December 1945 as a piano rebuilder and retailer. Today, Cunningham specializes in the restoration of high-quality American and European pianos, and produces the new Matchless Cunningham.

Designed by Frank Emerson, the Matchless Cunningham is based on the original Cunningham scale designs. "Matchless" is used in reference to an offer made by Patrick Cunningham over a century ago: that he would pay $10,000 to anyone who could build a better piano. Because no one ever took him up on his offer, Cunningham labeled his piano the Matchless. Today, Matchless also refers to a unique combination of high-quality parts and a successful American scale design, assembled in China at the world-class Hailun factory, and with quality control overseen by Cunningham in Philadelphia. The line consists of grands from 5' to 9' and two verticals, 44" and 50".

Cunningham grands have maple rims (arguably necessary for best sound), custom-designed German Abel Hammers, German music wire, agraffes, duplex scaling, and slow-close mechanisms on both the fallboard and lid. Cunningham regularly sends technical staff to the Ningbo Hailun factory to oversee production, and each piano undergoes a thorough final preparation by Cunningham in Philadelphia.

The special Heritage Series incorporates art cases that reflect late Victorian styling. Handcrafted cabinet parts are made and installed in Cunningham's Philadelphia facility, making each instrument unique. Customers have the option of customizing certain aspects of the cabinetry based on their personal preferences.

Warranty: 10 years, parts and labor.

EISENBERG — See Steinberg, Wilh.

ESSEX

Steinway & Sons
1133 Avenue of the Americas
New York, New York 10036
646-356-3960
essex@steinway.com
www.steinway.com/essex
Pianos made by: Guangzhou Pearl River Piano Group Ltd.,
Guangzhou, Guangdong Province, China

Essex pianos are designed by Steinway & Sons engineers and are made in China by Pearl River. Steinway introduced its Essex line of pianos in early 2001 with a limited offering of models made by Young Chang, and the brand kept an unusually low profile in the piano market for a number of years. In 2006, a major relaunch of Essex included a new and very complete line comprising 35 grand and 31 vertical models and finishes.

Today, two grand sizes and three vertical scales are made. The 42" model EUP-108 is a continental-style version of the 44" model EUP-111 console. The 46" model EUP-116 studio is available in 10 different and striking cabinets designed by Steinway & Sons and renowned furniture designer William Faber. Styles include: Classic, Queen Anne, Italian Provincial, French Country, Formal French, English Country, English Traditional, Contemporary, and Sheraton Traditional. These models incorporate various leg designs (including cabriole leg, spoon leg, and canopy-styled tapered leg and arm designs) and hand-carved trim (such as Acanthus leaf and tulip designs, and vertical bead molding), highly molded top lids, picture-frame front panels, and stylized, decorative music desks. The 48" model EUP-123 upright comes in a traditional style in five finishes, two with chrome hardware, along with Empire and French styles; an all-new school model, the EUP-123S, is offered in ebony polish only.

The Essex grands are available in 5' 1" (EGP-155) and 5' 8" (EGP-173) sizes in Classic and French Provincial styles. They come in a variety of regular and exotic veneers in high polish polyester and satin luster (semigloss) finishes.

Like Steinway's Boston pianos, the Essex line was designed with a lower tension scale and incorporates many Steinway-designed refinements. Included in these are a wide tail design that allows the bridges to be positioned closer to the more lively, central part of the soundboard, smoothing out the break between bass and treble. This and a thinner, tapered solid-spruce soundboard, and other scaling differences, produce a tone with a longer sustain. Other Steinway-designed features include an all-wood action with Steinway geometry, and with rosette-shaped hammer flanges, like those used in Steinway grands, to preserve hammer spacing; pear-shaped hammers with reinforced shoulders and metal fasteners; vertically laminated bridges with a solid maple cap; duplex scale; radial bracing (in grands); and staggered backposts (in verticals).

Steinway has put an immense amount of time and effort into the relaunch of Essex. The pianos are entirely new designs by Steinway engineers, not warmed-over designs from other companies. Steinway has a permanent office in Shanghai, China, and full-time employees who inspect the pianos made in the Asian factory. I expect that the quality of the Essex pianos will be toward the upper end of what these factories are capable of producing. So far, feedback from piano technicians confirms this expectation.

Steinway guarantees full trade-in value for an Essex piano toward the purchase of a Steinway grand within 10 years.

Warranty: 10 years, parts and labor, to original purchaser.

ESTONIA

Laul Estonia Piano Factory Ltd.
7 Fillmore Drive
Stony Point, New York 10980
845-947-7763
laulestoniapiano@aol.com
www.estoniapiano.com
Pianos made by: Estonia Klaverivabrik AS, Tallinn, Estonia

Estonia is a small republic in northern Europe on the Baltic Sea, near Scandinavia. For centuries it was under Danish, Swedish, German, or Russian domination, and finally gained its independence in 1918, only to lose it again to the Soviet Union in 1940. Estonia became free again in 1991 with the collapse of the Soviet Union.

Piano-making in Estonia goes back over 200 years under German influence, and from 1850 to 1940 there were nearly 20 piano manufacturers operating in the country. The most famous of these was Ernst Hiis-Ihse, who studied piano making in the Steinway Hamburg and Blüthner factories and established his own company in 1893. His piano designs gained international recognition. In 1950 the Communist-dominated Estonian government consolidated many smaller Estonian piano makers into a factory managed by Hiis, making pianos under the Estonia name for the first time. The instruments became prominent on concert stages throughout Eastern Europe and, amazingly, more than 7,400 concert grands were made. However, after Hiis's death, in 1964, the quality of the pianos gradually declined, partly due to the fact that high-quality parts and materials were hard to come by during the Communist occupation of the country. After Estonia regained its independence in 1991, the factory struggled to maintain production. In 1994 Estonia pianos were introduced to the U.S. market.

In 1994 the company was privatized under the Estonia name, with the managers and employees as owners. During the following years, Indrek Laul, an Estonian recording artist with a doctorate in piano performance from the Juilliard School of Music, gradually bought shares of the company from the stockholders until, in 2001, he became sole owner. Dr. Laul lives in the U.S. and represents the company here. In 2005, at its 100th-anniversary celebration, the Juilliard School named him one of the school's top 100 graduates; and in 2015, the President of Estonia awarded Laul the Presidential Medal, in recognition of the contribution Estonia pianos have made to awareness of that country. Estonia makes 200 to 300 pianos a year, all grands, mostly for sale in the U.S.

Estonia pianos have rims of laminated birch, sand-cast plates, Renner actions and hammers, laminated red beech pinblocks, and European solid spruce soundboards. They come in 5' 6", 6' 3", 6' 10" (new in 2013), 7' 4" (introduced in 2011), and 9' sizes. All have three pedals, including sostenuto, and come with a slow-close fallboard and an adjustable artist bench.

When I reported on Estonia pianos for the fourth edition of *The Piano Book* (2001), it was a good piano with much potential; but in the decade that followed, Dr. Laul introduced so many improvements to the piano that it became practically a different, much higher-level instrument. In 2010, Estonia began investing in designing new models, and the knowledge gained from designing the 6' 10" model L210, introduced in 2013, was used the following year to implement changes to most of the other models. These modifications included a complete soundboard redesign, new support beams of resonant spruce with improved doweled connection to the rim, and new specifications for hammer density. The model L190 also has a new, focused beam structure.

The Estonia factory makes a custom line of piano, offering exotic veneers such as rosewood, bubinga, pyramid mahogany, and Makassar ebony, and is willing to finish instruments to fit the desires of individual customers.

In the short time Estonia pianos have been sold here, they have gathered an unusually loyal and devoted following. Groups of owners of Estonia pianos, independent of the company, frequently hold musical get-togethers at different locations around the country.

The pianos have a rich, warm, singing tone and a wide dynamic range; are very well constructed and well prepared at the factory; and there is hardly a detail that the company has not examined and impressively perfected. The price has risen over the years, but they are still an unusually good value among higher-end instruments.

Warranty: 10 years, parts and labor, to original purchaser.

FANDRICH & SONS

Fandrich & Sons Pianos
7411 Silvana Terrace Road
Stanwood, Washington 98292
360-652-8980
877-737-1422
fandrich@fandrich.com
www.fandrich.com
Pianos made by: Pearl River

In the late 1980s, Darrell Fandrich, RPT, an engineer, pianist, and piano technician, developed a vertical piano action designed to play like a grand, for which 10 patents were issued. In July 2013, a new patent application was filed in the U.S. (along with an application for future international patents) on an improved version of the action. The improvement features use of a grand-piano knuckle, and results in improved touch and repetition, and the feel of aftertouch at the bottom of the keystroke.

You can see an illustration of the original Fandrich Vertical Action™, an explanation of how it works, and some history of its development in the third and fourth editions of *The Piano Book* and on the Fandrich & Sons website. Since 1994, Fandrich and his wife, Heather, have been installing Renner-made Fandrich actions in selected new pianos, selling them under the Fandrich & Sons label. They also sell some grands (with regular grand actions) under that name.

Over the years, the Fandrichs have installed their actions in over 300 instruments, including ones from Bohemia, Feurich, Klima, Pearl River, Wilh. Steinberg, and Steingraeber. At present, the action is being installed in 52" Pearl River uprights featuring Lothar Thomma scale designs (under the Fandrich & Sons label), and, by special order, in 51" Steingraeber uprights (under the Steingraeber & Söhne label). The converted pianos are available directly from the Fandrichs, as well as from their Canadian representative, in Montreal (contact the Fandrichs for information).

Playing a piano outfitted with a Fandrich Vertical Action is a very interesting experience. The action easily outperforms that of most other vertical pianos on the market, and some grands as well. The Fandrichs have now had 25 years of experience in refining and servicing the action, and reports suggest that customers are very satisfied with them.

Fandrich & Sons grand pianos are manufactured in China by the Pearl River Piano Group. These pianos feature Lothar Thomma scale designs, and are remanufactured at the Fandrich & Sons facility in Stanwood, Washington. The company offers three sizes of grand piano—models 170 (5' 7"), 188 (6' 2"), and 212 (7')—in two configurations: Standard (S) and Enhanced (E), the latter with Heller bass strings from Germany and/or Abel hammers, depending on customer preference. The tone of the S model is said to be powerful, dark, and sonorous; the E model, in contrast, is more brilliant and transparent. All models feature precision touchweighting using the Fandrich-Rhodes Weightbench™ system, which enables precise control of action inertia as well as traditional up- and downweight; redesigned pedal-lyre and trapwork systems; and a very extensive high-end preparation.

For those who wish a better musical experience at a lower cost, the Fandrichs also sell two vertical piano models with traditional actions that also receive the same high-end musical preparation as the more expensive models. The 46" model 118S and the 48" model 122 are designed by Lothar Thomma and built by Pearl River. All Fandrich & Sons pianos come with a matching bench.

The Fandrichs are passionate about their craft and choose the brands they work with carefully for musical potential. In addition to making standard modifications and refinements to remedy perceived shortcomings in the original Chinese-made instruments, the Fandrichs are inveterate tinkerers always searching for ways to make additional improvements, however subtle. As a result, many who play the pianos find them to be considerably more musical than their price and origin would suggest.

Warranty: 12 years, parts and labor, to original purchaser.

Note: Do not confuse the Fandrich & Sons pianos with the 48" Fandrich upright that was once manufactured with a Fandrich Vertical Action by Darrell Fandrich's brother, Delwin Fandrich. That piano has not been made since 1994.

FAZIOLI

Fazioli Pianoforti S.p.A.
Via Ronche 47
33077 Sacile (Pn), Italy
+39-0434-72026
info@fazioli.com
www.fazioli.com

In 1978, musician and engineer Paolo Fazioli of Rome, Italy, began designing and building pianos, with the object of making the finest-quality instruments possible. Now even the most famous piano makers of Western Europe are recognizing his accomplishment, and artists throughout the world are using the instruments successfully on the concert stage and elsewhere.

As a youth, Fazioli studied music and engineering, receiving advanced degrees in both subjects. He briefly attempted to make a living as a concert pianist, but instead joined his family's furniture company, rising to the position of factory manager in the Rome, Sacile, and Turin factories. But his creative ambitions, combined with his personal search for the perfect piano, finally led him to conclude that he needed to build his own piano. With advice and financial backing from his family, in 1977 Fazioli assembled a group of experts in woodworking, acoustics, and piano technology to study and scientifically analyze every aspect of piano design and construction. The following year, prototypes of his new instruments in hand, he began building pianos commercially in a factory housed at one end of the family's Sacile furniture factory, a top supplier in Italy of high-end office furniture.

In 2001, Fazioli built a new, expanded, modern piano-production facility, and in 2005 opened an adjoining 198-seat concert hall with a stage large enough for a chamber orchestra, where he maintains a regular concert schedule of well-known musicians who perform there. The concert hall is designed so that it can be adjusted acoustically with movable panels and sound reflectors to optimize the acoustics for performing, recording, or testing, and for different kinds of music, musical ensembles, and size of audience. The hall is used for the research and testing of pianos—every instrument Fazioli makes is tested here. In addition to these activities in the concert hall, the new factory also contains a department for ongoing research in piano design in cooperation with a number of educational institutions.

Fazioli builds only grands, about 150 per year, in six sizes from 5' 2" to 10' 2", the last one of the largest pianos in the world, with the further distinction of having four pedals. Three are the usual sustain, sostenuto, and una corda. The fourth is a "soft" pedal that brings the hammers closer to the strings—similar to the function in verticals and some older grands—to soften the sound without altering the tonal quality, as the una corda often does. A unique compensating device corrects for the action irregularity that would otherwise occur when the hammers are moved in this manner. The fourth pedal is available as an option on the other models. Fazioli also offers two actions and two pedal lyres as options on all models. Having two actions allows for more voicing possibilities without having to constantly revoice the hammers. A second pedal lyre containing only three pedals can be a welcome alternative for some pianists who might be confused by the presence of a fourth pedal.

All Fazioli pianos have inner and outer rims of maple, and seven-ply maple pinblocks from Bolduc, in Canada. The pianos have Renner actions and hammers and Kluge keyboards. The bronze capo d'astro bar is adjustable in the factory for setting the strike point and treble string length for best high-treble tone quality, and is removable for servicing if necessary; and the front and rear duplex scales can be tuned to maximize tonal color. A newly patented action rail structure is more resistant to moisture, and provides a more uniform touch across the keyboard. Also newly patented are double- and triple-layer, moisture-resistant soundboards, available by special order for pianos that will be used in extreme climates.

The company says that a critical factor in the sound of its pianos is the scientific selection of its woods, such as the "resonant spruce" obtained from the Val di Fiemme, where Stradivari reportedly sought woods for his violins. Each piece of wood is said to be carefully tested for certain resonant properties before being used in the pianos. Similarly, three different types of wood are used for the bridge caps, each chosen for the most efficient transmission of tonal energy for a particular register.

An incredible level of detail has gone into the design and construction of these pianos. For instance, in one small portion of the soundboard where additional stiffness is required, the grain of the wood runs perpendicular to that of the rest of the soundboard, cleverly disguised so as to be almost unnoticeable. The pianos are impeccably prepared at the factory, including very fine voicing—even perfect tuning of the duplex scales.

A series of stunning art-case pianos is a testament to the ability of the Fazioli artisans to execute virtually any custom-ordered artistic variation on the six Fazioli models.

Many artists, and others most familiar with Fazioli pianos, describe them as sources of inspiration with a wide color palette and dynamic range, and combining great power with great warmth in a way that causes music played on them to "make sense" in a way made possible by few other pianos.

Each Fazioli piano is built saving one ton of carbon dioxide, thanks to the use of electricity produced by a new photovoltaic system installed on the roof of the Fazioli factory.

Warranty: 10 years, parts and labor, transferable to future owners within the warranty period.

FEURICH

Feurich Pianoforte
Wendl & Lung
Kaiserstrasse 10/2
Vienna 1070
Austria
office@feurich.com   773-673-5564 (U.S.)
www.feurich.com   +43-1-523-3788 (Austria)

Pianos made by: Ningbo Hailun Musical Instruments Co. Ltd., Ningbo, Zhejiang Province, China

This German piano manufacturer was founded by Julius Feurich in 1851, in Leipzig. At its height in the early 20th century, the company employed 360 people, annually producing 1,200 upright and 600 grand pianos. Feurich was the first German manufacturer to produce an upright with an under-damper system, and was also a member of the so-called Group of Five—the leading German manufacturers who joined forces to provide selected renowned pianists with concert instruments worldwide. Like many German manufacturers, however, Feurich lost its factory during World War II. Following the war, the fourth generation of the Feurich family rebuilt in Langlau, in what became West Germany.

In 1991, Bechstein purchased Feurich and closed the Langlau factory, but in 1993 the name was sold back to the Feurich family. For a time, production was contracted out to other German manufacturers, including Schimmel, while the Feurich family marketed and distributed the pianos. In 1995, Feurich opened a new factory in Gunzenhausen, Germany. Under the direction of the fifth-generation Julius Feurich, the family-owned company once again began producing its own pianos.

In 2011, Feurich was acquired by Wendl & Lung, headquartered in Vienna, Austria, which distributed a line of pianos under that name made to their specifications by Hailun, in China. The Wendl & Lung pianos went through further development, and additional models were added to the line, before being rebranded as Feurich. Julius Feurich was granted a license to make a line of Feurich-branded pianos in Gunzenhausen, but soon thereafter terminated that license agreement, choosing instead to manufacture pianos independently under another name in a venture that did not last long.

Under the name Feurich Pianoforte, Wendl & Lung continues to make and distribute Feurich pianos, working on the design of its instruments with original Feurich designers such as Friedrich Steinbauer, as well as with other renowned European piano designers such as Jan Enzenauer, Rolf Ibach, and Stephen Paulello.

There are currently two lines of Feurich instruments on the market. Utilizing a separate production line within the Hailun factory in Ningbo, China, Feurich produces a line of high-quality, affordable uprights and grands distinguished by their strict quality control, the use of European tonewoods, and modern innovations, such as Paulello rust-free music wire. Feurich experts are present in the factory at all times, in order to perform a full quality-control inspection before shipping. In 2015, a new Feurich-designed action and keyboard was introduced for all Feurich uprights. New improvements and design modifications were made on all the instruments; for example, the new Feurich model 179 Dynamic II has a lighter frame and various other modern features, such as an integrated LED lamp.

The second line is made in Vienna, Austria. The first model in this line is the 48" model 123 Vienna upright, designed by the Feurich Vienna team of experts managed by master piano builder Emil Dimitrov and including Stephen Paulello and Clare Pichet. The strung back for this model is made in China by Hailun, but with a new design, more advanced CNC milling, and with Paulello rust-free strings. All other parts are European. The level of detail in the design can be seen in features such as the compensation in the action for the different proportions and leverages required for black and white keys, owing to their different lengths. The Feurich High-Speed KAMM Action, designed by master piano builder Udo Kamm, also features a new, patented system of springs and rollers that enable extremely fast repetition for an upright piano. The pianos are meticulously regulated and voiced in Vienna. The 50" model 128 Vienna, due to enter production in 2017, was designed by Friedrich Steinbauer (original designer from the Feurich factory in Germany) and Jan Enzenauer, and is based on original Feurich designs.

Feurich offers an optional fourth pedal on their grand pianos. The Harmonic Pedal is essentially the inverse of a sostenuto: instead of holding up the dampers of notes struck prior to depressing the pedal, it holds up all *but* those notes. This allows the player to create sympathetic resonance between strings, even while playing staccato.

Warranty: 5 years, parts and labor, to original purchaser.

FÖRSTER, AUGUST

August Förster GmbH
Jahnstrasse 8
02708 Löbau
Germany
+49-3585-86630
www.august-foerster.de
www.facebook.com/august.foerster

The August Förster factory was founded by Friedrich August Förster in 1859 in Löbau, Germany, after Förster studied the art of piano building. During the years of control by the government of East Germany, the factory was managed by the fourth-generation piano builder, Wolfgang Förster. After the reunification of Germany and privatization, Wolfgang and his family once again owned their company. August Förster GmbH is now managed in the fifth generation by Wolfgang's daughter, Annekatrin Förster.

With a workforce of 40 using a great deal of hand labor, Förster makes about 120 grands a year in four sizes, and 150 verticals a year in three sizes. The pianos are very well built structurally, and the cabinets are elegant. Rims and pinblocks are of beech, soundboards of solid mountain-grown spruce, and bridges are of hardrock maple (without graphite). Each string is individually terminated (single-strung). The actions are made by Renner with Renner hammers. A sostenuto pedal is standard on all grand models.

The tone of August Förster grands is unique, with a remarkable bass: dark, deep, yet clear. As delivered from the factory, the treble is often quite bright, and for some American tastes might be considered a bit thin—it is a less complex sound that emphasizes clarity. This, however, can be modified somewhat with voicing and a good dealer preparation. The instruments are quite versatile, at home with Mozart or Prokofiev, classical or jazz. The 6' 4" model is often said to have an especially good scale. The concert-quality 7' 2" and 9' 1" models are well balanced tonally, and over the years have been endorsed by many famous artists. The Renner actions are very responsive and arrive in exacting regulation. The new 53" model 134K anniversary upright, intended for pianists who don't have space for a grand, has such grand-piano–like features as a full sostenuto; a large, adjustable music desk; and black keys of real ebony.

Most of the comments regarding the quality of materials and workmanship of the Förster grands also apply to the verticals. The cabinet of the vertical is of exceptional width, with extra-thick side panels of solid-core stock. Counter bridges are used on the outside of the soundboard to increase its mass. The verticals have a full set of agraffes, and all the hardware and handmade wood parts are of elegant quality. The actions are built by Renner. The verticals possess the same warm, rich, deep bass tone as the grands.

Warranty: 5 years, parts and labor, to original purchaser.

FRIDOLIN— See Schimmel.

GEYER, A.
Piano Marketing Group, LLC
3227 Natoma Way
Orlando, Florida 32825
954-559-9553
s.shebeck@yahoo.com
www.geyer-pianos.com

Company Headquarters: Steffes & Schulz GmbH
Mühlgasse 11-13, D-65183 Wiesbaden, Germany
Phone: +49-611-992240
colintaylor@btconnect.com
Pianos made by: A piano factory in Zhejiang Province, China

The A. Geyer brand and factory were established by the Geyer family in 1877, in Eisenberg, Thuringia, Germany, and the brand was well known in the late 19th and early 20th centuries, when Eisenberg was a significant center for piano building. Also produced in the Geyer factory over the years were the brands of Fuchs & Mohr, Sassmann, Steinberg, and Weisbrod. In time, the Geyer factory became the Wilh. Steinberg factory, which continues to produce pianos today.

Today, A. Geyer is a new company, with headquarters in Wiesbaden, Germany. The company's founders are Christoph Schulz, a fifth-generation German piano maker; Frederik Steffes, the former owner of the Wilh. Steinberg factory; and Colin Taylor, formerly with Bösendorfer and Brodmann. Although the company is new, the three founders bring to it decades of combined experience in piano manufacturing, and a vision, they say, to create a piano wonderful in sound, touch, and style, with outstanding value for the money.

Although the pianos are designed in Germany, A. Geyer production is located near Hangzhou, in Zhejiang Province, China, a region just outside of Shanghai that has become a center of piano manufacturing. The company founders believe that their knowledge and experience of traditional German methods of piano making, combined with local Chinese resources, can result in a better piano at lower cost.

Currently, A. Geyer makes three upright pianos and five grands. All pianos use carefully selected Chinese parts that are subject to strict quality controls. German Wurzen felt is used for the upright hammers, and Abel hammers for the grands. All pianos have a solid-spruce-core veneered soundboard and Japanese Suzuki strings. The actions and keyboards have been designed by the company's German master piano builder. All pianos are inspected by the company's technicians before leaving the factory.

Warranty: 10 years, parts and labor, on main structural elements; 5 years, parts and labor, on other manufactured items.

GROTRIAN
including Friedrich Grotrian
Grotrian Piano Company GmbH
P.O. Box 5833
D-38049 Braunschweig, Germany
+49-531-210100
+49-531-2101040 (fax)
contact@grotrian.de
www.grotrian.de
Sales Agent for U.S. and Canada:
Mason & Hamlin Piano Co.
916-567-9999

Friedrich Grotrian was born in 1803 in Schöningen, Germany, and as a young man lived in Moscow, where he ran a music business and was associated with piano manufacturing. Later in his life he teamed up with C.F. Theodor Steinweg, son of Heinrich Steinweg, to build pianos. Heinrich had emigrated to the U.S. about 1850, soon to establish the firm of Steinway & Sons. Theodor followed in 1865, selling his share in the partnership to Wilhelm Grotrian, son of Friedrich, who had died in 1860. Thereafter, the firm became known as Grotrian-Steinweg. (In a legal settlement with Steinway & Sons, Grotrian-Steinweg agreed to use only the name Grotrian on pianos sold in North America.) Even as early as the 1860s, Grotrian pianos were well known and highly respected throughout Europe. Each successive generation of the Grotrian family maintained the company's high standards and furthered the technical development of the instrument.

In 2015, a majority interest in the Grotrian Piano Co. was purchased by Parsons Music Group, a Hong Kong–based piano manufacturer. Grotrian says that all pianos bearing its name will continue to be made in Braunschweig, Germany, and that the Parsons investment will be used to expand manufacturing capacity to better serve the burgeoning Asian piano market. A member of the sixth generation of the Grotrian family is also a shareholder, and will continue to participate in managing the company, as will the current CEO, who has been in that position for 18 years.

Grotrian grands have beech rims, solid spruce soundboards, laminated beech pinblocks, Renner actions, and are single-strung. Grotrian prides itself on what it calls its "homogeneous soundboard," in which each piece of wood is specially chosen for its contribution to the tone of the soundboard. The cast-iron plate is attached with screws along the outer edges of the rim, instead of on top of the rim, which the company says allows the soundboard to vibrate more freely. The vertical pianos have a unique star-shaped wooden back structure and a full-perimeter plate. Grotrian makes five sizes of grand and six sizes of vertical piano. New "studio" versions of grand models 192 (6' 3") and 208 (6' 10"), made for institutions, have scratch-resistant cabinet finishes, wider music desks, and more impervious soundboard finishes.

Grotrian also makes a lower-cost line, called Friedrich Grotrian, with a beech back frame but no back posts, and a simpler cabinet. It's available in a 43½" model in polished ebony with legs, and in 43½" and 45" models for institutional use, with satin finishes but without legs. The Friedrich Grotrian models are also completely made at the Grotrian factory in Braunschweig, Germany.

In the near future, the Friedrich Grotrian models described above, like all the other models that are entirely made in the Braunschweig factory, will be included under the Grotrian brand. A new, lower-cost Friedrich Grotrian line, to be introduced in 2017, will have the rim and finished cabinet, with cast-iron plate, soundboard, and pinblock installed, constructed by Parsons Music in China, then shipped to the Grotrian factory in Braunschweig, where German strings, keys, hammers, and Renner action parts will be installed, and the pianos tuned, regulated, and voiced. The amount of value added by German parts and labor will qualify these models for "Made in Germany" status under German law. At press time, prices for these models were not yet available.

The treble of Grotrian pianos has extraordinary sustaining characteristics. It also has a pronounced sound of attack, subtle and delicate. The tenor is darker than many other brands. The bass can be powerful, but without stridency. Overall, Grotrian pianos have a unique, expressive sound and are a pleasure to play. Over the years, many well-known pianists have endorsed or expressed appreciation for Grotrian pianos.

Warranty: 5 years, parts and labor, transferable to future owners.

HAESSLER — See Blüthner.

HAILUN
including Cline and Emerson

Hailun America
P.O. Box 1130
Richland, Washington 99352
509-946-8078
877-946-8078
info@hailun-pianos.com
www.hailun-pianos.com

Pianos made by: Ningbo Hailun Musical Instruments Co. Ltd., Ningbo, Zhejiang Province, China

Ningbo Hailun began making piano parts and components in 1986 under the Ningbo Piano Parts Factory name, and began assembling entire pianos in 1995. Its assembly facility converted to a full-scale piano manufacturing facility in 2000. Today, the Hailun factory has over 400,000 square feet of production capacity and 800 employees. A 200,000-square-foot expansion project is underway to accommodate distribution in the U.S. market. Additionally, a new cabinet factory is now complete and began production in 2008. In addition to making pianos under the Hailun name, the company also makes the Feurich brand (formerly Wendl & Lung—see **Feurich**). Hailun also makes pianos or components under contract for several other manufacturers and distributors. Hailun recently conducted an Initial Public Offering of stock on the Shenzen Stock Exchange.

Currently, the Hailun line consists of four vertical sizes (mostly larger uprights) and five grand sizes. In 2010, the company introduced the 52" model HU7-P, with a duplex scale, agraffes, and a steel capo bar for, the company says, a "lush and powerful sound in the American tradition." This model also has a middle pedal that operates a true sostenuto mechanism.

(Note: Model designations on the cast-iron plates of some Hailun pianos may differ from those in Hailun marketing materials and in this publication because the models may have different names in the Chinese and U.S. markets. In each such case, the scale designs are the same, but, according to Hailun, the U.S. models contain the higher-quality parts and materials advertised in U.S. marketing materials and on the Hailun America web page.)

Hailun America is in the process of introducing several new grand and vertical models under the Emerson brand name (formerly the Hailun Vienna Series). The W.P. Emerson Co. was founded in 1849 by William P. Emerson, later changing its name to the Emerson Piano Co. Located in Boston, the company became a meeting place of old-world artisans and new-world technology, and grew into one of the largest and most reputable piano manufacturers of its time, selling its pianos throughout the world. The distributor of today's Emerson piano says that it seeks to continue the tradition of bringing together the new and old worlds, combining European, American, and Asian resources to address the need for an exacting, quality instrument that "reflects the Western tradition of piano building" at a more favorable price, and to "create a warm tonal experience in the tradition of the Viennese sound."

Emerson pianos are designed by an international team of piano designers close to the Hailun factory, and are manufactured by Hailun. The wood for its soundboards is sourced from the North Austrian Alps. The grands are designed with a wide tail, vertically laminated maple bridges, a slightly firmer touch, and faster action speed. The vertical has a patented TriGon duplex scale, agraffes, a full-perimeter plate, and an enhanced soundboard design. Each purchaser of an Emerson may, within 18 months of purchase, request that a special highly qualified technician, known as a Vienna Concert Technician, spend a full day of concert-level regulation and voicing on the piano at the customer's home.

In 2011, Hailun introduced a slow-close piano lid in all its grand piano models. Graphically named the Hailun Limb Protection System (HLPS), this is a version of the Safety-Ease retrofit system, described **elsewhere** in this publication, built into the piano at the factory. HLPS allows even a child to easily lift the otherwise heavy lid of a grand piano without danger, and prevents a falling lid from crashing down onto arms and hands. A version of HLPS, called HLPS Plus, and available only in the Vienna models, allows the user to adjust a grand piano lid to any position without the need for a lid propstick. Apart from the safety benefit, HLPS Plus allows the user to modulate sound projection by adjusting the lid position.

Hailun is a little different from most of the other Chinese companies selling pianos in the U.S.: Its founder and owner, Chen Hailun, is an entrepreneur in the Western style, and deeply involved in every aspect of the business. Originally a maker of molds for industrial use, Chen got into the piano business when piano manufacturers started to use his services to make piano parts. In 1998 he bought out the government's position in his company to better control quality and hiring decisions.

While modern manufacturing methods are fully utilized, the factory also uses a large amount of skilled manual labor. Chen seeks out the best workers by paying considerably higher wages than other piano makers in China, he says, and provides an in-depth training program for his workers, conducted by piano builders and technicians from the U.S. and Europe. He also assists in the training of future piano technicians through an association with a local university. His greatest aspiration, Chen says, is to make the best piano in Asia.

Over the years, much of Chen's technical efforts have gone into maximizing the precision and stability of the pianos and parts his company makes. This is evidenced by the substantial investment in computer-controlled machinery used for precision cutting; the design of keys, keybeds, and other parts to resist warping; and the fact that grand piano actions are actually interchangeable between instruments of the same model (this requires an unusually high level of precision). The pianos themselves exhibit good quality control and intelligence in design. In terms of materials, the company uses maple in grand piano rims, a feature indicative of higher quality and arguably necessary for the best sound. In 2011, the company began sourcing its own supply of the highest-quality Austrian spruce, and plans to make its own soundboards with this spruce for select piano models. *Piano Buyer*'s reviewers have tried out several Hailun grands (see reviews in the **Fall 2009**, **Fall 2010**, and **Fall 2011** issues) and have been impressed with their musicality.

To help it reach the highest quality standards, Hailun has also hired an impressive group of experts from Japan (Ema Shigeru), Europe (Stephen Paulello, Claire Trichet, Sibin Zlatkovic, Peter Veletzky), and the U.S. (Frank Emerson). In 2009, to oversee and assist with quality control, Hailun hired Rolf Ibach, owner of Rud. Ibach Sohn, one of the oldest and most reputable European piano companies, which closed its doors in 2008 after more than 200 years in business.

Hailun USA has initiated several support programs designed to increase the speed at which service requests are handled, and to measure customer satisfaction. It has also introduced the Hailun Dream Assurance Program, in which the company guarantees, subject to certain limitations, that the sound of any purchased Hailun piano will be to the customer's liking or, within 90 days of purchase, the company will exchange the piano for another of the same model. Under the company's Gold Service Program, Hailun dealers are obligated to provide each customer with one free service call between 60 and 180 days after purchase of a piano.

Hailun America is reintroducing the Cline brand to the U.S. market in the form of entry-level models made by Hailun. Chester L. Cline began selling pianos in Tacoma, Washington, in the 1880s, and produced pianos under his own name beginning in 1889. He eventually expanded his retail chain throughout the Northwest and, in the 1920s, into California, becoming one of the largest piano dealers in the West. In the 1980s and '90s, pianos bearing the Cline name were made by several manufacturers of entry-level pianos.

Today, Cline makes 46½" and 48" verticals and a 4' 11" grand. The grand comes with the HLPS lid-support system. Both the 48" vertical and the grand are optionally available with the MG Silent System, which can turn the acoustic piano into a digital one that can be played with headphones at any time of day or night. It also features a metronome, and allows performances to be recorded and exported in MIDI format to share with others. (See the chapter on **Hybrid Pianos** for more information about silent systems.) Owners of Cline pianos in North America are entitled to receive a trade-in credit of the full amount paid for the instrument toward the purchase of a new grand made by Hailun, Emerson, Petrof, or Sauter (all of whom share a common distributor).

Warranty: Hailun— 15 years, parts and labor, to the original owner, transferable to the second owner within the warranty period. Cline—10 years, parts and labor, to original purchaser. Emerson—5 years, parts and labor, to original purchaser. Electronics—1 year, parts and labor, to original purchaser. See also the Dream Assurance Program, described above.

HALLET, DAVIS & CO.

Hallet Davis Pianos
11 Holt Drive
Stony Point, New York 10980
845-429-0106
usapianos@yahoo.com
www.halletdavispianos.com

Pianos made by: various makers (see text)

This famous old American piano brand dates back to at least 1843 in Boston, and has changed hands many times over the years. It eventually became part of the Aeolian group of piano brands, and instruments bearing the name were manufactured at Aeolian's Memphis plant until that company went out of business in 1985. Subsequently, North American Music began producing Hallet, Davis, & Co. pianos, first in Korea, and now in China.

The Heritage and Signature Collections are made by the Beijing Hsinghai Piano Group, Ltd. (see **Beijing Hsinghai**), and by the Silbermann Piano Co. The upper-level pianos, known as the Imperial Collection II, are manufactured by Parsons Music, a factory associated with a large chain of music stores in China and Hong Kong, and the third-largest producer of pianos in China.

HARDMAN, PECK & CO.

Hardman Pianos
11 Holt Drive
Stony Point, New York 10980
845-429-0106
info@hardmanpiano.com
www.hardmanpiano.com

Pianos made by: Beijing Hsinghai Piano Group, Ltd., Beijing, China

Hugh Hardman established the Hardman Piano Company in New York City in 1842. Leopold Peck joined the company in 1880, and became a partner in 1890, at which time the company was renamed Hardman, Peck & Company. In the early 20th century, Hardman, Peck was sold to the Aeolian Corporation, which eventually moved to Memphis, where it remained until it went out of business in 1985. Today's Hardman, Peck & Company pianos are manufactured in China by the Beijing Hsinghai Piano Group (see **Beijing Hsinghai**). The piano line offers a selection of vertical and grand pianos in a variety of styles and finishes to meet the needs of entry-level and mid-level pianists.

HEINTZMAN & CO.

including Gerhard Heintzman

Heintzman Distributor Ltd.
1-12351 Bridgeport Road
Richmond, British Columbia V6V 1J4
Canada
U.S.: 303-765-5775
Canada: 604-801-5393
info@hzmpiano.com
www.hzmpiano.com

Pianos made by: Heintzman Piano Company, Ltd., Beijing, China

Heintzman & Co. Ltd. was founded by Theodore August Heintzman in Toronto in 1866. By 1900, Heintzman was one of Toronto's larger manufacturing concerns, building 3,000 pianos per year and selling them throughout Canada and abroad through a network of company stores and other distributors. The pianos received high praise and won prizes at exhibitions. Even today, technicians frequently encounter old Heintzman pianos built in the early part of the 20th century and consider them to be of high quality. In the latter decades of the century, Heintzman, like other North American brands, struggled to compete with cheaper foreign imports. The factory finally closed its doors in 1986 and relocated to China. (For a few years thereafter, some pianos continued to be sold in Canada under the

Heintzman and Gerhard Heintzman names.) At first the company was a joint venture with the Beijing Hsinghai Piano Group (see **Beijing Hsinghai**), but when the Chinese government began allowing foreign ownership of manufacturing concerns, the Canadian partner bought back majority ownership and took control.

The new company, known as Heintzman Piano Company, Ltd., is Canadian owned and managed and has a private, independent factory dedicated to producing Heintzman-brand pianos. Heintzman makes pianos to the original Canadian Heintzman designs and scales using some of the equipment from Canada. James Moffat, plant manager of the Canadian Heintzman factory for 40 years, has been retained as a consultant and visits the factory in China several times a year. The company even uses some components from Canada, such as Bolduc soundboards, in grands and larger verticals. The factory makes about 5,000 pianos per year.

The smallest vertical made under the Heintzman name is 43½" tall, but pianos for export to North America typically start at 48" and contain a mixture of Chinese and imported parts, such as pinblocks and treble strings from Germany and Mapes bass strings from the U.S. Verticals 48½" and taller use Renner Blue or Abel Blue hammers, and the largest two sizes have Canadian Bolduc soundboards of solid Eastern white spruce. All verticals 50" and taller have a middle pedal that operates a bass-sustain mechanism, as well as a Silent Switch that operates a mute bar for silent practice.

The grands—5', 5' 6", 6' 1", 6' 8", and 9' long—also use German pinblocks and strings, Mapes bass strings, Renner Blue or Abel Blue hammers, and Canadian Bolduc or German Strunz soundboards of solid spruce.. The 9' concert grand comes with a full Renner action and Kluge keys from Germany. A Renner action is a higher-priced option on the other models. All grands come with a sostenuto pedal. A 6' 1" model patterned on the old Heintzman model D was introduced in 2007.

New in 2013, and aimed at a slightly more upscale audience, is the Royal series of verticals and grands, with two-tone cabinet trim and inlays on the inside of the lid, as well as a Bolduc or Strunz soundboard, Abel or Renner Blue hammers, and Mapes bass strings.

Heintzman Piano Company also makes the slightly less expensive Gerhard Heintzman brand. This line uses less expensive materials and components, such as Japanese hammers and a veneer-laminated spruce soundboard in the verticals (a Bolduc soundboard in some of the grands). The polished ebony grands have a silver plate and trim.

Warranty: Heintzman and Gerhard Heintzman—10 years, parts and labor, from the factory, transferable to future owners within the warranty period.

HESSEN, J.F

J.F. Hessen Piano
12816 SE 38th Street
Kirkland, Washington 98006
425-643-8113
info@jfhessenpiano.com
www.jfhessenpiano.com
In Canada, contact: Wayne Chen, **sales@pianokeyboard.com**

Pianos made by: Artfield Julius Feurich Piano Co., Shanghai, China, and Altenstadt, Hesse, Germany

In 2002, the Chinese piano manufacturer Artfield purchased a majority interest in Feurich from its owner, Julius Feurich, whose company had been making pianos in Germany since 1851. Artfield made exact copies of all the Feurich equipment and scale designs, and has since been manufacturing and distributing pianos in China under the Julius Feurich name. In 2008, Artfield transferred the Feurich company back to Julius Feurich in exchange for additional production equipment, but retained the right to use the Julius Feurich name in China. In 2011, Julius Feurich sold the remaining rights to the commercial use of his name to another party, and attempted to establish a new piano-building firm under a different name in Gunzenhausen, Germany, but that business failed. (See under **Feurich** for more information.) Now Artfield has hired Stephan Kühnlein, a production manager in Julius Feurich's former company, and other former Feurich employees, to complete the manufacture of pianos in Altenstadt, Germany, to the original Feurich designs. These pianos are to be called "J.F. Hessen," the "J.F." referring to Julius Feurich, and "Hessen" referring to the German state, Hesse, in which Altenstadt is located. Julius Feurich is not involved with the company.

Most of the assembly of J.F. Hessen pianos is performed in China by Artfield, and the pianos are similar to those Artfield makes under the Julius Feurich name. For the J.F. Hessen pianos, however, the nearly completed instruments are shipped to Germany, where the hammers are installed and all musical finishing work, such as tuning, voicing, and action regulating, is performed to German standards. The pianos contain the usual high-quality components often found in German pianos: Renner actions (standard in grands, optional in verticals), Renner or Abel hammers, Strunz Bavarian spruce soundboards, Röslau strings, and sharps of real ebony wood. Due to the amount of German materials and labor in the final product, the pianos qualify for "made in Germany" status under German law. At present, three vertical models (47", 48", and 52") and one grand model (5' 8") are available.

Warranty: Ten years, parts and labor, transferable between individuals with notification to dealer within the warranty period.

HOFFMANN, W. — See Bechstein, C.

HUPFELD — See Rönisch.

IRMLER
including Schiller
Blüthner USA LLC
5660 W. Grand River
Lansing, Michigan 48906
517-886-6000
800-954-3200
916-337-1086
info@irmler-piano.com
www.irmler-piano.com
In Canada, contact Bluethner Piano Canada Inc.
604-264-1138
rrgarvin@telus.net
www.bluethner.ca
Pianos made by: Irmler Piano GmbH, Leipzig, Germany, and other factories (see text)

Irmler is a sister company of Blüthner, and Irmler pianos are distributed through the Blüthner dealer network. The brand has recently been reintroduced to the market in two series: Studio and Professional.

The Studio series is largely made in a factory in China owned by Irmler. The pianos are then shipped to the Blüthner factory in Germany, where Abel hammers are installed and the pianos are inspected and adjusted as needed, prior to shipping to dealers. The pianos have Delignit pinblocks and veneer-laminated spruce soundboards. The grand rims are of Chinese oak and the grand actions are made with Renner parts. The Studio-series verticals include a number of models with interesting, modern cabinet designs.

The Professional series, also known as Irmler Europe, is assembled in Germany using strung backs (structural and acoustical elements) from Samick in Indonesia and cabinets from Poland (suppliers are subject to change). The pianos have Delignit pinblocks and solid spruce soundboards. Grands have rims of maple and beech, action parts by Renner (U.S. distribution only), and duplex scaling. Vertical actions are by Detoa.

The Irmler Studio series is also available from some dealers under the Schiller brand name, with a slightly modified cabinet; prices are comparable to those for Irmler.

Warranty: 10 years, parts and labor, to original purchaser.

KAWAI
including Shigeru Kawai
Kawai America Corporation
2055 East University Drive
Rancho Dominguez, California 90220
310-631-1771
800-421-2177
310-223-0900 (Shigeru Kawai)
acoustic@kawaius.com
www.kawaius.com
www.shigerukawai.com
Pianos made by: Kawai Musical Instrument Mfg. Co., Ltd.; Hamamatsu, Japan, and Karawan, Indonesia

Kawai was founded in 1927 by Koichi Kawai, an inventor and former Yamaha employee who was the first person in Japan to design and build a piano action. While Kawai is second in size to Yamaha among Japanese piano manufacturers, it has a well-deserved reputation all its own for quality and innovation. Nearly all Kawai grands and taller uprights are made in Japan; most consoles and studios are made in Indonesia. The company closed its North Carolina factory in 2005.

One of Kawai's most important innovations is the use of ABS Styran plastic in the manufacture of action parts. More than 40 years of use and scientific testing have shown this material to be superior to wood for this purpose. ABS does not swell and shrink with changes in humidity, so actions made with it are likely to maintain proper regulation better than wood actions. The parts are stronger and without glue joints, so breakage is rare. These parts are present in every Kawai piano. In the current Millennium III action found in some models, the ABS is reinforced with carbon fiber so it can be stronger with less mass. Having less mass to move (that is, less inertia), the action can be more responsive to the player's intentions, including faster repetition. Certain contact surfaces on the action parts are also micro-engineered for ideal shape and texture, resulting in a more consistent touch. Although it took a number of years to overcome the idea that plastic parts must be inferior, there is essentially no dispute anymore among piano technicians on this subject.

Kawai's vertical piano offerings change frequently and are sometimes confusing. At present there are three basic series of Kawai verticals. The console series begins with the 44½" model 506N, a basic entry-level console in an institutional-style cabinet (legs with toe blocks).

Model K-15 is a 44" version of this in a continental-style cabinet (no legs), and model 508 is a 44½" version in a simple furniture-style cabinet (freestanding legs). Model 607 is the same piano in a fancier furniture-style cabinet. All have the same internal workings. The action in this series is slightly smaller than a full-size action, so it will be slightly less responsive. However, it is more than sufficient for beginner or casual use.

Kawai has replaced both of its former studio models, the UST-7 and UST-8, with the 46" model UST-9, made in Indonesia. This model has the stronger back of the UST-7, rather than that of the UST-8, which was not known for its tuning stability. The UST-9 also contains the Millennium III action; an angled, leather-lined music desk to better hold music; and a stylish, reinforced bench. The 46½" model 907 is essentially the UST-9 in a fancy, furniture-style cabinet.

Kawai's K series of upright models has been updated in 2014, and the model names have been changed. The former K-2, K-3, K-5, K-6, and K-8, all sold in North America, have become the new K-200 (45"), K-300 (48"), K-400 (48"), K-500 (51"), and K-800 (53"). The K-400 is internally the same as the K-300, but its cabinet includes a grand-piano–style music desk (formerly available only with the K-8) and a folding, low-profile fallboard. The K-500—at 51", two inches taller than the old K-5—has been extensively redesigned internally, with longer bass strings, a larger soundboard, and a redesigned cast-iron plate. Several of the new K-series models are available in the AnyTime (ATX) series as silent/hybrid pianos. See the article on **Hybrid Pianos** for details.

As before, all K-series models include Kawai's Millennium III actions, made with carbon-fiber composites. The hammers in all models are now made with underfelt and mahogany moldings, which Kawai says improves the responsiveness of the action and the tonal sustain. All models have redesigned, tapered soundboards for improved tonal response; double-braced and steel-reinforced keybeds to prevent warping and flex; and come with slow-close fallboards and adjustable benches. The K-500 and K-800 both feature Kawai's Neotex ivory-substitute key material, and the K-800 comes with a sostenuto pedal. The K-series cabinets have been redesigned for a sleeker, more modern appearance.

Kawai makes two series of grand pianos: GX and GL. The GX line (formerly RX; see below), which is sold in North America in a version known as the BLAK series, is the most expensive and has the best features. It is designed for the best performance, whereas the GL series is designed more for efficiency in manufacturing, with fewer refinements. All the GX pianos feature a radial beam structure, converging together and connected

to the plate using a cast-iron bracket at the tenor break. This system makes for a more rigid structure, which translates into better tone projection. The soundboards in the GX models are tapered for better tonal response; and the rims are thicker and stronger than in the GL models, and are made of a blend of open- and closed-pore hardwoods to improve the tone. The Kawai Millennium III actions used in both series now have hammer-shank stabilizers, designed to retain power by keeping the shank from wavering under a heavy blow. All GX pianos have agraffes, duplex scaling, lighter hammers (less inertia), and Neotex synthetic ivory keptops; and come with a slow-close fallboard. The GX grands get more precise key weighting, plus more tuning, regulating, and voicing at the factory. The cabinetry is nicer looking and of better quality than that of the GL series pianos, with the polished ebony models in the new BLAK series receiving a UV-cured, scratch-resistant coating on the music rack.

In 2013, the GX BLAK models replaced the previous RX series—see our **review** in the Spring 2014 issue. The changes from RX to GX include a pinblock that is fitted to the plate flange and more securely attached to the case for better tuning stability, and the front stretcher has been made thicker, stiffening the structure, and thus both conserving tonal energy and contributing to tuning stability. The GX rims use alternating layers of two different hardwoods, one chosen for tonal power, the other for warmth. There have also been some changes to the scale designs and soundboard taper.

In the fall of 2015, Kawai consolidated its GM and GE piano lines into a single, new GL line of models: GL-10 (5'), GL-20 (5' 2"), GL-30 (5' 5"), GL-40 (5' 11"), and GL-50 (6' 2"). The GL models share some important features with the higher-end GX models: Millennium III action with hammer-shank stabilizers, agraffes, stronger pinblock/stretcher design, longer keys, full sostenuto pedal, and soft-close fallboard, among others. However, the GL models have a single-wood-variety hardwood rim, rather than the blended hardwoods of the GX series; a solid rather than a vertically laminated bridge, without cap; acrylic rather than Neotex keytops; a simpler beam structure in the smaller models (GL-10/20/30); and a simpler cabinet design and less elaborate interior finishing. The GL-20/30/40/50 models are all built in Japan; the GL-10 is made in Indonesia. The inclusion of several GX-level features makes the GL-10/20 models significant steps up from the discontinued GM models.

Kawai's quality control is excellent, especially in its Japanese-made pianos. Major problems are rare, and other than normal maintenance, after-sale service is usually limited to fixing the occasional minor buzz or squeak. Kawai's warranty service is also excellent, and the warranty is transferable to future owners within the warranty period (a benefit that is not common these days). The tone of most Kawai pianos, in my opinion, is not as ideal for classical music as some more expensive instruments, but when expertly voiced, it is not far off, and in any case is quite versatile musically. In part because the touch is so good, Kawai grands are often sought by classical pianists as a less-expensive alternative to a Steinway or other high-end piano. Kawai dealers tend to be a little more aggressive about discounting than their competition (Yamaha). There is also a thriving market for used Kawais. (If you're considering buying a used Kawai, please read "Should I Buy a Used 'Gray Market' Yamaha or Kawai Piano?" on pages 176–177 of *The Piano Book*, or the shorter version in "**Buying a Used or Restored Piano**" in this publication.)

The Shigeru Kawai line of grands represents Kawai's ultimate effort to produce a world-class piano. Named after Kawai's former chairman (and son of company founder Koichi Kawai), the limited-edition (fewer than 300 per year) Shigeru Kawai grands are made at the separate facility where Kawai's EX concert grands are built.

Although based on the Kawai RX designs, the Shigeru Kawai models are "hand made" in the extreme. Very high-grade soundboard spruce is air-dried for multiple years, then planed by hand by a worker who knocks on the wood and listens for the optimum tonal response. Ribs are also hand-planed for correct stiffness. String bearing is set in the traditional manner by planing the bridges by hand instead of having pre-cut bridges pinned by machine. Bass strings are wound by hand instead of by machine. Hammers are hand-pressed without heat for a wider voicing range, and the hammer weights are carefully controlled for even touch. Hammer shanks are thinned along the bottom so that their stiffness is matched to the hammer mass. These procedures represent a level of detail relatively few manufacturers indulge in.

In 2012, Kawai updated the Shigeru Kawai grands, changing the cabinet styling and some of the pianos' construction features. The inside of the rim is now finished with bird's-eye maple veneer, and the round legs have been changed to straight legs with brass trim. The rim itself is now made of alternating layers of rock maple and mahogany, which Kawai says provides more power without losing warmth in the tone. The structure at the front of the piano has been made stronger, and the beams underneath are now made from spruce instead of the laminated mahogany Kawai uses in its other models. The keys have been lengthened for a better touch, especially on the smaller models.

Each buyer of a Shigeru Kawai piano receives a visit within the first year by a Kawai master technician from the factory in Japan. These are the same factory technicians who do the final installation of actions in pianos, as well as the final voicing and regulation. According to those who have watched them work, these Japanese master technicians are amazingly skilled. Because the Shigeru Kawai pianos have been on the market only since 2000 and in very limited quantities, many piano technicians have yet to service one. Those who have, however, tend to rank them among the world's finest instruments, and Shigeru Kawai pianos are often chosen by pianists participating in international piano competitions.

Warranty: Kawai and Shigeru Kawai—10 years, parts and labor, transferable to future owners within the warranty period.

KAYSERBURG — See Pearl River

KINGSBURG
Piano Empire, Inc..
3035 East La Mesa Street
Anaheim, California 92806
800-576-3463
714-408-4599
info@pianoempire.com
www.kingsburgpianosusa.com

Pianos made by: Yantai Kingsburg Piano Co., Ltd., Yantai, Shandong Province, China

+86-535-6932912
kingsburgpiano@163.com
www.kingsburgpiano.com.cn

Yantai Kingsburg Piano Co., Ltd., formerly known as Yantai Longfeng, was established in 1988. It is located in a temperate area of northern China that is said to be ideal for piano making because of its moderate humidity level. The same factory, under previous ownership, made pianos for the West under various brand names for many years.

All Kingsburg pianos have been designed by well-known piano-design master Klaus Fenner, and scales have been further developed by a piano-design expert from a highly regarded overseas piano manufacturer. Components are sourced from around the world: from Germany, Röslau piano wire, Abel hammers, and Dehonit pinblocks; from the Czech Republic, Detoa actions; and from Japan, tuning pins and ivory-like mineral keytops. All pianos now feature keys of real ebony wood and come with a slow-close fallboard. Interesting design features include longer keys on upright models for more a grand-like playing experience, brass-bar duplex scale, and the company's exclusive Tri Board solid spruce soundboard, which, in the taller verticals, is unattached to the piano back at the bottom, for better bass tone and improved tuning stability.

To continue improving quality, Kingsburg has also invested in computerized manufacturing equipment and advanced scale-design software. With these tools, the company says, its goals are to achieve a smooth, comfortable touch from the keys and action; accurate downbearing and crown on the bridges and soundboard; and greater harmonic resonance and uniformity of sound volume.

At present, the Kingsburg line comprises four sizes of upright and three sizes of grand. Custom styles and finishes are also available.

A key focus of Yantai Kingsburg is that the final factory preparation of the pianos be done in such a manner that the dealer can deliver an instrument to the customer's home with very little additional work being required. To that end, the U.S. distributor's Asian affiliate sends highly trained technicians to the factory to fully tune, voice, and regulate Kingsburg pianos to their high standards before they are crated for shipment.

Warranty: 12 years, parts and labor, to original purchaser.

KNABE, WM.

See also **Samick**.

Samick Music Corp. (SMC)
1329 Gateway Drive
Gallatin, Tennessee 37066
615-206-0077
info@smcmusic.com
www.knabepianos.com

Pianos made by: Samick Musical Instrument Mfg. Co. Ltd., Inchon, South Korea; and Bogor, West Java, Indonesia

---

Founded in Baltimore in 1837 by Wilhelm (William) Knabe, a German immigrant, Wm. Knabe & Co. established itself in the 19th and early 20th centuries as one of the finest piano makers in America. Over the years, Knabe pianos have left an important mark on the music field, including over 40 years as the official piano of the Metropolitan Opera, sponsoring Tchaikovsky's appearance at the opening of Carnegie Hall, and their places inside the White House and Graceland. Today, Knabe is the official piano of the American Ballet Theatre at the Met. 2012 marks the company's 175th anniversary.

As part of the consolidation of the American piano industry in the early 20th century, Knabe eventually became part of the Aeolian family of brands. Following Aeolian's demise in 1985, the Knabe name became part of Mason & Hamlin, which was purchased out of bankruptcy in 1996 by the owners of PianoDisc. For a time, a line of Knabe pianos was made for PianoDisc by Young Chang in Korea and China. When the line was discontinued, Samick acquired the Wm. Knabe & Co. name. (Note: "Knabe" is pronounced using the hard K sound followed by "nobby.")

SMC (Samick's U.S. distribution subsidiary) began by using the Wm. Knabe name on some of the pianos formerly sold as the World Piano premium line of Samick instruments. In 2002, SMC developed the Concert Artist series for the Knabe name. Highlighting this series are the 5' 8" and 6' 4" grand models, which have been redesigned, based on the original 19th- and early 20th-century Knabe scale designs and cabinet styles in use when the company was based in Baltimore. Features include sand-cast plates, lacquer semigloss wood finishes, Renner actions on larger grands, German hammers, and rims of maple and oak. The company has added 5' 3", 7' 6", and 9' 2" models for the American market. The verticals feature unique cabinet designs with bird's-eye maple and mahogany inlays, rosewood key inserts, and tone escapement. The 52" upright includes a full sostenuto, hand-activated mute rail, and agraffes throughout the bass section of the piano.

For two years, SMC completed assembly of Concert Artist grands at its Tennessee facility, with strung backs made in Indonesia or Korea. Now, most Knabe pianos are made in their entirety in Indonesia but are still uncrated in the U.S., where they are inspected, tuned, regulated, and voiced before being shipped to dealers.

In 2011, SMC unveiled two additional product lines within the Knabe family: the Academy and Baltimore series. The Academy series has many of the same features and specifications as the popular, upper-end, Kohler & Campbell Millennium brand, also made by Samick: a maple or beech inner rim (grands); a premium soundboard of solid white spruce; German hammers; a Samick Premium Action; satin lacquer semigloss wood finishes; and a Samick-made hornbeam action rail (larger verticals). (See **Samick** for more about Kohler & Campbell.) The Academy series also boasts two institutional studio uprights, the WMV245 and WMV247, both with full-length music racks, the WMV247 also with agraffes through the bass section.

The Baltimore series offers a more modestly priced alternative to the institutional Academy series or upper-end Concert Artist series. This line features an all-spruce "surface tension" (veneered) soundboard. The grands provide a full sostenuto pedal, slow-close fallboard, fully adjustable music desk and rack, multiple finishes in both satin ebony and wood tones, and, recently, a new designer grand with accents of Bubinga or African Pommele. The verticals showcase a wide range of sizes and cabinet styles, including wood tones in French cherry, traditional mahogany, and Renaissance walnut.

Warranty: 10 years, parts and labor, transferable to future owners within the warranty period.

KOHLER & CAMPBELL — See Samick.

LOMENCE

J.D. Grandt Piano Supply Co.
181 King Road
Richmond Hill, Ontario L4E 2W1
Canada
905-773-0087
info@jdgrandt.com
www.jdgrandt.com

Pianos made by: Lomence Modern Crystal Piano Co., Ltd., Foshan, Guangdong Province, China

The Lomence factory is located in Foshan, China, approximately one hour north of Guangzhou, in the southern region of China. A manufacturer of traditional pianos since 1998, Lomence discovered great success in its local market after experimenting with more modern-looking cabinet designs. The distinguishing feature of Lomence pianos is that many of the cabinet parts, including the top lid, front panel, fallboard, and side gables, are made of clear acrylic. The sharps on the tallest vertical are also of clear acrylic, creating an interesting effect in which they appear black from above but clear from the side.

Lomence pianos are available in three vertical sizes, 47.5", 48.5", and 50.5", and a 6' grand. Material specifications include German Röslau music wire, Siberian spruce soundboard, laminated Austrian spruce keys, nickel-plated hardware, and a slow-close fallboard.

Warranty: 10 years, parts and labor, to the original purchaser.

MASON & HAMLIN

Mason & Hamlin Piano Company
35 Duncan Street
Haverhill, Massachusetts 01830
916-567-9999
www.masonhamlin.com

Pianos made by: Mason & Hamlin Piano Co., Haverhill, Massachusetts

Mason & Hamlin was founded in 1854 by Henry Mason and Emmons Hamlin. Mason was a musician and businessman and Hamlin was an inventor working with reed organs. Within a few years, Mason & Hamlin was one of the largest makers of reed organs in the U.S. The company began making pianos in 1881 in Boston, and soon became among the most prestigious of the Boston piano makers. By 1910, Mason & Hamlin was considered Steinway's chief competitor. Over the next 85 years, Mason & Hamlin changed hands many times. (You can read the somewhat lengthy and interesting history in *The Piano Book*.) In 1996 the Burgett brothers, owners of PianoDisc, purchased Mason & Hamlin out of bankruptcy and set about reestablishing manufacturing at the six-story factory in Haverhill, Massachusetts. The company emphasizes limited-quantity, handbuilt production, and currently manufactures from 200 to 350 pianos per year. Daily tours are offered to visitors.

Since acquiring the company, the Burgetts have brought back most of the piano models from the company's golden Boston era (1881–1932) that originally made the company famous. Refinements have been made to the original scale designs and other core design features. First came the 5' 8" model A and 7' model BB, both of which had been manufactured by the previous owner. Then, in fairly rapid succession, came the 6' 4" model AA, the 9' 4" model CC concert grand, and the 5' 4" model B. The development of these three models was an especially interesting and costly project: in the process, the engineering staff resurrected the original design of each model, constructed new rim presses, standardized certain features, refined manufacturing processes, and modernized jigs, fixtures, templates, and machinery, improvements that afterward were applied to the company's other models. The 50" model 50 vertical piano has also been reintroduced and redesigned, with longer keys for a more grand-like touch, and improved pedal leverage. Internal parts for the verticals are made in Haverhill, then assembled in the company's Sacramento factory, where it also installs PianoDisc systems.

All Mason & Hamlin grands have certain features in common, including a wide-tail design; a full-perimeter plate; an extremely thick and heavy maple rim; a solid spruce soundboard; a seven-ply, quartersawn maple pinblock; and the patented tension-resonator Crown Retention System. The tension resonator (illustrated in *The Piano Book*), invented by Richard Gertz in 1900, consists of a series of turnbuckles that connect to specific points on the inner rim. This system of turnbuckles is said to lock the rim in place so that it cannot expand with stress and age, thereby preserving the soundboard crown (curvature). (The soundboard is glued to the inner rim and would collapse if the rim expanded.) While there is no modern-day experimental evidence to confirm or deny this theory, anecdotal evidence and observations by piano technicians tend to validate it because, unlike most older pianos, the soundboards of old Mason & Hamlins almost always have plenty of crown.

In the early part of the 20th century, Wessell, Nickel & Gross was a major supplier of actions to American piano manufacturers, including Mason & Hamlin. Over the years, the name fell into disuse. In 2004 Mason & Hamlin revived the name by registering the trademark, which now refers to the design and specifications of Mason & Hamlin actions. The company manufactures a new line of carbon-fiber action parts of strikingly innovative design, which the company makes available to its dealers and to rebuilders as a high-performance upgrade to the traditional wood action. The company explained that it has moved to using composite parts because of the inherent shortcomings of wood: it's prone to breakage under constant pounding, the parts vary in strength and mass from one piece of wood to the next, and wood shrinks and swells with changing temperature and humidity. Composite parts, on the other hand, are more than ten times as strong as wood; are built to microscopic tolerances, so they are virtually identical; and are impervious to weather. According to the company, material scientists predict that in the benign environment of a piano, the minimum life expectancy of composite parts is 100 years. The Wessell, Nickel & Gross composite action is now standard on all new Mason & Hamlin pianos.

Mason & Hamlin grands are available in satin and high-polish ebony finishes, and in several standard and exotic wood finishes in high polish. Satin finishes are lacquer, the high-polish finishes are polyester. Most sizes are also available in a stylized case design called Monticello, which has fluted, conical legs, similar to Hepplewhite style, with matching lyre and bench. In 2009 Mason & Hamlin introduced the Chrome artcase design, in polished ebony with chrome and stainless-steel case hardware replacing the traditional brass hardware. This design also has art-deco case styling, a silver plate, and a new fallboard logo in a modern font. This modern-font logo, along with a new slow-close fallboard, is standard on all new Mason & Hamlin grands.

In 2014, to commemorate the company's 160th anniversary, Mason & Hamlin introduced the Cambridge Collection. Model designs in this series feature two-toned cabinets in hand-rubbed finishes of polished ebony and either bubinga or Macassar ebony. On the grands, the hand-selected exotic veneers appear on the fallboard, the music desk, the lid underside, and the inner rim; on the verticals, they appear on the upper and lower front panels.

The tone of Mason & Hamlin pianos is typically American—lush, singing, and powerful, not unlike the Steinway in basic character, but with an even more powerful bass and a clearer treble. The designers have done a good job of making a recognizable Mason & Hamlin sound that is consistent throughout the model line. The 5' 8" model A has a particularly powerful bass for a piano of its size. The treble, notably weak in prior versions, has been beefed up, but the bass is still the showpiece of the piano. The new 5' 4" model B also has a large-sounding bass for its size. The "growling" power of the Mason & Hamlin bass is most apparent in the 7' model BB. The 6' 4" model AA is a little better balanced between bass and treble, one reason why it is a favorite of mine.

The basic musical design of Mason & Hamlin pianos is very good, as is most of the workmanship. As with other American-made pianos, musical and cabinet detailing, such as factory voicing and regulation and plate and cabinet cosmetics, are reasonable but lag somewhat behind the company's European competitors in finesse. The company says it is standard procedure for final voicing and regulation to be finished off by thorough and competent dealer prep.

In recent years many companies have turned to China and other international sources for parts and materials, for several reasons: a domestic source is no longer available, to save money, to increase the security of supply, and, in some cases, to increase quality. Among makers of high-end pianos, Mason & Hamlin has been pioneering in this regard, though it is not the only company to do so. The company's worldwide sourcing of parts and materials, along with its investment in modernized equipment, has made the Mason & Hamlin a better instrument while keeping the piano's price at a reasonable level. It's a very good value among high-end instruments.

Warranty: 5 years, parts and labor, transferable to future owners within the warranty period.

MAY BERLIN — See Schimmel.

PALATINO

The Music Link
P.O. Box 57100
Hayward, California 94545
888-552-5465
piano@palatinousa.com
www.palatinousa.com

Pianos made by: AXL Musical Instrument Co., Ltd. Corp.,
Shanghai, China

PARSONS MUSIC

Parsons Music Corporation
8/F, Railway Plaza
39 Chatham Road South
Tsim Sha Tsui, Kowloon
Hong Kong
+852 2333 1863
mailto@parsonsmusic.com
www.parsonsmusic.com
www.parsonsmusic.com.cn

Although Palatino may be a relatively new name to the piano world, it is not a newcomer to the music business. For almost 20 years, parent company AXL has manufactured a full range of musical instruments under its own name and under a variety of other, recognizable brand names, including cooperative ventures with Schimmel and Renner. The company has a highly automated factory that employs CNC routers from Japan and Germany, and imports high-quality materials and components for its pianos from around the world.

Palatino makes over 10,000 pianos annually in two categories: Classic and Professional. The Classic series includes the 48" Torino upright (PUP-123T) and 5' Milano grand (PGD-50); the Professional series includes the 50" Capri upright (PUP-126), the 5' 9" Roma grand (PGD-59), and the 6' 2" Firenze grand (PGD-62). Features common to all Palatino pianos include a German or Canadian solid spruce soundboard, German Röslau steel strings, and hard rock-maple pinblock. In addition, Professional-series pianos have a Renner-style action and hammers; the Classic series uses British-designed customized BPA-style actions and hammers.

Based on personal observation and dealer reports, Palatino pianos appear to have good quality control and are prepared well at the factory before being shipped to dealers. The AXL factory is known as being one of China's higher-grade facilities for the manufacture of musical instruments. Our own reviewer tested a couple of the grand models and found them to be very musical and a pleasure to play (see **review** in the Fall 2009 issue).

Warranty: 10 years, parts and labor. Benches and slow-close fallboard mechanisms are warranted for one year.

Parsons Music Corporation, headquartered in Hong Kong, was founded in 1986 by Terence and Arling Ng as a small music-lesson studio. Since then it has become China's largest music retailer, with more than 100 retail locations and 80 music schools throughout China and Hong Kong. In 1997, the company expanded into manufacturing pianos and other musical instruments, and is now the third largest piano maker in China.

At present, all of the pianos Parsons makes for sale in this part of the world are made for and distributed by other companies under those companies' own brand names. However, Parsons manufactures and sells, in China and Hong Kong, its own house brands, Yangtze River, Toyama, and Schönbrunn; manufactures the brand Barrate & Robinson, which it licenses the right to sell in China; has a strategic alliance with Kawai, in which Parsons distributes Kawai pianos in China, and manufactures select Kawai models for sale only in Parsons Music's stores in China; is the majority shareholder of the German piano makers Grotrian and Wilh. Steinberg and manufactures some of the Wilh. Steinberg models in China; and cooperates in the manufacture of the Pianoforce electronic player-piano system, and distributes it in China and Hong Kong. Parsons Music's commitment to piano manufacturing is also demonstrated by its ownership of an iron-plate foundry, a wood-processing facility, and even the forests in which the wood for its instruments is grown. In recent years, Parsons has become known within the piano-manufacturing community as the source of some of the best-made pianos from China.

PEARL RIVER

including Ritmüller and Kayserburg

GW Distribution, LLC
P.O. Box 329
Mahwah, New Jersey 07430
845-429-3712
www.pearlriverusa.com
www.ritmullerusa.com
www.kayserburgusa.com
info@pearlriverusa.com

Pianos made by: Guangzhou Pearl River Piano Group Ltd.,
Guangzhou, China

Established in 1956, Pearl River Piano Group has become the largest piano manufacturer in the world, with a production of over 125,000 pianos annually by more than 2,000 workers. The company builds pianos under the Pearl River, Ritmüller, and Kayserburg names, as well as under a few other names for OEM contracts with distributors such as **Cristofori** (with Jordan Kitt's Music) and **Essex** (with Steinway). (See separate listings under those names.) Pearl River is the best-selling piano brand in China, and is exported to more than 100 countries. After a successful IPO in 2012, the formerly government-owned company completed construction of a new, state-of-the-art, 3.5 million sq. ft. factory, to which it will transition next year. The factory combines traditional craftsmanship with advanced CNC digital machinery, and complies with European high-level technology and process standards.

In recent years, Pearl River has revised and streamlined its model line with the assistance of European and American piano-design consultants. Many new models have been introduced, while older models have been reviewed and modified. Currently, Pearl River verticals begin with the 43" console model EU110 leg and toe continental (new in 2016) and the EU111 series in several traditional American furniture styles. They continue with a series of studio models, including the 45" model UP115M5 in a traditional institutional style (legs with toe blocks), and the 45" model UP115E in a school-friendly institutional style with special casters and a full-length music desk. Finally, there are the upright models, including the 46½" model EU118 (new in 2015), and the relatively new 48" model EU122 and 51½" model EU131 concert upright.

Pearl River grands come in six sizes, from 4' 11" to 9', and have been redesigned over the last three years to include features such as vertically laminated bridges with solid maple caps, lighter touchweights, German hammer felt, and new scale designs.

Pearl River also makes pianos under the Ritmüller name, a brand that originated in Germany in 1795. A European master piano designer was engaged in 2007 to design, from the ground up, a line of higher-end pianos that would be distinct from the Pearl River line. These instruments were introduced in North America in 2009 under the Ritmüller name. (In some parts of the world, these pianos are branded Kayserburg.)

Ritmüller pianos come in three distinct price categories: Premium, Performance, and Classic. The Premium models feature solid spruce soundboards, Renner hammers, hornbeam and maplewood actions, and real ebony sharps, among other higher-quality features. *Piano Buyer*'s reviewers have auditioned several of the new grand models and have been very impressed. See reviews in the **Fall 2009** issue of the grand models GH-160, 170, and 188; in the **Fall 2010** issue of the GH-148R; and in the **Fall 2011** issue of the GH-188R. In addition, the 48" model UH-121R vertical and the 4' 10" model GH-148R grand have been chosen as "Staff Picks." The Performance models, introduced in 2014, feature unique scales, offset backposts, ebony sharps, high-quality German Abel hammers, and a veneered and tapered all-spruce soundboard. The Classic series, introduced in 2011, is a line of lower-cost instruments currently comprising three vertical models. They feature a veneered all-spruce soundboard and German Röslau strings.

In 2013, Pearl River brought to North America the upper-level Kayserburg Artists series. These instruments are handmade by two dozen of Pearl River's most experienced craftsmen, personally managed by European piano experts, in what can be described only as a small "German" piano workshop inside a large Chinese piano factory. The Kayserburg Artists craftsmen have all completed a rigorous training that includes studying the world's finest pianos and working side by side with visiting European craftsmen. The Kayserburg Artists pianos contain such high-end features as soundboards of tight-grained, solid European spruce, Renner hammers, Laoureux (French) damper felt, German Röslau strings, vertically laminated maple bridges with wood cores and solid beech caps, German Ivory*Leit* natural keytops, and genuine ebony sharps.

Warranty: 10 years, parts and labor, to original purchaser.

PERZINA, GEBR.

including G. Steinberg

Perzina Pianos America LLC
70 SW Century Drive, Suite 100-278
Bend, Oregon 97702
541-639-3093
844-PER-ZINA
888-754-0654 (fax)
marti@bolpianos.nl
www.perzina-america.com

G. Steinberg
Freeburg Pianos
2314-D Asheville Highway
Hendersonville, North Carolina 28791
828-697-0110
levi@freeburgpianos.com
www.freeburgpianos.com

Pianos made by: Yantai Perzina Piano Manufacturing Co., Ltd., Yantai, Shandong Province, China

The Gebr. Perzina (Perzina Bros.) piano company was established in the German town of Schwerin in 1871, and was a prominent piano maker until World War I, after which its fortunes declined. In more recent times, the factory was moved to the nearby city of Lenzen and the company became known as Pianofabrik Lenzen GmbH. In the early 1990s the company was purchased by Music Brokers International B.V. of the Netherlands. Eventually it was decided that making pianos in Germany was not economically viable, so manufacturing was moved to Yantai, China, where, under license, Perzina verticals and grands were made for a number of years by another company. In 2003, Music Brokers International established Yantai-Perzina, a joint-venture factory in Yantai, where it now builds Perzina pianos.

Perzina verticals have several interesting features rarely found in other pianos, including a "floating" soundboard that is unattached to the back at certain points for freer vibration, and a reverse or concave soundboard crown. (There may be something to this; Perzina verticals sound very good, particularly in the bass.) The veneered soundboards are made entirely of Austrian white spruce, and the hammers are from Renner or Abel, in Germany.

A new line of Perzina grand pianos was introduced in 2011, designed and manufactured by Perzina in cooperation with a major European manufacturer. All contain veneered soundboards of Austrian white spruce, duplex scaling, and Abel hammers, among other high-quality components. All models come with a slow-close fallboard, and an adjustable artist bench. The distributor says that each grand is unpacked in the U.S., inspected, and adjusted as necessary before being shipped to the dealer.

The company's European headquarters says it ships many European materials to Yantai, including Degen copper-wound and Röslau strings, Delignit pinblocks, Renner and Abel hammers, English felts, European veneers, and Austrian white spruce soundboards. New manufacturing equipment is from Germany, Japan, and Italy. According to the company, all the piano designs are the original German scales.

The Perzina factory also manufactures G. Steinberg (formerly Gerh. Steinberg) pianos for distribution in the U.S. Gerhard Steinberg began making pianos in Berlin in 1908. The firm he established changed hands several times during the 20th century, most recently in 1993, when it was acquired by Music Brokers International. G. Steinberg grands are lower-cost versions of Perzina grands. They use standard factory hammers instead of Abel hammers, and the cabinets are cosmetically simpler. The verticals, also a lower-cost alternative, are of an entirely different scale design from that of Perzina verticals, and do not use Perzina's floating soundboard design.

Warranty: Gebr. Perzina and G. Steinberg: 10 years, parts and labor, to original purchaser, except for the soundboard, which carries a lifetime guarantee to original purchaser.

PETROF

Piano Royale Prague LLC
P.O. Box 1130
Richland, Washington 99352
509-946-8078
877-946-8078
www.petrof.com

Pianos made by: Petrof, spol. s.r.o., Hradec Králové, Czech Republic

The Petrof piano factory was founded in 1864 by Antonin Petrof in Hradec Králové, an old, historic town 100 kilometers east of Prague, in the present Czech Republic. Five generations of the Petrof family owned and managed the business, during which time the company kept pace with technical developments and earned prizes for its pianos at international exhibitions. The Czechs have long been known for their vibrant musical-instrument industry, which also includes makers of brass, woodwind, and stringed instruments.

In 1947, when all businesses in the Czech Republic were nationalized by the state, the Petrof family was forced out of the business. In 1965 Petrof, along with other piano manufacturers, was forced to join Musicexport, the state-controlled import-export company for musical instruments. Since the fall of the Soviet Union and the liberation of Eastern Europe, the various factories that were part of

Musicexport have been spun off as private businesses, including Petrof, which is once again owned and controlled by the Petrof family. Currently Petrof manufactures 5,000 vertical pianos and 900 grands annually.

Petrof recently introduced a series of six new grand piano models, named (in size order) Bora, Breeze, Storm, Pasat, Monsoon, and Mistral, from 5' 2" to 9' 2" in length. Most component parts are produced by Petrof or other Czech factories, including the hardware, plates, and cabinetry. Soundboards are of solid Bohemian spruce, grand rims are of laminated beech and birch, pinblocks are of compressed beech, plates are cast in wet sand, and hammers are from Renner or Abel. These pianos also boast several interesting features: The soundboard is custom-tapered and asymmetrically crowned for optimal resonance; the treble bridge is capped with genuine ebony for better transmission of treble tone; front and rear duplexes are tuned for tonal color; pianos are single-strung for tuning stability; an adjustable bolt has been added from the plate to the wooden cross block for additional tuning stability; and a decorative veneer has been added to the inner rim. The earlier series of Petrof grands with model numbers containing roman numerals will coexist with the new models as long as supplies last.

Actions in Petrof pianos are standard Detoa on the smaller verticals, Renner on the larger grands and larger verticals, and either Renner parts on a Petrof action frame or Petrof Original Actions made by Detoa on mid-size instruments.

Petrof has also invented and patented a version of its new grand action that uses tiny opposing magnets on the wippens and wippen rail. These magnets allow for the removal of the usual lead counterweights in the keys and, according to the company, significantly alter the action's dynamic properties. The new action also furthers the European Union's stated environmental goal of phasing out the use of lead in pianos. The action is adjusted in the factory for a standard touchweight and is serviced in exactly the same way as a standard action. The Magnetic Accelerated Action, as it is known, is a special-order option on the grands. Petrof also offers as an option the Magnetic Balanced Action, which allows the player to quickly and easily change the touchweight in the range of ±4–5 grams simply by turning a knob.

Petrofs are known for their warm, rich, singing tone, full of color. The pianos are solidly built and workmanship is good. After careful preparation, the pianos can sound and feel quite beautiful and hold their own against other European brands. Wages in the Czech Republic have risen in recent years, and with it the price of Petrof pianos, but the company has placed a greater emphasis on quality control and enhanced features in the new models in order to meet the higher expectations that come with higher prices.

Note: For years, Weinbach pianos were made by the Petrof company and were virtually identical to Petrof brand pianos. The Weinbach name is no longer being used in North America.

Warranty: 10 years, parts and labor, to original purchaser, from the manufacturer.

PRAMBERGER

See also **Samick**.

Samick Music Corp. (SMC)
1329 Gateway Drive
Gallatin, Tennessee 37066
615-206-0077
info@smcmusic.com
www.smcmusic.com

Pianos made by: Samick Musical Instrument Mfg. Co. Ltd., Bogor, West Java, Indonesia

The Pramberger name was used by Young Chang for its premium-level pianos under license from the late piano engineer Joseph Pramberger, who at one time was head of manufacturing at Steinway & Sons. When Pramberger died, in 2003, his estate terminated its relationship with Young Chang and signed up with Samick. However, since Young Chang still holds the rights to its piano designs, Samick has designed new pianos to go with the name.

The J.P. Pramberger Platinum piano is a higher-end instrument, formerly made in Korea, and now made in Indonesia under Korean supervision using the CNC equipment acquired by Samick during its partnership with Bechstein. It is then shipped to the U.S. for inspection, tuning, regulating, and voicing before being shipped to dealers. Several American technicians who had known and worked with Joe Pramberger went to Korea at Samick's request to design this piano. Benefiting by work previously done by Bechstein engineers at the Samick factory, they began with a modified Bechstein scale, then added several features found on current or older Steinways, such as an all-maple (or beech) rim, an asymmetrically tapered white spruce soundboard, vertically laminated and tunneled maple and mahogany bridges with maple cap, duplex scaling, a Renner/Pramberger action, and Renner or Abel hammers. One of the technicians told me that the group feels its design is an advancement of Pramberger's work that he would have approved of.

The Pramberger Signature (formerly known as J. Pramberger) is a more modestly priced instrument from Indonesia whose design is based on the former Korean-built

Young Chang version. This line uses Samick's Pratt-Reed Premium action, Renner or Abel hammers, and a Bolduc (Canadian) solid spruce soundboard. The institutional verticals in this line have all-wood cabinet construction and agraffes in the bass section, and the decorator versions include Renner hammers and a slow-close fallboard.

The Pramberger Legacy, the newest addition to the Pramberger line, has a veneer-laminated "surface tension" soundboard, and provides a reasonably priced option for the budget-minded consumer. These models were formerly sold under the Remington label. (The Remington brand is no longer a regular part of the Pramberger lineup, but is available to dealers on special order.)

[Note: Samick's Pratt-Reed Premium action should not be confused with the Pratt-*Read* action used in many American-made pianos in the mid to late 20th century and eventually acquired by Baldwin. Samick says its Pratt-Reed action, designed by its research and development team and based on the German Renner action, is made in Korea.]

See **Samick** for more information.

Warranty: 10 years, parts and labor, transferable to future owners within the warranty period.

RAVENSCROFT

Spreeman Piano Innovations, LLC
7898 East Acoma Drive, Suite 105
Scottsdale, Arizona 85260
480-664-3702
info@RavenscroftPianos.com
www.RavenscroftPianos.com

Handcrafted in Scottsdale, Arizona by piano builder Michael Spreeman, the Ravenscroft piano entered the market for high-end performance pianos in 2006. Two models are available, the 7' 3" model 220 and the 9' model 275. The 220 made its debut in 2007 in the Manufacturers' Showcase of the 50th Annual Convention of the Piano Technicians Guild. A custom-built model 275 is currently the official piano at the Tempe Center for the Arts.

While the general trend in the industry seems to be toward outsourcing to less expensive suppliers, Spreeman says his concept is the exact opposite. Appealing to the niche market of high-end consumers, Spreeman's approach is more along the lines of the early European small-shop builders, with an emphasis on quality and exclusivity.

The case and iron frame of the Ravenscroft piano are constructed in Germany by Sauter to Ravenscroft specifications and shipped to the Arizona facility. The Renner action and Kluge keys of each piano are computer-designed to optimize performance. The rib scale, soundboard, bridges, and string scale are designed by Spreeman, who meticulously hand-builds each instrument with his three-person team.

Currently, only four to six pianos are produced yearly, with pricing beginning at $230,000 for a model 220, and up to $550,000 for a model 275 with "all the extras," including titanium string terminations, exotic veneers, intarsia, artwork, and inlays of precious stones. Most instruments are custom ordered and can take up to a year to complete.

RITMÜLLER — See Pearl River.

RÖNISCH
including Hupfeld

Blüthner USA LLC
5660 West Grand River
Lansing, Michigan 48906
517-886-6000
800-954-3200
info@bluthnerpiano.com
www.roenisch-pianos.de
www.hupfeld-piano.com

In Canada, contact Bluethner Piano Canada Inc.
604-264-1138
rgarvin@telus.net
www.bluethner.ca

Pianos made by: Carl Rönisch Piano Manufacture GmbH, Leipzig, Germany, and other factories (see text)

In 2009, the German piano manufacturer Blüthner purchased the Rönisch and Hupfeld brands and, to manufacture them, set up a new legal entity and a factory next door to the Blüthner factory in Leipzig, Germany.

Rönisch was established in Dresden in 1845 by Carl Rönisch. In his day, Rönisch was a pioneer in piano building, and his instruments were sold throughout the world. Rönisch's son sold the company after World War I, and production was moved to Leipzig after the Dresden factory was bombed in 1945. During the Communist era, the company was taken over by the state and combined with other piano factories; it became privately owned again in the 1990s.

Since purchasing the brand, Blüthner has redesigned the pianos, which are now made in three sizes of vertical and three sizes of grand, in dozens of styles, woods, and finishes. Musically, and in terms of their quality, Rönisch pianos are very similar to Haessler, another Blüthner brand, but the cabinet styles and finishes offered are different. The pianos are entirely made in Germany, with such parts as rims, beams, and cabinets supplied by Blüthner. The pianos also use high-quality parts such as Renner actions, Delignit pinblocks, soundboards of solid European mountain spruce, and Abel hammers. Although new to North America, Rönisch pianos have been very popular in other parts of the world for decades. Approximately 600 verticals and 300 grands are made each year.

Ludwig Hupfeld became involved in the musical-instrument business in 1892, and purchased the Rönisch company in 1918. (Today, Hupfeld is a subdivision of Rönisch.) Hupfeld was one of the earliest and best-known makers of reproducing pianos—advanced pneumatic player pianos of the early 1900s that faithfully recorded the nuances of the playing of recording artists—and other automatic musical instruments.

Hupfeld pianos are made in two editions: Hupfeld Europe and Studio. The Hupfeld Europe line is entirely made in Europe, with strung backs and cabinets from Romania, and key and action assembly, final regulation, voicing, and inspection done at the Rönisch factory in Germany. The Studio line is made in Indonesia, using cast-iron plates, actions, and keys from Indonesian suppliers, and hammers, strings, pinblocks, and felt from Germany. The instruments are then sent to the Rönisch factory in Germany for final regulation, voicing, and inspection.

Warranty: 10 years, parts and labor, to original purchaser.

SAMICK

See separate listings for **Wm. Knabe**, **Pramberger**, and **Seiler**.

Samick Music Corp. (SMC)
1329 Gateway Drive
Gallatin, Tennessee 37066
615-206-0077
info@smcmusic.com
www.smcmusic.com

Pianos made by: Samick Musical Instrument Mfg. Co. Ltd., Inchon, South Korea; and Bogor, West Java, Indonesia

---

In 1958, in South Korea, Hyo Ick Lee founded Samick as a Baldwin distributor. Facing an immense challenge in an impoverished and war-torn country, in the early 1960s, using largely imported parts, Lee began to build and sell a very limited quantity of vertical pianos. As South Korea's economy improved, Lee expanded his operation, and in 1964 began exporting to other parts of the world, eventually becoming one of the world's largest piano manufacturers, now making most parts in-house. Over the next several decades, Samick expanded into manufacturing guitars and other instruments and opened factories in China and Indonesia, where it shifted much of its production as Korean wages rose. The Asian economic crisis of the late 1990s forced Samick into bankruptcy, from which the company emerged in 2002; it is now on a sound financial footing.

The company says that "Samick" means "three benefits" in Korean, symbolizing the management's wish that the activities of the company benefit not only the company itself, but also its customers and the Korean economy.

Samick Music Corporation (SMC), the North American sales and marketing arm of the Korean company, distributes Samick, Pramberger, Wm. Knabe, and Seiler pianos in North America (see separate listings for **Wm. Knabe**, **Pramberger**, and **Seiler**). Samick no longer distributes pianos under the names Bernhard Steiner, Conover Cable, Hazelton Bros., Remington, or Sohmer & Co. The Kohler & Campbell line has been discontinued in North America but is still sold elsewhere. (For historical information about the original Kohler & Campbell piano company, see *The Piano Book*.) Most Samick-made pianos destined for the U.S. market are made in Indonesia. Some of the company's upper-level Wm. Knabe and J.P. Pramberger instruments are still made in South Korea. SMC has a warehouse and office facility in Tennessee, at which it uncrates, inspects, tunes, regulates, and voices its upper-level pianos before shipping them to dealers.

Most dealers of Samick-made pianos carry the Wm. Knabe, Pramberger, and/or Seiler lines. The company's offerings under the Samick brand name are limited to three sizes of grand piano that the company calls its International Series. These models are made in Indonesia using the same German CNC (computer numerical control) equipment employed for the upper-level models of its other brands. These models have solid white-spruce soundboards.

In the 1980s Klaus Fenner, a German piano designer, was hired to revise the Samick scale designs to make the pianos sound more "European." Most Samick pianos now being made are based on these designs. Most Samicks also have veneer-laminated soundboards, which the company calls a "surface tension" soundboard—essentially, a solid spruce soundboard sandwiched by two very thin veneers. With Klaus Fenner's technical advice, Samick pioneered the use of this soundboard in early 1980, and it is now used by others as well. Tonally, it behaves much like a solid spruce soundboard, but won't crack or lose its crown.

Quality control in Samick's South Korean and Indonesian factories has steadily improved over the years, and the Indonesian product is said to be almost as good as the Korean. The company says that new CNC machinery installed in 2007 has revolutionized the consistency and accuracy of its manufacturing. Climate control in the tropically situated Indonesian factory, and issues of action geometry, are also among the areas that have seen improvement. Many of Samick's Indonesian pianos are priced similarly to low-cost pianos from China. The musical design and performance of Samick's upper-level pianos—J.P. Pramberger, Wm. Knabe, and Seiler—have met with very positive response.

[Note: Samick-made pianos are identified using an odd system of serial numbers and letters that appears to vary from factory to factory. Please contact SMC for information on the date of manufacture of a Samick-made piano.]

Warranty: 10 years, parts and labor, transferable to future owners within the warranty period.

SAUTER

Carl Sauter Pianofortemanufaktur GmbH & Co. KG
Max-Planck-Strasse 20
78549 Spaichingen
Germany
+49-7424-94820
+49-7424-948238 (fax)
info@sauter-pianos.de
www.sauter-pianos.de

The Sauter piano firm was founded in 1819 by Johann Grimm, stepfather to Carl Sauter I, and has been owned and managed by members of the Sauter family for six generations, currently by Ulrich Sauter. The factory produces about 800 vertical pianos and 120 grand pianos a year in its factory in the extreme south of Germany, at the foot of the Alps. Structural and acoustical parts are made of high-quality woods, including solid Bavarian spruce soundboards and beech pinblocks. Actions are made by Renner, and Sauter makes its own keys. The keybed is reinforced with steel to prevent warping, and all pianos are fully tropicalized for humid climates. The larger verticals use an action, designed and patented by Sauter, that contains an auxiliary jack spring to aid in faster repetition. Sauter calls this the R2 Double Escapement action. (Although the term *double escapement* does not apply here as it has historically been used, the mechanism has some of the same effects.)

Sauter pianos are especially known for the variety of finishes and styles in which they are available, many with intricate detail and inlay work. It is common to find such rare woods as yew, burl walnut, pyramid mahogany, and genuine ebony in the cabinets of Sauter pianos, as well as special engravings, which can be customized to any customer's desires. Sauter's M Line of vertical pianos features exclusive cabinet detailing and built-in features such as a hygrometer to measure

relative humidity. New Masterline institutional uprights, sold directly to institutions and not through dealers, include protective sidebars, industrial-grade casters, and locking mechanisms. Amadeus is a special-edition 6' 1" grand honoring the 250th anniversary of Mozart's birth, with styling reminiscent of that in Mozart's time. The natural keytops are of polished bone, the sharps of rosewood with ebony caps. Only 36 are to be made, one for each year of Mozart's life.

The company also has introduced versions of its 48" upright and 6' 11" and 7' 6" grands with cabinets designed by the famous European designer Peter Maly. Some recent designs include the 48" upright Vitrea, after the Latin word for glass, with a veneer of greenish glass covering the front of the cabinet; and Ambiente, a 7' 6" grand that is asymmetrically curved on both the bass and treble sides. In the recent past, Sauter has won several prestigious design awards for its Peter Maly–designed pianos.

A couple of extremely unusual models bear mentioning. The 7' 3" model 220 has colored lines painted on the soundboard and white inlays on the tops of the dampers as guides for musicians performing music for "prepared piano," ultramodern music requiring the insertion of foreign objects between the strings, or the plucking or striking of strings directly by the performer. The 1/16-tone microtonal piano is an upright with 97 keys that has a total pitch range, from its lowest to its highest note, of only one octave, the pitch difference from key to key being only 1/16 of a tone (1/8 of a semitone). You can read more about these strange instruments in *The Piano Book*.

Sauter pianos are high-quality instruments with a lush, full, singing tone, closer to an "American" sound than most other European pianos.

Note: At press time for this issue, Sauter had just decided to distribute directly from the factory (see contact info, above), and new prices were not yet available. For the time being, we are continuing to publish the prices from the former distributor.

Warranty: 5 years, parts and labor, to original purchaser.

SCHILLER — See Irmler.

SCHIMMEL

including Wilhelm Schimmel, Vogel, May Berlin

Schimmel Piano Corporation
329 North New Street
Lititz, Pennsylvania 17543
800-426-3205
schimmel@ptd.net
www.schimmel-piano.de

Pianos made by: Wilhelm Schimmel Pianofortefabrik GmbH, Braunschweig, Germany (Schimmel), and Kalisz, Poland (Wilhelm Schimmel); and Guangzhou Pearl River Piano Group Ltd., Guangzhou, China (Fridolin Schimmel)

Wilhelm Schimmel began making pianos in Leipzig in 1885, and his company enjoyed steady growth through the late 19th and early 20th centuries. The two World Wars and the Depression disrupted production several times, but the company has gradually rebuilt itself over the past 70 years while earning a strong reputation for quality. In 2016, the Chinese piano maker Pearl River purchased a majority interest in Schimmel, in which the Schimmel family remains shareholders. Today, Schimmel is managed by Hannes Schimmel-Vogel, the husband of Viola Schimmel. One of Europe's most prolific piano makers, Schimmel makes about 2,500 verticals and 500 grands per year.

Among European piano manufacturers, Schimmel has been a pioneer in the use of computer-aided design and manufacturing. The company has used its Computer Assisted Piano Engineering (CAPE) software to research, design, and implement virtually every aspect of making a piano, from keyboard layout and action geometry to soundboard acoustics and scale design. According to Schimmel, the combination of CNC machinery and handcraftsmanship leads to better results than handwork alone. Schimmel also believes that precision is aided by controlling as much of the production process as possible. For that reason, Schimmel produces its own piano-cabinet components and its own keyboards, which it also supplies to other German piano makers.

Schimmel's model line is organized into five categories: Konzert (K) and Classic (C), both made entirely in Germany; the Schimmel International series, made in Germany from parts sourced globally (this series is no longer exported to North America); Wilhelm Schimmel (formerly known as Vogel), made in Poland; and Fridolin Schimmel, made in China by Pearl River.

The company says that the purpose of the Konzert series is to expand the Schimmel line upward to a higher level of quality than it had previously attained, whereas the Classic series represents models that have been tested over time and are solid, traditional, high-quality instruments, but without all the latest refinements. The Konzert-series uprights—48" model K122, 49" model K125, and 52" model K132—are based on a more sophisticated philosophy of construction than the Classics, and incorporate triplex scaling and other advanced design features. Schimmel's philosophy for these uprights was to design them to be as much like the grands as possible. The treble scales, in fact, are exactly the same as in the Konzert grands. All uprights have adjustable gliders (to adjust to unevenness in the floor) and come with a matching adjustable bench.

All Konzert grand models are scaled to use the model 280's concert-grand action. The case sides are angled slightly to accommodate a larger soundboard, and all have tunable front and rear duplex or triplex scales for greater tonal color. Other advanced features include: improved soundboard and bridge materials, more time spent voicing the instruments in the factory, sharps of real ebony, and mineral white keytops to mimic the feel of ivory. The largest grands have reinforced keys for optimal energy transmission.

Schimmel grand pianos historically had a very bright, clear tone that was a bit thin, and lacking in color in the treble. The grands were redesigned, in part, to add color to the tone, and the result is definitely more interesting than before. Sustain is also very good. The pianos are being delivered to U.S. dealers voiced less bright than in the past, as this is what the American ear tends to prefer. As for the verticals, the smaller models tend to have very big bass for their size, with a tone that emphasizes the fundamental, giving the low end a warmer character. The 52" model K132, which features a grand-shaped soundboard, has a very big sound; listening to it, one might think one was in the presence of a medium-size grand.

In 2002, Schimmel acquired the PianoEurope factory in Kalisz, Poland, a piano-restoration and manufacturing facility. Schimmel at first used the Kalisz factory to manufacture its Vogel brand, a moderately priced line named for the company's president. This line has now been replaced by the Wilhelm Schimmel brand, named for the company's founder. Schimmel says that although the skill level of its Polish employees is high, the lower wages and other lower costs available in Poland result in a piano approximately 30% less costly than comparable Schimmel models. Wilhelm Schimmel grand pianos feature full Renner actions, with other parts mainly made by Schimmel, in Braunschweig or in Kalisz. The Wilhelm Schimmel pianos, though designed by Schimmel, don't have all the refinements and advanced features of the latest Schimmel models. Nevertheless, they have received praise from many quarters for their high-quality workmanship and sound.

The May Berlin line, made for Schimmel in China, has been discontinued. The Fridolin Schimmel line is named for Wilhelm Schimmel's younger brother, who emigrated to America in 1890, and in 1893 established his own piano-manufacturing business, in Faribault, Minnesota. Fridolin Schimmel instruments feature scales, actions, and cabinets designed by Schimmel in Germany, and are made to high quality standards by Pearl River in China.

Warranty: Schimmel, Wilhelm Schimmel, and Fridolin Schimmel—10 years, parts and labor, to original purchaser.

SCHULZE POLLMANN

North American Music Inc.
11 Holt Drive
Stony Point, New York 10980
845-429-0106
www.schulzepollmann.com
www.namusic.com

Pianos made by: Schulze Pollmann s.r.l., Borgo Maggiore, San Marino

Schulze Pollmann was formed in 1928 by the merger of two German piano builders who had moved to Italy. Paul Pollmann had worked first with Ibach, then with Steinway & Sons (Hamburg), before opening his own piano factory in Germany. He later moved to Italy, where he met Albert Schulze, another relocated German piano builder. Pollmann managed the combined firms until 1942, and was followed by his son Hans, who had managed the piano maker Schimmel before returning to his father's firm. Recently, the company relocated a short distance to San Marino, a tiny city-state entirely surrounded by Italy.

In North America, Schulze Pollmann offers two series of pianos: Masterpiece (grands) and Studio (verticals). The Masterpiece Series pianos, available only by special order, are made entirely in Italy and San Marino, and contain Delignit pinblocks, Renner actions and hammers from Germany, and Ciresa solid red-spruce soundboards from the Val di Fiemme, in Italy. The company uses both sophisticated technology and handwork in its manufacturing. All soundboards have finger-jointed construction to optimize stability and prevent cracking. Many of the cabinets have beautiful designs and inlays. The Studio series is partially made in Asia and finished off, including deluxe cabinetwork, in San Marino.

The uprights are well built and have a warm, colorful sound with a good amount of sustain. The treble is not nearly as brittle sounding as in some other European uprights. Schulze Pollmann grands are likewise very nicely crafted and arrive at the dealer in good condition, needing only solid preparation to sound their best.

In 2005, Italian auto manufacturer Ferrari Motor Car selected Schulze Pollmann as a partner in the launch of its new Ferrari 612 Scaglietti series of automobiles. For the occasion, Schulze Pollmann crafted a limited-edition version of its 6' 7" model 197/G5 grand piano, still available, with a case that sports Ferrari's racing red and a cast-iron plate in Ferrari gray carbon, the same color as the Scaglietti's engine. The car and the piano have been exhibited together in cities around the world.

Warranty: 10 years, parts and labor.

SEILER

including Johannes Seiler

Samick Music Corp. (SMC)
1329 Gateway Drive
Gallatin, Tennessee 37066
615-206-0077
info@smcmusic.com
www.seilerpianousa.com

Pianos made by: Ed. Seiler Pianofortefabrik, Kitzingen, Germany; with Samick Musical Instrument Mfg. Co. Ltd., Bogor, West Java, Indonesia

Eduard Seiler, the company's founder, began making pianos in 1849, in Liegnitz, Silesia, then part of Prussia. By 1923 the company had grown to over 435 employees, was producing up to 3,000 pianos per year, and was the largest piano manufacturer in Eastern Europe. In 1945 and after World War II, when Liegnitz (now Legnica) became part of Poland, the plant was nationalized by the Polish Communist government, and the Seiler family left their native homeland with millions of other refugees. In 1954, Steffan Seiler reestablished the company in Copenhagen under the fourth generation of family ownership, and began making pianos again. In 1962 he moved the company to Kitzingen, in Bavaria, Germany, where it resides today. Steffan Seiler died in 1999; the company was managed by his widow, Ursula, until its sale to Samick in 2008. Seiler now produces about 1,000 pianos annually. Samick continues Seiler's tradition of making high-quality pianos, while diversifying the product lineup to suit a wider range of buyers.

Seiler uses a combination of traditional methods and modern technology. The scale designs are of relatively high tension, producing a balanced tone that is quite consistent from one Seiler piano to the next. Although brilliant, the tone also sings well, due to, the company says, a unique, patented soundboard feature called the Membrator system, used in Seiler's SE and

ED lines: The perimeter of the soundboard is sculpted to be thicker and heavier in mass than the central portion of the board, forming an internal frame within the soundboard itself. The lighter, inner area becomes the vibrating membrane—a diaphragm on its own—unimpeded by the larger soundboard's attachment to the inner rim. Seiler says that its use of the Membrator system, as well as effective rib positioning, improves the soundboard's efficiency in radiating sound. It's easy to identify the Membrator by the tapered groove around the perimeter of the board.

The grands have wide tails, for greater soundboard area and string length. The German Seiler pianos feature Bavarian spruce soundboards, multi-laminated Delignit pinblocks, quartersawn beech bridges, full Renner actions, and slow-close fallboards. A few years ago, the grands were redesigned with a duplex scale for greater treble tonal color, and with longer keys and a lighter touch. Musically, these redesigns were very successful; they retained the typical Seiler clarity, but had longer sustain and a more even-feeling touch.

Beginning in 2010, Samick expanded the Seiler line to cover several additional price points. The top-level, SE-series instruments continue to be handcrafted at the Seiler factory in Kitzingen, Germany, just as they have been for many years. These come in two styles, Classic and Trend. The construction and specifications of the two styles are the same, but the Trends look a bit more modern, and sport a silver-colored plate and chrome hardware, whereas the Classics have the traditional gold- or bronze-colored plate and brass hardware. Both are available in dozens of special furniture styles with beautiful, exotic woods and inlays.

The mid-level Seiler pianos, the ED models, are also known as the Eduard Seiler line. The pianos are manufactured entirely at Samick's Indonesian factory, using German CNC machinery, to the exact scales and specifications of the hand-built German models. The actions include Renner wippen assemblies and an action rail of Delignit or hornbeam, with keys made by Samick.

New in 2016 is the custom model ED-186A, a specially prepared, limited-production version of the 6' 2" model ED-186, for the higher-level player who seeks a musical response greater than that generally found in regular factory-produced instruments. This model uses hand-selected Renner action parts, and higher-quality keys, keyframe, and hammers, all assembled, regulated, and voiced by Samick's Senior Technical Advisor at the company's facility in Tennessee.

In July 2013, the new Johannes Seiler line was introduced. Though it features cabinetry as beautiful as that of its more expensive brethren, this lower-cost line has its own scale design not shared by other Samick-owned brands, and is produced entirely in the company's Indonesian facility, using Samick's premium action and hammers from Abel. These three grand and three vertical models can be identified by the "Johannes Seiler" label on the fallboard.

At both the German and Indonesian factories, strung backs are inspected and cabinet parts carefully fitted to ensure that all specifications have been met to precise tolerances. Soundboard mass distribution and rib positioning are under strict quality control, to achieve consistency in the soundboard's acoustical properties. Pre-stretching of the strings is done several times, followed by multiple tunings, to ensure maximum stability. Hammer alignment, voicing, and key weighting and balancing are all carefully performed by experienced Seiler technicians, both at the factory and at the company's Tennessee distribution facility, before shipment to dealers.

Seiler's 52" upright is available by special order with the optional Super Magnet Repetition (SMR) action, a patented feature that uses magnets to increase repetition speed. During play, tiny magnets attached to certain action parts of each note repel each other, forcing the parts to return to their rest position faster, ready for the next keystroke.

Warranty: 10 years, parts and labor, to original purchaser.

STEINBERG, G. — See Perzina, Gebr.

STEINBERG, WILH.
including Eisenberg

Thüringer Pianoforte GmbH
Mozartstr. 3
07607 Eisenberg, Germany
+49 (0) 36691 / 595-0
+49 (0) 36691 / 595-40 (fax)
sales@wilh-steinberg.com
www.Wilh-Steinberg.com

Pianos made by: Thüringer Pianoforte GmbH, Eisenberg, Germany; and Parsons Music Ltd., China.

This company, formerly known as Wilh. Steinberg Pianofortefabrik, was formed after the reunification of Germany by the merger of several East German piano companies, the oldest of which traces its origins back to 1877. Since July 2013, the company has been owned by Parsons Music Ltd., a Hong Kong–based piano manufacturer. In addition to its own pianos, Thüringer Pianoforte makes several other European piano brands under OEM agreements. The company also specializes in custom cabinets and finishes. Piano production is about 500 verticals and 50 grands per year.

Wilh. Steinberg pianos are made in two levels of quality. The higher-quality level is the Signature series. These pianos are made in Germany with actions by Renner and keyboards by Kluge. Cabinets for the verticals are made by Thüringer Pianoforte in its own facilities; grand cabinets are supplied by Parsons Music. "Amadeus" and "Passione" are Signature series models that have special cabinet styles.

The lower-cost models, known as the P line (model numbers beginning with P), were formerly made under the Eisenberg brand name, a name no longer in use. P-line models are entirely made by Parsons Music in China using Thüringer designs.

Warranty: 5 years, parts and labor, to original purchaser.

STEINGRAEBER & SÖHNE

Steingraeber & Söhne
Steingraeberpassage 1
95444 Bayreuth, Germany
+49-921-64049
+49-921-58272 (fax)
steingraeber@steingraeber.de
www.steingraeber.de

Bayreuth is famous the world over for its annual summer Wagner festival. But tucked away in the old part of town is a second center of Bayreuth musical excellence and one of the world's best-kept secrets: Steingraeber & Söhne. The company was founded in 1852 by Eduard Steingraeber, though its roots date back to the 1820s, when Eduard's father and uncle opened a workshop for square pianos and organs in the city of Neustadt. Eduard was an innovative piano designer, exhibiting his first full-size cast-iron frame at the world exhibition in Paris in 1867. From 1872 on, Steingraeber was associated with, and built pianos for, Franz Liszt and Richard Wagner, and in 1873 opened its first concert hall in Bayreuth.

Steingraeber has worked with furniture designers since 1904, when it collaborated with Bruno Paul on his Art Nouveau furniture for the St. Louis World's Fair. More recently, the company built a piano designed by Jørn Utzon, architect of the Sydney Opera House, with features reminiscent of that building. The Steingraeber engineering department offers consulting services on the technical development of pianos. This service was created in 1991, after reunification, to assist piano manufacturers of the former East Germany, and has designed and manufactured prototypes of new piano models for a number of European piano manufacturers. These designs

are different from Steingraeber's own current models. In 2012, Steingraeber entered into a cooperative agreement with Pearl River, in China, to help that company design and manufacture a new line of premium pianos.

Steingraeber is one of the smaller piano manufacturers in the world, producing fewer than 80 grands and 60 verticals per year for the top end of the market. It is owned and operated by sixth-generation family member Udo Schmidt-Steingraeber, who still makes pianos using the traditional methods of his forebears at the company's present factory, which it has occupied since 1872.

Steingraeber makes three sizes of vertical piano: 48", 51", and 54". An interesting option on the vertical models is their "twist and change" panels: two-sided top and bottom panels, one side finished in polished ebony, the other in a two-toned combination of a wood veneer and ebony. The panels can be reversed as desired by the piano owner to match room décor, or just for a change of scenery.

The company also makes five sizes of grand piano: 5' 7", 6' 3", 7', 7' 7", and 8' 11". The 5' 7" model A-170 grand has an unusually wide tail, allowing for a larger soundboard area and longer bass strings than are customary for an instrument of its size. The 7' model C-212, known as the Chamber Concert Grand, and recently redesigned from the model 205, was intended to embody the tone quality of the Steingraeber Liszt grand piano of circa 1873, but with more volume in the bass register. The 8' 11" model E-272 concert grand was introduced in 2002 for Steingraeber's 150th anniversary. Unique features include a drilled capo bar for more sustain in the treble, unusually shaped rim bracing, and a smaller soundboard resonating area in the treble to better match string length. In 2007, Steingraeber introduced the 7' 7" D-232 concert grand to provide an additional smaller, concert-size instrument. Its design includes many of the innovations of the E-272. New in 2012 is the 6' 3" model B-192, which follows the design enhancements of the D-232 and C-212 in a size more comfortable for homes and smaller concert halls.

Steingraeber pianos have a unique sound, with an extensive tonal palette derived from a mixture of clarity and warmth.

Steingraeber is known for its many innovative technical improvements to the piano, one of which is a new action for uprights, available in all three vertical-piano models. This SFM action, as it is called, contains no jack spring, instead using magnets to return the jack more quickly under the hammer butt for faster repetition. Another innovation, introduced in 2013, is the optional sordino pedal, which inserts a thin strip of felt between hammers and strings. Popular in early 19th-century grand pianos, the purpose of this feature is not, as in most modern pianos, to damp the sound almost completely, but rather to create a distant, ethereal sound, and thus to expand the instrument's expressive possibilities. On a Steingraeber piano, the sordino can either replace the sostenuto as the middle pedal or, be operated by a fourth pedal or a knee lever. A knee lever can also be employed to activate the so-called Mozart Rail, which reduces both the hammer-blow distance and the key-touch depth to simulate the sound and touch of the pianos of Mozart's day. In 2014, Steingraeber introduced the world's lightest grand piano lid, made of modern aircraft material with a honeycomb interior, which makes the lid nearly 50% lighter than conventional lids. The company says that the new material also projects sound better. Steingraeber also specializes in so-called ecological or biological finishes, available as an option on most models. This involves the use of only organic materials in the piano, such as natural paints and glues in the case, and white keytops made from cattle bone.

Steingraeber pianos can also be special-ordered with a carbon-fiber soundboard, and with the Phoenix system of bridge agraffes (see **www.hurstwoodfarmpianos .co.uk** for more information on the Phoenix system).

In addition to its regular line of pianos, Steingraeber makes a piano that can be used by physically handicapped players who lack the use of their legs for pedaling. A wireless (Bluetooth) pedal actuator is operated by biting on a special denture.

Warranty: 5 years, parts and labor, transferable to future owners within the warranty period.

STEINWAY & SONS

Steinway & Sons
1133 Avenue of the Americas
New York, New York 10036
646-356-3960
www.steinway.com

Heinrich Engelhardt Steinweg, a cabinetmaker and piano maker from Seesen, Germany, emigrated with his family to the United States in 1850, and established Steinway & Sons in 1853. Within a relatively short time, the Steinways were granted patents that revolutionized the piano, and which were eventually adopted or imitated by other makers. Many of these patents concerned the quest for a stronger frame, a richer, more powerful sound, and a more sensitive action. By the 1880s, the Steinway piano was in most ways the modern piano we have today, and in the next generation the standards set by the founder were strictly adhered to. (The early history of Steinway & Sons is fascinating, and is intimately connected to the history of New York City and

the piano industry in general. You can read a summary of it in *The Piano Book;* there are also several excellent books devoted to the subject.)

In the 1960s the fourth generation of Steinways found themselves without any heirs willing or able to take over the business, and without enough capital to finance much-needed equipment modernization; eventually, in 1972, they sold their company to CBS. CBS left the musical instrument business in 1985, selling Steinway to an investment group. In 1995 the company was sold again, this time to Conn-Selmer, Inc., a major manufacturer of brass and woodwind instruments, and the combined company (called Steinway Musical Instruments, Inc.) was taken public on the New York Stock Exchange. In 2013, Paulson & Company, a private-equity firm led by Queens native John Paulson, purchased the public company and took it private once again. Paulson has said that he is committed to continuing the quality-first approach on which Steinway has built its reputation. Steinway also owns a branch factory in Hamburg, Germany, which serves the world market outside of the Americas, and two major suppliers: the Herman Kluge company, Europe's largest maker of piano keys; and the O.S. Kelly company, the only remaining piano plate foundry in the U.S.

Steinway makes two types of vertical piano in three sizes: a 45" model 4510 studio, a 46½" model 1098 studio, and a 52" model K-52 upright. Models 4510 and 1098 are technically identical, with differences only in the cabinets: the former is in a period style for home use, the latter in an institutional cabinet for school use or less furniture-conscious home use. In all three models, the middle pedal operates a sostenuto mechanism. All Steinway verticals use a solid spruce soundboard, have no particleboard, and in many other ways are similar in design, materials, and quality of workmanship to Steinway grands. Actions are made by Renner. Model K-52 in ebony, and model 1098 in ebony, mahogany, and walnut, come with an adjustable artist bench, the others with a regular bench.

Technicians have always liked the performance of Steinway verticals, but used to complain that the studio models in particular were among the most difficult pianos to tune and would unexpectedly jump out of tune. In recent years, Steinway has made small design changes to alleviate this problem. The pianos are now mechanically more normal to tune and are stable, but an excess of false beats (tonal irregularities) still make the pianos at times difficult to tune.

Steinway makes six sizes of grand piano. All ebony, mahogany, and walnut grand models come with an adjustable artist bench, the others with a regular bench.

The 5' 1" model S is very good for a small grand, but

has the usual limitations of any small piano and so is recommended only where space considerations are paramount. The 5' 7" model M is a full six inches longer, but costs little more than the S. Historically one of Steinway's more popular models, it is found in living rooms across the country. Its medium size makes the tone in certain areas slightly less than perfect, but it's an excellent home instrument.

The 5' 10½" model L has been replaced with the model O of the same size. Model O was first produced in 1902, but discontinued in 1924 in favor of the model L. Changes over time in both engineering and musical taste, as well as a desire to better synchronize the offerings of the New York factory with Hamburg (where the model O was never abandoned), seemed to dictate a return to the O. The main difference between the two models is in the shape of the tail—the L has a squared-off tail, the O a round tail—but this can also affect the soundboard and bridges and therefore the tone.

Reintroduction of the model O followed by one year the reintroduction of the legendary 6' 2" model A. First offered in 1878 and discontinued in New York in 1945, the model A revolutionized piano making by featuring, for the first time, the radial rim bracing and one-piece bent rim construction now used in all Steinway grands. Over the years the model A has gone through several makeovers, each of slightly different size and scaling. The version being reintroduced was made in New York from 1896 to 1914 and is the same size as the model A that has been made at the Hamburg factory for more than a century. Models O and A are suitable for larger living rooms, and for many school and teaching situations.

The 6' 10½" model B is the favorite of many piano technicians. It is the best choice for the serious pianist, recording or teaching studio, or small recital hall. Small design changes and other refinements to this model in recent years have brought a steady stream of accolades. The 8' 11¾" model D, the concert grand, is the flagship of the Steinway line and the piano of choice for the overwhelming majority of concert pianists. It's too large for most places other than the concert stage.

Steinway uses excellent materials and construction techniques in the manufacture of its grands. The rims, both inner and outer, are made in one continuous bend from layers of maple, and the beams are of solid spruce. The keybed is of quartersawn spruce planks freely mortised together, and the keys are of Bavarian spruce. The pinblock consists of seven laminations of maple with successive grain orientations of 45 and 90 degrees. The soundboard is of solid Sitka spruce, the bridges are vertically laminated of maple with a solid maple cap, and all models have duplex scaling.

It is well known that Steinway's principal competition comes from used and rebuilt Steinways, many of which come in exotic veneers or have elaborately carved or customized "art cases." The company has responded by expanding its product line to include modern-day versions of these collector's items. The Crown Jewel Collection consists of the regular models in natural (non-ebonized) wood veneers, many of them exotic. They are finished in a semigloss that Steinway calls Satin Lustre. In addition to satin and semigloss finishes, all regular Steinway grands are also now available in polyester high-polish ebony, lacquer high-polish ebony, and polyester high-polish white.

Limited Edition models, issued at irregular intervals, are reproductions of turn-of-the-century designs, or pianos with artistic elements that make them unique. A currently-available Limited Edition model, honoring the 70th anniversary of the birth of John Lennon, is the Imagine Series, a white piano that incorporates artwork by Lennon, along with other design elements.

During the early 1900s, ownership of art-case Steinways became a symbol of wealth and culture. Steinway has resumed this tradition by regularly commissioning noted furniture designers to create new art-case designs, usually around a theme. For example, in 1999 Frank Pollaro designed an art case called Rhapsody to commemorate the 100th anniversary of the birth of George Gershwin. The piano featured a blue-dyed maple veneer adorned with more than 400 hand-cut mother-of-pearl stars and a gilded silver plate. In 2016, another Pollaro-designed art-case model, the Fibonacci, was sold, for a record-setting $2.4 million, as Steinway's 600,000th piano. Each year sees new art-case pianos from Steinway, and they are truly stunning.

As another way of capitalizing on the popularity of older Steinways, the company also operates at its factory the world's largest piano rebuilding facility for the restoration of older Steinways. *The Piano Book* contains a great deal of additional information on the purchase of older or restored Steinways. See also "**Buying a Used or Restored Piano**" in this publication.

The underlying excellence of the Steinway musical designs and the integrity of the construction process are the hallmarks of the Steinway piano. Steinway pianos at their best have the quintessential American piano sound: a powerful bass, a resonant midrange, and a singing treble with plenty of tonal color. Although other brands have some of these characteristics, it is perhaps the particular combination of harmonics that comprise the Steinway's tonal coloration that, more than anything else, distinguishes it from other brands and gives it its richness, depth, and power. The construction process creates a very durable and rigid framework that also contributes to the power of its sound.

Musical and cabinet detailing, such as factory voicing and regulation, and plate and cabinet cosmetics, are reasonable, but have traditionally lagged somewhat behind the company's European competitors in finesse. Over the last couple of years, however, the company has been making a determined effort to remedy this by paying close attention to many small details, and by applying lessons learned from its European operations. Examples include: rounding the edges and corners of satin ebony models so they will better hold the finish and not prematurely wear through; more careful woodworking on the bottom of the piano, and applying a clear coat of lacquer to the bottom instead of painting it to cover imperfections; protecting the case and plate during stringing and other manufacturing operations so they don't have to be touched up, often imperfectly, later on; additional time spent playing-in pianos during manufacture in order to naturally harden the hammers so they don't need quite so much chemical hardening and voicing in the field; and other improvements too numerous to mention here. (See discussion and photo essay on this subject in the **Spring 2011 issue** of *Piano Buyer*.)

Steinway pianos require more preparation by the dealer than most pianos in their class, but, as mentioned above, the factory preparation has greatly improved, so the work required by the dealer is no longer excessive. Still, some dealers are more conscientious than others, and I occasionally hear of piano buyers who "can't find a good Steinway." How much of this is due to inherent weaknesses in some pianos, how much to lack of dealer preparation, and how much to customer bias or groundless complaining is hard to tell. I suspect it is a little of each. Piano technicians who work on these pianos do sometimes remark that some seem to have more potential than others. Many dealers do just enough regulating and voicing to make the instruments acceptable to the average customer, but reserve the highest level of work for those situations where a fussy customer for one of the larger models is trying to decide between a few particular instruments. Most customers for a Steinway will probably find one they like on the sales floor. However, if you are a discriminating buyer who has had trouble finding a Steinway that suits your preferences, I recommend letting the salesperson know, as precisely as you can, what you're looking for. Give the salesperson some time to have a few instruments prepared for you before making a decision. It may also help to tactfully let the salesperson know that you are aware that other options are available to you in the market for high-end pianos. By the way, customers seeking to purchase a model B or D Steinway who have not found the piano they are looking for at their local dealer can make arrangements with that dealer to visit the Steinway factory in New York, where a selection of the larger models is kept on hand for this purpose.

As mentioned earlier, Steinway owns a branch factory in Hamburg, Germany, established in 1880. The "fit and finish" (detailing) of the pianos at this factory is reputed to be better than at the one in New York, although pianists sometimes prefer the sound of the New York Steinway. Traditionally, the Hamburg factory has operated somewhat autonomously, but more recently the company has been synchronizing the two plants through technical exchanges, model changes, jointly built models, and materials that are shipped from New York to Hamburg. It's possible to special-order a Hamburg Steinway through an American Steinway dealer; or an enterprising American customer could travel to Europe, buy one there, and have it shipped back home.

In 2008 Steinway underwent a change in management, the first in 23 years. For the first time, the company's top executives were recruited from its European operations rather than from America. It is speculated that this may have signaled a subtle change of direction with regard to quality issues, and may be one of the reasons that European quality standards are appearing to be more strictly applied to the American-made instruments.

In 2016, in a major development for the company, Steinway unveiled its own electronic player-piano system, Spirio. For details, see **Spirio** in the chapter on electronic player-piano systems.

Warranty: 5 years, parts and labor, to original purchaser.

STORY & CLARK

Story & Clark Piano Co.
269 Quaker Drive
Seneca, Pennsylvania 16346
800-247-6557
814-676-6683
www.qrsmusic.com
Owned by: QRS Music Technologies, Inc.
Pianos made by: various German and Asian manufacturers

Hampton Story began making pianos in 1857 and was joined by Melville Clark in 1884. The business settled in Grand Rapids, Michigan, in 1901, where it remained, under various owners, until about 1990, when a new owner moved the company to its present location in Seneca, Pennsylvania. Over the years, pianos were manufactured under a number of different names, including, in recent years, Story & Clark, Gulbransen, Hobart M. Cable, Hampton, and Classic. In 1993 Story & Clark was purchased by QRS Piano Rolls, Inc., now QRS Music Technologies, Inc. (Ironically, QRS itself was founded in 1900 by Melville Clark, of the Story & Clark Piano Co. of old.) QRS, historically the nation's major source of music rolls for traditional player pianos, now manufactures an electronic player-piano system, called PNOmation, that can be retrofitted into any piano (see **"Buying an Electronic Player-Piano System"**).

Story & Clark offers two series of pianos, each series including verticals and grands made to its specifications by various Asian manufacturers. The Heritage Series is a popularly priced line of verticals and grands with a Storytone II soundboard—Story & Clark's name for a veneer-laminated, all-spruce soundboard.

The Signature Series also comes in both vertical and grand models. These pianos feature premium Renner hammers, Röslau strings, maple and mahogany rims, solid brass hardware, Bolduc tapered soundboards of solid spruce, sand-cast plates, and advanced low-tension scales. The Signature models have cabinet designs that offer lots of detail for the money and coordinate with major furniture trends. In spite of their beauty, the company says, these pianos are also appropriate for school and commercial applications.

In keeping with the tradition, established by Hampton Story and Melville Clark, of integrating the latest technology into pianos, all Story & Clark pianos now come equipped with QRS's latest connected systems. Grand pianos, and the 48" model H7 Academy upright, all have a PNOmation Studio reproducing-piano system, which includes the PNOmation3 playback system, the PNOscan™ record system, a keystop rail to prevent the hammers from striking the strings in Practice (Silent) mode, and a specially designed piano speaker. Most vertical pianos are standardly equipped with a connected PNOscan Studio system, which includes PNOscan, the PNOmation3 controller, a keystop rail, a specially designed piano speaker, headphones, and one year of PianoMarvel interactive piano lessons.

PNOscan is an optical sensor strip attached to the key frame directly under the keys. It senses the entire movement of each key so that it can precisely re-create every detail of an original performance, including the force, speed, and duration of each note played, without affecting the touch or response of the keyboard. The data captured by QRS's PNOmation3 controller can then be used in multiple ways: wirelessly transmitted via Bluetooth to third-party apps, auto-recorded, auto-saved locally, or auto-archived to the customer's free PNOcloud account. The PNOmation3 controller also features built-in sounds for practicing in silence or layering. Use of any Wi-Fi–enabled or hardwired device will give full access to all settings, setups, and content, and the systems can also be controlled by Apple Watch and Amazon Echo. A USB connection or MIDI output to a computer, general MIDI sound module, or other digital device is also available. PNOscan and PNOmation are both HD MIDI ready. The addition of these systems to every Story & Clark acoustic piano gives customers the potential to have all the features of a digital piano and more.

In all Story & Clark pianos with a factory-installed PNOmation system, the system will be fully concealed, with no solenoid-rail cover visible, no need to cut the legs to accommodate the entire 88-note system, and full use of the original pedals and trapwork. This is called the QRS ZERO installation.

In 2017 Story & Clark introduced its new Black-Tie series, made to its specifications in cooperation with the German manufacturer Blüthner. The new models are specifically designed to perform in the rigors of commercial venues. Premium features include Renner hammers, Röslau strings, beech rims, solid brass hardware, tapered spruce soundboards, sand-cast plates, and advanced low-tension scales. The new models will include PNOmation Studio or PNOscan Studio systems, as outlined above. Prices were not available at press time.

Warranty: 10 years on moving parts to original purchaser.

WALTER, CHARLES R.

Walter Piano Company, Inc.
25416 CR 6
Elkhart, Indiana 46514
574-266-0615
www.walterpiano.com

Charles Walter, an engineer, was head of Piano Design and Developmental Engineering at C.G. Conn in the 1960s, when Conn was doing important research in musical acoustics. In 1969 Walter bought the Janssen piano name from Conn, and continued to make Janssen pianos until 1981. In 1975 he brought out the Charles R. Walter line of consoles and studios, based on his continuing research in piano design. Walter began making grands in 1997.

The Walter Piano Company is fairly unique among U.S. piano manufacturers in that it is a family business, staffed by Charles and his wife, several of their grownup children, and various in-laws, in addition to unrelated production employees. The Walters say that each piano is inspected and signed by a member of their family before being shipped. Dealers and technicians report that doing business with the Walters is a pleasure in itself.

The Charles R. Walter line consists of 43" and 45" studio pianos in various decorator and institutional styles, and 5' 9" and 6' 4" grands. Note that both vertical models have full-size actions and therefore are studio pianos, not consoles, as I define those terms. In fact, they are identical pianos inside different cabinets. Walter calls the 43" model a console because of its furniture styling, but due to its larger action, it will outplay most real consoles on the market.

Although Mr. Walter is not oblivious to marketing concerns, his vertical piano bears the mark of being designed by an engineer who understands pianos and strives for quality. The pianos are built in a traditional manner, with heavy-duty, full-length spruce backposts; a solid spruce soundboard; and Delignit pinblock. Exceptionally long, thick keys that are individually lead-weighted provide a very even feel across the keyboard. The scale design is well thought out and the bass sounds good most of the way to the bottom. The cabinetry is substantial, contains no particleboard, and is beautifully finished. Some of the fancy consoles in particular, such as the Queen Anne models, are strikingly beautiful. The pianos are well prepared at the factory and so need minimal preparation by the dealer.

The vertical pianos now use Renner actions, but a Chinese-made action is available as a lower-cost option, reducing the price of the piano by about $1,500. The Chinese parts are virtually indistinguishable from the Renner parts, but they make the action feel just slightly lighter due to differing spring tensions.

The Walter 5' 9" and 6' 4" grands were designed by Del Fandrich, one of the nation's most respected piano-design engineers. Both models have high-quality features such as a maple rim, Renner action, Kluge keys, Delignit pinblock, tapered solid spruce soundboard, and Abel hammers (Ronsen hammers in the 5' 9" model). The 5' 9" grand also has a number of innovative features: A portion of the inner rim and soundboard at the bass end of the piano are separated from the rest of the rim and allowed to "float." Less restricted in its movement, the soundboard can reproduce the fundamental frequencies of the lower bass notes more as a larger piano does. A special extension of the tenor bridge creates a smoother transition from bass to treble. Eight plate nosebolts increase plate stability, helping to reduce energy loss to the plate and thus increase sustain. Inverted half-agraffes embedded in the capo bar maintain string alignment and reduce unwanted string noise. The Walter grands are competently built and play very well.

Warranty: 12 years, parts and labor, transferable to future owners within the warranty period.

WEBER — See Young Chang.

WENDL & LUNG — See Feurich.

WERTHEIM

Wertheim Piano
Level 3, 480 Collins Street
3000 Melbourne, Victoria, Australia
+61 (0) 418 350124
info@wertheimpiano.com
www.wertheimpianousa.com
Pianos for North American distribution made by: AXL Musical Instrument Co., Shanghai, China

Wertheim pianos were first produced in Germany from 1875 to 1908, and then in Richmond, Australia, a suburb of Melbourne, from 1908 to 1935. Approximately 18,000 uprights and grands were made during the Richmond period. They were popular, all-purpose pianos with a good reputation for easy maintenance, and were used in a wide variety of settings, including homes, schools, and public halls. The most famous exponent of the Wertheim brand was Dame Nellie Melba, who frequently requested Wertheim pianos for her performances.

The Wertheim brand is currently owned and distributed to the international market by John Martin, who revived it in 2002. In his more than 46 years in the music industry, Martin has owned full-line retail music stores, managed a buying group for music-store retailers, and manufactured and distributed Wertheim pianos. Martin says that Wertheim's aim is to make the best-value, top-class pianos, using the best designs, materials, and workmanship, and working with leading piano designers and technicians from Germany, the U.S., Australia, and New Zealand.

Most Wertheim pianos for the North American market are made by AXL Musical Instrument Co., in Shanghai, China, which also manufactures the better-known Palatino brand. These Wertheims come in three series: Gold (model numbers beginning with W), Euro (WE), and Platinum (WP). The Gold-series models are for the budget-conscious buyer, Euro and Platinum for those desiring higher performance and quality. All contain German Röslau strings, solid spruce soundboard, and an 18-ply pinblock. The Gold and Euro series models use a Chinese action, the Platinum series models use a Renner action, with the option of a Wessell, Nickel & Gross composite action. The Euro and Platinum series have German Strunz soundboards and Renner hammers, and real ebony wood sharps. Currently available in North

America are 48", 48½", and 49" verticals, and 5' 1", 5' 7", 5' 10", and 7' grands, each available in several popular finishes, and with some variation in cabinet design.

New in 2017 is the Wertheim/Fandrich series. These models, designed by internationally recognized piano designer Del Fandrich, are assembled in Wertheim's own new factory from the best internationally sourced components by workers who, the company says, are rewarded for high quality rather than high volume. The new models will be positioned to fill the mid- to upper range of the piano market.

Warranty: 5 years, parts and labor, to original purchaser.

YAMAHA
including Cable-Nelson. See separate listing for **Disklavier** in "**Buying an Electronic Player-Piano System.**"

Yamaha Corporation of America
P.O. Box 6600
Buena Park, California 90622
714-522-9011
800-854-1569
infostation@yamaha.com
www.yamaha.com

Pianos made by: Yamaha Corporation, Hamamatsu, Japan and other locations (see text)

Torakusu Yamaha, a watchmaker, developed Japan's first reed organ, and founded Yamaha Reed Organ Manufacturing in 1887. In 1899, Yamaha visited the U.S. to learn how to build pianos. Within a couple of years he began making grand and vertical pianos under the name Nippon Gakki, Ltd. Beginning in the 1930s, Yamaha expanded its operations, first into other musical instruments, then into other products and services, such as sporting goods and furniture, and finally internationally.

Export of pianos to the U.S. began in earnest about 1960. In 1973, Yamaha acquired the Everett Piano Co., in South Haven, Michigan, and made both Yamaha and Everett pianos there until 1986. In that year, the company moved its piano manufacturing to a plant in Thomaston, Georgia, where it made Yamaha consoles, studios, and some grands until 2007, when a depressed piano market and foreign competition forced it to close its doors. Since then, the company has introduced new models, made in other Yamaha factories, to replace those formerly made in Thomaston.

Yamaha is probably the most international of the piano manufacturers. In addition to its factories in Japan, Yamaha has plants in Mexico, China, and Indonesia. Yamaha pianos sold in the U.S. are made in Japan, China, and Indonesia. In 2009, Yamaha closed its factories in England (with Kemble) and Taiwan. Models

formerly made in those factories are now being produced in Yamaha's other Asian plants. Yamaha also owns the renowned Austrian piano maker, Bösendorfer.

Yamaha's console line consists of the 43" model b1, in continental style, with a laminated soundboard; and the 44" models M460 and M560 in furniture style (free-standing legs), representing two levels of cabinet sophistication and price. All are internally similar (except for the soundboard) and have a compressed action typical of a console, which means that the action will not be quite as responsive as in larger models.

The studio line consists of the popular 45" model P22 in institutional style (legs with toe blocks) with school-friendly cabinet; the furniture-style version P660; and the 45" model b2, with a less-expensive institutional-style cabinet. The b2 replaces the Chinese-made model T118. All studio models are internally similar, with a full-size action. All Yamaha verticals under 48" tall are now made in the company's Indonesian factory, which has been making pianos for more than 30 years and, according to Yamaha, adheres to the same quality standards as its Japanese plant.

The uprights are the very popular 48" model U1; the 48" model b3, which is made in Indonesia, has the same scale design as the U1, and replaces the Chinese-made model T121SC; and the 52" model U3. The U3 joins the YUS5 (see below) in having a "floating" soundboard—the soundboard is not completely attached to the back at the top, allowing it to vibrate a little more freely to enhance the tonal performance. A new Super U series of uprights (YUS1, YUS3, and YUS5) have different hammers and get additional tuning and voicing at the factory, including voicing by machine to create a more consistent, more mellow tone. The YUS5 has German Röslau music wire instead of Yamaha wire, also for a mellower tone. This top-of-the-line 52" upright also has agraffes, duplex scaling, and a sostenuto pedal (all other Yamaha verticals have a practice/mute pedal). The U- and YU-series uprights are all made in Japan and come with soft-close fallboards.

Yamaha verticals are very well made for mass-produced pianos. The taller uprights in particular are considered a "dream" to service by technicians, and are very much enjoyed by musicians. Sometimes the pianos can sound quite bright, though much less so now than in previous years. The current version of the model P22 school studio is said to have been redesigned to sound less bright and to have a broader spectrum of tonal color. Double-striking of the hammer in the low tenor on a soft or incomplete keystroke is a problem occasionally mentioned in regard to Yamaha verticals by those who play with an especially soft touch. This tendency is a characteristic of the action design, the trade-off being better-than-normal repetition for a vertical piano. If necessary, it's possible that a technician can lessen this problem with careful adjustment, but at the risk of sacrificing some speed of repetition.

Yamaha grands come in several levels of sophistication and size. The Classic Collection consists of the 5' model GB1K, the 5' 3" model GC1M, and the 5' 8" model GC2. The GB1K has simplified case construction and cabinetry, no duplex scale, and the middle pedal operates a bass-sustain mechanism. It does have a soft-close fallboard. It is currently the only Yamaha grand sold in the U.S. that is made in Indonesia. The GC1M and GC2 have regular case construction, duplex scale, soft-close fallboard, and sostenuto pedal.

The Conservatory Classic and Conservatory Concert Collections of C-series grands were replaced in 2012 with the CX series, consisting of the 5' 3" model C1X, the 5' 8" model C2X, the 6' 1" model C3X, the 6' 7" model C5X, the 7' model C6X, and the 7' 6" model C7X. The new CX series incorporates some of the design elements of the limited-production CF series (see below) into the higher-production C-series pianos to create a sound more like that of a high-end American or European instrument—see our **review** in the Spring 2014 issue. Features include a European spruce soundboard crowned using CF-series technology, a thicker rim and bracing, German music wire, additional time spent voicing, regulating, and tuning by very skilled craftsmen, and some changes in cabinet design.

Both the C and CX models have the advanced construction, scaling, and cabinetry mentioned earlier, including a true sostenuto pedal and a soft-close fallboard. Both also have vertically laminated bridges with maple or boxwood cap. The vertically laminated design is similar to that found in Steinways and other fine pianos, and is considered to give the bridges greater strength and resistance to cracking and better transmission of vibrational energy. All C and CX grands have keytops of Ivorite™, Yamaha's ivory alternative.

The new CF Series, one of two Yamaha Premium Collection lines, comprises the 9' model CFX (replacing model CFIIIS), and the 6' 3" model CF4 and 7' model CF6 (respectively replacing, in the U.S., models S4B and S6B, which will remain available by special order only). The pianos in this collection are made in a separate factory to much higher standards and with some different materials: e.g., maple and mahogany in the rim, which is made more rigid, for greater tonal power, than in the other collections; higher-grade soundboard material; a treble "bell" (as in the larger Steinways) to enhance treble tone; German strings, and hammer and scaling changes,

for a more mellow tone; as well as the more advanced features of the other collections. The result is an instrument capable of greater dynamic range, tonal color, and sustain than the regular Yamahas. The new CF-series pianos have a thicker rim and more substantial structure than their predecessors, for greater strength and tonal projection, and the method for developing the soundboard crown has been changed to allow the soundboard to vibrate more freely and with greater resonance. The models CF4 and CF6 have an open pinblock design reminiscent of some European pianos, which gives the tuner slightly greater control over the tuning pins. Yamaha says that the CF series represents 19 years of research and development by its craftsmen, designers, and engineers. The Yamaha concert grand is endorsed and used by a number of notable musicians, including Olga Kern, Michael Tilson Thomas, Chick Corea, and Elton John.

The second Premium Collection line, added in 2017, is the SX Series, positioned between the CX and CF lines and comprising the 6' 1" model S3X, the 6' 7" model S5X, and the 7' 6" model S7X. The SX series uses the same soundboard and scale-design approach as the flagship CFX model; has a completely new hammer design derived from testing more than 100 prototypes; and, most significant, has a new, thicker rim construction in which the wood is treated with a patented accelerated-aging process called Acoustic Resonance Enhancement, to give the piano a warmer, more romantic sound with a wider range of expression.

The price differences between the SX and CF models are related to their production processes: the CF instruments are fully handcrafted, whereas the SX pianos are built with a combination of handcraftsmanship and innovative technologies. Yamaha says that SX pianos are intended especially for institutions and smaller concert venues, the CF models for larger concert halls.

Yamaha grands have historically been a little on the percussive side and have been said not to "sing" as well as some more expensive pianos. The tone has been very clear and often bright, especially in the smaller grands, although the excessive brightness that once characterized Yamahas has long since been corrected. The clarity and percussiveness are very attractive but are less well suited for classical music, which tends to require a singing tone and lush harmonic color. On the other hand, Yamaha has long been the piano of choice for jazz and popular music, which may value clarity and brightness more than the other qualities mentioned.

In recent years, however, Yamaha has been trying to move away from this image of a "bright" piano whose sound is limited to jazz. First with its larger grands, and later with the smaller ones, Yamaha has changed such things as bridge construction and hammer density, and provided more custom voicing at the factory, to bring out a broader spectrum of tonal color. Now, with its Premium Collection models, and the innovative soundboard, hammer, and rim technologies used in their design and construction, Yamaha has come fully into the world of instruments suited for classical music (as well as jazz).

Both Yamaha's quality control and its warranty and technical service are legendary in the piano business. They are the standard against which every other company is measured. For general home and school use, piano technicians probably recommend Yamaha pianos more often than any other brand. Their precision, reliability, and performance make them a very good value for a consumer product.

Until recently, Yamaha made an entry-level line of pianos under the name Cable-Nelson. This is the name of an old American piano maker whose roots can be traced back to 1903. Yamaha acquired the name when it bought the Everett Piano Company, in 1973, and used the name in conjunction with Everett pianos until 1981. The most recent Cable-Nelson models were made in Yamaha's factories in China and Indonesia.

There is a thriving market for used Yamahas. If you're considering buying a used Yamaha, please read "Should I Buy a Used, 'Gray Market' Yamaha or Kawai Piano?" on pages 176–177 of *The Piano Book*, and "**Buying a Used or Restored Piano**" in this publication.

Yamaha also makes electronic player pianos called Disklaviers, as well as a variety of hybrid acoustic/digital instruments—including Silent Piano (formerly called MIDIPiano), the AvantGrand series, and the model NU1, that account for a substantial percentage of the company's sales. These products are separately reviewed in the articles "**Buying an Electronic Player-Piano System**" and "**Hybrid Pianos**."

Warranty: Yamaha—10 years, parts and labor, to original purchaser.

YOUNG CHANG
including Weber and Albert Weber

PAL Sound
6000 Phyllis Drive
Cypress, California 90630
657-200-3470
www.youngchang.com
www.weberpiano.com

Pianos made by: Young Chang Co., Ltd., Incheon, South Korea; and Tianjin, China

In 1956, three brothers—Jai-Young, Jai-Chang, and Jai-Sup Kim—founded Young Chang and began selling Yamaha pianos in Korea under an agreement with that Japanese firm. Korea was recovering from a devastating war, and only the wealthy could afford pianos. But the prospects were bright for economic development, and as a symbol of cultural refinement the piano was much coveted. In 1962 the brothers incorporated as Young Chang Akki Co., Ltd.

In 1964 Yamaha and Young Chang entered into an agreement in which Yamaha helped Young Chang set up a full-fledged manufacturing operation. Yamaha shipped partially completed pianos from Japan to the Young Chang factory in Incheon, South Korea, where Young Chang would perform final assembly work such as cabinet assembly, stringing, and action installation. This arrangement reduced high import duties. As time went by, Young Chang built more of the components, to the point where they were making virtually the entire piano. In 1975 the arrangement ended when Young Chang decided to expand domestically and internationally under its own brand name, thus becoming a competitor. Young Chang began exporting to the U.S. in the late 1970s, and established a North American distribution office in California in 1984. In addition to making pianos under its own name, Young Chang also made pianos for a time for Baldwin under the Wurlitzer name, for Samsung under the Weber name, and private-label names for large dealer chains and distributors worldwide.

Weber & Co. was established in 1852 by Albert Weber, a German immigrant, and was one of the most prominent and highly respected American piano brands of the late 19th and early 20th centuries. During the consolidation of the American piano industry in the early 20th century, Weber became part of the Aeolian family of brands. Following Aeolian's demise in 1985, Young Chang acquired the Weber name.

In 1995, in response to rising Korean wages and to supply a growing Chinese domestic market, Young Chang built a 750,000-square-foot factory in Tianjin, China, and gradually began to move manufacturing operations there for some of its models. Today, the Tianjin facility produces

Young Chang and Weber pianos, and components for the Albert Weber line, which is assembled in South Korea.

Hyundai Development Company, a Korean civil-engineering and construction firm, acquired Young Chang in 2006. The company says that Hyundai Development has brought the necessary capital for factory renovations and has instituted new advanced industrial quality-control systems.

In 2008 Young Chang hired noted American piano designer Delwin D. Fandrich to undertake a redesign of the entire Young Chang and Weber piano line. Highlights include extensively redesigned cast-iron plates, new string scales, and new rib designs. New directly-coupled bass bridges, along with unique "floating soundboard" configurations, improve soundboard mobility around the bass bridge for better bass tonal response. At the same time, a revised hammer-making process, in which the hammers are cold-pressed with less felt compression, provides for greater hammer resilience and improved tone, with less voicing required. Fandrich says that all of these features and processes contribute to his goal of building instruments with improved tonal balance and musicality, and provide opportunities to standardize manufacturing processes for better quality control. The new designs were phased in gradually from 2011 to 2013.

Along with being redesigned by Delwin Fandrich, former multiple piano lines were consolidated into just three lines: the Young Chang (Y) and Weber (W) series are entry- and mid-level instruments made in China, and the Albert Weber (AW) line comprises upper-level models made in Korea. The AW grands have lower-tension scales, maple rims, and Renner actions, and higher-quality hammer felt, soundboard material, and veneers (on wood-veneered models). The Y and W grands have lauan rims and Young Chang actions. The AW verticals use slightly better materials than the other verticals for the cabinets, hardware, music wire, and keys, though in general the differences are smaller than with the grands.

The Young Chang and Weber pianos distinctly differ from one another: the Weber models have a low-tension scale and softer, cold-pressed hammers, and the greater warmth and romantic tonal characteristics that often accompany that type of scale; the Young Chang models have a higher-tension scale and firmer cold-pressed hammers, and the greater brightness and stronger projection of a more modern sound. The Weber line, also known as the Premium Edition, also has agraffes in the bass section of the verticals, and beveled lids on the grands.

Quality control in Young Chang's Korean factory has improved little by little over the years, and is now nearly as good as that in Japan. Most of the problems currently encountered are minor ones that can be cured by a good dealer make-ready and a little follow-up service, and the pianos hold up well in the field, even in institutions. The Albert Weber pianos, in particular, have great musical potential and respond well to expert voicing. Pianos from the factory in China, like other pianos from that country, have been uneven in quality, but in recent years have greatly improved. Young Chang says that Hyundai Development Group has upgraded the factories in both countries, and that the pianos made at the Tianjin factory are now on a par with those made in Korea.

Young Chang also owns Kurzweil Music Systems, a manufacturer of professional keyboards and home digital pianos, which it acquired in 1990.

Warranty: Young Chang and Weber—10 years, parts and labor, to the original purchaser; Albert Weber—15 years, parts and labor, transferable to future owners during the warranty period, plus a lifetime warranty on parts to the original owner. 🎹

[*Online Edition readers*: After reading the following introduction, please click below to access the free searchable database of acoustic piano models and prices.]

[Acoustic Piano Database]

This guide contains price information for nearly every brand, model, style, and finish of new piano that has regular distribution in the United States and, for the most part, Canada. Omitted are some marginal, local, or "stencil" brands (brands sold only by a single dealership). Prices are in U.S. dollars and are subject to change. Prices include an allowance for the approximate cost of freight from the U.S. warehouse to the dealer, and for a minimal amount of make-ready by the dealer. The prices cited in this edition were compiled in August 2017 and apply only to piano sales in the U.S. Prices in Canada are often very different due to differences in duty, freight, sales practices, and competition.

Note that the prices of European pianos vary with the value of the dollar against the euro. For this edition, the exchange rate used by most manufacturers was approximately €1 = $1.05–1.10. Prices of European pianos include import duties and estimated costs of airfreight (where applicable) to the dealer. However, actual costs will vary depending on the shipping method used, the port of entry, and other variables. Also keep in mind that the dealer may have purchased the piano at an exchange rate different from the current one.

Unless otherwise indicated, cabinet styles are assumed to be traditional in nature, with minimal embellishment and straight legs. Recognizable furniture styles are noted, and the manufacturer's own trademarked style name is used when an appropriate generic name could not be determined. Please see the section on "Furniture Style and Finish" in the article "**Piano-Buying Basics**" for descriptions or definitions of terms relating to style and finish.

"Size" refers to the height of a vertical or the length of a grand. These are the only dimensions that vary significantly and relate to the quality of the instrument. The height of a vertical piano is measured from the floor to the top of the piano. The length of a grand piano is measured from the very front (keyboard end) to the very back (tail end) with the lid closed.

About Prices

The subject of piano pricing is difficult, complicated, and controversial. One of the major problems is that piano dealers tend to prefer that list prices be as high as possible so they can still make a profit while appearing to give very generous discounts. Honesty about pricing is resisted.

But even knowing what is "honest" is a slippery business because many factors can have a dramatic effect on piano pricing. For one thing, different dealerships can pay very different wholesale prices for the same merchandise, depending on:

- the size of the dealership and how many pianos it agrees to purchase at one time or over a period of time
- whether the dealer pays cash or finances the purchase
- the degree to which the dealer buys manufacturer overstocks at bargain prices
- any special terms the dealership negotiates with the manufacturer or distributor.

In addition to these variations at the wholesale level, retail conditions also vary from dealer to dealer or from one geographic area to another, including:

- the general cost of doing business in the dealer's area
- the level of pre- and post-sale service the dealer provides
- the level of professionalism of the sales staff and the degree to which they are trained and compensated
- the ease of local comparison shopping by the consumer for a particular type of piano or at a particular price level.

Besides the variations between dealerships, the circumstances of each sale at any particular dealership can vary tremendously due to such things as:

- how long a particular piano has been sitting around unsold, racking up finance charges for the dealer
- the dealer's financial condition and need for cash at the moment

- competing sales events going on at other dealerships in the area
- whether or not the customer is trading in a used piano.

As difficult as it might be to come up with accurate price information, confusion and ignorance about pricing for such a high-ticket item is intolerable to the consumer, and can cause decision-making paralysis. I strongly believe that a reasonable amount of price information actually greases the wheels of commerce by giving the customer the peace of mind that allows him or her to make a purchase. In this guide I've tried to give a level of information about price that reasonably respects the interests of both buyer and seller, given the range of prices that can exist for any particular model.

Prices include a bench except where noted. (Even where a price doesn't include a bench, the dealer will almost always provide one and quote a price that includes it.) Most dealers will also include delivery and one or two tunings in the home, but these are optional and a matter of agreement between you and the dealer. Prices do not include sales tax.

In this guide, two prices are given for each model: Manufacturer's Suggested Retail Price (MSRP) and Suggested Maximum Price (SMP).

Manufacturer's Suggested Retail Price (MSRP)

The MSRP is a price provided by the manufacturer or distributor and designed as a starting point from which dealers are expected to discount. I include it here for reference purposes—only rarely does a customer pay this price. The MSRP is usually figured as a multiple of the wholesale price, but the specific multiple used differs from company to company. **For that reason, it's fruitless to compare prices of different brands by comparing discounts from**

the MSRP. To see why, consider the following scenario:

Manufacturer A sells brand A through its dealer A. The wholesale price to the dealer is $1,000, but for the purpose of setting the MSRP, the manufacturer doubles the wholesale price and sets the MSRP at $2,000. Dealer A offers a 25 percent discount off the MSRP, for a "street price" of $1,500.

Manufacturer B sells brand B through its dealer B. The wholesale price to the dealer is also $1,000, but manufacturer B triples the wholesale price and sets the MSRP at $3,000. Dealer B offers a generous 50 percent discount, for a street price of, again, $1,500.

Although the street price is the same for both pianos, a customer shopping at both stores and knowing nothing about the wholesale price or how the MSRPs are computed, is likely to come away with the impression that brand B, with a discount of 50 percent off $3,000, is a more "valuable" piano and a better deal than brand A, with a discount of 25 percent off $2,000. Other factors aside, which dealer do you think will get the sale? It's important to note that there is nothing about brand B that makes it deserving of a higher MSRP than brand A—how to compute the MSRP is essentially a marketing decision on the part of the manufacturer.

Because of the deceptive manner in which MSRPs are so often used, some manufacturers no longer provide them. In those cases, I've left the MSRP column blank.

Suggested Maximum Price (SMP)

The Suggested Maximum Price (SMP) is a price I've created, based on a profit margin that I've uniformly applied to published wholesale prices. (Where the published wholesale price is believed to be bogus, as is sometimes

the case, I've made a reasonable attempt to find out what a typical small dealer actually pays for the piano, and use that price in place of the published one.) Because in the SMP, unlike in the MSRP, the same profit margin is applied to all brands, the SMP can be used as a "benchmark" price for the purpose of comparing brands and offers. The specific profit margin I've chosen for the SMP is one that dealers often try—but rarely manage—to attain. Also included in the SMP, in most cases, are allowances for duty (where applicable), freight charges, and a minimal amount of make-ready by the dealer. Although the SMP is my creation, it's a reasonable estimate of the **maximum** price you should realistically expect to pay. However, **most sales actually take place at a discount to the SMP**, as discussed below.

Actual Selling or "Street" Price

As you should know by now from reading this publication, most dealers of new pianos are willing—and expect—to negotiate. Only a handful of dealers have non-negotiable prices. For more information on negotiating, please see "**Negotiating Price and Trade-Ins**" in the article "**Piano Buying Basics.**" *The Piano Book* also gives advice about negotiating tactics.

How good a deal you can negotiate will vary, depending on the many factors listed earlier. But in order to make a budget, or to know which pianos are within your budget, or just to feel comfortable enough to actually make a purchase, you need some idea of what is considered normal in the industry. In most cases, discounts from the Suggested Maximum Price range from 10 to 30 percent. This does *not* mean that if you try hard enough, you can talk the salesperson into giving you a 30 percent discount. Rather, it reflects the wide range of prices possible in the marketplace due to the many factors discussed earlier. For budgeting purposes only, I suggest figuring a discount of about 15 or 20 percent. This will probably bring you within about 10 percent, one way or the other, of the final negotiated price. Important exception: Discounts on Steinway pianos generally range from 0 to 10 percent. For your convenience in figuring the effects of various discounts,

a discount calculator is included in the model and price database, accessible through the electronic edition of this publication.

There is no single "fair" or "right" price that can be applied to every purchase. The only fair price is that which the buyer and seller agree on. It's understandable that you would like to pay as little as possible, but remember that piano shopping is not just about chasing the lowest price. Be sure you are getting the instrument

that best suits your needs and preferences, and that the dealer is committed to providing the appropriate level of pre- and post-sale service.

For more information about shopping for a new piano and how to save money, please see pages 60–75 in *The Piano Book, Fourth Edition*.

[*Online Edition readers:* Click below to access the free searchable database of acoustic piano models and prices.]
[Acoustic Piano Database]

Model	Feet	Inches	Description	MSRP*	SMP*
BALDWIN					
Verticals					
B342		43	French Provincial Satin Cherry	9,895	7,190
B442		43	Satin Mahogany	9,895	7,190
BP1		47	Polished Ebony	8,625	6,390
B243		47	Satin Ebony/Walnut (school piano)	9,895	7,190
BH122		48	Polished Ebony	9,265	6,790
BP3		48	French Provincial Polished Rosewood	10,225	7,390
BP3T		48	Polished Ebony	9,895	7,190
BP3T		48	Polished Rosewood	10,225	7,390
BP5		49	Polished Ebony	10,225	7,390
BP5		49	Polished Rosewood	10,550	7,590
B252		52	Satin Ebony	12,495	8,790
Grands					
BP148	4	10	Satin Ebony	22,395	14,990
BP148	4	10	Polished Ebony	21,425	14,390
BP148	4	10	Polished Ebony with Silver Hardware	22,395	14,990
BP148	4	10	Polished Mahogany/Walnut/White	22,395	14,990
BP152	5		Satin Ebony	25,295	16,790
BP152	5		Polished Ebony	24,325	16,190
BP152	5		Polished Mahogany/Walnut/White	25,295	16,790
BP165	5	5	Satin Ebony	27,550	18,190
BP165	5	5	Polished Ebony	26,595	17,590
BP165	5	5	Polished Ebony with Silver Hardware	27,550	18,190
BP165	5	5	Polished Mahogany/Walnut/White	27,550	18,190
BP178	5	10	Satin Ebony	37,425	24,390
BP178	5	10	Polished Ebony	35,825	23,390
BP178	5	10	Polished Mahogany/Walnut	37,425	24,390
BP190	6	3	Satin Ebony	44,795	28,990
BP190	6	3	Polished Ebony	42,895	27,790
BP190	6	3	Polished Mahogany/Walnut	44,795	28,990
BP211	6	11	Polished Ebony	63,995	40,990

*See pricing explanation on page 188.

BECHSTEIN, (C.)

Models beginning with "B" say only "Bechstein" on the fallboard. Others say "C. Bechstein."

Bechstein Verticals

Model	Feet	Inches	Description	MSRP*	SMP*
B112 Modern		44	Polished Ebony		23,848
B112 Modern		44	Polished White		26,620
B112 Chrome Art		44	Polished Ebony		26,560
B112 Chrome Art		44	Polished White		29,120
B116 Accent		45.5	Polished Ebony		26,180
B116 Accent		45.5	Polished White		28,910
B116 Compact		45.5	Polished Ebony		26,180
B116 Compact		45.5	Polished White		28,910
B116 Compact		45.5	Satin and Polished Walnut/Mahogany/Cherry		31,198
B120 Select		47.5	Polished Ebony		27,754
B120 Select		47.5	Polished White		30,526
B124 Imposant		49	Polished Ebony		28,448
B124 Imposant		49	Polished White		30,274
B124 Style		49.5	Polished Ebony		29,624
B124 Style		49.5	Polished White		32,354
B124 Style		49.5	Satin and Polished Mahogany/Walnut/Cherry		34,642

C. Bechstein Verticals

Model	Feet	Inches	Description	MSRP*	SMP*
Millenium 116K		46	Polished Ebony		30,926
Millenium 116K		46	Polished White		35,168
Classic 118		46.5	Polished Ebony		32,836
Classic 118		46.5	Polished White		37,100
Classic 118		46.5	Satin and Polished Walnut/Mahogany/Cherry		37,100
Contour 118		46.5	Polished Ebony		32,836
Contour 118		46.5	Polished White		37,100
Contour 118		46.5	Satin and Polished Walnut/Mahogany/Cherry		37,100
Classic 124		49	Polished Ebony		42,412
Classic 124		49	Polished White		47,726
Classic 124		49	Satin and Polished Walnut/Mahogany/Cherry		47,726
Elegance 124		49	Polished Ebony		42,412
Elegance 124		49	Polished White		47,726
Elegance 124		49	Satin and Polished Walnut/Mahogany/Cherry		
Concert 8		51.5	Polished Ebony		70,070
Concert 8		51.5	Polished White		78,574
Concert 8		51.5	Satin and Polished Walnut/Mahogany/Cherry		
Concert 8		51.5	Satin and Polished Burl Walnut/Vavona		

Bechstein Grands

Model	Feet	Inches	Description	MSRP*	SMP*
B160	5	3	Polished Ebony		66,332
B160	5	3	Satin and Polished Mahogany/Walnut		83,972
B160	5	3	Polished White		79,708
B175	5	9	Polished Ebony		71,644
B175	5	9	Satin and Polished Walnut/Mahogany		89,704
B175	5	9	Polished White		85,462
B190	6	3	Polished Ebony		76,958
B190	6	3	Satin and Polished Mahogany/Walnut		97,138
B190	6	3	Polished White		92,896
B208	6	8	Polished Ebony		84,182
B208	6	8	Satin and Polished Mahogany/Walnut		102,472
B208	6	8	Polished White		98,210
B228	7	5	Polished Ebony		95,458
B228	7	5	Satin and Polished Mahogany/Walnut		119,462
B228	7	5	Polished White		110,978

*See pricing explanation on page 188.

BECHSTEIN, (C.) *(continued)*
C. Bechstein Grands

Model	Feet	Inches	Description	MSRP*	SMP*
L167	5	6	Polished Ebony		119,546
L167	5	6	Satin and Polished Mahogany/Walnut/Cherry		142,100
L167	5	6	Polished White		142,100
M/P192	6	4	Polished Ebony		139,538
M/P192	6	4	Satin and Polished Mahogany/Walnut/Cherry		162,070
M/P192	6	4	Polished White		162,070
B212	6	11	Polished Ebony		172,508
B212	6	11	Polished White		197,372
C234	7	7	Polished Ebony		210,328
C234	7	7	Polished White		249,242
D282	9	2	Polished Ebony		268,372
D282	9	2	Polished White		317,260

BLÜTHNER
Prices do not include bench.
Verticals

Model	Feet	Inches	Description	MSRP*	SMP*
D		45	Satin and Polished Ebony	32,664	30,398
D		45	Satin and Polished Walnut/Mahogany	35,277	32,749
D		45	Satin and Polished Cherry	35,441	32,897
D		45	Satin and Polished White	34,951	32,456
D		45	Satin and Polished Bubinga/Yew/Rosewood/Macassar	36,257	33,631
C		46	Satin and Polished Ebony	36,294	33,665
C		46	Satin and Polished Mahogany/Walnut	39,197	36,277
C		46	Satin and Polished Cherry	39,379	36,441
C		46	Satin and Polished White	38,834	35,951
C		46	Satin and Polished Bubinga/Yew/Rosewood/Macassar	40,286	37,257
C		46	Saxony Polished Pyramid Mahogany	46,093	42,484
C		46	Polished Burl Walnut/Camphor	48,996	45,096
A		49	Satin and Polished Ebony	41,817	38,635
A		49	Satin and Polished Mahogany/Walnut	45,162	41,646
A		49	Satin and Polished Cherry	45,371	41,834
A		49	Satin and Polished White	44,744	41,270
A		49	Satin and Polished Bubinga/Yew/Rosewood/Macassar	46,416	42,774
A		49	Saxony Polished Pyramid Mahogany	53,107	48,796
A		49	Polished Burl Walnut/Camphor	56,452	51,807
B		52	Satin and Polished Ebony	47,339	43,605
B		52	Satin and Polished Mahogany/Walnut	51,127	47,014
B		52	Satin and Polished Cherry	51,363	47,227
B		52	Satin and Polished White	50,653	46,588
B		52	Satin and Polished Bubinga/Yew/Rosewood/Macassar	52,547	48,292
B		52	Saxony Polished Pyramid Mahogany	60,121	55,109
B		52	Polished Burl Walnut/Camphor	63,908	58,517
S		57.5	Satin and Polished Ebony	63,615	58,254
S		57.5	Satin and Polished Mahogany/Walnut	68,704	62,834
S		57.5	Satin and Polished Cherry	69,022	63,120
S		57.5	Satin and Polished White	68,068	62,261
S		57.5	Satin and Polished Bubinga/Yew/Rosewood/Macassar	70,613	64,552
S		57.5	Saxony Polished Pyramid Mahogany	80,791	73,712
S		57.5	Polished Burl Walnut/Camphor	85,880	78,292
Verticals			e-volution Hybrid Piano System, add	8,200	7,380

*See pricing explanation on page 188.

Model	Feet	Inches	Description	MSRP*	SMP*
BLÜTHNER (continued)					
Grands					
11	5	1	Satin and Polished Ebony	82,234	75,011
11	5	1	Satin and Polished Mahogany/Walnut	88,812	80,931
11	5	1	Satin and Polished Cherry	89,223	81,301
11	5	1	Satin and Polished White	87,990	80,191
11	5	1	Satin and Polished Bubinga/Yew/Rosewood/Macassar	91,279	83,151
11	5	1	Saxony Polished Pyramid Mahogany	105,259	95,733
11	5	1	Polished Burl Walnut/Camphor	105,259	95,733
11	5	1	President Polished Ebony	93,422	85,080
11	5	1	President Polished Mahogany/Walnut	100,001	91,001
11	5	1	President Polished Bubinga	102,468	93,221
11	5	1	President Burl Walnut	116,448	105,803
11	5	1	Wilhelm II Satin and Polished Ebony	96,213	87,592
11	5	1	Wilhelm II Polished Mahogany/Walnut	103,910	94,519
11	5	1	Wilhelm II Polished Pyramid Mahogany	122,664	111,398
11	5	1	Wilhelm II Polished Burl Walnut	122,664	111,398
11	5	1	Ambassador Santos Rosewood	118,663	107,797
11	5	1	Ambassador Walnut	115,456	104,910
11	5	1	Nicolas II Satin Walnut with Burl Inlay	117,890	107,101
11	5	1	Louis XIV Rococo Satin White with Gold	127,271	115,544
11	5	1	Jubilee Polished Ebony	99,638	90,674
11	5	1	Jubilee Polished Mahogany/Walnut	106,217	96,595
11	5	1	Jubilee Burl Walnut	122,664	111,398
11	5	1	Julius Bluthner Edition	104,118	94,706
11	5	1	Crystal Edition Elegance	123,000	111,700
11	5	1	Crystal Edition Idyllic	144,000	130,600
10	5	5	Satin and Polished Ebony	94,797	86,317
10	5	5	Satin and Polished Mahogany/Walnut	102,381	93,143
10	5	5	Satin and Polished Cherry	102,855	93,570
10	5	5	Satin and Polished White	101,433	92,290
10	5	5	Satin and Polished Bubinga/Yew/Rosewood/Macassar	105,225	95,703
10	5	5	Saxony Polished Pyramid Mahogany	119,444	108,500
10	5	5	Polished Burl Walnut/Camphor	119,444	108,500
10	5	5	President Polished Ebony	105,986	96,387
10	5	5	President Polished Mahogany/Walnut	113,570	103,213
10	5	5	President Polished Bubinga	116,413	105,772
10	5	5	President Burl Walnut	130,633	118,570
10	5	5	Senator Walnut w/Leather	111,888	101,699
10	5	5	Senator Jacaranda Satin Rosewood w/Leather	121,212	110,091
10	5	5	Wilhelm II Satin and Polished Ebony	110,912	100,821
10	5	5	Wilhelm II Polished Mahogany/Walnut	119,785	108,807
10	5	5	Wilhelm II Polished Pyramid Mahogany	136,849	124,164
10	5	5	Wilhelm II Polished Burl Walnut	136,849	124,164
10	5	5	Ambassador Santos Rosewood	136,792	124,113
10	5	5	Ambassador Walnut	133,095	120,786
10	5	5	Nicolas II Satin Walnut with Burl Inlay	131,389	119,250
10	5	5	Louis XIV Rococo Satin White with Gold	146,715	133,044
10	5	5	Jubilee Polished Ebony	112,202	101,982
10	5	5	Jubilee Polished Mahogany/Walnut	119,786	108,807
10	5	5	Jubilee Burl Walnut	136,849	124,164
10	5	5	Julius Bluthner Edition	114,996	104,496
10	5	5	Crystal Edition Elegance	135,000	122,500
10	5	5	Crystal Edition Idyllic	156,000	141,400
PH	5	9	Paul Hennigsen Design	154,000	139,600
6	6	3	Satin and Polished Ebony	103,391	94,052
6	6	3	Satin and Polished Mahogany/Walnut	111,662	101,496
6	6	3	Satin and Polished Cherry	112,179	101,961
6	6	3	Satin and Polished White	110,628	100,565

*See pricing explanation on page 188.

Model	Feet	Inches	Description	MSRP*	SMP*
BLÜTHNER (continued)					
6	6	3	Satin and Polished Bubinga/Yew/Rosewood/Macassar	114,764	104,288
6	6	3	Saxony Polished Pyramid Mahogany	130,272	118,245
6	6	3	Polished Burl Walnut/Camphor	130,272	118,245
6	6	3	President Polished Ebony	114,580	104,122
6	6	3	President Polished Mahogany/Walnut	122,851	111,566
6	6	3	President Polished Bubinga	125,953	114,358
6	6	3	President Burl Walnut	141,461	128,315
6	6	3	Senator Walnut w/Leather	124,320	112,888
6	6	3	Senator Jacaranda Satin Rosewood w/Leather	133,644	121,280
6	6	3	Wilhelm II Satin and Polished Ebony	120,967	109,870
6	6	3	Wilhelm II Polished Mahogany/Walnut	130,645	118,581
6	6	3	Wilhelm II Polished Pyramid Mahogany	147,677	133,909
6	6	3	Wilhelm II Polished Burl Walnut	147,677	133,909
6	6	3	Ambassador Santos Rosewood	142,307	129,076
6	6	3	Ambassador Walnut	139,578	126,620
6	6	3	Nicolas II Satin Walnut with Burl Inlay	143,300	129,970
6	6	3	Louis XIV Rococo Satin White with Gold	160,016	145,014
6	6	3	Jubilee Polished Ebony	120,796	109,716
6	6	3	Jubilee Polished Mahogany/Walnut	129,067	117,160
6	6	3	Jubilee Burl Walnut	147,677	133,909
6	6	3	Julius Bluthner Edition	125,874	114,287
6	6	3	Crystal Edition Elegance	144,000	130,600
6	6	3	Crystal Edition Idyllic	180,000	163,000
6	6	3	Jubilee Plate, add	5,594	5,035
4	6	10	Satin and Polished Ebony	122,626	111,363
4	6	10	Satin and Polished Mahogany/Walnut	132,436	120,192
4	6	10	Satin and Polished Cherry	133,049	120,744
4	6	10	Satin and Polished White	131,210	119,089
4	6	10	Satin and Polished Bubinga/Yew/Rosewood/Macassar	136,115	123,504
4	6	10	Saxony Polished Pyramid Mahogany	154,509	140,058
4	6	10	Polished Burl Walnut/Camphor	154,509	140,058
4	6	10	President Polished Ebony	133,815	121,434
4	6	10	President Polished Mahogany/Walnut	143,625	130,263
4	6	10	President Polished Bubinga	147,304	133,574
4	6	10	President Burl Walnut	165,698	150,128
4	6	10	Senator Walnut w/Leather	142,968	129,671
4	6	10	Senator Jacaranda Satin Rosewood w/Leather	152,292	138,063
4	6	10	Wilhelm II Satin and Polished Ebony	143,472	130,125
4	6	10	Wilhelm II Polished Mahogany/Walnut	154,950	140,455
4	6	10	Wilhelm II Polished Pyramid Mahogany	171,914	155,723
4	6	10	Wilhelm II Polished Burl Walnut	171,914	155,723
4	6	10	Ambassador Santos Rosewood	166,060	150,454
4	6	10	Ambassador Walnut	161,572	146,415
4	6	10	Nicolas II Satin Walnut with Burl Inlay	169,960	153,964
4	6	10	Louis XIV Rococo Satin White with Gold	189,786	171,807
4	6	10	Jubilee Polished Ebony	140,031	127,028
4	6	10	Jubilee Polished Mahogany/Walnut	149,841	135,857
4	6	10	Jubilee Burl Walnut	171,914	155,723
4	6	10	Julius Bluthner Edition	147,630	133,867
4	6	10	Queen Victoria JB Edition Polished Rosewood	176,690	160,021
4	6	10	Crystal Edition Elegance	165,000	149,500
4	6	10	Crystal Edition Idyllic	204,000	184,600
2	7	8	Satin and Polished Ebony	137,056	124,350
2	7	8	Satin and Polished Mahogany/Walnut	148,020	134,218
2	7	8	Satin and Polished Cherry	148,706	134,835
2	7	8	Satin and Polished White	146,650	132,985
2	7	8	Satin and Polished Bubinga/Yew/Rosewood/Macassar	152,132	137,919
2	7	8	Saxony Polished Pyramid Mahogany	174,061	157,655

*See pricing explanation on page 188.

Model	Feet	Inches	Description	MSRP*	SMP*
BLÜTHNER (continued)					
2	7	8	Polished Burl Walnut/Camphor	174,061	157,655
2	7	8	President Polished Ebony	148,245	134,421
2	7	8	President Polished Mahogany/Walnut	159,209	144,288
2	7	8	President Polished Bubinga	163,321	147,989
2	7	8	President Burl Walnut	185,250	167,725
2	7	8	Senator Walnut w/Leather	155,400	140,860
2	7	8	Senator Jacaranda Satin Rosewood w/Leather	164,724	149,252
2	7	8	Wilhelm II Satin and Polished Ebony	160,355	145,320
2	7	8	Wilhelm II Polished Mahogany/Walnut	173,184	156,866
2	7	8	Wilhelm II Polished Pyramid Mahogany	191,466	173,319
2	7	8	Wilhelm II Polished Burl Walnut	191,466	173,319
2	7	8	Ambassador Santos Rosewood	185,601	168,041
2	7	8	Ambassador Walnut	180,585	163,527
2	7	8	Nicolas II Satin Walnut with Burl Inlay	191,467	173,320
2	7	8	Louis XIV Rococo Satin White with Gold	212,118	191,906
2	7	8	Jubilee Polished Ebony	154,461	140,015
2	7	8	Jubilee Polished Mahogany/Walnut	165,425	149,883
2	7	8	Jubilee Burl Walnut	191,466	173,319
2	7	8	Julius Bluthner Edition	170,940	154,846
2	7	8	Queen Victoria JB Edition Polished Rosewood	195,475	176,928
2	7	8	Crystal Edition Elegance	216,000	195,400
2	7	8	Crystal Edition Idyllic	255,000	230,500
1	9	2	Satin and Polished Ebony	175,185	158,667
1	9	2	Satin and Polished Mahogany/Walnut	189,200	171,280
1	9	2	Satin and Polished Cherry	190,076	172,068
1	9	2	Satin and Polished White	187,448	169,703
1	9	2	Satin and Polished Bubinga/Yew/Rosewood/Macassar	194,456	176,010
1	9	2	Saxony Polished Pyramid Mahogany	222,485	201,237
1	9	2	Polished Burl Walnut/Camphor	227,741	205,967
1	9	2	President Polished Ebony	187,173	169,456
1	9	2	President Polished Mahogany/Walnut	201,188	182,069
1	9	2	President Polished Bubinga	206,444	186,800
1	9	2	President Burl Walnut	223,747	202,372
1	9	2	Wilhelm II Satin and Polished Ebony	204,967	185,470
1	9	2	Wilhelm II Polished Mahogany/Walnut	221,364	200,228
1	9	2	Wilhelm II Polished Pyramid Mahogany	241,133	218,020
1	9	2	Wilhelm II Polished Burl Walnut	246,389	222,750
1	9	2	Ambassador Santos Rosewood	241,125	218,013
1	9	2	Ambassador Walnut	236,500	213,850
1	9	2	Nicolas II Satin Walnut with Burl Inlay	250,515	226,464
1	9	2	Jubilee Polished Ebony	193,833	175,450
1	9	2	Jubilee Polished Mahogany/Walnut	207,848	188,063
1	9	2	Jubilee Burl Walnut	246,389	222,750
1	9	2	Julius Bluthner Edition	216,373	195,736
1	9	2	Queen Victoria JB Edition Polished Rosewood	244,938	221,444
1	9	2	Crystal Edition Elegance	246,000	222,400
1	9	2	Crystal Edition Idyllic	285,000	257,500
Grands			e-volution Hybrid Piano System, add	8,800	7,920

*See pricing explanation on page 188.

Model	Feet	Inches	Description	MSRP*	SMP*
BÖSENDORFER					
Verticals					
130		52	Satin and Polished Ebony	73,999	70,998
130		52	Satin and Polished White, other colors	87,999	84,998
130		52	Polished, Satin, Open-pore: Walnut, Cherry, Mahogany, Pomele	93,999	88,998
130		52	Polished , Satin, Open-pore: Pyramid Mahogany, Burl Walnut, Birdseye Maple, Macassar, Madronna, Vavona, Wenge	99,999	95,598
Grands					
155	5	1	Satin and Polished Ebony	117,999	111,998
155	5	1	Satin and Polished White, other colors	131,999	124,998
155	5	1	Polished, Satin, Open-pore: Walnut, Cherry, Mahogany, Pomele	140,999	133,398
155	5	1	Polished , Satin, Open-pore: Pyramid Mahogany, Burl Walnut, Birdseye Maple, Macassar, Madronna, Vavona, Wenge	152,999	144,998
155	5	1	Chrome: Satin and Polished Ebony	129,999	125,798
170CS	5	7	Conservatory Satin Ebony	109,999	104,198
170	5	7	Satin and Polished Ebony	119,999	117,398
170	5	7	Satin and Polished White, other colors	135,999	130,398
170	5	7	Polished, Satin, Open-pore: Walnut, Cherry, Mahogany, Pomele	143,999	138,998
170	5	7	Polished , Satin, Open-pore: Bubinga, Pyramid Mahogany, Santos Rosewood, Burl Walnut, Birdseye Maple, Macassar, Madronna, Vavona, Wenge	154,999	150,198
170	5	7	Chrome: Satin and Polished Ebony	137,999	130,798
170	5	7	Johann Strauss: Satin and Polished Ebony w/Maple	147,999	140,398
170	5	7	Johann Strauss: Any finish and veneer	171,999	162,598
170	5	7	Liszt: Polished Vavona	175,999	166,598
170	5	7	Chopin, Louis XVI: Satin Pommele	199,999	189,998
170	5	7	Baroque: Light Satin Ivory; Vienna: Polished Amboyna	223,999	210,998
170	5	7	Artisan Satin and Polished	286,999	270,998
185CS	6	1	Conservatory Satin Ebony	113,999	108,598
185	6	1	Satin and Polished Ebony	128,999	122,598
185	6	1	Satin and Polished White, other colors	142,999	134,998
185	6	1	Polished, Satin, Open-pore: Walnut, Cherry, Mahogany, Pomele	151,999	143,998
185	6	1	Polished , Satin, Open-pore: Pyramid Mahogany, Burl Walnut, Birdseye Maple, Macassar, Madronna, Vavona, Wenge	163,999	155,598
185	6	1	Chrome: Satin and Polished Ebony	142,999	134,998
185	6	1	Johann Strauss: Satin and Polished Ebony w/Maple	152,999	144,998
185	6	1	Johann Strauss: Any finish and veneer	178,999	168,998
185	6	1	Liszt: Polished Vavona	182,999	172,998
185	6	1	Edge: Satin and Polished Ebony	204,999	193,598
185	6	1	Chopin, Louis XVI: Satin Pommele	208,999	196,998
185	6	1	Baroque: Satin Light Ivory; Vienna: Polished Amboyna	228,999	216,398
185	6	1	Porsche Design: Diamond Black Metallic Gloss	239,999	226,598
185	6	1	Artisan Satin and Polished	295,999	278,998
200CS	6	7	Conservatory Satin Ebony	119,999	114,198
200	6	7	Satin and Polished Ebony	139,999	132,598
200	6	7	Satin and Polished White, other colors	154,999	146,998
200	6	7	Polished, Satin, Open-pore: Walnut, Cherry, Mahogany, Pomele	165,999	156,798
200	6	7	Polished , Satin, Open-pore: Pyramid Mahogany, Burl Walnut, Birdseye Maple, Macassar, Madronna, Vavona, Wenge	179,999	169,798
200	6	7	Chrome Satin and Polished Ebony	145,596	120,744
200	6	7	Chrome: Satin and Polished Ebony	153,999	145,998
200	6	7	Johann Strauss: Satin and Polished Ebony w/Maple	164,999	155,998
200	6	7	Johann Strauss: Any finish and veneer	193,999	183,798
200	6	7	Liszt: Polished Vavona	199,999	188,998
200	6	7	Beethoven Polished Ebony, Klimt "Woman in Gold"	169,999	160,998
200	6	7	Beethoven: Chrome; Cocteau: White	197,999	186,998
200	6	7	Edge: Satin and Polished Ebony	224,999	212,998
200	6	7	Oscar Peterson Disklavier: Polished Ebony	209,999	198,998

*See pricing explanation on page 188.

PIANOBUYER.COM

Model	Feet	Inches	Description	MSRP*	SMP*
BÖSENDORFER (continued)					
200	6	7	Butterfly: Polished Ebony w/Maple	199,999	188,998
200	6	7	Chopin, Louis XVI: Satin Pommele	227,999	214,998
200	6	7	Baroque: Satin Light Ivory; Vienna: Polished Amboyna	249,999	235,998
200	6	7	Artisan Satin and Polished	314,999	296,998
214VC CS	7		Conservatory Satin Ebony	129,999	124,998
214VC	7		Satin and Polished Ebony	154,999	147,998
214VC	7		Satin and Polished White, other colors	174,999	164,998
214VC	7		Polished, Satin, Open-pore: Walnut, Cherry, Mahogany, Pomele	187,999	177,598
214VC	7		Polished , Satin, Open-pore: Pyramid Mahogany, Burl Walnut, Birdseye Maple, Macassar, Madronna, Vavona, Wenge	203,999	192,198
214VC	7		Chrome: Satin and Polished Ebony	174,999	165,398
214VC	7		Johann Strauss: Satin and Polished Ebony w/Maple	182,999	172,998
214VC	7		Johann Strauss: Any finish and veneer	219,999	207,998
214VC	7		Liszt: Polished Vavona	224,999	212,998
214VC	7		Beethoven: Polished Ebony, Klimt "Woman in Gold"	184,999	176,998
214VC	7		Beethoven: Chrome; Cocteau: White	216,999	204,998
214VC	7		Edge: Satin and Polished Ebony	249,999	238,998
214VC	7		Chopin, Louis XVI: Satin Pommele	257,999	242,998
214VC	7		Baroque: Satin Light Ivory; Vienna: Polished Amboyna	283,999	266,998
214VC	7		Porsche Design: Diamond Black Metallic Gloss	297,999	280,998
214VC	7		Audi Design Polished Ebony	359,999	340,998
214VC	7		Artisan Satin and Polished	359,999	340,998
225	7	4	Satin and Polished Ebony	172,999	163,998
225	7	4	Satin and Polished White, other colors	189,999	179,998
225	7	4	Polished, Satin, Open-pore: Walnut, Cherry, Mahogany, Pomele	204,999	193,798
225	7	4	Polished , Satin, Open-pore: Pyramid Mahogany, Burl Walnut, Birdseye Maple, Macassar, Madronna, Vavona, Wenge	221,999	209,798
225	7	4	Chrome: Satin and Polished Ebony	186,999	177,198
225	7	4	Johann Strauss: Satin and Polished Ebony w/Maple	198,999	187,398
225	7	4	Johann Strauss: Any finish and veneer	239,999	226,998
225	7	4	Liszt: Polished Vavona	245,999	232,398
225	7	4	Chopin, Louis XVI: Satin Pommele	281,999	265,998
225	7	4	Baroque: Satin Light Ivory; Vienna: Polished Amboyna	309,999	292,198
225	7	4	Artisan Satin and Polished	385,999	362,998
225	7	4	Grand Bohemian: Polished Ebony	420,000	420,000
280VC	9	2	Satin and Polished Ebony	224,999	212,598
280VC	9	2	Satin and Polished White, other colors	246,999	233,798
280VC	9	2	Polished, Satin, Open-pore: Walnut, Cherry, Mahogany, Pomele	265,999	250,998
280VC	9	2	Polished , Satin, Open-pore: Pyramid Mahogany, Burl Walnut, Birdseye Maple, Macassar, Madronna, Vavona, Wenge	287,999	271,998
280VC	9	2	Johann Strauss: Satin and Polished Ebony w/Maple	261,999	246,998
280VC	9	2	Johann Strauss: Any finish and veneer	312,999	294,998
280VC	9	2	Liszt: Polished Vavona	319,999	301,998
280VC	9	2	Chopin, Louis XVI: Satin Pommele	366,999	345,398
280VC	9	2	Baroque: Satin Light Ivory; Vienna: Polished Amboyna	399,999	378,798
280VC	9	2	Porsche Design: Diamond Black Metallic Gloss	424,999	400,998
280VC	9	2	Artisan Satin and Polished	457,999	430,998
290	9	6	Satin and Polished Ebony	255,999	240,998
290	9	6	Satin and Polished White, other colors	279,999	264,998
290	9	6	Polished, Satin, Open-pore: Walnut, Cherry, Mahogany, Pomele	302,999	286,198
290	9	6	Polished , Satin, Open-pore: Pyramid Mahogany, Burl Walnut, Birdseye Maple, Macassar, Madronna, Vavona, Wenge	327,999	308,998
290	9	6	Johann Strauss: Satin and Polished Ebony w/Maple	292,999	276,198
290	9	6	Johann Strauss: Any finish and veneer	356,999	334,998
290	9	6	Liszt: Polished Vavona	364,999	343,598
290	9	6	Chopin, Louis XVI: Satin Pommele	416,999	392,998
290	9	6	Baroque: Satin Light Ivory; Vienna: Polished Amboyna	457,999	430,998
290	9	6	Artisan Satin and Polished	519,999	490,998

*See pricing explanation on page 188.

Model	Feet	Inches	Description	MSRP*	SMP*
BÖSENDORFER (continued)					
200			Disklavier Enspire, add	39,999	37,998

BOSTON

Boston MSRP is the price at the New York retail store.

Verticals

Model	Feet	Inches	Description	MSRP*	SMP*
UP-118E PE		46	Satin and Polished Ebony	11,600	11,600
UP-118E PE		46	Polished Mahogany	13,400	13,400
UP-118E PE		46	Satin and Polished Walnut	13,400	13,400
UP-118S PE		46	Satin Black Oak/Honey Oak	7,600	7,600
UP-118S PE		46	Satin Mahogany	9,100	9,100
UP-126E PE		50	Polished Ebony	13,900	13,900
UP-126E PE		50	Polished Mahogany	16,100	16,100
UP-132E PE		52	Polished Ebony	15,400	15,400

Grands

Model	Feet	Inches	Description	MSRP*	SMP*
GP-156 PE	5	1	Satin and Polished Ebony	21,100	21,100
GP-163 PE	5	4	Satin and Polished Ebony	25,800	25,800
GP-163 PE	5	4	Satin and Polished Mahogany	28,200	28,200
GP-163 PE	5	4	Satin and Polished Walnut	28,600	28,600
GP-163 PE	5	4	Polished White	31,800	31,800
GP-178 PE	5	10	Satin and Polished Ebony	30,200	30,200
GP-178 PE	5	10	Satin and Polished Mahogany	32,600	32,600
GP-178 PE	5	10	Satin and Polished Walnut	33,100	33,100
GP-193 PE	6	4	Satin and Polished Ebony	39,200	39,200
GP-215 PE	7	1	Satin and Polished Ebony	51,400	51,400

BRODMANN

Verticals

Model	Feet	Inches	Description	MSRP*	SMP*
CE 118		47	Polished Ebony	7,350	5,900
PE 118V		47	Vienna Polished Ebony	10,170	7,780
PE 121		48	Polished Ebony	9,150	7,100
PE 121		48	Polished Mahogany/Walnut	10,050	7,700
PE 121		48	Polished White	10,350	7,900
PE 124V		48	Vienna Polished Ebony	11,670	8,780
PE 124V		48	ViennaPolished Bubinga	12,570	9,380
PE 125		49	Polished Ebony	10,050	7,700
PE 130		52	Polished Ebony	14,250	10,500
PE 132V		52	Vienna Polished Ebony	15,570	11,380
AS 132		52	Polished Ebony	23,970	16,980

Grands

Model	Feet	Inches	Description	MSRP*	SMP*
CE 148	4	10	Polished Ebony	18,270	13,180
CE 175	5	9	Polished Ebony	21,270	15,180
PE 150	5		Polished Ebony	21,870	15,580
PE 162	5	4	Polished Ebony	25,470	17,980
PE 162	5	4	Polished Mahogany/Walnut	28,170	19,780
PE 162	5	4	Polished White	27,270	19,180
PE 162	5	4	Polished Bubinga	28,470	19,980
PE 162	5	4	Polished Two Tone (Ebony/Bubinga)	26,070	18,380
PE 187	6	2	Polished Ebony	29,070	20,380
PE 187 IV	6	2	Polished Ebony w/Carbon-Fiber Action	34,440	23,960
PE 187	6	2	Polished Mahogany/Walnut	31,770	22,180
PE 187	6	2	Polished White	31,170	21,780
PE 187	6	2	Polished Bubinga	32,670	22,780
PE 187	6	2	Strauss Polished Ebony	31,170	21,780

*See pricing explanation on page 188.

Model	Feet	Inches	Description	MSRP*	SMP*
BRODMANN (continued)					
PE 187	6	2	Strauss Polished Two Tone (Ebony/Bubinga)	32,070	22,380
PE 212	7		Polished Ebony	45,870	31,580
PE 228	7	5	Polished Ebony	58,770	40,180
AS 188	6	2	Polished Ebony	53,970	36,980
AS 211	7		Polished Ebony	68,970	46,980
AS 227	7	6	Polished Ebony	77,970	52,980
AS 275	9		Polished Ebony	128,970	86,980
Grands			With Carbon-Fiber Action, add	5,370	3,580

CLINE
Verticals
Model	Feet	Inches	Description	MSRP*	SMP*
CL118		46.5	Polished Ebony		6,300
CL118		46.5	Polished Ebony w/Nickel		6,500
CL118		46.5	Polished Walnut/Mahogany		6,500
CL121/123		48	Polished Ebony		7,390
CL121/123		48	Polished Ebony w/Nickel		7,590
CL121/123		48	Polished Mahogany/Walnut		7,590
CL121/123		48	Polished Mahogany/Walnut w/Detail Trim		7,590

Grands
Model	Feet	Inches	Description	MSRP*	SMP*
CL 150	4	11	Polished Ebony		12,300
CL 150	4	11	Polished Mahogany/Walnut		12,500

CRISTOFORI
Verticals
Model	Feet	Inches	Description	MSRP*	SMP*
V430R		43	French Provincial Satin Cherry	4,999	4,999
V450		45	Polished Ebony	3,999	3,999
V450		45	Polished Mahogany	4,199	4,199
V465		46.5	Polished Ebony	4,499	4,220
V465		46.5	Polished Mahogany	4,699	4,442
V480LS		48	Polished Ebony	4,999	4,530
V480LS		48	Polished Mahogany	5,199	4,668

Grands
Model	Feet	Inches	Description	MSRP*	SMP*
G410L	4	10	Polished Ebony	8,990	8,750
G410L	4	10	Polished Mahogany	9,490	9,418
G53L	5	3	Satin and Polished Ebony	9,990	9,990
G53L	5	3	Polished Mahogany/Snow White	10,490	10,490
G57L	5	7	Satin and Polished Ebony	11,990	10,642
G57L	5	7	Polished Mahogany	12,490	11,406
G62L	6	2	Satin and Polished Ebony	13,990	11,902

CUNNINGHAM
Verticals
Model	Feet	Inches	Description	MSRP*	SMP*
Liberty Console		44	Satin Ebony	6,590	6,590
Liberty Console		44	Polished Ebony	5,890	5,890
Liberty Console		44	Satin Mahogany	6,890	6,890
Liberty Console		44	Polished Mahogany	6,190	6,190
Studio Upright		50	Satin Ebony	10,690	10,690
Studio Upright		50	Polished Ebony	9,890	9,890
Studio Upright		50	Satin Mahogany	10,990	10,990
Studio Upright		50	Polished Mahogany	10,190	10,190

Grands
Model	Feet	Inches	Description	MSRP*	SMP*
Baby Grand	5		Satin Ebony	20,390	20,390
Baby Grand	5		Polished Ebony	19,190	19,190

*See pricing explanation on page 188.

Model	Feet	Inches	Description	MSRP*	SMP*
Cunningham (continued)					
Baby Grand	5		Satin Mahogany	21,090	21,090
Baby Grand	5		Polished Mahogany	19,890	19,890
Studio Grand	5	4	Satin Ebony	22,090	22,090
Studio Grand	5	4	Polished Ebony	20,890	20,890
Studio Grand	5	4	Satin Mahogany	22,790	22,790
Studio Grand	5	4	Polished Mahogany	21,590	21,590
Parlour Grand	5	10	Satin Ebony	26,390	26,390
Parlour Grand	5	10	Polished Ebony	25,190	25,190
Parlour Grand	5	10	Satin Mahogany	27,090	27,090
Parlour Grand	5	10	Polished Mahogany	25,890	25,890
Chamber Grand	7		Satin Ebony	41,290	41,290
Chamber Grand	7		Polished Ebony	39,790	39,790
Concert Grand	9		Satin Ebony	62,990	62,990
Concert Grand	9		Polished Ebony	60,990	60,990

DISKLAVIER — see Yamaha; see also Bösendorfer

ESSEX

Essex MSRP is the price at the New York retail store.

Verticals

Model	Feet	Inches	Description	MSRP*	SMP*
EUP-108C		42	Continental Polished Ebony	5,490	5,490
EUP-111E		44	Polished Ebony	6,190	6,190
EUP-111E		44	Polished Sapele Mahogany	6,590	6,360
EUP-116E		45	Polished Ebony	6,990	6,580
EUP-116E		45	Polished Walnut	7,990	7,240
EUP-116E		45	Polished Sapele Mahogany	7,290	6,680
EUP-116E		45	Polished White	7,590	6,920
EUP-116FC		45	French Country Satin Lustre Cherry	7,990	7,440
EUP-116CT		45	Contemporary Satin Lustre Sapele Mahogany	7,990	7,400
EUP-116IP		45	Italian Provincial Satin LustreWalnut	7,590	7,400
EUP-116QA		45	Queen Anne Satin Lustre Cherry	7,690	7,540
EUP-116ST		45	Sheraton Traditional Satin Lustre Sapele Mahogany	7,590	7,400
EUP-116EC		45	English Country Satin Lustre Walnut	7,690	7,360
EUP-116ET		45	English Traditional Satin Lustre Sapele Mahogany	7,690	7,340
EUP-116FF		45	Formal French Satin Lustre Brown Cherry	7,990	7,580
EUP-116FF		45	Formal French Satin Lustre Red Cherry	7,990	7,580
EUP-123E		48	Satin Ebony w/Chrome Hardware	8,390	7,760
EUP-123E		48	Polished Ebony	7,490	7,100
EUP-123E		48	Polished Ebony w/Chrome Hardware	7,590	7,200
EUP-123E		48	Satin Sapele Mahogany	8,490	7,780
EUP-123E		48	Polished Sapele Mahogany	8,490	7,600
EUP-123E		48	Satin Walnut	8,490	7,620
EUP-123CL		48	French Satin Sapele Mahogany	8,590	7,860
EUP-123FL		48	Empire Satin Walnut	8,590	7,660
EUP-123FL		48	Empire Satin Sapele Mahogany	8,590	7,860
EUP-123S		48	Institutional Studio Polished Ebony	7,490	7,420

Grands

Model	Feet	Inches	Description	MSRP*	SMP*
EGP-155	5	1	Satin and Polished Ebony	13,500	13,500
EGP-155	5	1	Polished Sapele Mahogany	14,800	14,800
EGP-155	5	1	Satin Lustre Sapele Mahogany	15,100	15,100
EGP-155	5	1	Polished Kewazinga Bubinga	16,900	16,020
EGP-155	5	1	Polished White	18,000	16,020
EGP-155F	5	1	French Provincial Satin Lustre Brown Cherry	17,200	17,120
EGP-173	5	8	Satin Lustre and Polished Ebony	17,100	17,100
EGP-173	5	8	Polished Sapele Mahogany	18,900	18,900
EGP-173F	5	8	French Provincial Satin Lustre Brown Cherry	20,200	20,200

*See pricing explanation on page 188.

Model	Feet	Inches	Description	MSRP*	SMP*

ESTONIA

The Estonia factory can make custom-designed finishes with exotic veneers; prices upon request.
Prices here include Jansen adjustable artist benches.

Grands

Model	Feet	Inches	Description	MSRP*	SMP*
L168	5	6	Satin and Polished Ebony	41,715	39,608
L168	5	6	Satin and Polished Mahogany/Walnut/White	45,125	42,563
L168	5	6	Polished Kewazinga Bubinga	48,948	46,299
L168	5	6	Polished Pyramid Mahogany	54,165	51,299
L168	5	6	Hidden Beauty Polished Ebony w/Bubinga	46,165	43,479
L190	6	3	Satin and Polished Ebony	51,228	48,139
L190	6	3	Satin and Polished Mahogany/Walnut/White	54,569	51,678
L190	6	3	Polished Pyramid Mahogany	65,143	60,350
L190	6	3	Polished Santos Rosewood	65,143	60,187
L190	6	3	Polished Kewazinga Bubinga	58,750	55,530
L190	6	3	Hidden Beauty Polished Ebony w/Bubinga	53,877	50,904
L210	6	10	Satin and Polished Ebony	60,287	57,949
L210	6	10	Satin and Polished Mahogany/Walnut/White	66,315	63,646
L210	6	10	Satin and Polished Pyramid Mahogany	75,358	72,187
L210	6	10	Polished Kewazinga Bubinga	71,140	68,200
L210	6	10	Hidden Beauty Polished Ebony w/Bubinga	64,030	61,279
L225	7	4	Satin and Polished Ebony	75,894	70,807
L225	7	4	Satin and Polished Mahogany/Walnut/White	81,645	76,873
L225	7	4	Satin and Polished Pyramid Mahogany	90,625	86,438
L225	7	4	Polished Kewazinga Bubinga	82,000	79,664
L225	7	4	Hidden Beauty Polished Ebony w/Bubinga	80,605	75,715
L274	9		Satin and Polished Ebony	121,060	107,360
L274	9		Satin and Polished Mahogany/Walnut	132,790	118,595
L274	9		Polished Pyramid Mahogany	137,385	131,013
L274	9		Satin and Polished White	124,930	113,565

FANDRICH & SONS

These are the prices on the Fandrich & Sons website. Other finishes available at additional cost. See website for details.

Verticals

Model	Feet	Inches	Description	MSRP*	SMP*
118-S		46	Polished Ebony with Nickel Trim	5,640	5,640
122		48	Polished Ebony	6,640	6,640
122		48	Polished Mahogany/Walnut/Cherry	6,840	6,840
131-V		52	Polished Ebony	12,890	12,890

Grands

Model	Feet	Inches	Description	MSRP*	SMP*
170-S	5	7	Polished Ebony	18,890	18,890
188-S	6	2	Polished Ebony	22,490	22,490
212-S	7		Polished Ebony	34,990	34,990
212-E	7		Polished Ebony	36,490	36,490

FAZIOLI

Fazioli is willing to make custom-designed cases with exotic veneers, marquetry, and other embellishments.
Prices on request to Fazioli. Euro = $1.075

Grands

Model	Feet	Inches	Description	MSRP*	SMP*
F156	5	2	Satin and Polished Ebony	120,000	113,951
F156	5	2	Satin and Polished White/Red	138,000	130,609
F156	5	2	Satin and Polished Walnut/Cherry/Mahogany	150,000	141,414
F156	5	2	Satin and Polished Pyramid Mahogany/Macassar	168,000	157,846
F156	5	2	Satin and Polished Briers: Mahogany/California Walnut/Sequoia	180,000	168,651
F183	6		Satin and Polished Ebony	122,900	116,602
F183	6		Satin and Polished White/Red	141,300	133,260
F183	6		Satin and Polished Walnut/Cherry/Mahogany	153,600	144,515
F183	6		Satin and Polished Pyramid Mahogany/Macassar	172,100	161,173

*See pricing explanation on page 188.

Model	Feet	Inches	Description	MSRP*	SMP*
FAZIOLI (continued)					
F183	6		Satin and Polished Briers: Mahogany/California Walnut/Sequoia	184,300	172,428
F212	7		Satin and Polished Ebony	137,300	130,458
F212	7		Satin and Polished White/Red	151,000	142,839
F212	7		Satin and Polished Walnut/Cherry/Mahogany	164,800	155,220
F212	7		Satin and Polished Pyramid Mahogany/Macassar	178,500	167,600
F212	7		Satin and Polished Briers: Mahogany/California Walnut/Sequoia	192,200	179,981
F228	7	6	Satin and Polished Ebony	153,600	146,415
F228	7	6	Satin and Polished White/Red	169,000	160,372
F228	7	6	Satin and Polished Walnut/Cherry/Mahogany	184,300	174,553
F228	7	6	Satin and Polished Pyramid Mahogany/Macassar	199,700	188,510
F228	7	6	Satin and Polished Briers: Mahogany/California Walnut/Sequoia	215,000	202,466
F278	9	2	Satin and Polished Ebony	205,400	193,162
F278	9	2	Satin and Polished White/Red	225,900	211,846
F278	9	2	Satin and Polished Walnut/Cherry/Mahogany	246,500	230,529
F278	9	2	Satin and Polished Pyramid Mahogany/Macassar	267,000	249,213
F278	9	2	Satin and Polished Briers: Mahogany/California Walnut/Sequoia	287,600	267,897
F308	10	2	Satin and Polished Ebony	224,600	207,418
F308	10	2	Satin and Polished White/Red	247,100	227,677
F308	10	2	Satin and Polished Walnut/Cherry/Mahogany	269,500	247,712
F308	10	2	Satin and Polished Pyramid Mahogany/Macassar	292,000	267,521
F308	10	2	Satin and Polished Briers: Mahogany/California Walnut/Sequoia	314,400	287,330

FEURICH

Verticals

Model	Feet	Inches	Description	MSRP*	SMP*
115 Premiere	45		Polished Ebony	8,800	6,172
122 Universal	48		Polished Ebony	9,800	7,055
123 Vienna	48.5		Polished Ebony	15,500	15,128
133 Concert	52		Polished Ebony	12,500	9,956

Grands

Model	Feet	Inches	Description	MSRP*	SMP*
162 Dynamic I	5	4	Polished Ebony	19,500	15,380
179 Dynamic II	5	10	Polished Ebony	23,500	18,407
218 Concert I	7	2	Polished Ebony	37,900	31,021
Grands			Harmonic Pedal, add	3,000	1,892

FÖRSTER, AUGUST

Prices do not include bench. Euro = $1.09

Verticals

Model	Feet	Inches	Description	MSRP*	SMP*
116 C	46		Chippendale Satin Mahogany		26,975
116 C	46		Chippendale Satin Walnut		28,354
116 D	46		Continental Polished Ebony		20,457
116 D	46		Continental Satin Mahogany/Beech/Alder		20,959
116 D	46		Continental Polished Mahogany		20,959
116 D	46		Continental Satin and Polished Walnut/Oak/Cherry		22,388
116 D	46		Continental Polished White		21,961
116 E	46		Polished Ebony		23,917
116 E	46		Satin and Polished Mahogany/Beech/Alder		24,443
116 E	46		Satin and Polished Walnut/Oak/Cherry		25,822
116 E	46		Polished White		25,446
125 F	49		Polished Ebony		27,602
125 G	49		Polished Ebony		27,025
125 G	49		Satin Mahogany/Beech/Alder		27,602
125 G	49		Polished Mahogany/Beech/Alder		27,627
125 G	49		Satin and Polished Walnut/Oak/Cherry		29,583
125 G	49		Polished White		28,555
134 K	53		Polished Ebony		40,939

*See pricing explanation on page 188.

| --- | --- | --- | --- | --- | --- |

FÖRSTER, AUGUST (continued)

Grands

Model	Feet	Inches	Description	MSRP*	SMP*
170	5	8	Polished Ebony		56,307
170	5	8	Satin and Polished Walnut		59,717
170	5	8	Satin and Polished Mahogany		57,511
170	5	8	Polished White		59,742
170	5	8	Classik Polished Ebony		64,731
170	5	8	Classik Polished Walnut		74,458
170	5	8	Classik Polished Mahogany		69,093
170	5	8	Classik Polished White		68,617
190	6	4	Polished Ebony		63,578
190	6	4	Satin and Polished Walnut		66,812
190	6	4	Satin and Polished Mahogany		64,656
190	6	4	Polished White		66,761
190	6	4	Classik Polished Ebony		71,800
190	6	4	Classik Polished Mahogany		76,263
190	6	4	Classik Polished Walnut		81,553
190	6	4	Classik Polished White		75,711
215	7	2	Polished Ebony		76,338
275	9	1	Polished Ebony		138,136

GEYER, A.

Prices do not include bench. Other woods available on request.

Verticals

Model	Feet	Inches	Description	MSRP*	SMP*
GU 115		45	Polished Ebony	6,185	4,990
GU 115		45	Polished Mahogany/Walnut	6,685	5,290
GU 115		45	Polished White	6,485	5,190
GU 123		47	Polished Ebony	6,785	5,390
GU 123		47	Polished Mahogany/Walnut	7,235	5,690
GU 123		47	Polished White	7,085	5,590
GU 133		52	Polished Ebony	7,685	5,990
GU 133		52	Polished Mahogany/Walnut	8,285	6,390
GU 133		52	Polished White	7,985	6,190

Grands

Model	Feet	Inches	Description	MSRP*	SMP*
GG 150	4	11	Polished Ebony	12,785	9,590
GG 150	4	11	Polished Mahogany/Walnut	13,685	9,990
GG 150	4	11	Polished White	13,235	9,870
GG 160	5	3	Polished Ebony	14,535	10,590
GG 160	5	3	Polished Mahogany/Walnut	15,285	10,990
GG 160	5	3	Polished White	15,035	10,890
GG 170	5	7	Polished Ebony	16,385	11,790
GG 170	5	7	Polished Mahogany/Walnut	16,715	12,010
GG 170	5	7	Polished White	16,835	12,090
GG 185	6	1	Polished Ebony	18,785	13,390
GG 185	6	1	Polished Mahogany/Walnut	19,585	13,990
GG 185	6	1	Polished White	19,385	13,790
GG 230	7	7	Polished Ebony	29,225	25,990

*See pricing explanation on page 188.

Model	Feet	Inches	Description	MSRP*	SMP*
GROTRIAN					

Prices do not include bench. Other woods available on request. Euro = $1.10

Verticals

Model	Feet	Inches	Description	MSRP*	SMP*
Friedrich Grotrian	43.5		Open-pore Walnut		15,038
Cristal	44		Continental Satin Ebony		19,403
Cristal	44		Continental Polished Ebony		20,263
Cristal	44		Continental Open-pore Walnut		20,263
Cristal	44		Continental Polished Walnut/White		22,201
Contour	45		Polished Ebony		21,771
Contour	45		Open-pore Walnut		21,771
Contour	45		Polished Walnut/White		23,850
Canto	45		Satin Ebony		21,626
Canto	45		Polished Ebony		22,631
Canto	45		Open-pore Walnut		22,631
Carat	45.5		Polished Ebony		25,500
Carat	45.5		Open-pore Walnut		25,500
Carat	45.5		Polished Walnut/White		27,726
College	48		Satin Ebony		27,564
College	48		Polished Ebony		29,001
College	48		Open-pore Walnut		29,001
Classic	49		Polished Ebony		34,454
Classic	49		Open-pore Walnut		34,454
Classic	49		Polished Walnut/White		37,108
Concertino	52		Polished Ebony		43,384
Concertino	52		Open-pore Walnut		43,384
Verticals			Chippendale/Rococo/Empire, add		1,240
Verticals			Sostenuto, add		1,493

Grands

Model	Feet	Inches	Description	MSRP*	SMP*
Chambre	5	5	Satin Ebony		66,499
Chambre	5	5	Polished Ebony		73,387
Chambre	5	5	Open-pore Walnut		73,387
Chambre	5	5	Polished Walnut/White		80,425
Cabinet	6	3	Satin Ebony		77,281
Cabinet	6	3	Polished Ebony		86,117
Cabinet	6	3	Studio Lacquer Ebony		59,867
Cabinet	6	3	Open-pore Walnut		86,117
Cabinet	6	3	Polished Walnut/White		94,354
Charis	6	10	Satin Ebony		91,096
Charis	6	10	Polished Ebony		99,480
Charis	6	10	Studio Lacquer Ebony		73,117
Charis	6	10	Open-pore Walnut		99,480
Concert	7	4	Satin Ebony		108,491
Concert	7	4	Polished Ebony		122,834
Concert	7	4	Open-pore Walnut		122,834
Concert Royal	9	1	Polished Ebony		164,921
Concert Royal	9	1	Open-pore Walnut		164,921
Grands			Chippendale/Empire, add		4,488
Grands			CS Style, add		5,016
Grands			Rococo, add		15,048

HAESSLER

Prices do not include bench.

Verticals

Model	Feet	Inches	Description	MSRP*	SMP*
H 115	45		Polished Ebony	21,911	20,919
H 115	45		Satin Mahogany/Walnut	22,360	21,327
H 115	45		Polished Cherry	37,649	35,226
H 115	45		Satin Oak/Beech	23,258	22,144

*See pricing explanation on page 188.

PIANOBUYER.COM

Model	Feet	Inches	Description	MSRP*	SMP*
HAESSLER (continued)					
H 115		45	Polished White	22,809	21,735
H 115		45	Polished Mahogany w/Vavona Inlay	37,649	35,226
H 115		45	Polished Cherry and Yew	37,649	35,226
H 118		47	Polished Ebony	24,156	22,960
H 118		47	Satin Mahogany/Walnut	25,279	23,981
H 118		47	Polished Mahogany/Walnut	29,320	27,655
H 118		47	Satin Cherry	25,728	24,389
H 118		47	Polished Cherry	29,769	28,063
H 118		47	Satin Oak/Beech	23,977	22,797
H 118		47	Polished White	26,401	25,001
H 118		47	Polished Bubinga	29,993	28,266
H 118		47	Satin Mahogany w/Vavona Inlay	27,075	25,614
H 118		47	Polished Mahogany w/Vavona Inlay	30,667	28,879
H 118		47	Polished Burl Walnut	30,442	28,675
H 118		47	Satin Burl Walnut w/Walnut Inlay	27,075	25,614
H 118		47	Polished Burl Walnut w/Walnut Inlay	30,667	28,879
H 118		47	Satin Cherry and Yew	27,165	25,695
H 118		47	Polished Cherry and Yew	30,667	28,879
H 124		49	Polished Ebony	26,401	25,001
H 124		49	Satin Mahogany/Walnut	27,389	25,899
H 124		49	Polished Mahogany/Walnut	31,565	29,695
H 124		49	Satin Cherry	27,524	26,022
H 124		49	Polished Cherry	32,014	30,104
H 124		49	Satin Oak/Beech	27,299	25,817
H 124		49	Polished White	28,646	27,042
H 124		49	Polished Bubinga	32,238	30,307
H 124		49	Polished Pyramid Mahogany	35,696	33,451
H 124		49	Satin Mahogany w/Vavona Inlay	28,871	27,246
H 124		49	Polished Mahogany w/Vavona Inlay	34,034	31,940
H 124		49	Polished Burl Walnut	35,247	33,043
H 124		49	Satin Burl Walnut w/Walnut Inlay	28,871	27,246
H 124		49	Polished Burl Walnut w/Walnut Inlay	34,034	31,940
H 124		49	Satin Cherry and Yew	28,871	27,246
H 124		49	Polished Cherry and Yew	35,247	33,043
K 124		49	Polished Ebony	28,557	26,961
K 124		49	Satin Mahogany/Walnut	29,544	27,858
K 124		49	Polished Mahogany/Walnut	33,720	31,655
K 124		49	Satin Cherry	29,679	27,981
K 124		49	Polished Cherry	34,169	32,063
K 124		49	Satin Oak/Beech	29,455	27,777
K 124		49	Polished White	30,802	29,002
K 124		49	Polished Bubinga	34,394	32,267
K 124		49	Polished Pyramid Mahogany	37,851	35,410
K 124		49	Satin Mahogany w/Vavona Inlay	31,026	29,205
K 124		49	Polished Mahogany w/Vavona Inlay	36,190	33,900
K 124		49	Polished Burl Walnut	37,402	35,002
K 124		49	Satin Burl Walnut w/Walnut Inlay	31,026	29,205
K 124		49	Polished Burl Walnut w/Walnut Inlay	36,190	33,900
K 124		49	Satin Cherry and Yew	31,026	29,205
K 124		49	Polished Cherry and Yew	37,402	35,002
H 132		52	Polished Ebony	29,544	27,858
H 132		52	Satin Mahogany/Walnut	29,993	28,266
H 132		52	Polished Mahogany/Walnut	34,483	32,348
H 132		52	Satin Cherry	31,340	29,491
H 132		52	Polished Cherry	34,932	32,756
H 132		52	Polished White	31,789	29,899
H 132		52	Polished Bubinga	35,381	33,165
H 132		52	Palisander Rosewood	37,402	35,002

*See pricing explanation on page 188.

Model	Feet	Inches	Description	MSRP*	SMP*
HAESSLER (continued)					
H 132		52	Polished Pyramid Mahogany	38,300	35,818
H 132		52	Satin Mahogany w/Vavona Inlay	32,912	30,920
H 132		52	Polished Mahogany w/Vavona Inlay	37,402	35,002
H 132		52	Polished Burl Walnut	37,402	35,002
H 132		52	Satin Burl Walnut w/Walnut Inlay	32,912	30,920
H 132		52	Polished Burl Walnut w/Walnut Inlay	37,402	35,002
H 132		52	Satin Cherry and Yew	32,912	30,920
H 132		52	Polished Cherry and Yew	37,402	35,002
K 132		52	Polished Ebony	32,553	30,594
K 132		52	Satin Mahogany/Walnut	33,002	31,002
K 132		52	Polished Mahogany/Walnut	37,492	35,084
K 132		52	Satin Cherry	34,349	32,226
K 132		52	Polished Cherry	37,941	35,492
K 132		52	Polished White	34,798	32,635
K 132		52	Polished Bubinga	38,390	35,900
K 132		52	Palisander Rosewood	40,410	37,736
K 132		52	Polished Pyramid Mahogany	41,308	38,553
K 132		52	Satin Mahogany w/Vavona Inlay	35,920	33,655
K 132		52	Polished Mahogany w/Vavona Inlay	40,410	37,736
K 132		52	Polished Burl Walnut	40,410	37,736
K 132		52	Satin Burl Walnut w/Walnut Inlay	35,920	33,655
K 132		52	Polished Burl Walnut w/Walnut Inlay	40,410	37,736
K 132		52	Satin Cherry and Yew	35,920	33,655
K 132		52	Polished Cherry and Yew	40,410	37,736
Grands					
H 175	5	8	Polished Ebony	75,960	70,055
H 175	5	8	Satin Mahogany/Walnut	81,657	75,234
H 175	5	8	Polished Mahogany/Walnut	89,330	82,209
H 175	5	8	Satin Cherry	80,974	74,613
H 175	5	8	Polished Cherry	91,420	84,109
H 175	5	8	Polished White	81,277	74,888
H 175	5	8	Polished Bubinga	93,091	85,628
H 175	5	8	Palisander Rosewood	97,687	89,806
H 175	5	8	Polished Pyramid Mahogany	102,283	93,985
H 175	5	8	Polished Mahogany w/Vavona Inlay	111,893	102,721
H 175	5	8	Polished Burl Walnut	99,776	91,705
H 175	5	8	Polished Burl Walnut w/Walnut Inlay	111,893	102,721
H 175	5	8	Satin Cherry and Yew	106,043	97,403
H 175	5	8	Polished Cherry and Yew	111,893	102,721
H 175	5	8	Classic Alexandra Polished Ebony	91,002	83,729
H 175	5	8	Classic Alexandra Polished Walnut	104,372	95,884
H 175	5	8	Classic Alexandra Burl Walnut	114,818	105,380
H 175	5	8	Classic Alexandra Palisander	112,729	103,481
H 175	5	8	Louis XIV Satin White w/Gold	146,238	133,944
H 175	5	8	Satin and Polished Louis XV Mahogany	111,893	102,721
H 175	5	8	Ambassador Palisander	137,881	126,346
H 175	5	8	Ambassador Walnut	133,703	122,548
H 186	6	1	Polished Ebony	80,556	74,233
H 186	6	1	Satin Mahogany/Walnut	86,598	79,725
H 186	6	1	Polished Mahogany/Walnut	93,927	86,388
H 186	6	1	Satin Cherry	85,570	78,791
H 186	6	1	Polished Cherry	96,016	88,287
H 186	6	1	Polished White	86,195	79,359
H 186	6	1	Polished Bubinga	100,194	92,085
H 186	6	1	Palisander Rosewood	102,283	93,985
H 186	6	1	Polished Pyramid Mahogany	108,550	99,682
H 186	6	1	Polished Mahogany w/Vavona Inlay	116,489	106,899

*See pricing explanation on page 188.

Model	Feet	Inches	Description	MSRP*	SMP*
HAESSLER (continued)					
H 186	6	1	Polished Burl Walnut	104,372	95,884
H 186	6	1	Polished Burl Walnut w/Walnut Inlay	116,489	106,899
H 186	6	1	Satin Cherry and Yew	101,447	93,225
H 186	6	1	Polished Cherry and Yew	116,489	106,899
H 186	6	1	Classic Alexandra Polished Ebony	95,598	87,907
H 186	6	1	Classic Alexandra Polished Walnut	108,968	100,062
H 186	6	1	Classic Alexandra Burl Walnut	119,414	109,558
H 186	6	1	Classic Alexandra Palisander	117,325	107,659
H 186	6	1	Louis XIV Satin White w/Gold	150,416	137,742
H 186	6	1	Satin and Polished Louis XV Mahogany	116,489	106,899
H 186	6	1	Ambassador Palisander	150,416	137,742
H 186	6	1	Ambassador Walnut	146,238	133,944
H 210	6	10	Polished Ebony	93,801	86,274
H 210	6	10	Satin Mahogany/Walnut	100,836	92,669
H 210	6	10	Polished Mahogany/Walnut	110,974	101,885
H 210	6	10	Satin Cherry	101,949	93,681
H 210	6	10	Polished Cherry	112,729	103,481
H 210	6	10	Polished White	100,367	92,243
H 210	6	10	Polished Bubinga	114,400	105,000
H 210	6	10	Palisander Rosewood	123,174	112,976
H 210	6	10	Polished Pyramid Mahogany	129,441	118,674
H 210	6	10	Polished Mahogany w/Vavona Inlay	137,798	126,271
H 210	6	10	Polished Burl Walnut	121,085	111,077
H 210	6	10	Polished Burl Walnut w/Walnut Inlay	137,798	126,271
H 210	6	10	Satin Cherry and Yew	121,169	111,154
H 210	6	10	Polished Cherry and Yew	137,798	126,271
H 210	6	10	Classic Alexandra Polished Ebony	108,843	99,948
H 210	6	10	Classic Alexandra Polished Walnut	126,015	115,559
H 210	6	10	Classic Alexandra Burl Walnut	136,127	124,752
H 210	6	10	Classic Alexandra Palisander	138,216	126,651
H 210	6	10	Louis XIV Satin White w/Gold	183,842	168,129
H 210	6	10	Satin and Polished Louis XV Mahogany	129,734	118,940
H 210	6	10	Ambassador Palisander	162,951	149,137
H 210	6	10	Ambassador Walnut	158,773	145,339
HAILUN					
Verticals					
HU116		45.5	Institutional Polished Ebony	10,782	8,188
HU1-P		48	Polished Ebony	11,502	8,668
HU1-P		48	Polished Mahogany/Walnut	12,366	9,244
HU1-PS		48	Polished Ebony with Nickel Trim	11,970	8,980
HU1-EP		48	Polished Ebony w/mahogany leg, fallboard, cheekblocks	12,402	9,268
HU5-P		50	Polished Ebony	12,474	9,316
HU5-P		50	Polished Ebony with Nickel Trim	13,903	10,268
HU5-P		50	Polished Mahogany/Walnut	13,903	10,268
HU7-P		52	Polished Ebony w/Sostenuto	17,982	12,988
Grands					
HG151	4	11.5	Polished Ebony	22,296	15,864
HG151	4	11.5	Polished Mahogany/Walnut	23,955	16,970
HG151C	4	11.5	Chippendale Polished Mahogany/Walnut	24,750	17,500
HG161	5	4	Polished Ebony	24,981	17,656
HG161	5	4	Polished Mahogany/Walnut	26,842	18,548
HG161G	5	4	Georgian Polished Mahogany/Walnut	30,330	19,770
HG178	5	10	Polished Ebony	31,968	22,312
HG178	5	10	Polished Mahogany/Walnut	33,282	23,188
HG178B	5	10	Baroque Polished Ebony w/Birds-Eye Maple Accents	35,064	24,376

*See pricing explanation on page 188.

Model	Feet	Inches	Description	MSRP*	SMP*
HAILUN (continued)					
HG198	6	5	Emerson Polished Ebony	47,178	32,452
HG198	6	5	Emerson Polished Mahogany/Walnut	49,176	33,784
HG218	7	2	Paulello Polished Ebony	65,257	44,504

HALLET, DAVIS & CO.

Heritage Collection Verticals

Model	Feet	Inches	Description	MSRP*	SMP*
H108		43	Continental Polished Ebony	5,295	4,100
H108		43	Continental Polished Mahogany	5,495	4,190
HC43R		43	Satin Cherry (Roung Leg)	6,280	4,590
HC43F		43	French Provincial Satin Cherry	6,280	4,590
H117H		46	Polished Ebony	5,950	4,300
H117H		46	Polished Mahogany	6,150	4,390
H118F		46	Demi-Chippendale Polished Ebony	5,995	4,500
H118F		46	Demi-Chippendale Polished Mahogany	6,195	4,590

Signature Collection Verticals

Model	Feet	Inches	Description	MSRP*	SMP*
HS114E		45	Classic Studio Polished Mahogany/Walnut	5,995	4,500
HS115M2		45	Classic Studio Polished Ebony	6,995	4,590
HS115M2		45	Classic Studio Polished Mahogany/Walnut	7,195	4,790
HS118M		46.5	Polished Ebony	7,395	4,990
HS118M		46.5	Polished Mahogany/Walnut/White	7,595	5,190
HS121S		48	Polished Ebony	8,795	5,390
HS121S		48	Polished Mahogany/Walnut/White	9,095	5,590
HS131Y		52	Polished Ebony	9,495	6,190
HS132E		52	Polished Mahogany	9,995	6,300

Heritage Collection Grands

Model	Feet	Inches	Description	MSRP*	SMP*
H142C	4	7	Polished Ebony	13,195	8,990
H142C	4	7	Polished Mahogany	13,995	9,390
H142F	4	7	Queen Anne Polished Mahogany	14,995	9,790

Signature Collection Grands

Model	Feet	Inches	Description	MSRP*	SMP*
HS148	4	10	Satin Ebony	14,695	9,790
HS148	4	10	Polished Ebony	13,995	9,390
HS148	4	10	Polished Mahogany/Walnut/White	14,695	9,790
HS160	5	3	Satin Ebony	15,995	10,790
HS160	5	3	Polished Ebony	15,395	10,390
HS160	5	3	Polished Mahogany/Walnut/White	15,995	10,790
HS170	5	7	Satin Ebony	16,995	12,190
HS170	5	7	Polished Ebony	16,495	11,590
HS170	5	7	Polished Mahogany/Walnut/White	16,995	12,190
HS188	6	2	Satin Ebony	20,495	14,590
HS188	6	2	Polished Ebony	19,995	13,990
HS188	6	2	Polished Mahogany/Walnut	20,495	14,590
HS212	7		Polished Ebony	29,995	26,990

Imperial Collection Grands

Model	Feet	Inches	Description	MSRP*	SMP*
HD148B	4	10	Polished Ebony	14,995	10,990
HD152B	5		Polished Ebony	17,195	11,790
HD152T	5		Designer Birds-Eye Maple Two Tone	19,195	13,190
HD165B	5	5	Polished Ebony	19,495	12,990
HD165P	5	5	Polished Ebony (fluted leg)	20,995	14,390

HARDMAN, PECK & CO.

Verticals

Model	Feet	Inches	Description	MSRP*	SMP*
R110S		44	Polished Ebony	5,495	4,090
R110S		44	Polished Mahogany	5,595	4,190

*See pricing explanation on page 188.

PIANOBUYER.COM

Model	Feet	Inches	Description	MSRP*	SMP*
HARDMAN, PECK & CO. (continued)					
R45F		45	French Provincial Satin Cherry	6,695	4,790
R115LS		45	Polished Ebony	5,995	4,390
R115LS		45	Polished Mahogany	6,195	4,490
R116		46	School Polished Ebony	6,695	4,790
R116		46	School Satin Cherry	6,895	4,890
R117XK		46	Chippendale Polished Mahogany	6,695	4,790
RUE118H		46	Polished Ebony with Silver Hardware	6,695	4,790
R120LS		48	Polished Ebony	6,495	4,690
R120LS		48	Polished Mahogany	6,695	4,790
R132HA		52	Polished Ebony	9,495	6,390
Grands					
R143S	4	8	Polished Ebony	13,695	8,790
R143S	4	8	Polished Mahogany	14,995	9,390
R143F	4	8	French Provincial Polished Mahogany	15,395	9,790
R150S	5		Polished Ebony	15,095	9,590
R150S	5		Polished Mahogany	15,795	9,990
R150SGE	5		Polished Ebony w/Chrome	16,495	10,390
R158S	5	3	Polished Ebony	16,095	10,190
R158S	5	3	Polished Mahogany	16,795	10,590
R158F	5	3	French Provincial Polished Mahogany	17,495	10,990
R168S	5	7	Polished Ebony	17,495	10,990
R168S	5	7	Polished Mahogany	18,195	11,390
R185S	6	1	Polished Ebony	20,295	12,590
R185S	6	1	Polished Mahogany	20,995	12,990
HEINTZMAN & CO.					
Heintzman Verticals					
121DL		48	Satin Mahogany	7,995	7,380
123B		48.5	Polished Mahogany	8,795	7,580
123F		48.5	French Provincial Polished Mahogany	7,995	6,980
126C		50	Polished Ebony	8,795	7,600
126 Royal		50	Polished Ebony	9,795	8,200
132D		52	Polished Mahogany, Decorative Panel	11,795	8,980
132E		52	French Provincial Polished Ebony	11,795	8,780
132E		52	French Provincial Satin and Polished Mahogany	11,795	8,980
132 Royal		52	Satin Mahogany	12,795	9,580
140CK		55	Polished Mahogany	14,995	10,980
Gerhard Heintzman Verticals					
G118		47	Polished Ebony w/Silver Plate and Trim	4,995	4,995
G118		47	Polished Mahogany w/Silver Plate and Trim	5,195	5,195
G120		48	Polished Ebony w/Silver Plate and Trim	5,995	5,700
G120		48	Polished Mahogany w/Silver Plate and Trim	6,195	5,900
G126		50	Polished Ebony w/Silver Plate and Trim	7,995	6,400
G126		50	Polished Mahogany w/Silver Plate and Trim	8,195	6,600
G132		52	Polished Ebony w/Silver Plate and Trim	9,295	7,200
Heintzman Grands					
168	5	6	Polished Ebony	18,995	16,990
168	5	6	Polished Mahogany	19,995	17,390
168 Royal	5	6	Polished Ebony	23,995	17,990
186	6	1	Polished Ebony	21,995	18,980
186	6	1	Polished Mahogany	22,995	20,180
186 Royal	6	1	Polished Ebony	26,995	19,980
203	6	8	Polished Ebony	24,995	20,580
203 Royal	6	8	Polished Ebony	29,995	21,580
277	9		Polished Ebony	89,995	60,995

*See pricing explanation on page 188.

Model	Feet	Inches	Description	MSRP*	SMP*
HEINTZMAN & CO. (continued)					
Gerhard Heintzman Grands					
G152	5		Polished Ebony	9,995	9,995
G152	5		Polished White	11,995	11,995
G152R	5		Empire Polished Mahogany	11,995	11,995
G168	5	6	Polished Ebony	15,995	12,800
G168	5	6	Polished White	19,995	13,800
G168R	5	6	Empire Polished Mahogany	17,995	13,800
HESSEN, J.F.					
Verticals					
120		47	Polished Ebony	15,200	12,200
120		47	Polished Ebony with Round Edges	15,450	12,600
120		47	Polished Walnut	16,100	12,800
123		48	Polished Ebony	18,200	12,800
123		48	Polished Ebony with Round Edges	18,450	13,200
123		48	Polished Walnut	19,100	13,400
132		52	Polished Ebony	26,200	13,800
132		52	Polished Ebony with Round Edges	26,450	14,200
132		52	Polished Walnut	27,100	14,400
Verticals			Add'l for Renner action	1,400	1,400
Grands					
172	5	8	Polished Ebony	41,200	31,800
HOFFMANN, W.					
Vision Series Verticals					
V112		44.5	Polished Ebony		14,042
V112		44.5	Polished Mahogany/Walnut		16,246
V112		44.5	Polished White		15,806
V120		47.6	Polished Ebony		15,364
V120		47.6	Polished Mahogany/Walnut		17,590
V120		47.6	Polished White		17,150
V120		47.6	Chippendale Polished Mahogany/Walnut/White		20,260
V120		47.6	Rococo Satin White		21,320
V120		47.6	Rococo Satin White w/Gold Trim		21,556
V126		49.6	Polished Ebony		16,918
V126		49.6	Polished White		20,472
V131		51.8	Polished Ebony		19,354
Tradition Series Verticals					
T122		48	Polished Ebony		18,472
T122		48	Satin Mahogany/Walnut		21,350
T122		48	Polished Mahogany/Walnut		22,232
T122		48	Polished White		21,350
T128		50.4	Polished Ebony		20,236
T128		50.4	Satin Mahogany/Walnut		22,462
T128		50.4	Polished Mahogany/Walnut		22,904
T128		50.4	Polished White		22,462
Professional Series Verticals					
P114		45	Polished Ebony w/Chrome Hardware		19,626
P114		45	Polished White w/Chrome Hardware		21,532
P120		47.2	Polished Ebony w/Chrome Hardware		20,686
P120		47.2	Polished White w/Chrome Hardware		22,592
P126		49.6	Polished Ebony w/Chrome Hardware		22,806

*See pricing explanation on page 188.

HOFFMANN, W. (continued)

Vision Series Grands

Model	Feet	Inches	Description	MSRP*	SMP*
V158	5	2	Polished Ebony		33,236
V158	5	2	Polished Mahogany/Walnut/White		40,984
V175	5	9	Polished Ebony		38,002
V175	5	9	Polished Walnut/Mahogany/White		45,416
V183	6		Polished Ebony		42,770
V183	6		Polished Walnut/Mahogany/White		49,846

Tradition Series Grands

Model	Feet	Inches	Description	MSRP*	SMP*
T161	5	3	Polished Ebony		44,092
T161	5	3	Polished Mahogany/Walnut		53,606
T161	5	3	Polished White		51,400
T177	5	10	Polished Ebony		48,964
T177	5	10	Polished Mahogany/Walnut		58,478
T177	5	10	Polished White		56,272
T186	6	1	Polished Ebony		53,836
T186	6	1	Polished Mahogany/Walnut		63,350
T186	6	1	Polished White		61,144

Professional Series Grands

Model	Feet	Inches	Description	MSRP*	SMP*
P162	5	4	Polished Ebony w/Chrome Hardware		54,424
P188	6	2	Polished Ebony w/Chrome Hardware		61,648
P206	6	9	Polished Ebony w/Chrome Hardware		68,894

HUPFELD

Studio Edition Verticals

Model	Feet	Inches	Description	MSRP*	SMP*
HU 118		46.5	Polished Ebony	6,462	6,462
HU 121		47.5	Polished Ebony	6,725	6,725
HU 121		47.5	Polished White	6,865	6,865
HU 125		49	Polished Ebony	8,208	8,208
HU 132		52	Polished Ebony	9,563	9,500

Europe Edition Verticals

Model	Feet	Inches	Description	MSRP*	SMP*
HU 116E		45.5	Polished Ebony	11,086	10,854
HU 116E		45.5	Satin Mahogany/Walnut	11,086	10,854
HU 116E		45.5	Polished Mahogany/Walnut	11,782	11,473
HU 116E		45.5	Satin Cherry	11,782	11,473
HU 116E		45.5	Polished Cherry/White	13,174	12,710
HU 122E		48	Polished Ebony	12,304	11,937
HU 122E		48	Satin Mahogany/Walnut	12,304	11,937
HU 122E		48	Polished Mahogany/Walnut	13,000	12,556
HU 122E		48	Satin Cherry	13,000	12,556
HU 122E		48	Polished Cherry/White	14,392	13,793
HU 122E		48	Polished Bubinga	15,401	14,690
HU 132E		52	Polished Ebony	13,035	12,587
HU 132E		52	Satin Mahogany/Walnut	13,035	12,587
HU 132E		52	Polished Mahogany/Walnut	13,731	13,205
HU 132E		52	Satin Cherry	13,731	13,205
HU 132E		52	Polished Cherry/White	15,123	14,443
HU 132E		52	Polished Bubinga	18,185	17,164

Studio Edition Grands

Model	Feet	Inches	Description	MSRP*	SMP*
HU 148	4	10	Polished Ebony	17,989	16,990
HU 148	4	10	Polished Mahogany/Walnut	19,037	17,922
HU 148	4	10	Polished White	18,689	17,612
HU 160	5	3	Polished Ebony	20,783	19,474
HU 160	5	3	Polished Mahogany/Walnut	21,641	20,236
HU 160	5	3	Polished White	21,483	20,096

*See pricing explanation on page 188.

Model	Feet	Inches	Description	MSRP*	SMP*
HUPFELD (continued)					
HU 188	6	2	Polished Ebony	29,691	27,392
HU 188	6	2	Polished Mahogany/Walnut	30,303	27,936
HU 188	6	2	Polished White	30,391	28,014
HU 213	7		Polished Ebony	36,329	33,292
HU 213	7		Polished White	38,075	34,844
Europe Edition Grands					
HU 160E	5	3	Polished Ebony	34,724	31,866
HU 160E	5	3	Polished Mahogany/Walnut	37,197	34,064
HU 160E	5	3	Polished Cherry/Bubinga/White	40,083	36,629
HU 175E	5	9	Polished Ebony	38,022	34,797
HU 175E	5	9	Polished Mahogany/Walnut	40,495	36,996
HU 175E	5	9	Polished Bubinga/White	43,380	39,560
HU 186E	6	3	Polished Ebony	45,441	41,392
HU 186E	6	3	Polished Mahogany/Walnut	47,914	43,590
HU 186E	6	3	Polished Bubinga/White	50,799	46,155
HU 210E	6	10.5	Polished Ebony	50,799	46,155
HU 228E	7	6.5	Polished Ebony	59,043	53,483
IRMLER					
Studio Edition Verticals					
P112		44	Polished Ebony	6,318	6,318
P118		46.5	Polished Ebony	6,576	6,573
P118		46.5	Polished White	6,712	6,688
P125		49	Polished Ebony	8,026	7,802
Art Design Verticals					
Mia		47.5	Polished Ebony	8,725	8,394
Gina		48.5	Polished Ebony	9,095	8,708
Monique		49	Polished Ebony	9,095	8,708
Louis		49	Polished Ebony	8,725	8,394
Titus		49	Polished Ebony	9,095	8,708
Alexa		49	Polished Ebony	10,320	9,746
Carlo		49	Polished Ebony	10,320	9,746
Supreme Edition Verticals					
SP118		46.5	Polished Ebony	8,169	7,923
SP121		48	Polished Ebony	8,725	8,394
SP125		49	Polished Ebony	9,579	9,118
SP132		52	Polished Ebony	10,622	10,002
Professional Edition Verticals					
P116E		46	Polished Ebony	9,362	8,934
P116E		46	Satin Mahogany/Walnut	9,362	8,934
P116E		46	Satin Cherry	9,949	9,431
P116E		46	Polished Mahogany/Walnut	9,949	9,431
P116E		46	Polished Cherry/White	11,125	10,428
P122E		48	Polished Ebony	10,390	9,805
P122E		48	Satin Mahogany/Walnut	10,390	9,805
P122E		48	Satin Cherry	10,978	10,303
P122E		48	Polished Mahogany/Walnut	10,978	10,303
P122E		48	Polished Cherry/White	12,153	11,299
P122E		48	Polished Bubinga	13,005	12,021
P132E		52	Polished Ebony	11,007	10,328
P132E		52	Satin Mahogany/Walnut	11,007	10,328
P132E		52	Satin Cherry	11,595	10,826
P132E		52	Polished Mahogany/Walnut	11,595	10,826
P132E		52	Polished Cherry/White	12,770	11,822
P132E		52	Polished Bubinga	15,356	14,014

*See pricing explanation on page 188.

Model	Feet	Inches	Description	MSRP*	SMP*
IRMLER (continued)					
Studio Edition Grands					
F148	4	10	Polished Ebony	17,589	15,906
F148	4	10	Polished Mahogany/Walnut	18,614	16,775
F148	4	10	Polished White	18,273	16,486
F160	5	3	Polished Ebony	20,321	18,221
F160	5	3	Polished Mahogany/Walnut	21,160	18,932
F160	5	3	Polished White	21,006	18,802
F188	6	2	Polished Ebony	29,031	25,603
F188	6	2	Polished Mahogany/Walnut	29,630	26,110
F188	6	2	Polished White	29,715	26,182
F213	7		Polished Ebony	35,521	31,103
F213	7		Polished White	37,228	32,549
Professional Edition Grands					
F160E	5	3	Polished Ebony	32,409	28,465
F160E	5	3	Polished Mahogany/Walnut	34,718	30,422
F160E	5	3	Polished Cherry	37,410	32,703
F160E	5	3	Polished White	37,410	32,703
F160E	5	3	Polished Bubinga	37,410	32,703
F175E	5	9	Polished Ebony	35,487	31,074
F175E	5	9	Polished Mahogany/Walnut	37,795	33,030
F175E	5	9	Polished White	40,488	35,312
F175E	5	9	Polished Bubinga	40,488	35,312
F190E	6	3	Polished Ebony	42,412	36,942
F190E	6	3	Polished Mahogany/Walnut	44,720	38,898
F190E	6	3	Polished White	47,413	41,181
F190E	6	3	Polished Bubinga	47,413	41,181
F210E	6	10.5	Polished Ebony	47,413	41,181
F230E	7	6.5	Polished Ebony	55,107	47,701
KAWAI					
Verticals					
K-15		44	Continental Polished Ebony	5,495	5,390
K-15		44	Continental Polished Mahogany	5,695	5,590
506N		44.5	Satin Ebony/Mahogany	5,495	5,390
508		44.5	Satin Mahogany	6,195	5,990
607		44.5	French Renaissance Satin Cherry	7,495	6,990
607		44.5	Queen Anne Satin Mahogany	7,495	6,990
K-200		45	Satin and Polished Ebony	7,495	6,990
K-200		45	Satin and Polished Mahogany	8,195	7,590
K-200NKL		45	Satin and Polished Ebony with Nickel Trim	7,895	7,290
UST-9		46	Satin Ebony/Oak/Walnut/Cherry	7,995	7,390
907N		46.5	English Regency Satin Mahogany	10,695	9,590
907N		46.5	French Provincial Satin Cherry	10,695	9,590
K-300		48	Satin and Polished Ebony	11,195	9,990
K-300		48	Satin and Polished Mahogany	11,995	10,590
K-300		48	Polished Snow White	12,195	10,790
K-300NKL		48	Satin and Polished Ebony with Nickel Trim	11,595	10,390
K-400		48	Polished Ebony	11,995	10,590
K-400NKL		48	Polished Ebony with Nickel Trim	12,195	10,790
K-500		51	Satin and Polished Ebony	14,695	12,790
K-500		51	Polished Sapele Mahogany	16,495	14,190
K-800		53	Polished Ebony	23,195	19,590
AnyTime (Silent) Verticals					
K-200 ATX-CA		45	AnyTime Polished Ebony w/CA Sound	11,695	10,390
K-300 ATX-SS		48	AnyTime Polished Ebony w/Soundboard Speaker	16,495	14,190

*See pricing explanation on page 188.

Model	Feet	Inches	Description	MSRP*	SMP*
KAWAI (continued)					
Grands					
GL-10	5		Satin and Polished Ebony	15,095	14,190
GL-10	5		Polished Ebony with Nickel Trim	15,995	14,990
GL-10	5		Polished Mahogany/Snow White	16,795	15,590
GL-10	5		French Provincial Polished Mahogany	17,895	16,590
GL-20	5	2	Satin and Polished Ebony	20,395	18,990
GL-20	5	2	Polished Sapele Mahogany	23,895	21,990
GL-20	5	2	Polished Snow White	22,895	21,190
GL-30	5	5	Satin and Polished Ebony	27,295	24,990
GL-30	5	5	Polished Sapele Mahogany	32,895	29,990
GL-30	5	5	Satin Dark Walnut	32,895	29,990
GL-30	5	5	Polished Snow White	31,595	28,790
GX-1 BLK	5	5	Satin and Polished Ebony	36,695	30,390
GX-1 BLK	5	5	Polished Dark Walnut	42,995	35,390
GL-40	5	11	Satin and Polished Ebony	32,295	29,390
GL-40	5	11	Polished Sapele Mahogany	38,095	34,590
GL-40	5	11	Satin Dark Walnut	38,095	34,590
GX-2 BLK	5	11	Satin and Polished Ebony	42,495	34,990
GX-2 BLK	5	11	Satin Walnut/Cherry/Oak	46,995	38,590
GX-2 BLK	5	11	Polished Walnut/Sapeli Mahogany	48,995	40,190
GX-2 BLK	5	11	Polished Snow White	45,195	37,190
CR40-PL	6	1	Plexiglass Crystal Piano	231,495	186,190
GL-50	6	2	Polished Ebony	36,995	33,590
GX-3 BLK	6	2	Satin and Polished Ebony	54,495	44,590
GX-5 BLK	6	7	Satin and Polished Ebony	61,695	50,390
GX-6 BLK	7		Satin and Polished Ebony	69,195	56,390
GX-7 BLK	7	6	Satin and Polished Ebony	80,195	65,190
EX-L	9	1	Polished Ebony	218,995	176,190
AnyTime (Silent) Grands					
GL-30 ATX-SS	5	5	AnyTime Polished Ebony w/Soundboard Speaker	30,195	27,590

Model	Feet	Inches	Description	MSRP*	SMP*
KAWAI, SHIGERU					
Grands					
SK-2	5	11	Polished Ebony	64,000	52,200
SK-2	5	11	Polished Sapele Mahogany	73,800	60,000
SK-3	6	2	Polished Ebony	74,800	60,800
SK-3	6	2	Polished Sapele Mahogany	85,800	69,600
SK-3	6	2	Polished Pyramid Mahogany	99,500	80,600
SK-5	6	7	Polished Ebony	86,000	69,800
SK-6	7		Polished Ebony	97,000	78,600
SK-7	7	6	Polished Ebony	108,000	87,200
SK-EX	9	1	Polished Ebony	239,000	192,600

Model	Feet	Inches	Description	MSRP*	SMP*
KAYSERBURG					
Verticals					
KA-121B		48	Polished Ebony	15,995	12,990
KA-121B		48	Polished Dark Walnut	16,995	13,790
KA-126B		50	Polished Ebony	18,495	14,590
KA-126B		50	Polished Cherry	19,995	15,390
KA-132B		52	Polished Ebony	20,995	16,190
KA-132C		52	Polished Ebony w/Sostenuto	21,495	16,990
Grands					
KA-180	5	11	Polished Ebony	59,995	52,990

*See pricing explanation on page 188.

PIANOBUYER.COM

Model	Feet	Inches	Description	MSRP*	SMP*
KINGSBURG					
Verticals					
LM 116		46	Chippendale Polished Walnut	6,295	5,660
KG 120		48	Polished Ebony	9,009	7,025
KU 120		48	Polished Ebony	8,395	5,870
KU 120		48	Satin and Polished Mahogany/Walnut	8,710	6,080
KG 122		48	Polished Ebony	9,605	7,340
KF 123		50	Polished White & Red	12,838	9,440
KG 123		50	Decorator Satin Walnut	11,811	8,925
KU 123		50	Decorator Satin Walnut	9,445	6,710
KG 125		50	Polished Ebony	9,873	7,665
KU 125		50	Polished Ebony	9,445	6,500
KU 125		50	Polished Ebony w/Inlay	10,097	6,920
KU 125		50	Satin and Polished Mahogany/Walnut	9,970	6,710
KF 126		50	Satin Walnut	14,019	10,280
KF 128		50	Polished Ebony	13,808	11,120
KF 133		52	Polished Ebony	15,698	11,960
KG 133		52	Polished Ebony	11,902	9,020
KU 133		52	Polished Ebony	10,070	7,130
KU 133		52	Polished Mahogany/Walnut	10,479	7,340
Grands					
KF 158	5	3	Polished Ebony	24,675	24,675
KG 158	5	3	Polished Ebony	18,895	13,010
KG 158	5	3	Polished Ebony w/Inlay	19,945	13,640
KG 158	5	3	Polished Mahogany/Walnut	19,420	13,430
KF 185	6	1	Polished Ebony	31,448	31,448
KG 185	6	1	Polished Ebony	23,095	14,690
KG 185	6	1	Polished Ebony w/Inlay	24,670	15,320
KG 185	6	1	Polished Mahogany/Walnut	24,145	15,110
KF 228	7	4	Polished Ebony	66,150	61,186
KNABE, WM.					
Baltimore Series Verticals					
WV 43		43	Continental Polished Ebony	5,695	5,198
WV 243F		43	French Provincial Satin Cherry	6,195	5,598
WV 243T		43	Satin Mahogany/Walnut	6,195	5,598
WV 115		45	Satin Ebony	6,795	5,998
WV 115		45	Polished Ebony	6,195	5,598
WV 118H		46.5	Satin Ebony	7,295	6,398
WV 118H		46.5	Polished Ebony	6,795	5,998
Verticals			Other finishes, add		1,500
Academy Series Verticals					
WMV 245		45	Satin Ebony	6,795	5,998
WMV 245		45	Polished Ebony	6,495	5,798
WMV 247		46.5	Satin Ebony	7,795	6,798
WMV 247		46.5	Polished Ebony	7,595	6,598
WMV 247		46.5	Satin Walnut	8,095	6,998
WMV 647F		46.5	French Provincial Satin Cherry	7,695	6,598
WMV 647R		46.5	Renaissance Satin Walnut	7,695	6,598
WMV 647T		46.5	Satin Mahogany	7,695	6,598
WMV 121M		47.5	Satin Ebony	7,895	6,798
WMV 121M		47.5	Polished Ebony	7,595	6,598
WMV 132		52	Satin Ebony	9,795	8,198
WMV 132		52	Polished Ebony	9,195	7,798
Verticals			Other finishes, add		1,500

*See pricing explanation on page 188.

Model	Feet	Inches	Description	MSRP*	SMP*

KNABE, WM. *(continued)*

Concert Artist Series Verticals

Model	Feet	Inches	Description	MSRP*	SMP*
WKV 118F		46.5	French Provincial Lacquer Semigloss Cherry	10,495	8,798
WKV 118R		46.5	Renaissance Lacquer Satin Ebony	10,495	8,798
WKV 118R		46.5	Renaissance Lacquer Semigloss Walnut	10,495	8,798
WKV 118T		46.5	Lacquer Semigloss Mahogany	10,495	8,798
WKV 121		48	Satin Ebony	11,095	9,198
WKV 121		48	Polished Ebony	10,495	8,798
WKV 132MD		52	Satin Ebony	12,195	9,998
WKV 132MD		52	Polished Ebony	11,095	9,198
Verticals			Other finishes, add		1,500

Baltimore Series Grands

Model	Feet	Inches	Description	MSRP*	SMP*
WG 50	5		Satin Ebony	14,595	11,798
WG 50	5		Polished Ebony	13,795	11,198
WG 54	5	4	Satin Ebony	15,995	12,798
WG 54	5	4	Polished Ebony	14,595	11,798
WG 54	5	4	Polished Ebony w/Bubinga or Pommele Accents	18,195	14,598
WG 54	5	4	Polished Fire Red	19,295	15,398
WSG 54	5	4	M Leg w/Bubinga or Pommele Accents	20,695	16,398
WG 59	5	9	Satin Ebony	18,995	14,998
WG 59	5	9	Polished Ebony	17,895	14,198
WG 61	6	1	Satin Ebony	19,895	15,598
WG 61	6	1	Polished Ebony	18,795	14,998
Grands			Other finishes, add		2,000

Academy Series Grands

Model	Feet	Inches	Description	MSRP*	SMP*
WMG 610	5	9	Satin Ebony	21,395	16,798
WMG 610	5	9	Polished Ebony	20,295	15,998
WMG 660	6	1	Satin Ebony	23,795	18,598
WMG 660	6	1	Polished Ebony	22,695	17,798
WFM 700T	6	10	Satin Ebony	28,095	21,798
WFM 700T	6	10	Polished Ebony	26,495	20,598
Grands			Other finishes, add		2,000

Concert Artist Series Grands

Model	Feet	Inches	Description	MSRP*	SMP*
WKG 53	5	3	Satin Ebony	25,395	19,798
WKG 53	5	3	Polished Ebony	24,595	19,198
WKG 58	5	8	Satin Ebony	31,095	23,998
WKG 58	5	8	Polished Ebony	30,295	23,398
WKG 70	7		Satin Ebony	42,695	32,598
WKG 70	7		Polished Ebony	41,895	31,998
WKG 76	7	6	Satin Ebony	44,795	34,198
WKG 76	7	6	Polished Ebony	43,495	33,198
WKG 90	9	2	Satin Ebony	111,795	83,798
WKG 90	9	2	Polished Ebony	108,795	81,598
Grands			Other finishes, add		2,000

LOMENCE

Verticals

Model	Feet	Inches	Description	MSRP*	SMP*
121		47.5	Polished Black/White/Red	9,450	8,560
121		47.5	Polished Orange/Blue/Lavender	9,490	8,592
123		48.5	Polished Black	9,650	8,720
123		48.5	Polished White	9,785	8,830
123		48.5	Polished Red/Orange	9,740	8,790
123		48.5	Polished Blue	9,970	8,976
123		48.5	Polished Lavender	10,085	9,066
125		50.5	Polished Black	11,063	9,850

*See pricing explanation on page 188.

Model	Feet	Inches	Description	MSRP*	SMP*
LOMENCE (continued)					
125		50.5	Polished White/Red	11,188	9,950
125		50.5	Polished Lavender/Blue	11,375	10,100
Grands					
TRS 186	6		Any Color	44,995	44,995

Model	Feet	Inches	Description	MSRP*	SMP*
MASON & HAMLIN					
Verticals					
50		50	Satin and Polished Ebony	28,210	25,881
Verticals			Cambridge Collection, add	3,061	2,700
Grands					
B	5	4	Satin and Polished Ebony	62,802	53,314
B	5	4	Polished Mahogany/Walnut	67,120	56,911
B	5	4	Polished Pyramid Mahogany	76,624	64,828
B	5	4	Polished Rosewood	70,431	59,669
B	5	4	Polished Bubinga	73,035	61,838
B	5	4	Polished Macassar Ebony	76,624	64,828
A	5	8	Satin and Polished Ebony	72,334	61,255
A	5	8	Polished Mahogany/Walnut	77,132	65,252
A	5	8	Polished Pyramid Mahogany	93,653	79,013
A	5	8	Polished Rosewood	85,515	72,233
A	5	8	Polished Bubinga	88,508	74,727
A	5	8	Polished Macassar Ebony	93,653	79,013
AA	6	4	Satin and Polished Ebony	82,566	69,779
AA	6	4	Polished Mahogany/Walnut	87,025	73,493
AA	6	4	Polished Pyramid Mahogany	99,996	84,297
AA	6	4	Polished Rosewood	91,836	77,500
AA	6	4	Polished Bubinga	94,823	79,989
AA	6	4	Polished Macassar Ebony	99,996	84,297
BB	7		Satin and Polished Ebony	93,694	79,047
BB	7		Polished Mahogany/Walnut	97,009	81,810
BB	7		Polished Pyramid Mahogany	115,504	97,215
BB	7		Polished Rosewood	108,595	91,460
BB	7		Polished Bubinga	111,289	93,704
BB	7		Polished Macassar Ebony	115,504	97,215
CC	9	4	Satin and Polished Ebony	139,302	117,039
CC	9	4	Polished Mahogany/Walnut	149,104	125,204
CC	9	4	Polished Pyramid Mahogany	169,752	142,404
CC	9	4	Polished Rosewood	157,581	132,266
CC	9	4	Polished Bubinga	162,863	136,665
CC	9	4	Polished Macassar Ebony	169,752	142,404
Grands			Monticello Art Case, add	8,000	6,800
Grands			Cambridge Collection, add	8,000	6,800

Model	Feet	Inches	Description	MSRP*	SMP*
PALATINO					
Verticals					
PUP-22C		48	Polished Mahogany/Cherry	5,000	5,000
PUP-22C		48	Satin Walnut	5,000	5,000
PUP-123T		48	Torino Polished Ebony	5,900	5,900
PUP-123T		48	Torino Polished Dark Walnut	6,200	6,200
PUP-125		50	Satin and Polished Ebony	5,950	5,950
PUP-125		50	Polished Mahogany/White	5,950	5,950
PUP-126		50	Capri Polished Ebony	6,900	6,900
PUP-126		50	Capri Polished Dark Walnut	7,500	7,500

*See pricing explanation on page 188.

Model	Feet	Inches	Description	MSRP*	SMP*
PALATINO (continued)					
Grands					
PGD-50	5		Milano Polished Ebony	12,000	12,000
PGD-50	5		Milano Polished Dark Walnut	12,500	12,500
PGD-59	5	9	Roma Polished Ebony	13,400	13,400
PGD-62	6	2	Firenze Polished Ebony	15,400	15,400
PEARL RIVER					
Verticals					
EU 110		43	Polished Ebony	4,495	4,390
EU 111PA		43	French Provincial Satin Cherry	5,995	5,190
EU 111PB		43	Mediterranean Satin Walnut	5,995	5,190
EU 111PC		43	Italian Provincial Satin Mahogany	5,995	5,190
UP 115E		45	Satin Ebony/Mahogany (School)	5,995	5,190
UP 115M5		45	Polished Ebony	4,995	4,590
UP 115M5		45	Polished Mahogany/Walnut/White	5,395	4,790
EU 118S		46.5	Polished Ebony w/Silver Hardware	5,595	4,990
EU 118S		46.5	Polished Mahogany/Walnut w/Silver Hardware	5,795	5,190
EU 122		48	Polished Ebony	6,495	5,590
EU 122		48	Polished Mahogany/Walnut/White	6,695	5,790
EU 122		48	Satin Cherry	6,695	5,790
EU 122S		48	Polished Ebony w/Silver Hardware	6,695	5,790
EU 122 Silent		48	Polished Ebony w/Silent System	8,995	7,990
EU 131		52	Polished Ebony	7,395	6,190
Grands					
GP 150	4	11	Hand-rubbed Satin Ebony	11,995	9,590
GP 150	4	11	Polished Ebony	11,495	9,190
GP 150	4	11	Polished Mahogany/Walnut/White	11,995	9,590
GP 150	4	11	Polished Sapele Mahogany/Artisan Walnut	12,495	9,990
GP 150S	4	11	Polished Ebony w/Silver Hardware	11,995	9,590
GP 160	5	3	Hand-rubbed Satin Ebony	13,395	10,390
GP 160	5	3	Polished Ebony	12,995	9,990
GP 160	5	3	Polished Mahogany/Walnut/White	13,495	10,390
GP 160	5	3	Polished Sapele Mahogany/Artisan Walnut	13,995	10,790
GP 170	5	7	Hand-rubbed Satin Ebony	15,495	11,990
GP 170	5	7	Polished Ebony	14,995	11,590
GP 170	5	7	Polished Mahogany/Walnut	15,495	11,990
GP 170	5	7	Polished Sapele Mahogany/Artisan Walnut	15,995	12,390
GP 188A	6	2	Polished Ebony	18,495	13,990
GP 212	7		Polished Ebony	29,995	22,990
GP 275	9		Polished Ebony	79,995	60,990
PERZINA, GEBR.					
Verticals					
GP-112 Kompact		45	Continental Polished Ebony	8,890	8,000
GP-112 Kompact		45	Continental Polished Walnut/Mahogany	9,450	8,250
GP-112 Kompact		45	Continental Polished White	9,780	8,490
GP-115 Merit		45	Polished Ebony	9,660	8,430
GP-115 Merit		45	Polished Mahogany/Walnut	10,220	8,690
GP-115 Merit		45	Polished White	10,550	8,900
GP-115 Merit		45	Queen Anne Polished Ebony	10,220	8,600
GP-115 Merit		45	Queen Anne Polished Mahogany/Walnut	11,045	8,920
GP-115 Merit		45	Queen Anne Polished White	11,375	9,140
GP-122 Konsumat		48	Polished Ebony	10,990	9,090
GP-122 Konsumat		48	Polished Ebony with Chrome Hardware	12,090	10,000
GP-122 Konsumat		48	Polished Mahogany/Walnut	11,375	9,400

*See pricing explanation on page 188.

Model	Feet	Inches	Description	MSRP*	SMP*
PERZINA, GEBR. (continued)					
GP-122 Konsumat		48	Polished White	11,580	9,590
GP-122 Konsumat		48	Queen Anne Polished Ebony	11,375	9,380
GP-122 Konsumat		48	Queen Anne Polished Mahogany/Walnut	12,200	9,590
GP-122 Konsumat		48	Queen Anne Polished White	12,500	9,800
GP-122 Balmoral		48	Designer Polished Ebony	12,285	9,300
GP-122 Balmoral		48	Designer Polished Ebony/Bubinga (two-tone)	13,300	10,840
GP-129 Kapitol		51	Polished Ebony	12,240	10,220
GP-129 Kapitol		51	Polished Mahogany/Walnut	12,860	10,420
GP-129 Kapitol		51	Polished White	13,520	10,630
GP-129 Kapitol		51	Queen Anne Polished Ebony	13,520	10,420
GP-129 Kapitol		51	Queen Anne Polished Mahogany/Walnut	13,565	10,630
GP-129 Kapitol		51	Queen Anne Polished White	14,290	10,840
GP-130 Konzert		51	Polished Ebony	14,840	11,460
Grands					
GBT-152 Prysm	5	1	Polished Ebony	22,570	16,440
GBT-152 Prysm	5	1	Polished Mahogany/Walnut	24,680	17,650
GBT-152 Prysm	5	1	Polished White	26,750	17,860
GBT-152 Prysm	5	1	Designer Polished Ebony/Bubinga (two-tone)	28,620	18,480
GBT-152 Prysm	5	1	Designer Polished Mahogany/Walnut with Burled Walnut Inlay	29,920	19,520
GBT-152 Prysm	5	1	Designer Queen Anne or Empire Polished Ebony	23,090	16,760
GBT-152 Prysm	5	1	Designer Queen Anne or Empire Polished Mahogany/Walnut	25,160	17,980
GBT-152 Prysm	5	1	Designer Queen Anne or Empire Polished White	27,260	18,180
GBT-160 Sylvr	5	5	Polished Ebony	29,360	18,690
GBT-160 Sylvr	5	5	Polished Mahogany/Walnut	31,460	19,850
GBT-160 Sylvr	5	5	Polished White	33,590	20,020
GBT-160 Sylvr	5	5	Designer Polished Ebony/Bubinga (two-tone)	37,610	23,900
GBT-160 Sylvr	5	5	Designer Polished Mahogany/Walnut with Burled Walnut Inlay	38,930	24,930
GBT-160 Sylvr	5	5	Designer Queen Anne or Empire Polished Ebony	30,330	19,020
GBT-160 Sylvr	5	5	Designer Queen Anne or Empire Polished Mahogany/Walnut	32,500	20,170
GBT-160 Sylvr	5	5	Designer Queen Anne or Empire Polished White	34,670	20,320
GBT-175 Granit	5	10	Polished Ebony	31,940	19,640
GBT-175 Granit	5	10	Polished Mahogany/Walnut	34,720	20,790
GBT-175 Granit	5	10	Polished White	37,160	20,980
GBT-175 Granit	5	10	Designer Polished Ebony/Bubinga (two-tone)	40,190	24,840
GBT-175 Granit	5	10	Designer Polished Mahogany/Walnut with Burled Walnut Inlay	41,300	25,880
GBT-175 Granit	5	10	Designer Queen Anne or Empire Polished Ebony	32,660	19,960
GBT-175 Granit	5	10	Designer Queen Anne or Empire Polished Mahogany/Walnut	35,340	12,120
GBT-175 Granit	5	10	Designer Queen Anne or Empire Polished White	38,810	21,300
GBT-187 Royal	6	2	Polished Ebony	35,770	20,590
GBT-187 Royal	6	2	Polished Mahogany/Walnut	37,270	21,750
GBT-187 Royal	6	2	Polished White	39,910	21,930
GBT-187 Royal	6	2	Designer Polished Ebony/Bubinga (two-tone)	44,020	25,780
GBT-187 Royal	6	2	Designer Polished Mahogany/Walnut with Burled Walnut Inlay	45,650	26,820
GBT-187 Royal	6	2	Designer Queen Anne or Empire Polished Ebony	36,720	20,910
GBT-187 Royal	6	2	Designer Queen Anne or Empire Polished Mahogany/Walnut	37,940	22,070
GBT-187 Royal	6	2	Designer Queen Anne or Empire Polished White	40,350	22,250

PETROF

Most models are also available in finishes other than those shown here.

Verticals

Model	Feet	Inches	Description	MSRP*	SMP*
P 118 C1		46.25	Chippendale Polished Ebony	28,258	20,824
P 118 D1		46.25	Demi-Chippendale Polished Ebony	27,530	20,294
P 118 G2		46.25	Polished Ebony	26,794	19,760
P 118 M1		46.25	Polished Ebony	25,504	18,820
P 118 P1		46.25	Polished Ebony	24,980	18,440
P 118 R1		46.25	Rococo Satin White w/Gold Trim	29,930	22,046

*See pricing explanation on page 188.

Model	Feet	Inches	Description	MSRP*	SMP*
PETROF (continued)					
P 118 S1		46.25	Continental Polished Ebony/White	21,968	16,250
P 122 N1		47.75	Polished Ebony	26,100	19,240
P 125 F1		49.25	Polished Ebony	26,990	19,900
P 125 G1		49.25	Polished Ebony	28,490	20,990
P 125 M1		49.25	Polished Ebony	28,090	20,700
P 127 NEXT		49.5	Satin Ebony with Chrome Legs	39,540	29,030
P 127 NEXT		49.5	Satin Wood Tones with Chrome Legs	43,790	32,120
P 131 M1		51	Polished Ebony	38,570	28,326
P 135 K1		53	Polished Ebony	45,980	33,714
Grands					
P 159	5	2	Bora Polished Ebony	75,910	55,480
P 159	5	2	Bora Demi-Chippendale Polished Ebony	81,990	58,778
P 173	5	6	Breeze Polished Ebony	79,990	58,448
P 173	5	6	Breeze Chippendale Polished Ebony	90,958	68,424
P 173	5	6	Breeze Demi-Chippendale Polished Ebony	88,700	68,780
P 173	5	6	Breeze Klasik Polished Ebony	89,240	70,776
P 173	5	6	Breeze Rococo Satin White w/Gold Trim	94,190	68,780
P 194	6	3	Storm Polished Ebony	83,964	61,336
P 194	6	3	Storm Styl Polished Ebony	96,060	70,136
P 210	6	10	Pasat Polished Ebony	119,990	87,500
P 237	7	9	Monsoon Polished Ebony	157,390	120,740
P 284	9	2	Mistral Polished Ebony	217,084	158,152
Grands All Models			Mahogany/Walnut Upcharge	2,400	2,400
Grands All Models			White or Color Upcharge	1,600	1,600
PRAMBERGER					
Legacy Series Verticals					
LV-110		43	Continental Polished Ebony	5,995	5,398
LV-43F		43	French Provincial Satin Cherry	6,495	5,798
LV-43T		43	Satin Mahogany/Walnut	6,795	5,798
LV-115		45	Satin Ebony	6,795	5,998
LV-115		45	Polished Ebony	6,495	5,798
LV-118		46.5	Satin Ebony	7,295	6,398
LV-118		46.5	Polished Ebony	6,795	5,998
Signature Series Verticals					
PV-118F/R/T		46.5	Decorator Satin Cherry/Mahogany/Walnut	7,895	6,798
PV-118S		46.5	Satin Ebony	8,095	6,998
PV-118S		46.5	Polished Ebony	7,595	6,598
PV-121		47.5	Satin Ebony	9,195	7,798
PV-121		47.5	Polished Ebony	8,695	7,398
PV-132		52	Satin Ebony	10,295	8,598
PV-132		52	Polished Ebony	9,795	8,198
J.P. Pramberger Platinum Series Verticals					
JP-132		52	Satin Ebony	12,395	10,198
JP-132		52	Polished Ebony	11,295	9,398
Verticals			Other wood finishes, add		1,500
Legacy Series Grands					
LG-150	5		Satin Ebony	14,895	11,998
LG-150	5		Polished Ebony	13,995	11,398
LG-157	5	2	Satin Ebony	15,895	12,798
LG-157	5	2	Polished Ebony	14,895	11,998
LG-157	5	2	Polished Ebony w/Bubinga or Pommele Accents	17,795	14,198
LG-157	5	2	Polished Fire Red	19,195	15,198
LG-175	5	9	Satin Ebony	18,395	14,598
LG-175	5	9	Polished Ebony	17,295	13,798

*See pricing explanation on page 188.

Model	Feet	Inches	Description	MSRP*	SMP*
PRAMBERGER *(continued)*					
Signature Series Grands					
PS-157	5	2	Satin Ebony	19,195	15,198
PS-157	5	2	Polished Ebony	18,195	14,398
PS-157	5	2	Polished Ebony w/Bubinga or Pommele Accents	21,095	16,598
PS-175	5	9	Satin Ebony	20,795	16,398
PS-175	5	9	Polished Ebony	19,695	15,598
PS-185	6	1	Satin Ebony	21,595	16,998
PS-185	6	1	Polished Ebony	20,595	16,198
PS-208	6	10	Satin Ebony	28,095	21,798
PS-208	6	10	Polished Ebony	26,495	20,598
J.P. Pramberger Platinum Series Grands					
JP-179L	5	10	Satin Ebony	32,395	24,998
JP-179L	5	10	Polished Ebony	31,595	24,398
JP-179LF	5	10	French Provincial Satin Ebony	37,795	28,998
JP-179LF	5	10	French Provincial Lacquer Semigloss Cherry	37,795	28,998
JP-208B	6	10	Satin Ebony	40,995	31,398
JP-208B	6	10	Polished Ebony	40,295	30,798
JP-228C	7	6	Satin Ebony	44,795	34,198
JP-228C	7	6	Polished Ebony	44,295	33,798
JP-280E	9	2	Polished Ebony	132,295	98,998
Grands			Other wood finishes, add		2,000
RITMÜLLER					
Classic Verticals					
UP 110RB1		43	Italian Provincial Satin Walnut	6,995	5,390
UP 110RB		43	French Provincial Satin Cherry	6,995	5,390
UP 120RE		47.25	Satin Mahogany	7,995	5,990
UP 121RB		47.6	Polished Ebony	6,995	5,790
UP 121RB		47.6	Polished Mahogany/Walnut/White	7,495	5,990
Performance Verticals					
R1		47	Polished Ebony	8,595	6,790
R2		49	Polished Ebony w/Butterfly Lid	9,595	7,390
RB		49	Polished Ebony	9,595	7,390
Premium Verticals					
UH 121R		48	Chippendale Polished Ebony	9,795	7,900
UH 121R		48	Chippendale Polished Sapele Mahogany	9,995	8,190
UH 121RA		48	Polished Ebony	9,695	7,790
UH 121RA Silent		48	Silent Polished Ebony	12,995	10,190
UH 132R		52	Polished Ebony	11,995	8,990
Performance Grands					
R8	4	11	Polished Ebony	13,495	9,990
R8	4	11	Polished Mahogany/White	13,995	10,590
R9	5	3	Polished Ebony	15,495	10,790
R9	5	3	Polished Mahogany/White	15,995	11,390
Premium Grands					
GH 148R	4	10	Polished Ebony	15,995	11,590
GH 148R	4	10	Polished Sapele Mahogany	16,495	12,390
GH 160R	5	3	Hand-rubbed Satin Ebony	18,995	14,390
GH 160R	5	3	Polished Ebony	18,495	13,590
GH 160R	5	3	Polished Sapele Mahogany	18,995	14,390
GH 160RA	5	3	Polished Ebony (round leg)	18,995	14,390
GH 170R	5	7	Polished Ebony	20,995	15,990
GH 188R	6	2	Polished Ebony	25,995	19,590

*See pricing explanation on page 188.

Model	Feet	Inches	Description	MSRP*	SMP*
RITMÜLLER (continued)					
GH 212R	7		Polished Ebony	31,995	25,990
GH 275R	9		Polished Ebony	84,995	66,990

RÖNISCH

Verticals

Model	Feet	Inches	Description	MSRP*	SMP*
118 K		46.5	Polished Ebony	18,084	17,440
118 K		46.5	Satin Mahogany	18,810	18,100
118 K		46.5	Polished Mahogany	21,945	20,950
118 K		46.5	Satin Walnut	18,975	18,250
118 K		46.5	Polished Walnut	22,110	21,100
118 K		46.5	Satin European Cherry	19,305	18,550
118 K		46.5	Polished European Cherry	22,440	21,400
118 K		46.5	Satin German Oak	18,645	17,950
118 K		46.5	Polished White	19,734	18,940
118 K		46.5	Waxed Alder	17,985	17,350
118 K		46.5	Satin Heart Beech	18,315	17,650
118 K		46.5	Satin Ash	18,480	17,800
118 K		46.5	Satin Swiss Pear/Indian Apple	19,800	19,000
118 K		46.5	Polished Indian Apple	22,935	21,850
125 K		49	Polished Ebony	19,899	19,090
125 K		49	Satin Mahogany	20,229	19,390
125 K		49	Polished Mahogany	23,529	22,390
125 K		49	Satin Walnut	20,394	19,540
125 K		49	Polished Walnut	23,694	22,540
125 K		49	Satin European Cherry	20,724	19,840
125 K		49	Polished European Cherry	24,024	22,840
125 K		49	Polished White	21,549	20,590
125 K		49	Satin Bubinga	20,889	19,990
125 K		49	Polished Bubinga	24,189	22,990
125 K		49	Satin Swiss Pear/Indian Apple	21,219	20,290
125 K		49	Polished Indian Apple	24,519	23,290
125 K		49	Carl Ronisch Edition Satin Burl Walnut	23,859	22,690
125 K		49	Carl Ronisch Edition Polished Burl Walnut	27,159	25,690
132 K		52	Polished Ebony	22,275	21,250
132 K		52	Satin Mahogany	22,605	21,550
132 K		52	Polished Mahogany	25,905	24,550
132 K		52	Satin Walnut	22,770	21,700
132 K		52	Polished Walnut	26,070	24,700
132 K		52	Polished White	23,925	22,750
132 K		52	Satin Bubinga	23,265	22,150
132 K		52	Polished Bubinga	26,565	25,150
132 K		52	Carl Ronisch Edition Satin Burl Walnut	26,565	25,150
132 K		52	Carl Ronisch Edition Polished Burl Walnut	29,865	28,150

Grands

Model	Feet	Inches	Description	MSRP*	SMP*
175 K	5	9	Polished Ebony	59,730	55,300
175 K	5	9	Satin Mahogany	61,050	56,500
175 K	5	9	Polished Mahogany	70,290	64,900
175 K	5	9	Satin Pyramid Mahogany	76,890	70,900
175 K	5	9	Polished Pyramid Mahogany	86,130	79,300
175 K	5	9	Satin Walnut	62,040	57,400
175 K	5	9	Polished Walnut	71,280	65,800
175 K	5	9	Satin European Cherry	63,690	58,900
175 K	5	9	Polished European Cherry	72,930	67,300
175 K	5	9	Polished White	63,030	58,300
175 K	5	9	Satin Bubinga	64,680	59,800
175 K	5	9	Polished Bubinga	73,920	68,200

*See pricing explanation on page 188.

Model	Feet	Inches	Description	MSRP*	SMP*
RÖNISCH *(continued)*					
175 K	5	9	Satin Rosewood	70,290	64,900
175 K	5	9	Polished Rosewood	79,530	73,300
175 K	5	9	Carl Ronisch Edition Satin Burl Walnut	73,590	67,900
175 K	5	9	Carl Ronisch Edition Polished Burl Walnut	82,830	76,300
186 K	6	1	Polished Ebony	64,680	59,800
186 K	6	1	Satin Mahogany	66,000	61,000
186 K	6	1	Polished Mahogany	75,240	69,400
186 K	6	1	Satin Pyramid Mahogany	81,840	75,400
186 K	6	1	Polished Pyramid Mahogany	91,080	83,800
186 K	6	1	Satin Walnut	66,990	61,900
186 K	6	1	Polished Walnut	76,230	70,300
186 K	6	1	Satin European Cherry	68,640	63,400
186 K	6	1	Polished European Cherry	77,880	71,800
186 K	6	1	Polished White	67,980	62,800
186 K	6	1	Satin Bubinga	69,630	64,300
186 K	6	1	Polished Bubinga	78,870	72,700
186 K	6	1	Satin Rosewood	75,240	69,400
186 K	6	1	Polished Rosewood	84,480	77,800
186 K	6	1	Carl Ronisch Edition Satin Burl Walnut	78,540	72,400
186 K	6	1	Carl Ronisch Edition Polished Burl Walnut	87,780	80,800
210 K	6	10.5	Polished Ebony	82,830	76,300
210 K	6	10.5	Polished White	86,130	79,300
SAMICK					
Grands					
NSG 158	5	2	Satin Ebony	25,495	19,198
NSG 158	5	2	Polished Ebony	23,995	18,198
NSG 175	5	7	Satin Ebony	27,995	20,998
NSG 175	5	7	Polished Ebony	26,495	19,998
NSG 186	6	1	Satin Ebony	30,795	22,998
NSG 186	6	1	Polished Ebony	29,395	21,998
Grands			Other wood finishes, add	2,000	2,000
SAUTER					
Standard wood veneers are walnut, mahogany, ash, and alder.					
Verticals					
119		46	Peter Maly Concent Satin Ebony	32,000	32,000
119		46	Peter Maly Concent Polished Ebony	34,000	34,000
122		48	Ragazza Polished Ebony	36,500	36,500
122		48	Ragazza Satin Cherry	36,500	36,500
122		48	Ragazza Polished Cherry/Yew	43,000	43,000
122		48	Vista Polished Ebony	40,000	40,000
122		48	Vista Satin Maple	38,500	38,500
122		48	Vista Satin Cherry	40,000	40,000
122		48	Master Class Polished Ebony	47,000	47,000
122		48	Peter Maly Artes Polished Ebony	52,000	52,000
122		48	Peter Maly Artes Polished Palisander/Macassar	53,500	53,500
122		48	Peter Maly Artes Polished White	53,500	53,500
122		48	Peter Maly Pure Noble Polished Ebony/Veneers	49,000	49,000
122		48	Peter Maly Pure Noble Polished White/Red	50,000	50,000
122		48	Peter Maly Pure Basic Satin Ebony/Walnut	39,900	39,900
122		48	Peter Maly Pure Basic Satin White	39,900	39,900
122		48	Peter Maly Pure Basic Satin White/Maple	39,900	39,900
122		48	Peter Maly Rondo Polished Ebony	43,500	43,500

*See pricing explanation on page 188.

Model	Feet	Inches	Description	MSRP*	SMP*

SAUTER (continued)

Model	Feet	Inches	Description	MSRP*	SMP*
122		48	Peter Maly Rondo Satin Wenge	40,500	40,500
122		48	Peter Maly Vitrea Colored Ebony with Glass	41,000	41,000
122		48	Schulpiano Satin Beech/Black Ash	32,000	32,000
130		51	Master Class Polished Ebony	53,000	53,000
130		51	Competence Polished Ebony	45,500	45,500
130		51	Competence Satin Walnut	43,000	43,000
130		51	Sonder Polished Ebony w/Sostenuto	39,900	39,900
130		51	Sonder Polished Ebony w/o Sostenuto	36,000	36,000

Grands

Model	Feet	Inches	Description	MSRP*	SMP*
160	5	3	Alpha Polished Ebony	95,000	95,000
160	5	3	Alpha Satin Standard Wood Veneers	88,000	88,000
160	5	3	Chippendale Satin Cherry	99,000	99,000
160	5	3	Chippendale Satin Standard Wood Veneers	96,000	96,000
160	5	3	Noblesse Satin Cherry	106,000	106,000
160	5	3	Noblesse Polished Cherry	115,000	115,000
160	5	3	Noblesse Satin Burl Walnut	111,000	111,000
160	5	3	Noblesse Satin Standard Wood Veneers	106,000	106,000
160	5	3	Noblesse Polished Standard Wood Veneers	114,000	114,000
185	6	1	Delta Polished Ebony	106,000	106,000
185	6	1	Delta Polished Ebony w/Burl Walnut	110,000	110,000
185	6	1	Delta Polished Pyramid Mahogany	117,000	117,000
185	6	1	Delta Polished Bubinga	116,000	116,000
185	6	1	Delta Polished Rio Palisander	117,000	117,000
185	6	1	Delta Satin Maple with Silver	99,000	99,000
185	6	1	Delta Polished White	110,000	110,000
185	6	1	Delta Satin Standard Wood Veneers	98,000	98,000
185	6	1	Chippendale Satin Cherry	109,000	109,000
185	6	1	Chippendale Satin Standard Wood Veneers	105,000	105,000
185	6	1	Noblesse Satin Cherry	116,000	116,000
185	6	1	Noblesse Polished Cherry	129,000	129,000
185	6	1	Noblesse Satin Burl Walnut	121,000	121,000
185	6	1	Noblesse Satin Standard Wood Veneers	112,000	112,000
185	6	1	Noblesse Polished Standard Wood Veneers	126,000	126,000
210	6	11	Peter Maly Vivace Polished Ebony	150,000	150,000
210	6	11	Peter Maly Vivace Satin Wood Veneers	140,000	140,000
210	6	11	Peter Maly Vivace Polished White	150,000	150,000
220	7	3	Omega Polished Ebony	135,000	135,000
220	7	3	Omega Polished Burl Walnut	149,000	149,000
220	7	3	Omega Polished Pyramid Mahogany	148,000	148,000
220	7	3	Omega Satin Standard Wood Veneers	129,000	129,000
230	7	7	Peter Maly Ambiente Polished Ebony	170,000	170,000
230	7	7	Peter Maly Ambiente Polished Ebony w/Crystals	195,000	195,000
275	9		Concert Polished Ebony	230,000	230,000

SCHIMMEL

Classic Series Verticals

Model	Feet	Inches	Description	MSRP*	SMP*
C 116		46	Tradition Polished Ebony	24,308	20,446
C 116		46	Tradition Polished Mahogany/White	27,398	22,918
C 116		46	Tradition Satin Walnut/Cherry/Beech/Alder	27,398	22,918
C 116		46	Modern Cubus Polished Ebony	28,171	23,537
C 116		46	Modern Cubus Polished White	31,261	26,009
C 120		48	Tradition Polished Ebony	26,368	22,094
C 120		48	Tradition Polished Mahogany/White	29,458	24,566
C 120		48	Tradition Satin Walnut/Cherry/Beech/Alder	29,458	24,566
C 120		48	Tradition Marketerie Polished Mahogany w/Inlay	31,518	26,214
C 120		48	Elegance Manhattan Polished Ebony	25,467	21,374

*See pricing explanation on page 188.

Model	Feet	Inches	Description	MSRP*	SMP*
SCHIMMEL (continued)					
C 120		48	Elegance Manhattan Polished Mahogany/White	28,557	23,846
C 120		48	Modern Polished Ebony	30,746	25,597
C 120		48	Modern Polished White	33,836	28,069
C 120		48	NWS Edition 80	32,419	26,935
C 120		48	Royal Polished Ebony	28,943	24,154
C 120		48	Royal Polished Mahogany/White	32,033	26,626
C 120		48	Royal Intarsie Flora Polished Mahogany w/Inlays	34,093	28,274
C 126		50	Tradition Polished Ebony	32,033	26,626
C 126		50	Tradition Polished Mahogany/White	35,123	29,098
C 130		51	Tradition Polished Ebony	34,608	28,686
C 130		51	Tradition Polished Mahogany/White	37,698	31,158
Konzert Series Verticals					
K 122		48	Tradition Polished Ebony	35,510	29,408
K 122		48	Tradition Polished Mahogany/White	39,630	32,704
K 122		48	Elegance Polished Ebony	35,510	29,408
K 122		48	Elegance Polished White	39,630	32,704
K 125		49	Tradition Polished Ebony	38,085	31,468
K 125		49	Tradition Polished Mahogany/White	42,205	34,764
K 132		52	Tradition Polished Ebony	43,493	35,794
K 132		52	Tradition Polished Mahogany/White	47,613	39,090
Fridolin Schimmel Verticals					
F 116		46	Polished Ebony	7,838	7,270
F 116		46	Polished White	8,213	7,570
F 121		48	Polished Ebony	8,963	8,170
F 121		48	Polished Walnut/White	9,338	8,470
F 123		49	Polished Ebony	10,088	9,070
F 123		49	Polished Mahogany/White	10,463	9,370
Wilhelm Schimmel Verticals					
W 114		46	Modern Swing Polished Ebony	15,682	13,180
W 114		46	Modern Swing Polished White	18,257	15,180
W 114		46	Tradition Polished Ebony	16,712	13,980
W 114		46	Tradition Polished Mahogany/White	19,287	15,980
W 118		48	Tradition Polished Ebony	18,257	15,180
W 118		48	Tradition Polished Mahogany/White	20,832	17,180
W 123		49	Tradition Polished Ebony	19,802	16,380
W 123		49	Tradition Polished Mahogany/White	22,377	18,380
Classic Series Grands					
C 169	5	7	Tradition Polished Ebony	66,280	54,024
C 169	5	7	Tradition Polished Mahogany/White	72,718	59,174
C 169	5	7	NWS Edition 80	73,233	59,586
C 189	6	3	Tradition Polished Ebony	70,143	57,114
C 189	6	3	Tradition Polished Mahogany/White	76,580	62,264
C 189	6	3	NWS Edition 80	77,095	62,676
C 213	7		Tradition Polished Ebony	76,580	62,264
C 213	7		Tradition Polished Mahogany/White	83,018	67,414
C 213	7		NWS Edition 80	83,533	67,826
Konzert Series Grands					
K 175	5	9	Tradition Polished Ebony	84,750	68,800
K 175	5	9	Tradition Polished Mahogany/White	92,250	74,800
K 195	6	5	Tradition Polished Ebony	92,250	74,800
K 195	6	5	Tradition Polished Mahogany/White	99,750	80,800
K 213	7		Glas Clear Acrylic and White or Black and Gold	312,500	251,000
K 213	7		Otmar Alt Polished Ebony w/Color Motifs	225,000	181,000
K 219	7	2	Tradition Polished Ebony	99,750	80,800
K 219	7	2	Tradition Polished Mahogany/White	107,250	86,800

*See pricing explanation on page 188.

Model	Feet	Inches	Description	MSRP*	SMP*
SCHIMMEL *(continued)*					
K 230	7	7	Tradition Polished Ebony	114,750	92,800
K 256	8	4	Tradition Polished Ebony	129,750	104,800
K 280	9	2	Tradition Polished Ebony	149,750	120,800
Wilhelm Schimmel Grands					
W 180	6		Tradition Polished Ebony	40,402	32,380
W 180	6		Tradition Polished Mahogany/White	45,552	36,380
W 206	6	10	Tradition Polished Ebony	49,414	39,380
W 206	6	10	Tradition Polished Mahogany/White	54,564	43,380
SCHULZE POLLMANN					
Studio Series Verticals					
SU115		45	Polished Peacock Ebony	9,595	7,790
SU115		45	Polished Peacock Mahogany	10,495	8,390
SU118A		46	Polished Peacock Ebony	10,995	8,990
SU118A		46	Polished Peacock Mahogany/Walnut	11,995	9,590
SU122A		48	Polished Peacock Ebony	13,995	10,390
SU122A		48	Polished Peacock Mahogany/Walnut	14,995	10,990
SU122A		48	Polished Feather Mahogany	15,895	11,590
Masterpiece Series Grands					
160/GK	5	3	Polished Ebony (spade leg)	55,995	55,995
160/GK	5	3	Polished Briar Mahogany (spade leg)	59,995	59,995
160/GK	5	3	Polished Feather Mahogany (spade leg)	63,995	63,995
197/G5	6	6	Polished Ebony (spade leg)	77,995	76,990
197/G5	6	6	Polished Briar Mahogany (spade leg)	80,995	80,995
197/G5	6	6	Polished Feather Mahogany (spade leg)	84,995	84,995
SEILER					
Seiler Verticals					
SE-116		45	Primus, Polished Ebony	28,895	22,398
SE-116		45	Mondial, Polished Ebony	30,495	23,598
SE-116		45	Mondial, Polished Rosewood	41,295	31,598
SE-116		45	Konsole, Polished Ebony	34,595	26,598
SE-116		45	Impuls, Polished Ebony	30,495	23,598
SE-116		45	Clou, Polished Ebony	35,895	27,598
SE-116		45	Accent, Polished Ebony	35,895	27,598
SE-122		48	Primus, Polished Ebony	38,595	29,598
SE-126		49	Konsole, Polished Ebony	42,695	32,598
SE-126		49	Konsole, Satin Walnut	43,995	33,598
SE-126		49	Attraction, Polished Ebony	45,695	34,798
SE-132		52	Consert, Polished Ebony	52,395	39,798
SE-132		52	Consert, Polished Ebony w/SMR	52,495	40,398
SE-132		52	Consert, Polished Ebony w/Rec Panel	54,995	41,798
SE-132		52	Consert, Polished Ebony w/Rec Panel/SMR	55,795	42,398
Eduard Seiler ED Series Verticals					
ED-126		49	Primus, Satin Ebony	14,495	10,998
ED-126		49	Primus, Polished Ebony	12,695	10,398
ED-132		52	Konzert, Satin Ebony	15,795	11,398
ED-132		52	Konzert, Polished Ebony	14,995	10,998
Verticals			Other wood finishes, add		1,500
Johannes Seiler Verticals					
GS-116N		45.5	Satin Ebony w/Nickel Hardware	9,999	8,398
GS-116N		45.5	Polished Ebony w/Nickel Hardware	9,395	7,998
GS-247		46.5	Satin Ebony	10,795	8,998
GS-247		46.5	Polished Ebony	9,995	8,398

*See pricing explanation on page 188.

Model	Feet	Inches	Description	MSRP*	SMP*
SEILER *(continued)*					
GS-247		46.5	Satin Walnut	10,795	8,998
GS-118		47	Satin Ebony	10,195	8,598
GS-118		47	Polished Ebony	9,695	8,198
GS-121		47.5	Ditto, Polished Ebony w/Silver accent	11,595	9,598
GS-122		48.5	Satin Ebony	10,995	9,198
GS-122		48.5	Polished Ebony	10,195	8,598
Verticals			Other wood finishes, add		1,500
Seiler Grands					
SE-168	5	6	Virtuoso, Polished Ebony	96,395	72,398
SE-168	5	6	Virtuoso, Polished Mahogany	115,795	86,798
SE-186	6	2	Maestro, Polished Ebony	113,195	84,798
SE-186	6	2	Maestro, Polished Mahogany	121,295	90,798
SE-186	6	2	Maestro, Polished Rosewood	129,595	96,998
SE-186	6	2	Ziricote, Polished Ebony	122,595	91,798
SE-186	6	2	Louvre, Polished Cherry	152,895	114,198
SE-186	6	2	Florenz, Polished Mahogany	152,895	114,198
SE-208	6	10	Professional, Polished Ebony	126,895	94,998
SE-242	8		Konzert, Polished Ebony	167,895	125,398
SE-278	9	2	Konzert, Polished Ebony	272,695	202,998
Eduard Seiler ED Series Grands					
ED-168	5	6	Virtuoso, Satin Ebony	36,995	28,398
ED-168	5	6	Virtuoso, Polished Ebony	36,495	27,998
ED-168HS	5	6	Heritage, Satin Ebony	45,995	34,998
ED-168HS	5	6	Heritage, Polished Ebony	44,895	34,198
ED-186	6	2	Maestro, Satin Ebony	45,095	34,398
ED-186	6	2	Maestro, Polished Ebony	43,495	33,198
ED-186A	6	2	Custom, Polished Ebony	83,495	62,798
Grands			Other wood finishes, add		2,000
Johannes Seiler Grands					
GS-160	5	3	Satin Ebony	25,395	19,798
GS-160	5	3	Polished Ebony	23,995	18,798
GS-160LN	5	3	Satin Ebony (M Leg Style)	28,595	22,198
GS-160LN	5	3	Polished Ebony (M Leg Style)	27,295	21,198
GS-175	5	9	Satin Ebony	27,795	21,598
GS-175	5	9	Polished Ebony	26,395	20,598
GS-186	6	2	Satin Ebony	29,695	22,998
GS-186	6	2	Polished Ebony	28,595	22,198
Grands			Other wood finishes, add		2,000
STEINBERG, G.					
Verticals					
RH-111 Nicosia		45	Polished Ebony	8,240	7,220
RH-111 Nicosia		45	Polished Mahogany/Walnut	8,460	7,430
RH-111 Nicosia		45	Polished White	8,680	7,640
RH-115 Slate		45	Polished Ebony	8,460	7,430
RH-115 Slate		45	Polished Mahogany/Walnut	8,680	7,550
RH-115 Slate		45	Polished White	9,010	7,780
RH-115 Slate		45	Queen Anne Polished Ebony	8,680	7,550
RH-115 Slate		45	Queen Anne Polished Mahogany/Walnut	8,900	7,660
RH-115 Slate		45	Queen Anne Polished White	9,120	7,880
RH-119 Splendit		47	Polished Ebony	8,900	7,860
RH-119 Splendit		47	Polished Mahogany/Walnut	9,120	8,070
RH-119 Splendit		47	Polished White	9,230	8,280
RH-119 Splendit		47	Queen Anne Polished Ebony	9,120	7,970
RH-119 Splendit		47	Queen Anne Polished Mahogany/Walnut	9,340	8,180

*See pricing explanation on page 188.

Model	Feet	Inches	Description	MSRP*	SMP*
STEINBERG, G. *(continued)*					
RH-119 Splendit	47		Queen Anne Polished White	9,450	8,380
RH-123 Performance	49		Polished Ebony	9,340	8,070
RH-123 Performance	49		Queen Anne Polished Ebony	9,670	8,280
RH-126 Sienna	50		Polished Ebony	10,440	8,700
RH-126 Sienna	50		Queen Anne Polished Ebony	10,770	8,900
Grands					
GBT-152 Sovereign	5	1	Polished Ebony	19,470	14,710
GBT-152 Sovereign	5	1	Polished Mahogany/Walnut	21,200	15,820
GBT-152 Sovereign	5	1	Polished White	22,960	16,160
GBT-152 Sovereign	5	1	Queen Anne or Empire Polished Ebony	19,855	15,120
GBT-152 Sovereign	5	1	Queen Anne or Empire Polished Mahogany/Walnut	21,615	16,290
GBT-152 Sovereign	5	1	Queen Anne or Empire Polished White	23,485	16,560
GBT-160 Stockholm	5	5	Polished Ebony	25,160	16,910
GBT-160 Stockholm	5	5	Polished Mahogany/Walnut	26,975	17,950
GBT-160 Stockholm	5	5	Polished White	28,790	18,160
GBT-160 Stockholm	5	5	Queen Anne or Empire Polished Ebony	26,015	17,190
GBT-160 Stockholm	5	5	Queen Anne or Empire Polished Mahogany/Walnut	27,855	18,450
GBT-160 Stockholm	5	5	Queen Anne or Empire Polished White	29,670	18,660
GBT-175 Schwerin	5	10	Polished Ebony	28,460	17,620
GBT-175 Schwerin	5	10	Polished Mahogany/Walnut	29,725	19,080
GBT-175 Schwerin	5	10	Polished White	31,870	19,280
GBT-175 Schwerin	5	10	Queen Anne or Empire Polished Ebony	27,965	18,160
GBT-175 Schwerin	5	10	Queen Anne or Empire Polished Mahogany/Walnut	30,275	19,410
GBT-175 Schwerin	5	10	Queen Anne or Empire Polished White	33,190	19,620
GBT-187 Amsterdam	6	2	Polished Ebony	30,635	18,790
GBT-187 Amsterdam	6	2	Polished Mahogany/Walnut	31,870	19,820
GBT-187 Amsterdam	6	2	Polished White	34,155	20,030
GBT-187 Amsterdam	6	2	Queen Anne or Empire Polished Ebony	31,430	19,100
GBT-187 Amsterdam	6	2	Queen Anne or Empire Polished Mahogany/Walnut	32,475	20,240
GBT-187 Amsterdam	6	2	Queen Anne or Empire Polished White	34,510	20,450
STEINBERG, WILH.					
Verticals					
P118	45.5		Polished Ebony	9,043	9,043
Signature 117	46		Polished Ebony	18,955	18,955
Signature 117	46		Satin Alder	21,307	21,307
Signature 117	46		Satin Walnut/Mahogany	20,702	20,702
Signature 117	46		Polished White	20,702	20,702
P121	47.5		Polished Ebony	9,883	9,883
Signature 125	49		Polished Ebony	20,467	20,467
Signature 125	49		Satin Alder	23,138	23,138
Signature 125	49		Satin Walnut/Mahogany	22,366	22,366
Signature 125	49		Polished White	22,366	22,366
P125E	49.5		Polished Ebony	10,387	10,387
Signature 130	51		Polished Ebony	24,163	24,163
Signature 130	51		Satin Alder	27,372	27,372
Signature 130	51		Satin Walnut/Mahogany	26,431	26,431
Signature 130	51		Polished White	26,431	26,431
Amadeus	51		Polished Ebony	27,523	27,523

*See pricing explanation on page 188.

Model	Feet	Inches	Description	MSRP*	SMP*
STEINBERG, WILH. (continued)					
Passione	51		Polished Ebony	30,043	30,043
Grands					
P152	5		Polished Ebony	21,492	21,492
P165	5	5	Polished Ebony	23,172	23,172
P178	5	10	Polished Ebony	24,852	24,852
Signature 188	6	2	Polished Ebony	46,692	46,692
Signature 212	6	11	Polished Ebony	55,932	55,932
Signature 275	9		Polished Ebony		

STEINGRAEBER & SÖHNE
Prices include bench. Euro = $1.10

Verticals

Model	Feet	Inches	Description	MSRP*	SMP*
122 T		48	Satin and Polished Ebony	44,104	42,854
122 T		48	Satin and Polished White	44,839	43,589
122 T		48	Polished Ebony w/Twist & Change Panels	49,543	48,293
122 T		48	Satin Ordinary Veneers	53,491	52,241
122 T		48	Polished Ordinary Veneers	58,699	57,449
122 T		48	Satin Special Veneers	55,297	54,047
122 T		48	Polished Special Veneers	60,484	59,234
122 T		48	Satin Extraordinary Veneers	66,868	65,618
122 T		48	Polished Extraordinary Veneers	72,076	70,826
122 T-SFM		48	Satin and Polished Ebony	46,540	45,290
122 T-SFM		48	Satin and Polished White	47,254	46,004
122 T-SFM		48	Polished Ebony w/Twist & Change Panels	52,000	50,750
122 T-SFM		48	Satin Ordinary Veneers	55,948	54,698
122 T-SFM		48	Polished Ordinary Veneers	61,114	59,864
122 T-SFM		48	Satin Special Veneers	57,733	56,483
122 T-SFM		48	Polished Special Veneers	62,920	61,670
122 T-SFM		48	Satin Extraordinary Veneers	69,325	68,075
122 T-SFM		48	Polished Extraordinary Veneers	74,491	73,241
130 T-PS		51	Satin and Polished Ebony	55,864	54,614
130 T-PS		51	Satin and Polished White	56,683	55,433
130 T-PS		51	Polished Ebony w/Twist & Change Panels	61,303	60,053
130 T-PS		51	Satin Ordinary Veneers	65,251	64,001
130 T-PS		51	Polished Ordinary Veneers	70,438	69,188
130 T-PS		51	Satin Special Veneers	67,036	65,786
130 T-PS		51	Polished Special Veneers	72,202	70,952
130 T-PS		51	Satin Extraordinary Veneers	78,628	77,378
130 T-PS		51	Polished Extraordinary Veneers	83,815	82,565
130 T-SFM		51	Satin and Polished Ebony	56,914	55,664
130 T-SFM		51	Satin and Polished White	57,754	56,504
130 T-SFM		51	Polished Ebony w/Twist & Change Panels	62,374	61,124
130 T-SFM		51	Satin Ordinary Veneers	66,322	65,072
130 T-SFM		51	Polished Ordinary Veneers	71,509	70,259
130 T-SFM		51	Satin Special Veneers	68,107	66,857
130 T-SFM		51	Polished Special Veneers	73,273	72,023
130 T-SFM		51	Satin Extraordinary Veneers	79,699	78,449
130 T-SFM		51	Polished Extraordinary Veneers	84,865	83,615
138 K		54	Satin and Polished Ebony	59,161	57,911
138 K		54	Satin and Polished White	59,917	58,667
138 K		54	Polished Ebony w/Twist & Change Panels	64,600	63,350
138 K		54	Satin Ordinary Veneers	68,569	67,319
138 K		54	Polished Ordinary Veneers	73,735	72,485
138 K		54	Satin Special Veneers	70,333	69,083
138 K		54	Polished Special Veneers	75,541	74,291
138 K		54	Satin Extraordinary Veneers	81,904	80,654

*See pricing explanation on page 188.

Model	Feet	Inches	Description	MSRP*	SMP*
STEINGRAEBER & SÖHNE (continued)					
138 K		54	Polished Extraordinary Veneers	87,112	85,862
138 K-SFM		54	Satin and Polished Ebony	61,597	60,347
138 K-SFM		54	Satin and Polished White	62,374	61,124
138 K-SFM		54	Polished Ebony w/Twist & Change Panels	67,057	65,807
138 K-SFM		54	Satin Ordinary Veneers	71,005	69,755
138 K-SFM		54	Polished Ordinary Veneers	76,192	74,942
138 K-SFM		54	Satin Special Veneers	72,790	71,540
138 K-SFM		54	Polished Special Veneers	77,956	76,706
138 K-SFM		54	Satin Extraordinary Veneers	84,382	83,132
138 K-SFM		54	Polished Extraordinary Veneers	89,548	88,298
Grands					
A-170 N	5	7	Satin and Polished Ebony	102,014	100,764
A-170 N	5	7	Satin and Polished White	103,904	102,654
A-170 N	5	7	Satin and Polished Ordinary Veneers	115,937	114,687
A-170 N	5	7	Satin and Polished Special Veneers	117,470	116,220
A-170 N	5	7	Satin and Polished Extraordinary Veneers	125,534	124,284
A-170 S	5	7	Studio Lacquer Anti-Scratch	99,263	98,013
B-192 N	6	3	Satin and Polished Ebony	117,953	116,703
B-192 N	6	3	Satin and Polished White	120,179	118,929
B-192 N	6	3	Satin and Polished Ordinary Veneers	133,283	132,033
B-192 N	6	3	Satin and Polished Special Veneers	134,984	133,734
B-192 N	6	3	Satin and Polished Extraordinary Veneers	144,035	142,785
B-192 S	6	3	Studio Lacquer Anti-Scratch	115,097	113,847
C-212 N	7		Satin and Polished Ebony	134,291	133,041
C-212 N	7		Satin and Polished White	136,811	135,561
C-212 N	7		Satin and Polished Ordinary Veneers	150,692	149,442
C-212 N	7		Satin and Polished Special Veneers	152,582	151,332
C-212 N	7		Satin and Polished Extraordinary Veneers	162,578	161,328
C-212 S	7		Studio Lacquer Anti-Scratch	131,015	129,765
D-232 N	7	7	Satin and Polished Ebony	162,591	161,341
D-232 N	7	7	Satin and Polished White	164,922	163,672
D-232 N	7	7	Satin and Polished Ordinary Veneers	180,756	179,506
D-232 N	7	7	Satin and Polished Special Veneers	182,772	181,522
D-232 N	7	7	Satin and Polished Extraordinary Veneers	193,776	192,526
D-232 S	7	7	Studio Lacquer Anti-Scratch	159,147	157,897
E-272	8	11	Satin and Polished Ebony	233,382	232,132
E-272	8	11	Satin and Polished White	234,054	232,804
E-272	8	11	Satin and Polished Ordinary Veneers	255,180	253,930
E-272	8	11	Satin and Polished Special Veneers	256,902	255,652
E-272	8	11	Satin and Polished Extraordinary Veneers	271,119	269,869

STEINWAY & SONS

These are the prices at the Steinway retail store in New York City, often used as a benchmark for Steinway prices throughout the country. Model K-52 in ebony; model 1098 in ebony, mahogany, and walnut; and grand models in ebony, mahogany, and walnut include adjustable artist benches. Other models include regular wood bench. Wood-veneered models are in a semigloss finish called "satin lustre."

Verticals

Model	Feet	Inches	Description	MSRP*	SMP*
4510		45	Sheraton Satin Ebony	34,200	34,200
4510		45	Sheraton Mahogany	37,900	37,900
4510		45	Sheraton Walnut	38,400	38,400
1098		46.5	Satin Ebony	32,300	32,300
1098		46.5	Mahogany	35,900	35,900
1098		46.5	Walnut	36,400	36,400
K-52		52	Satin Ebony	37,600	37,600
K-52		52	Mahogany	42,400	42,400
K-52		52	Walnut	43,900	43,900

*See pricing explanation on page 188.

Model	Feet	Inches	Description	MSRP*	SMP*
STEINWAY & SONS *(continued)*					
Grands					
S	5	1	Satin Ebony	65,600	65,600
S	5	1	Polyester Polished Ebony	67,700	67,700
S	5	1	Polyester Polished Ebony w/Sterling Hardware	69,500	69,500
S	5	1	Polyester Polished White	75,300	75,300
S	5	1	Mahogany	76,600	76,600
S	5	1	Walnut	77,400	77,400
S	5	1	Kewazinga Bubinga	81,800	81,800
S	5	1	East Indian Rosewood	92,500	92,500
S	5	1	Macassar Ebony	100,800	100,800
S	5	1	Figured Sapele	81,200	81,200
S	5	1	Dark Cherry	81,900	81,900
S	5	1	Santos Rosewood	91,900	91,900
S	5	1	African Pommele	95,200	95,200
M	5	7	Satin Ebony	69,700	69,700
M	5	7	Polyester Polished Ebony	72,100	72,100
M	5	7	Polyester Polished Ebony w/Sterling Hardware	73,900	73,900
M	5	7	Polyester Polished Ebony w/Spirio	87,100	87,100
M	5	7	Polyester Polished White	81,500	81,500
M	5	7	Mahogany	83,100	83,100
M	5	7	Walnut	83,900	83,900
M	5	7	Kewazinga Bubinga	88,600	88,600
M	5	7	East Indian Rosewood	99,500	99,500
M	5	7	Macassar Ebony	108,700	108,700
M	5	7	Figured Sapele	89,500	89,500
M	5	7	Dark Cherry	90,100	90,100
M	5	7	Santos Rosewood	99,300	99,300
M	5	7	African Pommele	102,900	102,900
M 1014A	5	7	Chippendale Mahogany	100,200	100,200
M 1014A	5	7	Chippendale Walnut	102,200	102,200
M 501A	5	7	Louis XV Walnut	128,600	128,600
M 501A	5	7	Louis XV East Indian Rosewood	149,500	149,500
M	5	7	Pops Polished Ebony w/White Accessories	85,900	85,900
M	5	7	Pops Polished Ebony w/Color Accessories	86,500	86,500
M	5	7	John Lennon Imagine Polished White	112,900	112,900
M	5	7	Onyx Duet Polished Ebony	106,900	106,900
O	5	10.5	Satin Ebony	78,400	78,400
O	5	10.5	Polyester Polished Ebony	80,900	80,900
O	5	10.5	Polyester Polished Ebony w/Sterling Hardware	82,700	82,700
O	5	10.5	Polyester Polished White	89,900	89,900
O	5	10.5	Mahogany	90,200	90,200
O	5	10.5	Walnut	91,100	91,100
O	5	10.5	Kewazinga Bubinga	95,700	95,700
O	5	10.5	East Indian Rosewood	108,100	108,100
O	5	10.5	Macassar Ebony	117,900	117,900
O	5	10.5	Figured Sapele	96,900	96,900
O	5	10.5	Dark Cherry	97,400	97,400
O	5	10.5	Santos Rosewood	107,400	107,400
O	5	10.5	African Pommele	111,900	111,900
O	5	10.5	Pops Polished Ebony w/White Accessories	93,200	93,200
O	5	10.5	Pops Polished Ebony w/Color Accessories	94,100	94,100
O	5	10.5	John Lennon Imagine Polished White	121,200	121,200
O	5	10.5	Onyx Duet Polished Ebony	112,100	112,100
A	6	2	Satin Ebony	89,700	89,700
A	6	2	Polyester Polished Ebony	92,500	92,500
A	6	2	Polyester Polished Ebony w/Sterling Hardware	94,300	94,300
A	6	2	Polyester Polished White	103,400	103,400

*See pricing explanation on page 188.

Model	Feet	Inches	Description	MSRP*	SMP*
STEINWAY & SONS *(continued)*					
A	6	2	Mahogany	101,600	101,600
A	6	2	Walnut	102,900	102,900
A	6	2	Kewazinga Bubinga	108,700	108,700
A	6	2	East Indian Rosewood	122,800	122,800
A	6	2	Macassar Ebony	134,100	134,100
A	6	2	Figured Sapele	109,100	109,100
A	6	2	Dark Cherry	110,700	110,700
A	6	2	Santos Rosewood	122,400	122,400
A	6	2	African Pommele	127,500	127,500
A	6	2	Pops Polished Ebony w/White Accessories	105,700	105,700
A	6	2	Pops Polished Ebony w/Color Accessories	106,500	106,500
A	6	2	John Lennon Imagine Polished White	136,100	136,100
A	6	2	Onyx Duet Polished Ebony	122,700	122,700
B	6	10.5	Satin Ebony	101,800	101,800
B	6	10.5	Polyester Polished Ebony	105,500	105,500
B	6	10.5	Polyester Polished Ebony w/Sterling Hardware	109,300	109,300
B	6	10.5	Polyester Polished Ebony w/Spirio	120,500	120,500
B	6	10.5	Polyester Polished White	117,500	117,500
B	6	10.5	Mahogany	116,500	116,500
B	6	10.5	Walnut	117,800	117,800
B	6	10.5	Kewazinga Bubinga	123,900	123,900
B	6	10.5	East Indian Rosewood	140,900	140,900
B	6	10.5	Macassar Ebony	152,800	152,800
B	6	10.5	Figured Sapele	123,800	123,800
B	6	10.5	Dark Cherry	124,600	124,600
B	6	10.5	Santos Rosewood	137,800	137,800
B	6	10.5	African Pommele	143,900	143,900
B	6	10.5	Fibonacci 600K	575,000	575,000
B	6	10.5	Pops Polished Ebony w/White Accessories	119,900	119,900
B	6	10.5	Pops Polished Ebony w/Color Accessories	120,900	120,900
B	6	10.5	John Lennon Imagine Polished White	153,300	153,300
B	6	10.5	Onyx Duet Polished Ebony	136,100	136,100
D	8	11.75	Satin Ebony	164,100	152,800
D	8	11.75	Polyester Polished Ebony	165,300	157,600
D	8	11.75	Polyester Polished Ebony w/Sterling Hardware	169,100	161,400
D	8	11.75	Polyester Polished White	182,200	173,400
D	8	11.75	Mahogany	191,900	185,000
D	8	11.75	Walnut	193,200	185,000
D	8	11.75	Kewazinga Bubinga	202,600	196,400
D	8	11.75	East Indian Rosewood	230,500	221,200
D	8	11.75	Macassar Ebony	249,100	242,200
D	8	11.75	Figured Sapele	195,500	189,600
D	8	11.75	Dark Cherry	198,700	191,600
D	8	11.75	Santos Rosewood	216,800	213,200
D	8	11.75	African Pommele	227,800	221,800
D	8	11.75	Pops Polished Ebony w/White Accessories	172,600	172,600
D	8	11.75	Pops Polished Ebony w/Color Accessories	173,700	173,700
D	8	11.75	John Lennon Imagine Polished White	211,800	211,800

*See pricing explanation on page 188.

Model	Feet	Inches	Description	MSRP*	SMP*

Steinway (Hamburg) Grands

I frequently get requests for prices of pianos made in Steinway's branch factory in Hamburg, Germany. Officially, these pianos are not sold in North America, but it is possible to order one through an American Steinway dealer, or to go to Europe and purchase one there. The following list shows approximately how much it would cost to purchase a Hamburg Steinway in Europe and have it shipped to the United States. The list was derived by taking the published retail price in Europe, subtracting the value-added tax not applicable to foreign purchasers, converting to U.S. dollars (the rate used here is 1 Euro = $1.06, but is obviously subject to change), and adding approximate charges for duty, air freight, crating, insurance, brokerage fees, and delivery. Only prices for grands in polished ebony are shown here. Caution: This list is published for general informational purposes only. The price that Steinway would charge for a piano ordered through an American Steinway dealer may be different. (Also, the cost of a trip to Europe to purchase the piano is not included.)

Model	Feet	Inches	Description	MSRP*	SMP*
S-155	5	1	Polished Ebony	72,300	72,300
M-170	5	7	Polished Ebony	74,500	74,500
O-180	5	10.5	Polished Ebony	83,800	83,800
A-188	6	2	Polished Ebony	86,000	86,000
B-211	6	11	Polished Ebony	99,000	99,000
C-227	7	5.5	Polished Ebony	111,400	111,400
D-274	8	11.75	Polished Ebony	149,000	149,000

STORY & CLARK

All Story & Clark pianos include PNOscan, and USB and MIDI connectivity. In addition, all grands now include a QRS PNOmation player-piano system. Prices shown are those for online sales **www.qrsmusic.com**.

Heritage Series Verticals

Model	Feet	Inches	Description	MSRP*	SMP*
H7		46	Academy Polished Ebony		5,395

Signature Series Verticals

Model	Feet	Inches	Description	MSRP*	SMP*
S8		48	Cosmopolitan Polished Ebony		5,395

Heritage Series Grands

Model	Feet	Inches	Description	MSRP*	SMP*
H50A	4	11	Prelude Polished Ebony/Mahogany		16,695
H60 QA	5		French Provincial Polished Ebony		17,495
H60 QA	5		French Provincial Satin Lacquer and Polished Mahogany		17,595
H60A	5	3	Academy Satin and Polished Ebony		17,495
H60A	5	3	Academy Polished Mahogany		17,495
H60A	5	3	Academy Polished White		17,995
H70A	5	7	Conservatory Polished Ebony		18,895
H80	6	1	Professional Polished Ebony		21,395
H90	6	10	Semi-Concert Polished Ebony		28,795

Signature Series Grands

Model	Feet	Inches	Description	MSRP*	SMP*
S500	4	11	Manhattan Semigloss Ebony w/Birdseye Maple Accents		25,095
S600	5	4	Cosmopolitan Polished Ebony		24,395
S600	5	4	Melrose Polished Ebony/Mahogany		26,995
S600	5	4	Park West Satin Ebony		24,195
S600	5	4	Park West Polished Ebony		24,495
S700	5	9	Fairfax Polished Ebony w/Bubinga Accents		26,695
S700	5	9	Versailles Satin Lacquer Cherry		26,295
S700	5	9	Park West Polished Ebony		24,695
S800	6	2	Islander British Colonial Satin Walnut		27,895
S800	6	2	Park West Polished Ebony		25,395
S900	7		Park West Satin Ebony		38,495

WALTER, CHARLES R.

Verticals

Model	Feet	Inches	Description	MSRP*	SMP*
1520		43	Satin and Polished Walnut		18,477
1520		43	Satin and Polished Cherry		18,420
1520		43	Satin and Polished Oak		17,803
1520		43	Satin and Polished Mahogany		18,813
1520		43	Italian Provincial Satin and Polished Walnut		18,514
1520		43	Italian Provincial Satin and Polished Mahogany		18,850

*See pricing explanation on page 188.

Model	Feet	Inches	Description	MSRP*	SMP*
WALTER, CHARLES R. *(continued)*					
1520		43	Italian Provincial Satin and Polished Oak		17,823
1520		43	Country Classic Satin and Polished Cherry		18,253
1520		43	Country Classic Satin and Polished Oak		17,923
1520		43	French Provincial Satin and Polished Oak		18,514
1520		43	French Provincial Satin and Polished Cherry/Walnut/Mahogany		19,072
1520		43	Riviera Satin and Polished Oak		17,752
1520		43	Queen Anne Satin and Polished Oak		18,666
1520		43	Queen Anne Satin and Polished Mahogany/Cherry		19,072
1500		45	Satin Ebony		17,172
1500		45	Semi-Gloss Ebony		17,506
1500		45	Polished Ebony (Lacquer)		17,707
1500		45	Polished Ebony (Polyester)		18,084
1500		45	Satin and Polished Oak		16,329
1500		45	Satin and Polished Walnut		17,358
1500		45	Satin and Polished Mahogany		17,619
1500		45	Satin and Polished Gothic Oak		17,380
1500		45	Satin and Polished Cherry		17,561
Verticals			Renner (German) action, add		1,925–2,150
Grands					
W-175	5	9	Satin Ebony		77,781
W-175	5	9	Semi-Polished and Polished Ebony (Lacquer)		79,776
W-175	5	9	Polished Ebony (Polyester)		80,863
W-175	5	9	Satin Mahogany/Walnut/Cherry		81,263
W-175	5	9	Semi-Polished & Polished Mahogany/Walnut/Cherry		83,334
W-175	5	9	Open-Pore Walnut		79,303
W-175	5	9	Satin Oak		74,766
W-175	5	9	Chippendale Satin Mahogany/Cherry		83,769
W-175	5	9	Chippendale Semi-Polished & Polished Mahogany/Cherry		85,804
W-190	6	4	Satin Ebony		82,731
W-190	6	4	Semi-Polished and Polished Ebony (Lacquer)		84,817
W-190	6	4	Polished Ebony (Polyester)		85,947
W-190	6	4	Satin Mahogany/Walnut/Cherry		86,339
W-190	6	4	Semi-Polished & Polished Mahogany/Walnut/Cherry		88,485
W-190	6	4	Open-Pore Walnut		84,310
W-190	6	4	Satin Oak		79,598
W-190	6	4	Chippendale Satin Mahogany/Cherry		88,990
W-190	6	4	Chippendale Semi-Polished & Polished Mahogany/Cherry		91,051
WEBER					
Weber Verticals					
W114		45	Satin Ebony	6,210	5,780
W114		45	Polished Ebony	5,950	5,580
W114		45	Polished Mahogany/Walnut/White	6,210	5,780
W114E		45	Polished Ebony w/Chrome	6,470	5,980
W114F		45	Designer Satin Mahogany/Cherry	6,990	6,380
W121		48	Satin Ebony	7,250	6,580
W121		48	Polished Ebony	6,990	6,380
W121		48	Polished Mahogany/Walnut/White	7,250	6,580
W121E		48	Polished Ebony w/Chrome	8,290	7,380
W121N		48	Polished Ebony	7,250	6,580
W131		52	Satin Ebony	8,030	7,180
W131		52	Polished Ebony	7,510	6,780
W131		52	Polished Mahogany	8,030	7,180

*See pricing explanation on page 188.

WEBER (continued)

Albert Weber Verticals

Model	Feet	Inches	Description	MSRP*	SMP*
AW 121		48	Polished Ebony	11,410	9,780
AW 121		48	Satin Mahogany	11,930	10,180
AW 121E		48	Polished Ebony w/Chrome	12,710	10,780
AW 131		52	Satin Ebony	15,050	12,580
AW 131		52	Polished Ebony	14,010	11,780

Weber Grands

Model	Feet	Inches	Description	MSRP*	SMP*
W150	4	11	Satin Ebony	14,270	11,980
W150	4	11	Polished Ebony	13,750	11,580
W150	4	11	Polished Mahogany/Walnut/White	14,270	11,980
W150E	4	11	Polished Ebony w/Chrome	14,530	12,180
W157	5	2	Satin Ebony	15,570	12,980
W157	5	2	Polished Ebony	14,790	12,380
W157	5	2	Polished Mahogany	15,570	12,980
W175	5	9	Satin Ebony	17,910	14,780
W175	5	9	Polished Ebony	16,870	13,980
W185	6	1	Satin Ebony	21,810	17,780
W185	6	1	Polished Ebony	20,770	16,980

Albert Weber Grands

Model	Feet	Inches	Description	MSRP*	SMP*
AW 185	6	1	Satin Ebony	38,970	30,980
AW 185	6	1	Polished Ebony	37,670	29,980
AW 208	6	10	Satin Ebony	47,290	37,380
AW 208	6	10	Polished Ebony	45,990	36,380
AW 228	7	6	Satin Ebony	66,530	52,180
AW 228	7	6	Polished Ebony	65,230	51,180
AW 275	9		Polished Ebony	119,570	92,980

WERTHEIM

Verticals

Model	Feet	Inches	Description	MSRP*	SMP*
W121		48	Polished Ebony	6,999	6,499
W121		48	Polished Mahogany/Walnut/White	7,499	6,899
W121		48	French Polished Ebony	6,999	6,499
W121		48	French Polished Mahogany/Walnut/White	7,499	6,899
WE123		48.5	Polished Ebony	9,999	8,499
WE123		48.5	Polished Mahogany/Walnut/White	10,499	8,949
WE123		48.5	French Polished Ebony	9,999	8,499
WE123		48.5	French Polished Mahogany/Walnut/White	10,499	8,949
WP125		49	San and Polished Ebony	13,999	11,999

Grands

Model	Feet	Inches	Description	MSRP*	SMP*
W153	5	1	Polished Ebony	12,499	10,999
W153	5	1	Polished Mahogany/Walnut/White	12,400	11,999
WE170	5	7	Polished Ebony	18,999	14,999
WE170	5	7	Polished Mahogany/Walnut/White	19,999	15,999
WP180	5	10	Satin and Polished Ebony	29,999	22,999
WP213	7		Polished Ebony	39,999	34,999

YAMAHA

Including Disklavier, Silent, and TransAcoustic Pianos

Verticals

Model	Feet	Inches	Description	MSRP*	SMP*
b1		43	Continental Polished Ebony	4,599	4,599
b1		43	Continental Polished Ebony with Chrome Accents	4,799	4,799
M560		44	Hancock Satin Brown Cherry	6,999	6,999
b2		45	Polished Ebony	6,549	6,398

*See pricing explanation on page 188.

Model	Feet	Inches	Description	MSRP*	SMP*
YAMAHA *(continued)*					
b2		45	Polished Ebony with Chrome Accents	6,749	6,749
b2		45	Polished Mahogany/Walnut	6,959	6,798
P22		45	Satin Ebony/Walnut/Oak	7,349	7,198
P660		45	Sheraton Satin Brown Mahogany	8,929	8,929
P660		45	Queen Anne Satin Brown Cherry	8,929	8,929
b3		48	Polished Ebony	8,159	7,598
b3		48	Polished Ebony with Chrome Accents	8,359	7,998
b3		48	Polished Mahogany/Walnut	9,029	8,198
U1		48	Satin and Polished Ebony	11,199	11,199
U1		48	Satin American Walnut	13,299	13,299
U1		48	Polished Mahogany/White	13,299	13,299
YUS1		48	Satin and Polished Ebony	15,299	14,798
YUS1		48	Satin American Walnut	18,799	17,930
YUS1		48	Polished Mahogany/White	18,799	17,930
U3		52	Polished Ebony	14,259	13,918
U3		52	Satin American Walnut	16,299	16,198
U3		52	Polished Mahogany	16,299	16,198
YUS3		52	Polished Ebony	18,599	17,738
YUS3		52	Polished Mahogany	21,499	20,598
YUS5		52	Polished Ebony	20,699	19,578
SU7		52	Polished Ebony	39,999	38,390
Disklavier Verticals					
DU1E3		48	Satin and Polished Ebony	27,399	25,398
DU1E3		48	Satin American Walnut	29,399	27,398
DU1E3		48	Polished Mahogany/Walnut/White	29,399	27,398
DU1ENST		48	Satin and Polished Ebony	28,199	26,658
DU1ENST		48	Satin American Walnut	30,299	28,858
DU1ENST		48	Polished Mahogany/White	30,299	28,858
DYUS1ENST		48	Satin and Polished Ebony	32,299	29,798
DYUS1ENST		48	Satin American Walnut	35,799	32,930
DYUS1ENST		48	Polished Mahogany/White	35,799	32,930
Silent and TransAcoustic Verticals					
b1SG2		43	Polished Ebony	8,599	8,598
b1SG2		43	Polished Ebony with Chrome Accents	8,799	8,799
b2SG2		45	Polished Ebony	10,549	9,498
b2SG2		45	Polished Ebony with Chrome Accents	10,749	9,898
b2SG2		45	Polished Mahogany/Walnut	10,959	9,898
b3SG2		48	Polished Ebony	12,159	10,698
b3SG2		48	Polished Ebony with Chrome Accents	12,359	11,098
b3SG2		48	Polished Mahogany/Walnut	13,029	11,298
U1SH		48	Satin and Polished Ebony	15,199	14,758
U1SH		48	Satin American Walnut	17,299	16,958
U1SH		48	Polished Mahogany/White	17,299	16,958
U1TA		48	Polished Ebony	17,199	16,758
YUS1SH		48	Satin and Polished Ebony	19,299	17,898
YUS1SH		48	Satin American Walnut	22,799	21,030
YUS1SH		48	Polished Mahogany/White	22,799	21,030
YUS1TA		48	Polished Ebony	21,299	19,898
YUS1TA		48	Polished White	24,799	23,030
U3SH		52	Polished Ebony	18,259	17,018
U3SH		52	Polished Mahogany	20,299	19,298
U3SH		52	Satin American Walnut	20,299	19,298
YUS3SH		52	Polished Ebony	22,599	20,838
YUS3SH		52	Polished Mahogany	25,499	23,698
YUS3TA		52	Polished Ebony	24,599	22,838
YUS5SH		52	Polished Ebony	24,699	22,678
YUS5TA		52	Polished Ebony	26,699	24,678

*See pricing explanation on page 188.

PIANOBUYER.COM

Model	Feet	Inches	Description	MSRP*	SMP*
YAMAHA *(continued)*					
Grands					
GB1K	5		Polished Ebony	14,799	13,858
GB1K	5		Polished American Walnut/Mahogany/White	17,339	16,198
GB1K	5		French Provincial Satin Cherry	19,179	18,598
GB1K	5		Georgian Satin Mahogany	18,359	18,198
GC1M	5	3	Satin and Polished Ebony	23,999	23,598
GC1M	5	3	Satin American Walnut	30,599	28,198
GC1M	5	3	Polished Mahogany/White	30,599	28,198
C1X	5	3	Satin and Polished Ebony	37,499	33,598
C1X	5	3	Satin American Walnut	46,369	41,118
C1X	5	3	Polished Mahogany/White	46,369	41,118
GC2	5	8	Satin and Polished Ebony	28,559	26,650
GC2	5	8	Satin American Walnut	33,559	30,998
GC2	5	8	Polished Mahogany/White	33,559	30,998
C2X	5	8	Satin and Polished Ebony	43,399	39,598
C2X	5	8	Polished Ebony w/Chrome Accents	45,699	41,398
C2X	5	8	Satin American Walnut	53,399	47,938
C2X	5	8	Polished Mahogany/White	53,399	47,938
C3X	6	1	Satin and Polished Ebony	56,999	51,470
C3X	6	1	Satin American Walnut	69,999	62,798
C3X	6	1	Polished Mahogany/White	69,999	62,798
S3X	6	1	Polished Ebony	77,999	74,998
CF4	6	3	Polished Ebony	105,599	105,599
C5X	6	7	Satin and Polished Ebony	62,899	57,198
C5X	6	7	Satin American Walnut	77,799	69,560
C5X	6	7	Polished Mahogany/White	77,799	69,560
S5X	6	7	Polished Ebony	84,999	80,998
C6X	7		Satin and Polished Ebony	70,199	63,718
C6X	7		Satin American Walnut	85,999	77,718
C6X	7		Polished Mahogany/White	85,999	77,718
CF6	7		Polished Ebony	119,999	119,598
C7X	7	6	Satin and Polished Ebony	81,999	73,598
C7X	7	6	Satin American Walnut	99,999	89,478
C7X	7	6	Polished Mahogany/White	99,999	89,478
S7X	7	6	Polished Ebony	104,999	100,998
CFX	9		Polished Ebony	179,999	179,999
Disklavier Grands					
DGB1KE3C	5		Classic Polished Ebony	19,999	19,998
DGB1KENCL	5		Classic Polished Ebony	23,799	22,858
DGB1KE3	5		Polished Ebony	25,399	23,998
DGB1KE3	5		Polished Mahogany/American Walnut/White	32,949	30,698
DGB1KENST	5		Polished Ebony	27,799	25,858
DGB1KENST	5		Polished Mahogany/American Walnut/White	30,339	28,198
DGC1E3S	5	3	Satin and Polished Ebony	39,549	36,798
DGC1E3S	5	3	Satin American Walnut	50,549	46,738
DGC1E3S	5	3	Polished Mahogany/White	50,549	46,738
DGC1ENST	5	3	Satin and Polished Ebony	40,999	38,598
DGC1ENST	5	3	Satin American Walnut	47,599	43,198
DGC1ENST	5	3	Polished Mahogany/White	47,599	43,198
DC1XE3S	5	3	Satin and Polished Ebony	53,549	50,398
DC1XE3S	5	3	Satin American Walnut	60,549	57,798
DC1XE3S	5	3	Polished Mahogany/White	60,549	57,798
DC1XENST	5	3	Satin and Polished Ebony	54,499	48,598
DC1XENST	5	3	Satin American Walnut	63,369	56,118
DC1XENST	5	3	Polished Mahogany/White	63,369	56,118
DGC2E3S	5	8	Satin and Polished Ebony	46,599	43,598
DGC2E3S	5	8	Satin American Walnut	53,099	49,998

*See pricing explanation on page 188.

Model	Feet	Inches	Description	MSRP*	SMP*
YAMAHA (continued)					
DGC2E3S	5	8	Polished Mahogany/White	53,099	49,998
DGC2ENST	5	8	Satin and Polished Ebony	45,559	41,650
DGC2ENST	5	8	Satin American Walnut	50,559	45,998
DGC2ENST	5	8	Polished Mahogany/White	50,559	45,998
DC2XE3S	5	8	Satin and Polished Ebony	63,899	56,198
DC2XE3S	5	8	Polished Ebony w/Chrome Accents	66,899	58,798
DC2XE3S	5	8	Satin American Walnut	73,899	64,998
DC2XE3S	5	8	Polished Mahogany/White	73,899	64,998
DC2XENST	5	8	Satin and Polished Ebony	60,399	54,598
DC2XENST	5	8	Polished Ebony w/Chrome Accents	62,699	56,398
DC2XENST	5	8	Satin American Walnut	70,399	62,938
DC2XENST	5	8	Polished Mahogany/White	70,399	62,938
DC3XE3PRO	6	1	Satin and Polished Ebony	77,999	65,298
DC3XE3PRO	6	1	Satin American Walnut	91,999	77,798
DC3XE3PRO	6	1	Polished Mahogany/White	91,999	77,798
DC3XENPRO	6	1	Satin and Polished Ebony	78,999	69,470
DC3XENPRO	6	1	Satin American Walnut	91,999	80,798
DC3XENPRO	6	1	Polished Mahogany/White	91,999	80,798
DCF4ENPRO	6	3	Polished Ebony	145,599	144,198
DC5XE3PRO	6	7	Satin and Polished Ebony	87,999	73,498
DC5XE3PRO	6	7	Satin American Walnut	100,999	85,698
DC5XE3PRO	6	7	Polished Mahogany/White	100,999	85,698
DC5XENPRO	6	7	Satin and Polished Ebony	84,899	75,198
DC5XENPRO	6	7	Satin American Walnut	99,799	87,560
DC5XENPRO	6	7	Polished Mahogany/White	99,799	87,560
DC6XE3PRO	7		Satin and Polished Ebony	94,999	80,998
DC6XE3PRO	7		Satin American Walnut	110,199	93,898
DC6XE3PRO	7		Polished Mahogany/White	110,199	93,898
DC6XENPRO	7		Satin and Polished Ebony	92,199	81,718
DC6XENPRO	7		Satin American Walnut	107,999	95,718
DC6XENPRO	7		Polished Mahogany/White	107,999	95,718
DCF6ENPRO	7		Polished Ebony	159,999	157,598
DC7XE3PRO	7	6	Satin and Polished Ebony	102,999	87,798
DC7XE3PRO	7	6	Satin American Walnut	117,999	101,898
DC7XE3PRO	7	6	Polished Mahogany/White	117,999	101,898
DC7XENPRO	7	6	Satin and Polished Ebony	103,999	91,598
DC7XENPRO	7	6	Satin American Walnut	121,999	107,478
DC7XENPRO	7	6	Polished Mahogany/White	121,999	107,478
DCFXE3PRO	9		Polished Ebony	259,999	232,598
DCFXENPRO	9		Polished Ebony	219,999	218,998
Silent and TransAcoustic Grands					
GB1KSG2	5		Polished Ebony	18,499	16,558
GB1KSG2	5		Polished Mahogany/Walnut/White	20,999	19,098
GC1SH	5	3	Satin and Polished Ebony	27,579	25,898
GC1SH	5	3	Satin American Walnut	33,999	31,098
GC1SH	5	3	Polished Mahogany/White	33,999	31,098
GC1TA	5	3	Polished Ebony	31,999	30,698
C1XSH	5	3	Satin and Polished Ebony	40,739	36,098
C1XSH	5	3	Satin American Walnut	50,369	44,218
C1XSH	5	3	Polished Mahogany/White	50,369	44,218
C1XTA	5	3	Polished Ebony	45,499	40,698
C1XTA	5	3	Polished White	54,369	48,218
GC2SH	5	8	Satin and Polished Ebony	31,999	29,298
GC2SH	5	8	Satin American Walnut	37,199	34,098
GC2SH	5	8	Polished Mahogany/White	37,199	34,098
C2XSH	5	8	Satin and Polished Ebony	46,499	42,098
C2XSH	5	8	Polished Ebony w/Chrome Accents	48,799	44,098
C2XSH	5	8	Satin American Walnut	57,419	51,038

*See pricing explanation on page 188.

Model	Feet	Inches	Description	MSRP*	SMP*
YAMAHA (continued)					
C2XSH	5	8	Polished Mahogany/White	57,419	51,038
C3XSH	6	1	Satin and Polished Ebony	62,929	53,678
C3XSH	6	1	Satin American Walnut	78,239	65,838
C3XSH	6	1	Polished Mahogany/White	78,239	65,838
C3XTA	6	1	Polished Ebony	64,999	58,570
C3XTA	6	1	Polished White	77,999	69,898
C5XSH	6	7	Satin and Polished Ebony	65,639	59,198
C5XSH	6	7	Satin American Walnut	81,739	72,660
C5XSH	6	7	Polished Mahogany/White	81,739	72,660
C6XSH	7		Satin and Polished Ebony	72,879	65,578
C6XSH	7		Satin American Walnut	90,979	80,818
C6XSH	7		Polished Mahogany/White	90,979	80,818
C7XSH	7	6	Satin and Polished Ebony	83,999	75,298
C7XSH	7	6	Satin American Walnut	105,199	92,578
C7XSH	7	6	Polished Mahogany/White	105,199	92,578

YOUNG CHANG

Verticals

Model	Feet	Inches	Description	MSRP*	SMP*
Y114		45	Polished Ebony	5,370	5,300
Y114		45	Polished Mahogany/Walnut/White	5,870	5,700
Y114E		45	Polished Ebony w/Chrome	6,120	5,900
Y116		46	Polished Ebony	6,870	6,500
Y116		46	Satin Ebony/Walnut	6,870	6,500
Y118		47	Satin Ebony	6,120	5,900
Y118		47	Polished Ebony	5,870	5,700
Y118		47	Polished Mahogany/Walnut	6,120	5,900
Y118R		47	Designer French Satin Cherry	6,870	6,500
Y118R		47	Designer Satin Mahogany	6,870	6,500
Y121		48	Satin Ebony	6,620	6,300
Y121		48	Polished Ebony	6,370	6,100
Y121		48	Polished Mahogany/Walnut	6,620	6,300
Y131		52	Satin Ebony	7,120	6,700
Y131		52	Polished Ebony	6,870	6,500
Y131		52	Polished Mahogany	7,120	6,700

Grands

Model	Feet	Inches	Description	MSRP*	SMP*
Y150	4	11	Satin Ebony	12,870	11,300
Y150	4	11	Polished Ebony	12,370	10,900
Y150	4	11	Polished Mahogany/Walnut/White	12,870	11,300
Y150E	4	11	Polished Ebony w/Chrome	13,120	11,500
Y157	5	2	Satin Ebony	14,370	12,500
Y157	5	2	Polished Ebony	13,370	11,700
Y157	5	2	Polished Mahogany	14,370	12,500
Y175	5	9	Satin Ebony	16,370	14,100
Y175	5	9	Polished Ebony	15,370	13,300
Y185	6	1	Satin Ebony	20,370	17,300
Y185	6	1	Polished Ebony	19,120	16,300

*See pricing explanation on page 188.

IF YOU'VE READ any of the "**Brand and Company Profiles**" on the acoustic side, you'll see that discussions of digital makes and models are of a very different nature. For one thing, although a few manufacturers of digital pianos can trace their roots back over 100 years, such histories, while occasionally fascinating, have little or no relevance to a type of instrument that has existed for only a few dozen years. For another, whereas acoustic piano makers may boast of using slowly grown spruce carefully harvested from trees on north-facing slopes in the Bavarian Alps, there are no stories from digital piano makers of silicon carefully harvested from isolated south-facing beaches during the second low tide of October; no tales of printed circuit boards still crafted by hand as they've been for generations, or descriptions of internal cable harnesses made of only the finest German wire. And while it's interesting to know who was the first to introduce a particular feature, digital pianos, like all modern electronic products, are very much a matter of "What have you done for me *lately*?"

Even more than in the section dedicated to acoustic pianos, the descriptions provided here are only half the story, and must be used in conjunction with the chart of "**Digital Piano Specifications and Prices**" if you are to have a clear picture of a given brand's offerings. In some cases, little information is available or forthcoming regarding a brand, and much that could have been included would simply be a reiteration of marketing statements. In others, specifications or descriptions available from a manufacturer have been in conflict, as when specifications on their website say one thing and the owner's manual says something else. While every effort has been made to ensure the accuracy of these listings and descriptions, some discrepancies will have undoubtedly slipped through.

Blüthner

Blüthner USA LLC
5660 West Grand River
Lansing, Michigan 48906
517-886-6000
800-954-3200
info@bluthnerpiano.com
www.bluthnerpiano.com

Blüthner, one of the world's preeminent piano makers, has released its first line of digital pianos, called the e-Klavier. (For company background, see the Blüthner listing in the "**Brand and Company Profiles**" for acoustic pianos.) Engineered and manufactured in Leipzig, Germany, the e-Klavier line comprises eight models in five styles: a slab, three standard verticals, a decorator vertical called the Pianette, a vertical called Homeline with a solid wood cabinet, and two grand-shaped models.

Blüthner says it has developed a unique approach to sampling and sound modeling, called Authentic Acoustic Behavior, that allows the e-Klavier to reproduce the effect of the aliquot (fourth) string of Blüthner's acoustic pianos. This system also permits the reproduction of advanced harmonics, such as the coincidental partials produced when two notes are played simultaneously, and the sound the dampers make when lifting off the strings. The e-Klavier actions, sourced from Fatar, feature escapement, and wooden keys with "ivory feel" in some models. In the near future, users will be able to download new sounds to the e-Klaviers via the Internet at no charge, and store the sounds of turn-of-the-century Blüthner pianos and other Blüthner models of interest.

The e-Klavier 2 and 3 also contain an actual piano soundboard, which enables these instruments to produce certain aspects of acoustic-piano tone that are difficult or impossible to simulate by purely electronic means.

Blüthner also makes a hybrid-piano system, called "e-volution," that can be installed in any of its acoustic upright or grand models. For more information, see the Blüthner listing in the Acoustic Pianos: Brand and Company Profiles section of this issue.

Casio

Casio USA
570 Mount Pleasant Avenue
Dover, New Jersey 07801
973-361-5400
www.casiomusicgear.com

Kashio Tadao established Casio in 1946. Originally a small subcontractor factory that made parts and gears for microscopes, Casio built Japan's first electric calculator in 1954, which began the company's transformation into the consumer-electronics powerhouse it is today. Perhaps best known for its calculators, digital cameras, and watches, Casio entered the musical instrument business with the launch of the Casiotone in 1980.

Casio's current line of digital pianos consists of nine vertical and five slab models. The Privia line's PX-160 slab is the least expensive ensemble model, and four of the five Privia slabs offer an optional stand-and-pedal module that turns them into three-pedal pianos with support for half-pedaling. At a mere 24 or 25 pounds, they are also some of the lightest digital pianos available. The AP and GP models are marketed under the Celviano label. All Casio digital pianos use a three-sensor, weighted, and scaled (graded) Tri-Sensor hammer action with ebony- and ivory-feel keys. Casio digital pianos are available at music retailers, consumer electronics stores, warehouse clubs, and online.

Dexibell

Dexibell North America
President: Antonio Ferranti
888-588-4099
818-304-1039 (direct)
antonio.ferranti@dexibell.com
www.dexibell.com

Dexibell, made in Italy, was established in 2013 by the R&D and engineering team of the former Roland Europe, with financial backing from parent company Proel S.p.A., an Italian manufacturer of leading brands of professional audio and lighting equipment, musical instruments, and accessories. In 2017, after several years of international success, Proel began distributing the Dexibell brand in North America.

Dexibell uses a suite of patented technologies, called T2L (True to Life), to increase acoustic-piano realism in its instruments. First, whereas the industry standard for sound resolution is 16-bit/44.1kHz (CD quality), Dexibell uses 24-bit/48kHz resolution, resulting in 256 times greater sound resolution and clarity. Second, in comparison to the industry-standard sampling time per note of five seconds or less, Dexibell's samples run for 15 seconds, capturing virtually the entire natural decay of a note, and eliminating the need for the artificial looping found in most of today's digital pianos. Last, Dexibell's Quad Core sound engine contains 320 digital oscillators, allowing for virtually unlimited polyphony and sympathetic resonance.

Dexibell partnered with Ferrari's design firm to create a look for its instruments that is uniquely Italian, with sleek curved lines, and striking color options that include black, white, red, pink, and blue, in matte and polished finishes.

Dexibell produces digital pianos, keyboards, and organs. Its digital piano line is called VIVO (Italian for *alive*), and is available in home, portable, and stage versions. All are Bluetooth-equipped, record and play digital audio, and come with two original apps: the VIVO Editor, for modifying any of the instruments' sound elements, and XMURE, for recording songs and play-along backing tracks with smart accompaniment.

Dynatone

Dynatone America Corporation
15203 Severyns Road
Tustin, California 92782
949-679-5500
www.dynatoneusa.com

Distributed by:
Piano Marketing Group, Inc.
3227 Natoma Way
Orlando, Florida 32825
954-559-9553
scott.shebeck@dynatoneUSA.com

Dynatone, headquartered in Seoul, South Korea, was founded in 1987 as the Electric Instruments Division of the global semiconductor manufacturer Korean Electronics Company (KEC), and was the first maker of electric musical instruments in Korea. It became an independent company in 2000. In addition to digital pianos and MIDI keyboards, Dynatone makes percussion, string, woodwind, and brass instruments, which it exports to more than 30 countries.

Dynatone is offering in the U.S. market two vertical and three grand models, some as standard digital and some as ensemble models. The cabinets come in a variety of finishes and distinctive, contemporary designs, including some with smaller, sleeker designs suitable when space is limited. The new ROS V.5 Plus sound engine contains the clean, realistic sound of a 12-megabyte grand piano sound sample. The wooden-key, triple-sensor, Real Hammer Action (RHA-3W) uses the hammer weight, not springs, to reproduce the touch and feel of an acoustic piano. The flagship model VGP-4000 digital grand is one of the only digital pianos on the market to contain a player-piano feature, and its USB memory stick can store a library of 1,300 songs. All Dynatone models come with a three-year parts and labor warranty.

Flychord

Flychord Instrument Company
327 N. First Street #B
Alhambra, California 91801
626-223-2445
admin@flychord.com
www.flychord.com

Flychord, a new brand of digital piano, is a subsidiary of a company headquartered in Shenzhen, Guangdong Province, China. Flychord currently offers two models in the U.S., the DP330 and DP420K, both ensemble verticals. The DP330 has 500 voices and 210 auto-accompaniment styles. The DP420K, with 40 voices and 50 styles, is more limited as an ensemble instrument, but with its triple-sensor and ivory-textured keys, support for half pedaling, and more elegant furniture styling, it has greater acoustic-piano realism in performance and appearance.

Flychord pianos are distributed in the U.S. by a network of sales agents—piano dealers, studios, and schools—who have demonstrator models to show potential buyers, but who do not stock the instruments themselves. When the customer places an order with the sales agent, the instrument is delivered directly from Flychord, which also handles any future warranty issues. The instruments are also available for purchase from Amazon.com, and directly from the Flychord website.

Galileo

GW Distribution, LLC
P.O. Box 329
Mahwah, New Jersey 07430
845-429-3712
www.galileopianos.com

Galileo is a division of Viscount International, an Italian company that traces its roots back to accordion builder Antonio Galanti, who built his first keyboard instrument in 1890. Today, Viscount is run by the fourth generation of the Galanti family, and distribution in the U.S. is handled by members of the fifth generation. Viscount also makes Physis digital pianos and Viscount organs.

The Galileo collection of digital pianos includes verticals, grands, and ensembles in a variety of colors, finishes, and elegant Italian styling.

Galileo recently introduced VEGA high-definition sound-generation technology, currently available on its new YP and GYP series of digitals.

Kawai

Kawai America Corporation
2055 East University Drive
Rancho Dominguez, California 90220
310-631-1771
800-421-2177
info@kawaius.com
www.kawaius.com

For company background, see the **Kawai** listing in the "**Brand and Company Profiles**" for acoustic pianos.

After more than 50 years as a renowned builder of acoustic pianos, in 1985 Kawai entered the market with its first digital piano. Today, Kawai's digital lineup for North America comprises models in four main groups: Concert Performer (CP), Concert Artist (CA), Classic Series (CS), and CN Series. Other digital models include the CL26, KDP90, KCP90 and CE220. Portable digitals include the ES100 and ES8, and professional models include the MP Series stage pianos and the VPC1 virtual piano controller.

Kawai created the first digital piano to use a transducer-driven soundboard for a more natural piano sound, a feature available in the flagship CA97 and the CS11. Many models offer USB digital audio recording and playback. And if you want a huge library of voices, the models at the upper end of the CP series come with over 1,000 sounds.

Several different types of actions appear in Kawai's digital pianos. Kawai is well-known for its wooden-key digital piano actions, with current versions being the Grand Feel (GF), GFII, RM3II, and AWA PROII. These actions can be found in upper-end models. The Responsive Hammer II (RHII), RHIII, and AHA-IV actions use an industry-standard graded hammer design with plastic keys, and are found in lower-cost and portable models.

Kawai's main lines of digital pianos are sold through a network of authorized local dealers, with certain models also available from Kawai's online store. Professional products and certain other digitals are sold through a combination of authorized online and bricks-and-mortar retailers.

Korg
Korg USA, Inc.
316 South Service Road
Melville, New York 11747
631-390-6800
www.korg.com

Korg was founded in 1962 to produce its first product, an automatic rhythm machine, and in 1972 entered the electronic-organ market. The LP-10 stage piano appeared in 1980, and its first digitally sampled piano, the SG1, was introduced in 1986. Korg now offers seven models of 88-key digital piano, plus several models with shorter keyboards. Following Kawai's lead, Korg recently announced plans to sell its home digital pianos online.

Kurzweil
Kurzweil Music Systems
6000 Phyllis Drive
Cypress, California 90630
657-200-3470
800-874-2880
www.kurzweilmusicsystems.com

Legendary American inventor Ray Kurzweil, perhaps best known for having developed a reading machine for the blind, and hailed by Forbes magazine as "a modern-day Edison," launched Kurzweil Music Systems in 1983, following conversations with Stevie Wonder about the potential for combining the control and flexibility of the computer with the sounds of acoustic instruments. The result, in 1984, was the Kurzweil K250, recognized as the world's first digital piano. In 1990, Boston-based Kurzweil Music Systems was purchased by Young Chang, which continues to operate the division today. Young Chang is part of Korean-based Hyundai Development Company (HDC), one of the largest companies in the world.

Designed and engineered in Boston, Massachusetts, by a team of American sound architects, all Kurzweil home pianos feature the award-winning PC3X sound engine. Kurzweil piano models also feature USB and audio inputs to allow easy expansion via iPads and other external peripherals. Kurzweil pianos and keyboards are available through a combination of musical instrument dealers, piano-specialty stores, and online sources.

Lowrey
Lowrey
989 AEC Drive
Wood Dale, Illinois 60191
708-352-3388
info@lowrey.com
www.lowrey.com

Early research by Chicago industrialist Frederick C. Lowrey produced a working model of an electronic sound source in 1918. The company bearing his name made organs for many years and, for a brief time in the 1980s, pianos. In 1988, Lowrey joined the Kawai family of companies, and is a developer and distributor of Lowrey Virtual Orchestra and digital piano products designed for the consumer market.

Nord
American Music & Sound
22020 Clarendon Street, Suite 305
Woodland Hills, California 91367
800-431-2609
nord@americanmusicandsound.com
www.americanmusicandsound.com
www.nordkeyboards.com

The Nord Piano 2 HA88, successor to the Nord Piano 88, is a professional stage piano that comes with a library of more than 1,000 sounds on a DVD, or downloadable from the Nord Piano website to the instrument via USB. Nord Keyboards are made in Sweden by Clavia DMI AB.

Omega
Piano Empire, Inc.
3035 E. La Mesa Street
Anaheim, California 92806
800-576-3463
714-408-4599
info@omegapianos.com
www.kainopianos.com

Omega is the brand name used in the U.S. for Kaino digital pianos. Established in 1986, Kaino, located in Guangzhou, China, began as a manufacturer of portable keyboards. In 1996, the company expanded to manufacture a full line of 88-note digital pianos, quickly becoming a major provider of keyboards throughout China. In 2010, the Omega brand was established for distribution in North America and Europe.

Physis

Physis Piano
11 Holt Drive
Stony Point, New York 10980
508-457-6771
sales.us@viscount.it
www.viscountinstruments.us

Physis is a division of Viscount International, an Italian company that also makes Galileo digital pianos, among other brands. It has factories and research facilities in San Marino and Italy.

Physis uses physical modeling as the sound source for its instruments. Instead of recorded samples, physical modeling uses advanced mathematical algorithms to reproduce the physical properties of sound, and requires immense computational power that, until recently, was not technologically available. Two international patents have been granted for the Physis technology.

The Physis physical model combines more than 100 elements of the traditional acoustic grand piano sound; e.g., hammer density, string resonance, soundboard size, damper noise, duplex vibration, etc. One of the key advantages of physical modeling is that these elements can be modified by users to create their own unique sounds, and the resulting models can be shared with others, allowing for their continuing evolution. Other advantages include unlimited polyphony, unlimited pedal resolution, and the greater expressiveness that results from the real-time interaction of the physical elements.

Some Physis models have wooden keys with ivory-like keytops and triple sensors, for better expression and a more natural, realistic feel. The H- and V-series pianos have a customizable, multitouch, glass-panel interface that gives the user control of all items on the panel, including display colors. These models also have USB thumb-drive connections for audio and data storage and playback. The Pro and Stage versions are ergonomically designed for portability, and allow maximum flexibility of inputs and outputs.

Physis pianos are sold through a network of professional music retailers.

Roland

Roland Corporation U.S.
5100 South Eastern Avenue
Los Angeles, California 90040
323-890-3700
www.rolandus.com

To simply say that Roland Corporation was established in 1972 is to ignore one of the most compelling stories in the realm of digital pianos. Ikutaro Kakehashi started down the path to Roland Corporation at the age of 16, when he began repairing watches and clocks in postwar Japan. However, his enthusiasm for music meant that his business soon evolved into the repair of radios. At the age of 20, Kakehashi contracted tuberculosis. After three years in the hospital, he was selected for the trial of a new drug, streptomycin, and within a year he was out of the hospital.

In 1954, Kakehashi opened Kakehashi Musen (Kakehashi Radio). Once again, his interest in music intervened, this time leading to his development of a prototype electric organ. In 1960, Kakehashi Radio evolved into Ace Electronic Industries. The FR1 Rhythm Ace became a standard offering of the Hammond Organ Company, and Ace Electronic Industries flourished. Guitar amplifiers, effects units, and more rhythm machines were developed, but as a result of various business-equity involvements, Ace was inadvertently acquired by a company with no interest in musical products, and Kakehashi left in March 1972. One month later, he established Roland Corporation. The first Roland product, not surprisingly, was a rhythm box.

In 1973, Roland introduced its first all-electronic combo piano, the EP-10, followed in 1974 by the EP-30, the world's first electronic piano with a touch-sensitive keyboard. Japan's first genuinely digital pianos for home use were released by Roland in 1975 as part of the early HP series. Next came Roland's portable EP-09 electronic piano in 1980, and the debut of the wood-finish HP-60 and HP-70 compact pianos in 1981. In 1983, Roland released the HP-300 and HP-400, the very first digital pianos with MIDI.

When introduced in 1986, the RD-1000 stage piano was Roland's first entry in what would become the digital piano category. Today, Roland offers more than two dozen models of digital piano covering every facet of the category: slab, vertical, grand, ensemble, and stage instruments.

Of particular interest to those looking for educational features is Roland's HPi model, which includes a substantial suite of educational capabilities supported by an LCD screen mounted on a music desk. The new LX models add traditional-looking vertical pianos to the line. Roland offers one of the widest selections of digital pianos in the industry. The chart of "**Digital Piano Specifications and Prices**" will give you a clear breakdown of the various models and features.

The Roland V-Piano is the first digital piano to rely entirely on physical modeling as its tonal source. Physical modeling breaks down the sound of a piano note into discrete elements that can be represented by mathematical equations, and creates the tone in real time based on a complex series of calculations. There are no acoustic piano samples. For more information about physical modeling, please see, elsewhere in this issue, "**Digital Basics, Part 1: Imitating the Acoustic Piano**" and "**My Other Piano Is a Computer: An Introduction to Software Pianos.**"

The HP models are the core of Roland's offerings in home digital pianos; the latest models, including the new GP607 Digital Grand, share the company's hallmark SuperNATURAL® piano sound engine, premium Progressive Hammer Action with Escapement, and built-in Bluetooth wireless capability, and differ from each other primarily in the specifications of their audio systems and cabinet-types.

Samick

Samick Music Corporation
1329 Gateway Drive
Gallatin, Tennessee 37066
615-206-0077
www.samickdigital.com

Established in 1958, Samick Musical Instrument Mfg. Co. Ltd. is one of the world's leading producers of pianos and guitars (see under **Samick** in the acoustic-piano listings). The company has factories in China, Germany, Indonesia, Korea, and the U.S.

Samick is in the process of revamping its digital piano line, and currently sells one vertical and two grand models. The grands are ensemble digitals with six or eight speakers; the vertical has four speakers and an acoustic-piano–style soundboard. All three have Fatar keyboards with triple-sensor keys and are equipped with Bluetooth.

Samick has instituted a new sales method for its digital pianos. Sales agents—who could be traditional piano dealers, or music teachers, or anyone connected with the music business—have demonstrator models that prospective buyers can try out, but the agents do not stock or deliver the instruments. Instead, the agents assist customers in going online and buying directly from the manufacturer at a non-negotiable price. The piano is then delivered by the manufacturer to the customer's home with "white-glove service": the mover unboxes and sets up the instrument where the customer desires it, then removes the packing materials from the premises. If there is ever a warranty issue, the customer contacts the manufacturer, who uses the same white-glove service to replace the instrument.

Suzuki

Suzuki Corporation
P.O. Box 710459
Santee, California 92072
800-854-1594
www.suzukimusic.com

Suzuki sells its line of digital pianos on its website, through other online outlets, and through Costco. Models change frequently.

Williams

Williams Pianos
P.O. Box 5111
Thousand Oaks, California 91359
www.williamspianos.com

Williams digital pianos are available from Guitar Center stores and the Musician's Friend e-commerce website. The company offers five models, including two verticals, two slabs with optional stand, and one ensemble grand. The sounds on Williams instruments are from the Williams Custom Sound Library, a large collection of high-definition sounds carefully sampled from sought-after acoustic, electric, and vintage keyboards, and unique to Williams digital pianos. Also unique to Williams pianos is the Mod/FX control interface, which enables authentic rotary effects on organs and vibrato on electric pianos. All models come with a free introduction to McCarthy Music educational software.

Yamaha

Yamaha Corporation of America
P.O. Box 6600
Buena Park, California 90622
714-522-9011
800-854-1569
infostation@yamaha.com
usa.yamaha.com

For company background, see the Yamaha listing in the "Brands and Company Profiles" for acoustic pianos.

Yamaha Corporation is the world's largest producer of musical instruments—from the obvious (pianos) to the slightly obscure (bassoon), Yamaha makes it. Yamaha entered the world of electronic instruments in 1959, when it introduced the first all-transistor organ. In 1971, because no manufacturer would develop an integrated circuit (IC) for Yamaha's relatively low-volume demand, the company built its own IC plant. Jumping ahead to 1983, the introduction of the first Yamaha Clavinova, the YP-40, marked the beginning of what we now call the digital piano. Today, Yamaha's three dozen or so models of digital piano (not counting different finishes) constitute the broadest range of any manufacturer. The downside is that deciphering the variety of options—slabs, verticals, grands, stage pianos, ensemble pianos, designer digitals, hybrids—can be a bit daunting. And then there are the sub-brands: Clavinova, Modus, and Arius.

Clavinova digital pianos include the standard CLP line and the ensemble CVP line, and are available only through piano dealers. The Modus models (model numbers beginning with F, H, and R), Yamaha's series of designer digitals, are functionally similar to the CLP line but with modern-looking cabinets. (The Modus H01 and H11 are perhaps the most striking visual designs among digital pianos.) They are now available online through authorized dealers. Arius (model numbers beginning with YDP) represents Yamaha's entry-level line of digital verticals, with the long-popular YDP223 now replaced by the YDP181.

The CP and CP stage models are intended for situations that require a portable instrument. Available at several price points, they are suitable for a wide range of applications, from live performance to studio recording. Some of the models in this line feature Yamaha's new Spectral Component Modeling (SCM) technology, or a combination of SCM and Advanced Wave Memory (AWM) sampling. The model CP1 also includes the NW-Stage action.

Yamaha's apps for iPad, iPhone, and iPod Touch are unique in the digital-piano world. The NoteStar app brings sheet music into the 21st century, and puts you in the band with real audio backing tracks that you can slow down or transpose. MusicSoft Manager lets you manage the content of your CVP Clavinova, while Repertoire Finder provides complete keyboard setups for songs you want to play.

Seven different actions are used in Yamaha digitals. In order of increasing quality, they are: Graded Hammer Standard (GHS), Graded Hammer (GH), Graded Hammer 3 (GH3), Natural Wood (NW), Natural Wood Stage (NW-Stage), Natural Wood Linear Graded Hammer (NW-LGH), and the grand piano action used in the AvantGrand models.

A few years ago, Yamaha introduced its AvantGrand hybrid piano. For more information about the Avant-Grand, see the article on "Hybrid Pianos" elsewhere in this issue.

IN THE SPECIFICATION CHART for each brand of digital piano, we have included those features and specifications about which buyers, in our experience, are most likely to be curious. However, many models have more features than are shown. See the various articles on digital pianos elsewhere in this publication for more information about each of the terms defined below, shown in the order in which they appear in the charts.

Form The physical form of the model: G=Grand, V= Vertical (Console), S=Slab.

Ensemble A digital piano with easy-play and auto-accompaniments (not just rhythms).

Finish The wood finishes or colors available for a particular model (not always specified for slab models). Multiple finish options are separated by a slash (/). A manufacturer's own color term is used where a generic term could not be determined. See the box below for finish codes.

Estimated Price This is our estimate of the price you will pay for the instrument. For digitals sold online or through chain and warehouse outlets, this price is the Minimum Advertised Price (MAP) and is shown in italics. For digitals sold only through bricks-and-mortar piano dealers, the price shown is based on a profit margin that piano dealers typically aspire to when selling digitals, including an allowance for incoming freight and setup. Discounts from this price, if any, typically are small. For more information on MAP and other pricing issues, please read "Buying a Digital Piano," elsewhere in this issue.

MSRP Manufacturer's Suggested Retail Price, also known as "list" or "sticker" price. Not all manufacturers use them.

Sound Source Indicates whether the sound source is Sampling (S) or Physical Modeling (M).

Voices The number of different musical voices the user can select from the instrument panel, plus (if applicable) the number of General MIDI (GM) or XG voices that are not user-selectable but are available for playback of MIDI files.

Key Off Indicates the presence of samples or simulation of Key Off sounds—acoustic piano keys and dampers returning to rest position and cutting off the sounds of vibrating strings.

FINISH CODES	
A	Ash
AG	Amber Glow
Al	Alder
Bl	Blue
Bk	Black
C	Cherry
DB	Deep Brunette
E	Ebony
G	Gold
Iv	Ivory
L	Laquor (used with a wood or color designation)
M	Mahogany
MD	Mahogany Decor
O	Oak
Or	Orange
P	Polished (used with a wood or color designation)
R	Rosewood
Rd	Red
S	Satin (used with a wood or color designation)
Sr	Silver
VR	Velvette Rouge
W	Walnut
WG	Wood Grain (wood type not specified)
Wt	White

Sustain Indicates the presence of samples or simulation of the sound with the sustain pedal depressed (allowing the strings to vibrate sympathetically).

String Resonance Indicates the presence of samples or simulation of String Resonance—the resonance sound of the strings of non-played notes.

Rhythms/Styles The number of rhythms in a standard digital, or the number of auto-accompaniment styles available in an ensemble digital.

Polyphony The maximum number of sounds the instrument can produce simultaneously. UL=Unlimited

Total Watts Total combined amplifier power.

Speakers The number of individual speakers.

Piano Pedals The number of piano pedals supplied with the model. A number in parentheses indicates the availability of an optional pedal unit with additional pedals.

Half Pedal Indicates that the model supports half-pedaling.

Action Indicates the type of action used, if specified.

Triple-Sensor Keys Indicates the presence of three key sensors, instead of the usual two, for greater touch realism.

Escapement Indicates the presence of an acoustic piano action's escapement feel.

Wood Keys Indicates actions with wooden keys.

Ivory Texture Indicates actions with ivory-textured keytops.

Bluetooth Indicates that the instrument is equipped with Bluetooth for connecting to the Internet.

Vocal Support The model supports some level of vocal performance. This support can vary from the piano simply having a microphone input, to its having the ability to produce the vocalist's voice in multi-part harmony, to pitch-correct the notes sung by the vocalist, or to alter the original voice.

Educational Features The model includes features that specifically support the learning experience. Note that while the ability to record and play back is an important learning tool, it is present on almost all models and so is not included in this definition.

External Storage Indicates the type of external memory storage accessible, such as USB or SanDisk.

USB to Computer Indicates the model's ability to interface with a Mac or PC via USB cable.

USB Digital Audio Indicates the ability to record and play back digital audio via a USB flash drive.

Recording Tracks The number of internal recordable tracks for recording of MIDI files.

Warranty (Parts/Labor) Indicates the manufacturer's warranty coverage period: the first number is the length of the parts coverage; the second number is the length of the labor coverage.

Dimensions Width, Depth, and Height are rounded to the nearest inch.

Weight Weight of the model rounded to the nearest pound.

Blüthner

Brand & Model	Form	Ensemble	Finish	Estimated Price	MSRP	Sound Source	Voices	Key Off	Sustain	String Resonance	Rhythms/Styles	Polyphony	Total Watts	Speakers	Piano Pedals	Half Pedal
e-Klavier PRO-88 EX	S		ESL		3,326	S	35+ 256GM	Y	Y	Y		256	60	2	3 (5)	Y
e-Klavier 1	V		ESL/WtSL		5,037	S	21	Y	Y	Y		256	60	2	3	Y
e-Klavier 2	V		ESL/WtSL		6,381	S	35+ 256GM	Y	Y	Y		256	100	4	3	Y
e-Klavier 2	V		EPL		7,389	S	35+ 256GM	Y	Y	Y		256	100	4	3	Y
e-Klavier 3	V		ESL/WtSL		7,358	S	25+ 127GM	Y	Y	Y		256	180	4	3	Y
e-Klavier 3	V		EPL		8,366	S	25+ 127GM	Y	Y	Y		256	180	4	3	Y
e-Klavier Pianette	V		EPL		18,782	S	35+ 256GM	Y	Y	Y		256	200	4	3	Y
e-Klavier Homeline	V		ES		4,701	S	35+ 256GM	Y	Y	Y		256	60	4	3	Y
e-Klavier Homeline	V		Stained wood		5,037	S	35+ 256GM	Y	Y	Y		256	60	4	3	Y
e-Klavier Homeline	V		Waxed beechwood		5,373	S	35+ 256GM	Y	Y	Y		256	60	4	3	Y
e-Grand Studio	V		ESL/WtSL		12,936	S	25+ 127GM	Y	Y	Y		256	150	4	3	Y
e-Grand Studio	V		EPL/WtPL		15,960	S	25+ 127GM	Y	Y	Y		256	150	4	3	Y
e-Grand Concert	G		ESL/WtSL		18,648	S	25+ 127GM	Y	Y	Y		256	150	4	3	Y
e-Grand Concert	G		EPL/WtPL		22,638	S	25+ 127GM	Y	Y	Y		256	150	4	3	Y

Casio

Brand & Model	Form	Ensemble	Finish	Estimated Price	MSRP	Sound Source	Voices	Key Off	Sustain	String Resonance	Rhythms/Styles	Polyphony	Total Watts	Speakers	Piano Pedals	Half Pedal
PX-5S	S		Wt	999	1,399	S	242+ 128GM	Y	Y	Y		256			1(2)	
PX-160	S		Bk/G	499	799	S	18		Y			128	16	2	1(3)	Y
PX-350	S	E	Bk/Wt	699	1,099	S	122+ 128GM		Y	Y	180	128	16	2	1(3)	Y
PX-360	S	E	Bk	899	1,199	S	422+ 128GM	Y	Y	Y	200	128	16	4	1(3)	Y
PX-560	S	E	Bl	1,199	1,599	S	522+ 128GM	Y	Y	Y	230	256	16	4	1(3)	Y
PX-760	V		Bk/W/Wt	699	1,099	S	18		Y	Y		128	16	2	3	Y
PX-770	V		Bk/W/Wt	699	1,099	S	19		Y			128	16	2	3	Y
PX-780	V	E	Bk	899	1,399	S	122+ 128GM		Y	Y	180	128	40	4	3	Y
PX-860	V		Bk/W/Wt	999	1,499	S	18	Y	Y	Y		256	40	4	3	Y
PX-870	V		Bk/W/Wt	999	1,499	S	19	Y	Y	Y		256	40	4	3	Y

Brand & Model	Action	Triple-Sensor Keys	Escapement	Wood Keys	Ivory Texture	Bluetooth	Vocal Support	Educational Features	External Storage	USB to Computer	USB Digital Audio	Recording Tracks	Warranty (Parts/Labor)	Dimensions WxDxH (Inchees)	Weight (Pounds)
Blüthner															
e-Klavier PRO-88 EX	4-zone graded				Y				USB	Y	Y	1	2	55x17x5	30
e-Klavier 1	4-zone graded		Y							Y		1	2	57x22x35	198
e-Klavier 2	4-zone graded			Y	Y	Y			USB	Y	Y	1	2	55x25x42	220
e-Klavier 2	4-zone graded			Y	Y	Y			USB	Y	Y	1	2	55x25x42	220
e-Klavier 3	4-zone graded			Y	Y	Y			USB	Y	Y	1	2	55x25x42	230
e-Klavier 3	4-zone graded			Y	Y	Y			USB	Y	Y	1	2	55x25x42	230
e-Klavier Pianette	4-zone graded			Y	Y	Y			USB	Y	Y	1	2	55x25x42	220
e-Klavier Homeline	4-zone graded		Y			Y			USB	Y	Y	1	2	140x60x35	135
e-Klavier Homeline	4-zone graded		Y			Y			USB	Y	Y	1	2	140x60x35	135
e-Klavier Homeline	4-zone graded		Y			Y			USB	Y	Y	1	2	140x60x35	135
e-Grand Studio	4-zone graded			Y	Y	Y			USB	Y	Y	1	2	51x33x35	225
e-Grand Studio	4-zone graded			Y	Y	Y			USB	Y	Y	1	2	51x33x35	225
e-Grand Concert	4-zone graded			Y	Y	Y			USB	Y	Y	1	2	51x55x35	248
e-Grand Concert	4-zone graded			Y	Y	Y			USB	Y	Y	1	2	51x55x35	248
Casio															
PX-5S	Weighted, Scaled, Hammer Action	Y			Y				USB	Y	Y	8	3/3	52x11x5	24
PX-160	Weighted, Scaled, Hammer Action	Y			Y			Y		Y		2	3/3	52x12x6	26
PX-350	Weighted, Scaled, Hammer Action	Y			Y			Y	USB	Y	Y	17	3/3	52x11x6	25
PX-360	Weighted, Scaled, Hammer Action	Y			Y			Y	USB	Y	Y	17	3/3	52x12x6	26
PX-560	Weighted, Scaled, Hammer Action	Y			Y			Y	USB	Y	Y	17	3/3	52x12x6	27
PX-760	Weighted, Scaled, Hammer Action	Y			Y			Y		Y		2	3/3	53x12x33	71
PX-770	Weighted, Scaled, Hammer Action	Y			Y			Y		Y		12	3/3	55x12x31	69
PX-780	Weighted, Scaled, Hammer Action	Y			Y			Y	USB	Y	Y	17	3/3	53x12x33	70
PX-860	Weighted, Scaled, Hammer Action	Y			Y			Y	USB	Y	Y	2	3/3	53x12x33	82
PX-870	Weighted, Scaled, Hammer Action	Y			Y			Y	USB	Y	Y	2	3/3	55x12x30	76

Brand & Model	Form	Ensemble	Finish	Estimated Price	MSRP	Sound Source	Voices	Key Off	Sustain	String Resonance	Rhythms/Styles	Polyphony	Total Watts	Speakers	Piano Pedals	Half Pedal
Casio (*continued*)																
CGP-700	V	E	Bk	799	1,099	S	422+ 128GM		Y		200	128	40	6	1(3)	Y
AP-260	V		Bk/W	1,049	1,499	S	18		Y			128	16	2	3	Y
AP-270	V		Bk/W/Wt	1,049	1,499	S	22		Y			192	16	2	3	Y
AP-460	V		Bk/W	1,499	1,899	S	18	Y	Y	Y		256	40	4	3	Y
AP-650	V	E	Bk	1,899	2,299	S	122+ 128GM	Y	Y	Y	180	256	60	4	3	Y
AP-700	V		Bk	2,499	2,999	S	26	Y	Y	Y		256	60	6	3	Y
GP-300	V		Bk/Wt	3,636	3,999	S	26	Y	Y	Y		256	100	6	3	Y
GP-400	V		Bk	4,273	4,999	S	35	Y	Y	Y		256	100	6	3	Y
GP-500	V		BkP	4,909	5,999	S	35	Y	Y	Y		256	100	6	3	Y
Dexibell																
VIVO S7	S	E	Bk	1,799	2,199		79	Y	Y	Y		UL	0	0	0 (3)	Y
VIVO P7	S	E	Bk	1,499	1,699		79	Y	Y	Y		UL	70	2	0 (2)	Y
VIVO H3	V	E	Bk/Wt		2,399		79	Y	Y	Y		UL	70	4	3	Y
VIVO H7	V	E	Bk/Wt/		2,999		79	Y	Y	Y		UL	112	5	3	Y
VIVO H7	V	E	EP/WtP		3,499		79	Y	Y	Y		UL	112	5	3	Y
Dynatone																
SDP-600	V		EP	3,809	5,795	S	33+ 128GM		Y	Y		256	100	4	3	Y
SDP-600	V		WtP	3,991	6,095	S	33+ 128GM		Y	Y		256	100	4	3	Y
SLP-210	V		R	1,627	2,195	S	18+ 128GM					81	24	2	3	
SLP-250H	V		Bk	2,173	3,095	S	33+ 128GM		Y	Y		256	30	4	3	Y
DPR-3200H	V	E	Bk	2,900	4,195	S	188	Y	Y	Y	80	256	100	4	3	Y
DPR-3500	V	E	Bk	3,445	5,095	S	188	Y	Y	Y	80	256	100	6	3	Y
SGP-500	G		EP	4,991	7,395	S	33+ 128GM					128	100	4	3	
SGP-600	G		EP	5,173	7,695	S	33+ 128GM		Y	Y		256	100	4	3	Y
SGP-600	G		WtP	5,355	7,995	S	33+ 128GM		Y	Y		256	100	4	3	Y
GPR-3500	G	E	EP	5,900	8,895	S	188	Y	Y	Y	80	256	100	6	3	Y
GPR-3500	G	E	WtP	6,082	9,195	S	188	Y	Y	Y	80	256	100	6	3	Y
VGP-4000	G	E	EP	9,173	14,495	S	188	Y	Y	Y	80	256	100	6	3	Y
VGP-4000	G	E	WtP	9,355	14,795	S	188	Y	Y	Y	80	256	100	6	3	Y

Brand & Model	Action	Triple-Sensor Keys	Escapement	Wood Keys	Ivory Texture	Bluetooth	Vocal Support	Educational Features	External Storage	USB to Computer	USB Digital Audio	Recording Tracks	Warranty (Parts/Labor)	Dimensions WxDxH (Inchees)	Weight (Pounds)
Casio *(continued)*															
CGP-700	Weighted, Scaled, Hammer Action	Y			Y			Y	USB	Y	Y	16	3/3	52x12x31	57
AP-260	Weighted, Scaled, Hammer Action	Y			Y			Y		Y		2	5/5	54x17x33	87
AP-270	Weighted, Scaled, Hammer Action	Y			Y			Y		Y		2	5/5	56x17x32	81
AP-460	Weighted, Scaled, Hammer Action	Y			Y			Y	USB	Y	Y	2	5/5	54x17x33	89
AP-650	Weighted, Scaled, Hammer Action	Y			Y			Y	USB	Y	Y	17	5/5	54x17x36	111
AP-700	Weighted, Scaled, Hammer Action	Y			Y			Y	USB	Y	Y	2	5/5	54x17x36	106
GP-300	Weighted, Scaled, Hammer Action	Y		Y	Y			Y	USB	Y	Y	2	5/5	57x19x38	171
GP-400	Weighted, Scaled, Hammer Action	Y		Y	Y			Y	USB	Y	Y	2	5/5	58x19x39	189
GP-500	Weighted, Scaled, Hammer Action	Y		Y	Y			Y	USB	Y	Y	2	5/5	57x19x38	171
Dexibell															
VIVO S7	Weighted	Y			Y	Y		Y	USB	Y	Y		3	52x15x5	39
VIVO P7	Weighted	Y				Y		Y	USB	Y	Y		3	52x15x5	32
VIVO H3	Weighted	Y				Y		Y	USB	Y	Y		5	56x14x31	97
VIVO H7	Weighted, graded	Y			Y	Y		Y	USB	Y	Y		5	56x14x31	137
VIVO H7	Weighted, graded	Y			Y	Y		Y	USB	Y	Y		5	56x14x31	137
Dynatone															
SDP-600	RHA-3W	Y		Y				Y		Y		1	3/3	55x16x39	218
SDP-600	RHA-3W	Y		Y				Y		Y		1	3/3	55x16x39	218
SLP-210	New RHA							Y		Y		2	3/3	54x16x33	75
SLP-250H	ARHA-I				Y			Y		Y		1	3/3	54x16x33	95
DPR-3200H	ARHA-3I	Y			Y			Y	USB	Y		2	3/3	55x19x35	127
DPR-3500	RHA-3W	Y		Y			Y	Y	USB	Y		2	3/3	55x19x35	119
SGP-500	ARHA									Y		1	3/3	55x36x11	176
SGP-600	RHA-3W	Y		Y				Y		Y		1	3/3	55x36x31	176
SGP-600	RHA-3W	Y		Y				Y		Y		1	3/3	55x36x31	176
GPR-3500	RHA-3W	Y		Y			Y	Y	USB	Y		2	3/3	56x46x36	209
GPR-3500	RHA-3W	Y		Y			Y	Y	USB	Y		2	3/3	56x46x36	209
VGP-4000	RHA-3W	Y		Y			Y	Y	USB	Y		2	3/3	60x56x40	440
VGP-4000	RHA-3W	Y		Y			Y	Y	USB	Y		2	3/3	60x56x40	440

Brand & Model	Form	Ensemble	Finish	Estimated Price	MSRP	Sound Source	Voices	Key Off	Sustain	String Resonance	Rhythms/Styles	Polyphony	Total Watts	Speakers	Piano Pedals	Half Pedal
Flychord																
DP330	V	E	R	999	1,499	S	500		Y		210	128	90	4	3	
DP420K	V	E	W	1,199	1,699	S	40		Y	Y	50	128	130	4	3	Y
Galileo																
YP200	V		R	2,495	3,495	S	19		Y	Y		128	80	4	3	
YP300	V		R	2,995	3,995	S	20		Y	Y		128	100	4	3	
YP300	V		EP	3,495	4,495	S	20		Y	Y		128	100	4	3	
Milano II	V	E	R	4,995	5,995	S	138				100	64	40	4	3	
GYP300	G		EP/MP/WtP	6,995	8,995	S	20		Y	Y		128	120	4	3	
Aria	G		EP	8,995	10,495	S	16		Y	Y		64	180	4	3	
Milano 3G	G	E	EP	5,995	7,995	S	138				100	64	120	4	3	
Maestro II	G	E	EP	9,995	11,995	S	128		Y	Y	128	128	250	5	3	
Maestro II	G	E	WtP	10,495	12,495	S	128		Y	Y	128	128	250	5	3	
Maestro II	G	E	MP	11,995	13,995	S	128		Y	Y	128	128	250	5	3	
Kawai																
ES110	S			729	1,049	S	19	Y	Y	Y	100	192	26	2	1	Y
MP7	S			1,799	2,199	S	256	Y	Y	Y	100	256			1	Y
MP11	S			2,799	3,299	S	40	Y	Y	Y	100	256			3	Y
VPC1	S			1,849	2,149		0								3	Y
ES8	S		Bk/Wt	1,999	2,499	S	34	Y	Y	Y	100	256	30	2	1 (3)	Y
CL26	V		R	1,099	1,495	S	8		Y			96	30	2	1	Y
CE220	V		ES	1,899	2,199	S	22		Y	Y	100	192	40	2	3	Y
KDP90	V		R	1,149	1,499	S	15	Y		Y		192	26	2	3	Y
CN27	V		R	1,899	2,299	S	19	Y		Y		192	40	2	3	Y
CN37	V		R	2,599	3,199	S	352	Y	Y	Y	100	256	40	4	3	Y
CN37	V		W/ES	2,699	3,299	S	352	Y	Y	Y	100	256	40	4	3	Y
CA67	V		R	3,464	4,199	S	60	Y	Y	Y	100	256	100	4	3	Y
CA67	V		M/ES	3,555	4,299	S	60	Y	Y	Y	100	256	100	4	3	Y
CA97	V		R	4,655	5,899	S	80	Y	Y	Y	100	256	135	6	3	Y
CA97	V		ES	4,755	5,999	S	80	Y	Y	Y	100	256	135	6	3	Y
CS8	V		EP	4,536	5,699	S	60	Y	Y	Y	100	256	100	4	3	Y
CS11	V		EP	6,536	8,499	S	80	Y	Y	Y	100	256	135	6	3	Y
KCP90	V	E	R	2,536	2,999	S	381	Y		Y	100	192	40	2	3	Y
CP3	V	E	R	4,354	5,999	S	700+	Y	Y	Y	183	256	100	2	3	Y
CP3	V	E	ES	4,445	6,099	S	700+	Y	Y	Y	215	256	100	2	3	Y
CP2	V	E	R	5,809	8,999	S	900+	Y	Y	Y	425	256	100	4	3	Y
CP2	V	E	M/ES	5,900	9,199	S	900+	Y	Y	Y	425	256	100	4	3	Y
CP1	G	E	EP	16,690	21,999	S	1000+	Y	Y	Y	425	256	200	9	3	Y

Brand & Model	Action	Triple-Sensor Keys	Escapement	Wood Keys	Ivory Texture	Bluetooth	Vocal Support	Educational Features	External Storage	USB to Computer	USB Digital Audio	Recording Tracks	Warranty (Parts/Labor)	Dimensions WxDxH (Inches)	Weight (Pounds)
Flychord															
DP330	Weighted, scaled							Y		Y	Y	1	1/1	54x19x33	92
DP420K	Weighted, scaled	Y	Y		Y			Y		Y	Y	1	1/1	55x20x35	130
Galileo															
YP200	Grand Response									Y			4/1	54x17x39	119
YP300	Graded Hammer									Y		3	4/1	54x20x41	137
YP300	Graded Hammer									Y		3	4/1	54x20x41	137
Milano II	Graded Hammer									Y		3	4/1	56x20x34	154
YP300G	Graded Hammer									Y		3	4/1	56x29x35	209
Aria	AGT Pro		Y	Y						Y		2	4/1	54x38x56	315
Milano 3G	Graded Hammer									Y		3	4/1	56x29x35	200
Maestro II	AGT Pro		Y				Y	Y	USB	Y		5	4/1	54x39x35	345
Maestro II	AGT Pro		Y				Y	Y	USB	Y		5	4/1	54x39x35	345
Maestro II	AGT Pro		Y				Y	Y	USB	Y		5	4/1	54x39x35	345
Kawai															
ES110	RHC					Y		Y				1	3/3	52x11x6	26
MP7	RHII	Y	Y		Y				USB	Y	Y	1	3/1	53x13x7	45
MP11	GF	Y	Y	Y	Y				USB	Y	Y	1	3/1	58x18x8	77
VPC1	RM3II	Y	Y	Y	Y				USB	Y			3/1	54x18x8	65
ES8	RHIII	Y	Y		Y				USB	Y	Y	2	3/3	54x15x6	46
CL26	AHA IV-F												3/3	51x11x31	63
CE220	AWA PROII			Y					USB	Y		2	3/3	54x20x35	137
KDP90	AHA IV-F							Y		Y		1	3/3	56x16x34	84
CN27	RHIII	Y	Y		Y	Y		Y		Y		1	5/5	54x16x34	99
CN37	RHIII	Y	Y		Y	Y		Y	USB	Y	Y	2	5/5	55x19x36	122
CN37	RHIII	Y	Y		Y	Y		Y	USB	Y	Y	2	5/5	55x19x36	122
CA67	GFII	Y	Y	Y	Y			Y	USB	Y	Y	2	5/5	57x19x36	161
CA67	GFII	Y	Y	Y	Y			Y	USB	Y	Y	2	5/5	57x19x36	161
CA97	GFII	Y	Y	Y	Y			Y	USB	Y	Y	2	5/5	58x19x37	192
CA97	GFII	Y	Y	Y	Y			Y	USB	Y	Y	2	5/5	58x19x37	192
CS8	GFII	Y	Y	Y	Y			Y	USB	Y	Y	2	5/5	57x19x37	176
CS11	GFII	Y	Y	Y	Y			Y	USB	Y	Y	2	5/5	60x21x41	225
KCP90	AHA IV-F									Y		2	3/3	54x19x34	105
CP3	RHII	Y	Y		Y			Y	USB	Y		16	5/5	56x23x38	224
CP3	RHII	Y	Y		Y			Y	USB	Y		16	5/5	56x23x38	224
CP2	GF	Y	Y	Y	Y		Y	Y	USB	Y	Y	16	5/5	56x23x38	248
CP2	GF	Y	Y	Y	Y		Y	Y	USB	Y	Y	16	5/5	56x23x38	248
CP1	GF	Y	Y	Y	Y		Y	Y	USB	Y	Y	16	5/5	59x63x39	430

Brand & Model	Form	Ensemble	Finish	Estimated Price	MSRP	Sound Source	Voices	Key Off	Sustain	String Resonance	Rhythms/Styles	Polyphony	Total Watts	Speakers	Piano Pedals	Half Pedal
Korg																
B1	S		Bk/Wt	500	700	S	8		Y	Y		120	9	2	1	
SP280	S		Bk/Wt	700	980	S	30					120	22	2	1	Y
SV-1-88	S		Bk	1,750	2,380	S	36		Y	Y		80	15	2	1 (3)	Y
LP180	V		Bk/Wt	600	980	S	10					120	11	2	3	Y
LP380	V		Bk/Wt/R	850	1,400	S	30					120	22	2	3	Y
B1SP	V		Bk/Wt	600	850	S	8		Y	Y		120	9	2	3	
G1 Air	V		Bk/Wt/WG	1,400	2,000	S	32	Y	Y	Y		120	20	4	3	Y
Kurzweil																
MPS-10	S		Bk	699	999	S	88	Y	Y		78	64	30	2	1	
MPS-10F	S		Bk	799	1,799	S	88	Y	Y		78	64	30	2	1	
MPS-20	S		Bk	999	1,499	S	200	Y	Y		100	64	30	4	1	
MPS-20F	S		Bk	1,199	1,799	S	200	Y	Y		100	64	30	4	1	
KA-90	S	E	Bk	599	699	S	20		Y		50	128	60	4	1	
KA-110	S	E	Bk	699	899	S	583		Y		230	128	80	4	1	
CUP-1	V		EP	2,999	3,999	S	1		Y	Y		256	100	4	3	Y
CUP-2	V		R	2,999	4,499	S	88	Y	Y		78	64	140	4	3	
CUP-2	V		EP	3,499	5,299	S	88	Y	Y		78	64	140	4	3	
CUP-2A	V		EP	3,999	5,999	S	88	Y	Y			128	150	6	3	
CUP-110	V		R	1,199	2,799	S	88	Y	Y			128	45	4	3	
CUP-110	V		EP	2,299	3,395	S	88	Y	Y			128	45	4	3	
CUP-120	V		R	1,399	2,599	S	88	Y	Y		78	128	45	4	3	
CUP-120	V		EP	1,499	3,399	S	88	Y	Y		78	128	45	4	3	
CUP-220	V		R	1,199	3,999	S	88	Y	Y			128	45	4	3	
CUP-310	V		R	2,799	2,799	S	88	Y	Y		69	128	50	4	3	Y
CUP-320	V		R	2,499	3,999	S	88	Y	Y		69	128	50	4	3	Y
KA-130	V		R	899	1,199	S	16		Y			32	30	2	3	Y
KA-150	V		R	899	1,099	S	128		Y		26	68	40	2	3	
M-130	V		R	899	1,199	S	20		Y			128	40	2	3	
M-210	V	E	R	1,299	1,599	S	20		Y		12	128	30	2	3	
M-230	V	E	R	1,299	1,599	S	30		Y		40	128	20	2	3	
M3W	V		R	1,999	3,699	S	200	Y	Y		100	64	50	4	3	
M3W	V		Wt	1,899	3,699	S	200	Y	Y		100	64	50	4	3	
MP-10	V		R	1,299	2,299	S	88	Y	Y		78	64	30	4	3	
MP-10	V		EP	1,499	2,799	S	88	Y	Y		78	64	30	4	3	
MP-10F	V		R	1,499	2,499	S	88	Y	Y		78	64	30	4	3	
MP-10F	V		EP	1,699	2,999	S	88	Y	Y		78	64	30	4	3	
MP-15	V		R	1,599	2,399	S	128	Y	Y		60	64	30	4	3	
MP-20	V		R	1,799	2,799	S	200	Y	Y	Y	100	64	45	4	3	

Brand & Model	Action	Triple-Sensor Keys	Escapement	Wood Keys	Ivory Texture	Bluetooth	Vocal Support	Educational Features	External Storage	USB to Computer	USB Digital Audio	Recording Tracks	Warranty (Parts/Labor)	Dimensions WxDxH (Inches)	Weight (Pounds)
Korg															
B1	NH												1/1	52x14x5	27
SP280	NH												1/1	54x16x31	42
SV-1-88	RH3									Y			1/1	53x14x6	45
LP180	NH												1/1	54x11x31	51
LP380	RH3												1/1	53x14x30	82
B1SP	NH												1/1	52x14x30	45
G1 Air	RH3					Y				Y			1/1	53x15x33	91
Kurzweil															
MPS-10	Weighted/LK									Y		1	3/2	51x14x4	40
MPS-10F	Weighted/Fatar									Y		1	3/2	51x14x4	40
MPS-20	Weighted/LK		Y							Y		2	3/2	52x14x4	40
MPS-20F	Weighted/Fatar		Y							Y		2	3/2	52x14x4	40
KA-90	Weighted								SD			1	3/2	54x14x5	27
KA-110	Weighted						Y		SD	Y		6	3/2	54x15x6	44
CUP-1	Weighted, graded					Y	Y			Y	Y		3/2	56x17x42	221
CUP-2	Weighted, graded		Y	Y						Y		1	3/2	56x17x42	214
CUP-2	Weighted, graded		Y	Y						Y		1	3/2	56x17x42	214
CUP-2A	Weighted, graded		Y	Y			Y			Y		1	3/2	56x17x42	225
CUP-110	Weighted							Y		Y		1	3/2	56x20x35	132
CUP-110	Weighted							Y		Y		1	3/2	56x20x35	132
CUP-120	Weighted							Y		Y		1	3/2	56x20x35	132
CUP-120	Weighted							Y		Y		1	3/2	56x20x35	132
CUP-220	Weighted, graded		Y	Y				Y		Y		1	3/2	55x17x34	115
CUP-310	Weighted, graded	Y						Y		Y		1	3/2	56x19x35	105
CUP-320	Weighted, graded	Y		Y				Y		Y		1	3/2	56x19x35	105
KA-130	Weighted							Y		Y		1	3/2	54x17x34	96
KA-150	Weighted						Y	Y		Y			3/2	54x20x34	119
M-130	Weighted									Y			3/2	56x17x34	135
M-210	Weighted, graded							Y		Y		1	3/2	55x16x33	112
M-230	Weighted, graded					Y	Y	Y		Y		1	3/2	55x19x33	124
M3W	Weighted, graded		Y	Y						Y		2	3/2	54x35x19	135
M3W	Weighted, graded		Y	Y						Y		2	3/2	54x35x19	135
MP-10	Weighted/LK									Y		1	3/2	56x19x35	115
MP-10	Weighted/LK									Y		1	3/2	56x19x35	115
MP-10F	Weighted/Fatar									Y		1	3/2	56x19x35	115
MP-10F	Weighted/Fatar									Y		1	3/2	56x19x35	115
MP-15	Weighted									Y		2	3/2	54x20x34	104
MP-20	Weighted, graded/LK		Y							Y		2	3/2	55x20x35	156

Brand & Model	Form	Ensemble	Finish	Estimated Price	MSRP	Sound Source	Voices	Key Off	Sustain	String Resonance	Rhythms/Styles	Polyphony	Total Watts	Speakers	Piano Pedals	Half Pedal
Kurzweil (continued)																
MP-20	V		EP	1,999	2,999	S	200	Y	Y	Y	100	64	45	4	3	
MP-20F	V		R	1,999	3,499	S	200	Y	Y	Y	100	64	45	4	3	
MP-20F	V		EP	2,499	3,999	S	200	Y	Y	Y	100	64	45	4	3	
KAG-100	G	E	EP	2,499	3,999	S	200		Y		100	64	35	4	3	
MPG-100	G	E	EP	3,999	5,999	S	500		Y		200	128	60	4	3	
MPG-200	G		EP	5,995	6,999	S	200	Y	Y		100	64	200	4	3	
CGP-220W	G		EP	5,999	6,999	S	128	Y	Y		100	128	200	4	3	
Lowrey																
EZP7	V	E	Bk	2,909	2,995	S	72				24	256	30	2	3	
Nord																
Nord Piano 2 HA88	S		Rd	2,499	2,999	S	1000+			Y		40-60			3	Y
Nord Piano 3	S		Rd	2,999	3,399	S	1000+			Y		40-60			3	Y
Omega																
CR-202	V	E	M	1,960	2,595	S	96				96	128	40	2	3	
CR-301	V	E	M	2,520	3,360	S	128				100	128	40	2	3	
LX-502	V	E	M	3,240	4,050	S	128				100	128	80	4	3	
LX-505	V	E	M	3,560	4,620	S	128				200	128	80	4	3	
LX-505	V	E	EP	4,388	5,620	S	128				200	128	80	4	3	
LX-802	G	E	EP	6,888	8,610	S	128				200	128	80	4	3	
Physis																
H1	S		Alu	4,390	4,995	M	192	Y	Y	Y		UL			3	Y
H2	S		Alu	3,800	4,295	M	192	Y	Y	Y		UL			3	Y
K4EX	S		Bl	3,250	3,795	M	192	Y	Y	Y		UL			3	Y
V100	V		PE/PRd/PWt/ SG/PBl	9,695	9,695	M	192	Y	Y	Y		UL	150	6	3	Y
Roland																
RD-2000	S		Bk	2,499	2,999	M/S	1100+	Y	Y	Y	200	UL/128	0	0	1 (3)	Y
V-Piano	S		Bk	6,999	7,999	M	24	Y	Y	Y		264	0	0	3	Y
FP-30	S	E	Bk/Wt	699	899	M/S	35	Y	Y	Y	8	128	22	2	1 (3)	Y
FP-30C	V	E	Bk/Wt	875	1,137	M/S	35	Y	Y	Y	8	128	22	2	3	Y
FP-50	S	E	Bk/Wt	1,299	1,799	M/S	372	Y	Y	Y	90	128	24	2	1 (3)	Y
FP-50C	V	E	Bk/Wt	1,499	2,099	M/S	372	Y	Y	Y	90	128	24	2	1 (3)	Y

Brand & Model	Action	Triple-Sensor Keys	Escapement	Wood Keys	Ivory Texture	Bluetooth	Vocal Support	Educational Features	External Storage	USB to Computer	USB Digital Audio	Recording Tracks	Warranty (Parts/Labor)	Dimensions WxDxH (Inchees)	Weight (Pounds)
Kurzweil *(continued)*															
MP-20	Weighted, graded/ LK		Y							Y		2	3/2	55x20x35	156
MP-20F	Weighted, graded/ Fatar									Y		2	3/2	55x20x35	156
MP-20F	Weighted, graded/ Fatar									Y		2	3/2	55x20x35	156
KAG-100	Weighted					Y		Y	USB	Y	Y	2	3/2	56x30x35	150
MPG-100	Weighted, graded	Y						Y		Y		6	3/2	56x36x35	212
MPG-200	Weighted, graded									Y		2	3/2	55x35x34	221
CGP-220W	Weighted, graded		Y	Y						Y		2	3/2	55x35x34	221
Lowrey															
EZP7	RHA				Y			Y					2/1	54x14x31	80
Nord															
Nord Piano 2 HA88										Y			1/1	51x13x5	40
Nord Piano 3		Y								Y			1/1	51x13x5	40
Omega															
CR-202	Graded Weighted								USB	Y		1	1/90		
CR-301	Fatar Graded								USB	Y		5	1/90		
LX-502	Fatar Graded								USB	Y	Y	7	1/90		
LX-505	Premium Fatar Graded								USB	Y	Y	7	1/90		
LX-505	Premium Fatar Graded								USB	Y	Y	7	1/90		
LX-802	Premium Fatar Graded								USB	Y	Y	7	1/90		
Physis															
H1	Tri-sensor, Hybrid	Y	Y	Y	Y				USB	Y	Y	16	3/1	54x13x4	58
H2	Lightweight Hammer, 3 sensors	Y	Y						USB	Y	Y	16	3/1	54x13x4	45
K4EX	Tri-sensor, Hybrid	Y	Y						USB	Y	Y	16	3/1	51x14x5	40
V100	Tri-sensor, Hybrid	Y	Y	Y	Y				USB	Y	Y	16	3/1	58x17x46	233
Roland															
RD-2000	PHA-50 Concert	Y	Y	Y	Y				USB	Y	Y	1	3/2	56x15x6	55
V-Piano	PHA III	Y	Y		Y				USB	Y	Y	0	3/2	56x21x7	84
FP-30	PHA-4 Standard	Y	Y		Y	Y		Y	USB	Y	Y	1	5/2	51x11x6	31
FP-30C	PHA-4 Standard	Y	Y		Y	Y		Y	USB	Y	Y	1	5/2	51x13x36	57
FP-50	Ivory Feel-G	Y	Y		Y				USB		Y	2	5/2	53x12x5	37
FP-50C	Ivory Feel-G	Y	Y		Y				USB		Y	2	5/2	53x16x37	64

Roland (continued)

Brand & Model	Form	Ensemble	Finish	Estimated Price	MSRP	Sound Source	Voices	Key Off	Sustain	String Resonance	Rhythms/Styles	Polyphony	Total Watts	Speakers	Piano Pedals	Half Pedal
FP-60	S	E	Bk/Wt	1,399	1,699	M/S	355	Y	Y	Y	21	288	26	2	1 (3)	Y
FP-90	S	E	Bk/Wt	1,799	2,199	M	355	Y	Y	Y	21	UL/384	60	4	1 (3)	Y
FP-90C	V	E	Bk/Wt	2,140	2,627	M	355	Y	Y	Y	21	UL/384	60	4	3	Y
DP-603	V	E	Bk	2,399	2,899	M	319	Y	Y	Y	21	UL/384	24	2	3	Y
DP-603	V	E	EP/WtP	3,199	3,699	M	319	Y	Y	Y	21	UL/384	24	2	3	Y
HP-504	V		R/ES	2,199	2,499	M/S	350	Y	Y	Y		128	24	2	3	Y
HP-601	V	E	R/ES/Wt	2,199	2,599	M/S	319	Y	Y	Y	21	288	28	2	3	Y
HP-603	V	E	R/ES/Wt	2,999	3,399	M	319	Y	Y	Y	21	UL/384	60	2	3	Y
HP-603A	V	E	R/ES/Wt	2,999	3,399	M	319	Y	Y	Y	21		60	2	3	Y
HP-605	V	E	EP	4,199	4,699	M	319	Y	Y	Y	21	UL/384	74	6	3	Y
HP-605	V	E	R/ES/Wt	3,699	4,199	M	319	Y	Y	Y	21	UL/384	74	6	3	Y
HPi-50e	V	E	R	4,499	4,999	M/S	350	Y	Y	Y	50	128	74	4	3	Y
LX-7	V	E	EP	5,799	6,599	M	319	Y	Y	Y	21		74	6	3	Y
LX-7	V	E	W/ES	5,299	5,999	M	319	Y	Y	Y	21	UL/384	74	6	3	Y
LX-17	V	E	EP/WtP	6,299	7,299	M	319	Y	Y	Y	21	UL/384	74	8	3	Y
F-140R	V	E	ES/Wt	1,199	1,399	M/S	316	Y	Y	Y	72	128	24	2	3	Y
RP-102	V	E	Bk	999	1,199	M/S	318	Y	Y	Y	21	128	12	2	3	Y
RP-501R	V	E	Bk/Wt/R	1,499	1,799	M/S	316	Y	Y	Y	72	128	24	2	3	Y
GP-7 (V-Piano Grand)	G		EP	19,950	22,999	M	30	Y	Y	Y		264	240	8	3	Y
GP-607 (Mini Grand)	G	E	EP/WtP	5,999	6,999	M	319	Y	Y	Y	21		70	5	3	Y

Samick

Brand & Model	Form	Ensemble	Finish	Estimated Price	MSRP	Sound Source	Voices	Key Off	Sustain	String Resonance	Rhythms/Styles	Polyphony	Total Watts	Speakers	Piano Pedals	Half Pedal
Ebony NEO	V		EP	3,816	4,395	S	10	Y	Y	Y		135	80	4	3	Y
SG-120	G	E	EP/WtP/RdP	2,995	3,695	S	377	Y	Y	Y	353	128	60	6	3	Y
SG-500	G	E	EP/WtP/RdP	3,995	5,295	S	377	Y	Y	Y	352	128	80	8	3	Y

Suzuki

Brand & Model	Form	Ensemble	Finish	Estimated Price	MSRP	Sound Source	Voices	Key Off	Sustain	String Resonance	Rhythms/Styles	Polyphony	Total Watts	Speakers	Piano Pedals	Half Pedal
SCP-88	V		Bk	899	1,099	S	24					128	30	2	3	
CTP-88	V	E	M	999	1,200	S	122+128GM		Y	Y	100	128	60	4	3	
SDP-2000ts	V	E	R	1,799		S	672+256GM				240	128	220	4	3	
MDG-250	G	E	EP	1,499		S	500				200	128	90	4	3	
MDG-300	G	E	EP	1,799	3,390	S	122+128GM		Y	Y	100	128	120	6	3	
MDG-300	G	E	MP/RdP/BlP	1,899	3,390	S	122+128GM		Y	Y	100	128	120	6	3	
MDG-330	G	E	EP	2,499	3,500	S	122+128GM		Y	Y	100	128	120	6	3	
MDG-400	G		EP	2,999	4,200	S	122+128GM		Y	Y	100	128	120	6	3	
MDG-400	G		W	3,299		S	122+128GM		Y	Y	100	128	120	6	3	

Brand & Model	Action	Triple-Sensor Keys	Escapement	Wood Keys	Ivory Texture	Bluetooth	Vocal Support	Educational Features	External Storage	USB to Computer	USB Digital Audio	Recording Tracks	Warranty (Parts/Labor)	Dimensions WxDxH (Inchees)	Weight (Pounds)
Roland *(continued)*															
FP-60	PHA-4 Standard	Y	Y		Y	Y		Y	USB	Y	Y	1	5/2	51x14x5	42
FP-90	PHA-50 Concert	Y	Y	Y	Y	Y	Y	Y	USB	Y	Y	2	5/2	53x15x5	52
FP-90C	PHA-50 Concert	Y	Y	Y	Y	Y	Y	Y	USB	Y	Y	2	5/2	53x15x37	83
DP-603	PHA-50 Concert	Y	Y	Y	Y	Y		Y	USB	Y	Y	3	5/2	55x14x31	104
DP-603	PHA-50 Concert	Y	Y	Y	Y	Y		Y	USB	Y	Y	3	5/2	55x14x31	104
HP-504	PHA4-Premium	Y	Y		Y			Y	USB	Y	Y	3	5/2	55x17x41	114
HP-601	PHA-50 Concert	Y	Y	Y	Y	Y		Y	USB	Y	Y	3	5/2	54x17x40	110
HP-603	PHA-50 Concert	Y	Y	Y	Y	Y		Y	USB	Y	Y	3	10/10	54x17x42	110
HP-603A	PHA-50 Concert	Y	Y	Y	Y	Y		Y	USB	Y	Y	3	10/10	54x17x42	110
HP-605	PHA-50 Concert	Y	Y	Y	Y	Y		Y	USB	Y	Y	3	10/10	54x17x44	119
HP-605	PHA-50 Concert	Y	Y	Y	Y	Y		Y	USB	Y	Y	3	10/10	54x17x44	119
HPi-50e	PHA4-Concert	Y	Y		Y			Y	USB	Y	Y	16	5/2	55x17x43	127
LX-7	PHA-50 Concert	Y	Y	Y	Y	Y		Y	USB	Y	Y	3	10/10	55x18x41	170
LX-7	PHA-50 Concert	Y	Y	Y	Y	Y		Y	USB	Y	Y	3	10/10	55x18x41	170
LX-17	PHA-50 Concert	Y	Y	Y	Y	Y		Y	USB	Y	Y	3	10/10	55x19x42	193
F-140R	PHA-4-Standard	Y	Y		Y	Y		Y	USB	Y	Y	1	5/2	54x14x31	76
RP-102	PHA4-Standard	Y	Y		Y	Y		Y		Y			5/2	54x17x39	83
RP-501R	PHA-4 Standard	Y	Y		Y	Y		Y	USB	Y	Y	1	5/2	54x12x31	81
GP-7 (V-Piano Grand)	PHA III	Y	Y		Y				USB	Y	Y	1	5/2	59x59x61	375
GP-607 (Mini Grand)	PHA-50 Concert	Y	Y	Y	Y	Y		Y	USB	Y	Y	3	10/10	55x37x35	223
Samick															
Ebony NEO	Graded	Y			Y	Y	Y		USB	Y	Y	2	3/3	57x19x41	170
SG-120	Graded	Y			Y	Y	Y		USB	Y	Y	5	3/3	56x35x29	170
SG-500	Graded	Y			Y	Y	Y		USB	Y	Y	5	3/3	56x49x35	290
Suzuki															
SCP-88	Weighted									Y			1/1	54x18x34	
CTP-88	Graded						Y		SD	Y		3	1/1	54x20x40	175
SDP-2000ts	Graded						Y		SD	Y		16	1/1	55x24x36	152
MDG-250	Graded							Y		Y		6	1/1	55x30x31	112
MDG-300	Graded						Y		SD	Y		3	1/1	55x30x36	218
MDG-300	Graded						Y		SD	Y		3	1/1	55x30x36	218
MDG-330	Graded						Y		SD	Y		3	1/1	57x39x36	330
MDG-400	Graded						Y		SD	Y		3	1/1	55x49x35	315
MDG-400	Graded						Y		SD	Y		3	1/1	55x49x35	315

Brand & Model	Form	Ensemble	Finish	Estimated Price	MSRP	Sound Source	Voices	Key Off	Sustain	String Resonance	Rhythms/Styles	Polyphony	Total Watts	Speakers	Piano Pedals	Half Pedal
Suzuki (*continued*)																
MDG-400	G		EP	2,999	4,200	S	122+128GM		Y	Y	100	128	120	6	3	
MDG-400	G		W	3,299		S	122+128GM		Y	Y	100	128	120	6	3	
MDG-4000ts	G		EP	3,699	5,899	S	672+256GM				240	128	250	6	3	
Williams																
Legato	S		Bk	199	400	S	5		Y			32	40	2	(1)	
Allegro 2	S		Bk	299	500	S	10		Y			64	60	2	(1)	
Rhapsody 2	V		WG	499	900	S	12		Y			64	60	2	2	
Overture 2	V		EP	699	1,200	S	19+128GM		Y			64	60	4	3	
Symphony Grand	G	E	EP	1,499	1,999	S	46+128GM	Y	Y	Y	120	128	60	6	3	
Yamaha																
P45B	S		Bk	450	499	S	10					64	12	2	1	Y
P115	S		Bk/Wt	600	999	S	14				14/10	192	14	4	1(3)	Y
P255	S		Bk&EP/Wt	1,300	1,999	S	24	Y	Y	Y	10	256	30	4	1	Y
CP300	S		Bk	2,499	3,499	S	50+480XG	Y	Y	Y		128	60	2	3	Y
CP40 Stage	S		Bk	1,699	2,399	M/S	297	Y	Y			128			1(2)	Y
CP4 Stage	S		Bk	1,999	2,699	M/S	433	Y	Y			128			1(2)	Y
CP1	S		Bk	4,999	5,999	M/S	17	Y	Y	Y		128			3	Y
YDP143	V		BkW/R	1,100	1,499	S	10					192	12	2	3	Y
YDP163	V		BkW/R	1,500	1,999	S	10					192	40	4	3	Y
YDPS52	V		Bk/Wt	1,350	2,199	S	10					192	40	2	3	Y
YDP181	V		R	1,700	2,199	S	14					128	40	2	3	Y
CSP150	V	E	Bk	3,500	3,999	S	721+480XG	Y	Y	Y	470	256	60	2	3	Y
CSP150	V	E	EP	4,000	4,599	S	721+480XG	Y	Y	Y	470	256	60	2	3	Y
CSP170	V	E	Bk	4,700	5,399	S	721+480XG	Y	Y	Y	470	256	180	4	3	Y
CSP170	V	E	EP	5,300	5,999	S	721+480XG	Y	Y	Y	470	256	180	4	3	Y
CLP625	V		EP	2,400	2,699	S	10	Y	Y	Y		256	40	2	3	Y
CLP625	V		Bk/R	2,000	2,299	S	10	Y	Y	Y		256	40	2	3	Y
CLP635	V		EP	3,200	3,599	S	36	Y	Y	Y	20	256	60	2	3	Y
CLP635	V		Bk/R/W	2,700	2,999	S	36	Y	Y	Y	20	256	60	2	3	Y
CLP645	V		EP	4,000	4,599	S	36	Y	Y	Y	20	256	100	4	3	Y
CLP645	V		Bk/R/W	3,500	3,999	S	36	Y	Y	Y	20	256	100	4	3	Y
CLP675	V		EP	5,300	5,999	S	36	Y	Y	Y	20	256	210	6	3	Y

Brand & Model	Action	Triple-Sensor Keys	Escapement	Wood Keys	Ivory Texture	Bluetooth	Vocal Support	Educational Features	External Storage	USB to Computer	USB Digital Audio	Recording Tracks	Warranty (Parts/Labor)	Dimensions WxDxH (Inchees)	Weight (Pounds)
Suzuki *(continued)*															
MDG-400	Graded						Y		SD	Y		3	1/1	55x49x35	315
MDG-400	Graded						Y		SD	Y		3	1/1	55x49x35	315
MDG-4000ts	Fatar Graded						Y		SD	Y		16	1/1	58x48x37	311
Williams															
Legato	Semi-Weighted									Y			1/1	50x11x4	19
Allegro 2	Weighted									Y		2	1/1	52x5x13	30
Rhapsody 2	Weighted									Y		2	1/1	54x16x31	83
Overture 2	Weighted						Y		USB	Y		2	1/1	55x19x34	117
Symphony Grand	Graded, Weighted					Y	Y		USB	Y	Y	4	1/1	54x35x36	163
Yamaha															
P45B	GHS									Y			3/3	52x12x6	26
P115	GHS									Y		2	3/3	52x12x6	26
P255	GH				Y				USB	Y	Y	2	3/3	53x14x6	38
CP300	GH									Y		16	3/3	54x18x7	72
CP40 Stage	GH								USB	Y	Y		3/3	52x14x6	36
CP4 Stage	NW-GH3	Y		Y	Y				USB	Y	Y		3/3	52x14x6	39
CP1	NW-Stage			Y	Y				USB	Y			3/3	55x17x7	60
YDP143	GHS									Y		2	3/3	54x17x32	84
YDP163	GH3	Y			Y					Y		2	3/3	54x17x33	93
YDPS52	GH				Y					Y		2	3/3	55x12x31	80
YDP181	GH								USB	Y		2	3/3	54x34x20	110
CSP150	GH3X	Y	Y		Y		Y	Y	USB-Tablet	Y	Y	16	5/5	56x18x40	127
CSP150	GH3X	Y	Y		Y		Y	Y	USB-Tablet	Y	Y	17	5/6	56x18x40	127
CSP170	NWX	Y	Y	Y	Y		Y	Y	USB-Tablet	Y	Y	18	5/7	56x18x40	147
CSP170	NWX	Y	Y	Y	Y		Y	Y	USB-Tablet	Y	Y	19	5/8	56x18x40	147
CLP625	GH3X	Y	Y		Y					Y		2	5/5	53x16x33	95
CLP625	GH3X	Y	Y		Y					Y		2	5/5	53x16x33	99
CLP635	GH3X	Y	Y		Y			Y	USB	Y	Y	16	5/5	58x18x37	123
CLP635	GH3X	Y	Y		Y			Y	USB	Y	Y	16	5/5	58x18x37	137
CLP645	NWX	Y	Y	Y	Y	Y		Y	USB	Y	Y	16	5/5	58x18x37	132
CLP645	NWX	Y	Y	Y	Y	Y		Y	USB	Y	Y	16	5/5	58x18x37	146
CLP675	GrandTouch	Y	Y	Y	Y	Y		Y	USB	Y	Y	16	5/5	58x19x38	152

Brand & Model	Form	Ensemble	Finish	Estimated Price	MSRP	Sound Source	Voices	Key Off	Sustain	String Resonance	Rhythms/Styles	Polyphony	Total Watts	Speakers	Piano Pedals	Half Pedal
Yamaha *(continued)*																
CLP675	V		BK/R/W	4,700	5,199	S	36	Y	Y	Y	20	256	210	6	3	Y
CLP685	V		EP	6,600	7,499	S	49+ 480XG	Y	Y	Y	20	256	300	6	3	Y
CLP685	V		WtP	7,600	8,474	S	49+ 480XG	Y	Y	Y	20	256	300	6	3	Y
CLP685	V		Bk	5,800	6,499	S	49+ 480XG	Y	Y	Y	20	256	300	6	3	Y
R01	V		Wt	4,900	7,199	S	1	Y	Y			128	24	2	3	Y
F02	V		EP/BlP/ RdP/OrP	5,000	7,699	S	20	Y	Y			128	80	4	3	Y
F11	V		EP/BlP/ RdP/OrP	7,500	13,999	S	20	Y	Y			128	80	4	3	Y
NU1	V		EP	5,816	6,499	S	5	Y	Y	Y		256	160	4	3	Y
DGX660	S	E	Bk&R/ Bk&Wt	800	1,299	S	151+ 388XG				205	192	12	4	1(3)	Y
CVP701	V	E	W	4,127	5,399	S	777+ 480XG	Y	Y	Y	310	256	50	2	3	Y
CVP701	V	E	EP	4,636	6,199	S	777+ 480XG	Y	Y	Y	310	256	50	2	3	Y
CVP705	V	E	W	6,455	8,699	S	984+ 480XG	Y	Y	Y	470	256	140	6	3	Y
CVP705	V	E	EP	7,245	9,699	S	984+ 480XG	Y	Y	Y	470	256	140	6	3	Y
CVP709	V	E	W	10,091	14,499	S	1270+ 480XG	Y	Y	Y	600	256	200	9	3	Y
CVP709	V	E	EP	11,087	15,999	S	1270+ 480XG	Y	Y	Y	600	256	200	9	3	Y
H01	G		AG/VR/DB	7,500	13,199	S	10	Y	Y				80	4	3	Y
H11	G		AG/VR/DB	10,000	20,799	S	10	Y	Y				80	4	3	Y
N1	G		EP	8,453	9,999	S	5	Y	Y	Y		256	175	6	3	Y
N2	G		EP	12,635	14,999	S	5	Y	Y	Y		256	500	12	3	Y
N3X	G		EP	18,816	22,199	S	10	Y	Y	Y		256	500	12	3	Y
CLP665GP	G		EP	5,500	6,199	S	36	Y	Y	Y	20	256	70	4	3	Y
CLP665GP	G		WtP	6,300	6,999	S	36	Y	Y	Y	20	256	70	4	3	Y
CVP709GP	G	E	EP	15,224	20,999	S	1270+ 480XG	Y	Y	Y	600	256	200	9	3	Y

Brand & Model	Action	Triple-Sensor Keys	Escapement	Wood Keys	Ivory Texture	Bluetooth	Vocal Support	Educational Features	External Storage	USB to Computer	USB Digital Audio	Recording Tracks	Warranty (Parts/Labor)	Dimensions WxDxH (Inches)	Weight (Pounds)
Yamaha *(continued)*															
CLP675	GrandTouch	Y	Y	Y	Y	Y		Y	USB	Y	Y	16	5/5	58x19x38	157
CLP685	GrandTouch	Y	Y	Y	Y	Y		Y	USB	Y	Y	16	5/5	58x19x41	183
CLP685	GrandTouch	Y	Y	Y	Y	Y		Y	USB	Y	Y	16	5/5	58x19x41	183
CLP685	GrandTouch	Y	Y	Y	Y	Y		Y	USB	Y	Y	16	5/5	58x19x41	196
R01	NW			Y	Y									55x15x38	88
F01	NW			Y					USB	Y		1	5/5	56x16x39	168
F11	NW			Y					USB	Y		1	5/5	56x16x39	198
NU1	Specialized Upright	Y	Y	Y					USB	Y	Y	1	5/5	60x18x40	240
DGX660	GHS						Y	Y	USB	Y		6	3/3	55x18x30	61
CVP701	GH3X		Y		Y		Y	Y	USB	Y	Y	16	5/5	53x24x36	130
CVP701	GH3X	Y	Y		Y		Y	Y	USB	Y	Y	16	5/5	53x24x36	130
CVP705	NWX	Y	Y	Y	Y		Y	Y	USB	Y	Y	16	5/5	56x24x34	170
CVP705	NWX	Y	Y	Y	Y		Y	Y	USB	Y	Y	16	5/5	56x24x34	170
CVP709	NWX	Y	Y	Y	Y		Y	Y	USB	Y	Y	16	5/5	56x24x34	174
CVP709	NWX	Y	Y	Y	Y		Y	Y	USB	Y	Y	16	5/5	56x24x34	174
H01	NW	Y		Y					USB				5/5	58x30x30	181
H11	NW			Y					USB				5/5	58x30x30	216
N1	Specialized Grand	Y	Y	Y					USB			1	5/5	58x24x39	266
N2	Specialized Grand	Y	Y	Y	Y				USB			1	5/5	58x21x40	313
N3X	Specialized Grand	Y	Y	Y	Y				USB	Y	Y	1	5/5	58x47x40	439
CLP665GP	GH3X	Y	Y		Y	Y		Y	USB	Y	Y	16	1	56x45x37	227
CLP665GP	GH3X	Y	Y		Y	Y		Y	USB	Y	Y	16	1	56x45x37	227
CVP709GP	NWX	Y	Y	Y	Y		Y	Y	USB	Y	Y	16	5/5	56x45x36	242

ADVERTISER INDEX

PHOTO CREDITS

Cover: Grand, Shigeru Kawai SK-5; Vertical, Ritmuller UH121R; Digital, Samick Ebony NEO

Page 5: www.baileyworld.com

Page 6: Mark Duffy

Page 12: Samick Music Corp.

Page 16: Douglas Gilbert

Page 31: www.nasa.gov

Page 51: header, Young Chang; Cristofori, Metropolitan Museum of Art; Sq. Grand, www.liveauctioneers.com

Page 68: © Schnapps2012, iStock

Page 73: © Keith Tsuji, iStock

Page 83: Faust Harrison Pianos

Page 89: © Galina Stepanova

Page 97: header, © Tatiana Popova; Regulating, © Brent Bossom

Page 102: © Ryan Lane

Page 111: Yamaha

Page 120: © Carl Keyes

Page 128: Yamaha

Page 133: PianoDisc

Page 134: © Martina Nehls-Sahabandu

*(continued from **page 2**)*
of used pianos for sale. If you're in need of piano-related services—tuning, rebuilding, sales, teaching, or moving—use our Local Services Directory. And when you're ready to take a break, treat yourself to some comic relief with our blog, *Piano-Buying Stories*.

Finally, if you're reading this online, consider buying a print copy of **Piano Buyer**. It's a handsome volume, printed in color on glossy paper, and will make a great reference, coffee-table book, or gift. You can purchase it through the website or in bookstores.

Piano Buyer exists to make shopping for a piano easier and more enjoyable. If you have a suggestion for how we can do that better, please e-mail me at ***larry@pianobuyer.com***.

—Larry Fine, *Publisher*